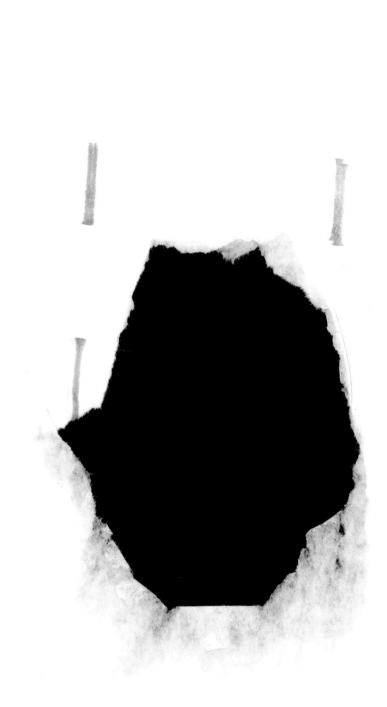

Cinema and Social Change
in Latin America

Special Publication
Institute of Latin American Studies
The University of Texas at Austin

CINEMA AND SOCIAL CHANGE IN LATIN AMERICA

Conversations with Filmmakers

Edited by

Julianne Burton

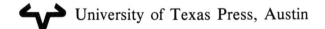 University of Texas Press, Austin

Library of Congress Cataloging-in-Publication Data

Cinema and social change in Latin America.

(Special publication)
Bibliography: p.
Includes index.
1. Moving-pictures—Social aspects—Latin America.
2. Moving-pictures—Political aspects—Latin America.
3. Moving-picture producers and directors—Latin America—Interviews.
I. Burton, Julianne. II. Series: Special publication (University of Texas at Austin. Institute of Latin American Studies)
PN1993.5.L3C49   1986   302.2'343'098   86-11297
ISBN 0-292-72453-5
ISBN 0-292-72454-3 (pbk.)

First Edition, 1986
Requests for permission to reproduce material from this work should be sent to:

Permissions
University of Texas Press
P.O. Box 7819
Austin, Texas 78713-7819

The publication of this book was assisted by a grant from the Andrew W. Mellon Foundation.

CONTENTS

Acknowledgments   vii

Introduction   ix

Part I.   The Documentary Impulse: The Drama of Reality

1. Fernando Birri (Argentina), *The Roots of Documentary Realism*   1
2. Mario Handler (Uruguay), *Starting from Scratch: Artisanship and Agitprop*   13
3. Jorge Silva and Marta Rodríguez (Colombia), *Cine-Sociology and Social Change*   25
4. Jorge Sanjinés (Bolivia), *Revolutionary Cinema: The Bolivian Experience*   35
5. Patricio Guzmán (Chile), *Politics and the Documentary in People's Chile*   49
6. Emilio Rodríguez Vázquez and Carlos Vicente Ibarra (Puerto Rico and Nicaragua), *Filmmaking in Nicaragua: From Insurrection to INCINE*   69
7. Helena Solberg-Ladd (Brazil and United States), *The View from the United States*   81

Part II.   Fictional Filmmaking: The Reality of Drama

8. Glauber Rocha (Brazil), *Cinema Novo and the Dialectics of Popular Culture*   105
9. Tomás Gutiérrez Alea (Cuba), *Beyond the Reflection of Reality*   115
10. Nelson Pereira dos Santos (Brazil), *Toward a Popular Cinema*   133
11. Humberto Solás (Cuba), *Every Point of Arrival Is a Point of Departure*   143
12. Antonio Eguino (Bolivia), *Neorealism in Bolivia*   161
13. Carlos Diegues (Brazil), *The Mind of Cinema Novo*   171

14. Raúl Ruiz (Chile and France), *Between Institutions* 181

15. Marcela Fernández Violante (Mexico), *Inside the Mexican Film Industry: A Woman's Perspective* 195

Part III. Behind the Scenes

16. Nelson Villagra (Chile), *The Actor at Home and in Exile* 211

17. Walter Achugar (Uruguay and Latin America at Large), *Using Movies to Make Movies* 221

18. Enrique Colina (Cuba), *The Film Critic on Prime Time* 237

19. Julio García Espinosa (Cuba), *Theory and Practice of Film and Popular Culture in Cuba* 243

20. Alfonso Gumucio Dagrón (Bolivia and Latin America at Large), *A Product of Circumstances: Reflections of a Media Activist* 259

For Further Reading 285

Appendix: Films and Writings by Latin American Directors 287

Index of Films 291

General Index 296

Acknowledgments

Portions of this project were completed while I was the recipient of fellowships from the Tinker Foundation (1977–1978) and the Joint Council on Latin American Studies of the American Council of Learned Societies and the Social Science Research Council (1980–1981). I also want to acknowledge the continued support of the Committee on Research at my home institution, the University of California at Santa Cruz, and the invaluable secretarial assistance of the staff at both Merrill and Kresge colleges there. Judy Burton, Janice Robinson, and Betsy Shipley provided cheerful and efficient assistance. I would like especially to thank Peter W. Rose for his timely encouragement. Most of all, I am indebted to the Latin American filmmakers, both those represented and those omitted from this volume, whose creativity, commitment, and cooperation have made this work possible.

Introduction

More, perhaps, than in other regions of the world, culture in Latin America inhabits a politicized zone, for Latin American artists and intellectuals acknowledge how profoundly history and politics inflect creativity. Over the past quarter century, no sector of artistic activity has been more explicit about its political dimension and goals than film. Those Latin American artists and intellectuals who, in their commitment to transform their society, have turned to film as the most promising instrument have also become deeply engaged in transforming that instrument. They have not only developed new contents and new forms but also new processes of production, diffusion, and reception. This double commitment to artistic innovation and social transformation accounts for both the interest and the importance of what is loosely called the New Latin American Cinema movement.

Convinced that (Hollywood) movies were the primary vehicle of cultural domination, and following the developmentalist logic of "import substitution" promulgated after World War II, progressive Latin Americans sought "modernization" and autonomy through the national production of cultural as well as consumer goods. Film was the most industrialized sector of the "culture industry," the most massive of the mass media in its accessibility to all social strata. It was clearly "the most important art," the most appropriate cultural means of social transformation.

Film was not a new industry to the region. Mass consumption of the movies in Latin American capitals began just months after the first successful Lumière screening in turn-of-the-century Paris. Because in that early period camera and projector were a single piece of equipment, and because audiences were avid for constantly replenished "views" of people, places, and events, local film production began almost immediately. In the years before World War I, several Latin American countries boasted a healthy output of primarily fictional films. Brazil was foremost among these, averaging one hundred films per year between 1900 and 1912.

As North American distributors moved into Latin American markets with increasing tenacity after World War I, national film production dwindled in many countries. It was further diminished by the transition to sound in the early thirties, which demanded access to large quantities of investment capital. Only in the largest and wealthiest nations—Brazil, Mexico, and Argentina—were film companies able to convert successfully to sound production; in most of the smaller countries, output never equaled what it had been before the introduction of the talkies. World War II gave an unexpected boost to domestic film production throughout Latin America, despite shortages of film stock. With Hollywood's energies channeled into the war effort, local film products had a unique opportunity to reclaim and expand their audiences. The three major genres indigenous to the region all date from this period and center on regional musical expressions: the Argentine tango film, the Brazilian *chanchada* (a musical comedy usually based on a carnival motif), and the Mexican *comedia ranchera* (a period musical featuring mariachi bands and set at a wealthy hacienda).

The postwar years witnessed rising nationalism, heightened regional identification, and increased militancy throughout Latin America. Momentous political events punctuated the decade of the 1950s: the uprising in Colombia in 1949 known as the *bogotazo*; the unfinished worker-peasant revolution in Bolivia, which began in 1952; the peasant columns of Luiz Carlos Prestes in Brazil; the liberal reforms in Guatemala in 1954, which provoked U.S. military intervention in defense of United Fruit Company's interests; the overthrow of Gen. Juan Perón in Argentina at mid-decade; and—most significant—the guerrilla war in Cuba, which began in 1956 and by 1 January 1959 had overthrown a despised dictator who in his brutality, corruption, and close ties to Washington was all too prototypical of a species that flourished in the region.

This was also the decade when talented young people, acutely conscious of social and economic inequities and anxious to remedy them, began redefining the role of the film medium in the Latin American context. The nature of their project was shaped by the fierce rejection of one model of filmmaking and the equally passionate emulation of another. In their view, the studio-based production system developed in Hollywood was hierarchical and overly compartmentalized. Directors seemed subordinate to studio bosses and stars. The priority given to purely commercial and technical concerns guaranteed an artificial, insular, alienating product. The Italian Neorealists, in contrast, abandoned the cloistered studio for natural sets, replaced professional actors with nonprofessionals, and adopted the kind of inexpensive, flexible equipment that had previously been used only by documentarists and news photographers. Fewer intermediaries came between directors and screenwriters and the embodiment of their creative visions. The resulting films seemed more authentic, more urgent, more real than what Hollywood was producing at the time because postwar Italy, like much of Latin America, was in the throes of profound social transformation, and filmmakers like DeSica, Rossellini, and Zavattini adapted their medium to those tumultuous times.

Turning their backs on local commercial efforts, which they condemned as alienated and alienating imitations of the Hollywood model, scores of young Latin American filmmakers assembled the minimum equipment necessary and undertook to produce films about and for and eventually with the disenfranchised Latin American masses. They sought to express "national reality," which they believed to be hidden, distorted, or negated by the dominant sectors and the media they controlled. Intent on capturing the plight of the rural and urban poor, these artists ventured beyond the confines of their own privileged urban milieu. Yet the journey that began in the backlands and slums, in the remote mountain and jungle regions, did not end there. These socially conscious filmmakers would eventually take the entire past and present of their countries and their region as their subject matter, probing the privileged as well as the marginalized sectors, examining historical and contemporary as well as invented examples of exploitation and rebellion, complicity, and refusal, all in the name of the discovery or recovery of a more authentic national identity.

Fernando Birri, who in the mid-1950s founded the first film school for socially committed filmmaking in Latin America, called for a new kind of cinema in the documentary mode—"realist, national, and popular." Beginning in the early 1960s, Uruguayan documentarists Mario Handler and Ugo Ulive adapted *cinéma vérité* and agitprop to the Latin American context, working in an artisanal mode that was the antithesis of filmmaking as an industrialized art form. In Colombia in the late 1960s, Jorge Silva and Marta Rodríguez, another pair of artisanal filmmakers, blended realist and illusionist modes in ethnographic documentaries that challenged and subverted that genre. Meanwhile, Argentine Fernando Solanas and Spanish-born Octavio Getino postulated a "third cinema." This cinema, instead of privileging the producer (like classical Hollywood or "first cinema") or the director (like auteurist or "second cinema"), would emphasize the interaction between film and audience in open, essay-style documentaries that would spur spectators to political action. As the 1960s were drawing to a close, Bolivians Jorge Sanjinés and Ricardo Rada rejected both documentary and fictional approaches in favor of historical reconstructions that enlist the participation of Andean peasants in the reenactment of events from the "popular memory" that would otherwise remain unrecorded. In the early 1970s, Chilean director Patricio Guzmán and his five-person crew, the Grupo Tercer Año, undertook to capture social transformation on a national scale, history in the making, as it were, by amalgamating existing documentary approaches and visually "mapping" what were in their opinion the critical sectors of social conflict in their country. *The Battle of Chile* ends up documenting not the democratic transition to socialism under Allende's Popular Unity government, which the filmmakers hoped to record, but instead the most violent and antidemocratic counterrevolution in recent history. In subsequent struggles for revolutionary change in Nicaragua and El Salvador, the new Super-8 and especially video technologies have played an important role in counterinformation and consolidation. The anonymous, collaborative methods and new synthetic forms produced out of necessity in this region are exerting their influence in other areas, where they are being adopted by choice.

Glauber Rocha, flamboyant genius of Brazil's Cinema Novo (New Cinema) movement, which made its debut in the early 1960s, celebrated the rediscovery of the minimal conditions necessary to filmmaking—"a camera in your hand and an idea in your head." If Nelson Pereira dos Santos, inspired by the example of the Italian Neorealist filmmakers during and after World War II, was the leading spokesman and practitioner of the realist mode, the films Rocha made throughout the 1960s vindicated the opposite—illusionism, allegory, visual and aural hyperbole. Many Cuban directors, including Tomás Gutiérrez Alea and Humberto Solás, managed to incorporate these apparently antithetical poles into their best work, where contrasts in styles and modalities create an internal resonance that challenges and enriches the viewers' understanding of the film medium. Wary of the international acclaim garnered by Gutiérrez Alea's *Memories of Underdevelopment* and Solás's *Lucía*, Cuban filmmaker and theorist Julio García Espinosa called for an "imperfect cinema," which would emphasize process over predigested analysis, experimentation and participation over the polish and compartmentalization of the Hollywood and European traditions. Admiring Hollywood's appeal even while deploring its impact, he argued in the early 1970s for films that "make a spectacle out of the destruction of the spectacle, perform[ing] this process jointly with the viewer." By mid-decade, Brazilian filmmakers like Carlos Diegues and the versatile Pereira dos Santos, working in collaboration with the newly established state film agency, Embrafilme, sought to realign the concept of popular or people's cinema with the persistent appeal of mass entertainment forms, vindicating the spectacle *as* spectacle.

Filmmakers in countries throughout Latin America and the Caribbean have followed these directions and initiated others. Individual trajectories, and the quantity and quality of films produced, have been shaped by the degree of space for political contestation permitted in the public arena at any given moment. During the 1970s, when repressive military governments proliferated throughout the region, scores of filmmakers were jailed for their activities. Many were made to disappear and subsequently, surreptitiously, murdered while in unofficial custody. Large numbers, including half of the people interviewed in this book, were compelled to choose the difficult detours of exile, attempting to continue their work in other Latin American countries, in Europe, or in North America (see especially the chapters dealing with filmmakers Raúl Ruiz and Alfonso Gumucio Dagrón, the actor Nelson Villagra, and the distributor Walter Achugar). Latin American and Caribbean filmmakers from Hispanic, French, Portuguese, and other linguistic traditions are increasingly making their presence felt on the independent film and television scene in the United States (for an example, see the interview with Helena Solberg-Ladd).

Filmmakers from throughout the Americas and the world have recently responded to the Central American crisis by putting their skills at the service of progressive forces in Nicaragua and El Salvador (see the interview with Emilio Rodríguez Vázquez and Carlos Vicente Ibarra for an early glimpse of the veritable revolution in the role of the visual media that is taking place in Central America). At the other end of the continent, the return to democratic government in the 1980s has breathed new life into film culture in countries like Argentina, which has periodically been at the forefront of both commercial and alternative cinema. Attempts to provide national film production with a solid economic base through state intervention, whether in socialist Cuba or in dependent capitalist countries like Brazil, Venezuela, and Mexico, are proving difficult to sustain, despite impressive accomplishments. (The interview with Marcela Fernández Violante presents one perspective on the crisis in the Mexican film industry.) Film production in the developed as well as the underdeveloped world is threatened by increased costs and new modes of reception that may soon make theatrical viewing obsolete. (See the interview with Julio García Espinosa for a Cuban slant on the preservation of popular culture and the challenge of the new mass media.) Increasingly, media activists throughout Central and South America are taking advantage of the newer Super-8 and video formats to break down hierarchical divisions between the filmmaker/technician and the subject/recipient to whom those skills have been directed. Filmmakers like the Bolivian Alfonso Gumucio Dagrón or the anonymous members of El Salvador's Radio Venceremos Film and Video Collective subordinate their own personal identities as creative artists to the larger goal of workers' and peasants' cinema, which can exist only outside the established (and rapidly changing) international political economy of the medium.

The specific approaches and priorities of what continues to call itself the New Latin American Cinema movement vary from period to period, from country to country, and from filmmaker to filmmaker as well as *within* periods and countries and individual careers—from realism to expressionism, from scientifically rigorous observation to fantastic invention, from "imperfect cinema" to high-gloss production values, from experimental and self-reflexive styles to the "transparency" of classical forms, from highly

industrialized to purely artisanal modes of production. What does not vary
is the commitment to the film medium as a vehicle for social transformation
and the expression of national and regional cultural autonomy. This is the
invisible thread that connects these various individuals and groups across
regional, technological, and generational frontiers. This same thread binds
the interviews presented here.

The following twenty chapters span thirty years of Latin American
filmmaking as theorized and practiced in Argentina, Uruguay, Colombia,
Bolivia, Chile, Nicaragua, Brazil, Cuba, and Mexico. Parts I and II, which
distribute fifteen filmmakers according to whether their most important
work has been primarily fictional or documentary, establish a loose
chronology based on the date of the interview or the date of the work or
works on which the interview focuses. Part III supplements the concentration
on filmmakers in the preceding sections with a sampling of associated
professionals—an actor, a distributor, a critic, a cultural minister, and
finally a jack-of-all-cinematic-trades for whom the film medium is but one of
several instruments for effecting social change. Many of the filmmakers
featured in this volume enjoy a worldwide reputation; others are not well
known outside their country of residence. No single volume of this sort can
encompass all who are worthy of inclusion. The filmmakers and associated
professionals included here are representative of important accomplishments
and tendencies within contemporary Latin American film culture.

Because many of the interviews endeavor to trace the career trajectory of
individual cineasts, the collection may appear to have an auteurist emphasis.
There is in most of the interviews, however, a counterbalancing stress on
contextual factors—an attempt to probe the historical, political, social, and
economic circumstances that have shaped a particular career trajectory.
Each of the chapters explores the politics, economics, and social
organization of cinematic production as well as the more personal factors
that shape creative expression. Among the principal issues and concerns
that recur throughout the collection are colonization and decolonization as
historical phenomena and as determinants of cultural expression; the
relation of practical and ideological constraints (for example, limited
resources, institutionalized or internalized censorship mechanisms) to
questions of form and aesthetics; variations in the social relations and
organization of film production (for example, under capitalism, socialism,
mixed economies; in independent and state-supported production units);
attempts to transform conventional modes of distribution (in favor of
domestic over imported productions) and exhibition (in favor of a greater
degree of audience participation); the impact of the new electronic
technologies; the role of ethnic, class, and gender differences in specific uses
of the film medium; the personal and professional impact of exile; the
impact of different cultural and economic contexts upon film reception; the

transformative potential of the mass media in general and the film medium in particular. Finally, the selection and organization of the interviews seek to make manifest a cross-weave of relationships between particular figures, movements, and approaches, which has yet to be fully explored by historians and critics.

Many changes have occurred over the past three decades. Hollywood no longer exists as the kind of unified process and product that practitioners of the New Latin American Cinema denounced and reacted against. Perhaps at the current historical moment, the very concept of the New Latin American Cinema movement is only slightly less heuristic than its founders' idea of Hollywood. Certainly neither is monolithic and both are more interrelated than previously recognized. International distribution structures continue to marginalize Latin American cinema within Latin America. Because film is not simply a mode of expression but also part of an international communications apparatus, the film products and practices of the underdeveloped world cannot be understood in isolation from those of the developed world. Dominant and oppositional, marginal and mainstream cultures are not independent but interdependent phenomena. Antithetical to one another, that very adversarial quality locks them together in a mutually hostile embrace. Mainstream cultural manifestations appropriate examples of marginal creativity without acknowledging—and often actively concealing—the source. Oppositional cultural practice defines itself as a denial of and an alternative to dominant practice, a stance that requires constant monitoring of its adversary. Mainstream cultures thus establish the terms of marginal cultures to a significant degree. Culture can be marginal without being oppositional, but cannot be mainstream without being in some degree dominant.

Rather than becoming more cohesive over the past three decades, Latin American cinema has become more diffuse, demonstrating varying degrees of marginality and oppositionality. In a number of countries—Brazil, Venezuela, Peru, Colombia, not to mention the longer-standing examples of Mexico and Cuba—the state has entered into film production. Though many believe that national film production in the underdeveloped sector cannot survive without state intervention, others fear the limitations this may set on autonomy of expression. Independents who chose to remain outside state systems of support assume a double marginality vis-à-vis both the developed sector outside their country and the state-financed sector within it. What aspired to be a single movement seems more than ever to be an amorphous grouping of mutually supportive individuals and groups brought together by the common economic and political difficulties they face.

The old Hollywood studios have been absorbed into multinational corporations intent on diversifying their holdings. Hollywood as a geographical locale is now only one of many sites of visual media production in the United States. Both it and the New Latin American Cinema, to the degree that they exist as entities, are increasingly embattled, yet the struggle each is waging is less and less against the other. Dominant and oppositional film-producing sectors are equally threatened by the prospect that the center will not hold. The most important art form of the twentieth century is being displaced, at the threshold of the twenty-first, by electronic successors. As with the Great Depression of the 1930s, or today's debt crisis, the impact of these violent "adjustments" is most acutely felt not in the center but in the periphery.

What is most remarkable to me as I look on Latin America at the current historical juncture is the tenacity with which artists and intellectuals cling to the film medium in the face of mounting obstacles to sustained production. Film (increasingly combined with video) remains the preferred medium for catalyzing and attesting to new sociopolitical alignments—the victory of the Sandinista insurrection in Nicaragua in 1979; the return to civilian democracy in Argentina, Brazil, and Uruguay in the 1980s; the resurgence of mass protests in Chile; the growing Hispanic presence in the United States. Yet increasingly, this most sensuous of media, in Latin American hands, affirms its potential for ensuring continuity as well as sparking change. Many citizens of Latin America (and other regions of the underdeveloped and developed world) continue to embrace the cinema as an incomparable vehicle for the assertion of cultural idiosyncrasy and the preservation of difference in a world where cultural variety is being rapidly assimilated into deadening, dehumanizing monotony. One of the most fascinating aspects of Latin American culture is its sense of unity within diversity. I hope the voices collected here effectively convey both the commonality of ends and essences and the multiplicity of experience and expression.

I conducted all interviews in Spanish (except the interview with Helena Solberg-Ladd) and have extensively rearranged them in the editing process to enhance clarity and thematic continuity. I have submitted all of my interviews to the interviewees for emendations and approval. I have made minor editorial modifications in some of the interviews conducted by others and have added notes where clarification seemed necessary.

Part I

THE DOCUMENTARY IMPULSE
The Drama of Reality

Chapter 1

Fernando Birri
(Argentina)

The Roots of Documentary Realism

Plate 1. Fernando Birri, founder of the Documentary Film School of Santa Fe, Argentina, at the First International Festival of the New Latin American Cinema, Havana, 1979. Photo by Julianne Burton.

As founder of the Documentary Film School at the National University of the Littoral in Santa Fe, Argentina, Fernando Birri is recognized as a pioneer of what was to become the New Latin American Cinema movement. Though political developments interrupted his work in Latin America, even in his absence his example bore fruit in a number of countries across the hemisphere. His most important films are *Tire dié* (*Throw Me a Dime*, 1960), *La pampa gringa* (1963), the Neorealist feature *Los inundados* (*Flooded Out*, 1962), and the experimental *Org* (1978). Birri has been living in Rome since 1964, with frequent and prolonged visits to Cuba, Mexico, and Venezuela since 1979. In 1986 Birri was named director of the Escuela de Cine y Televisión (School of Film and Television) to be constructed at San Antonio de los Baños, Cuba.

Of Puppets and Poetry

In the beginning, I was a puppeteer. I'd had a puppet theater since I was a child. In the early forties, when I began my studies at the university, what had earlier been limited to my own household and neighborhood became a much more public activity. Somewhat in imitation of La Barraca, the traveling theater group founded in Pre-Civil War Spain by Federico García Lorca, a group of us would take that puppet theater on tour—to schools, orphanages, insane asylums, jails—around the city of Santa Fe and the province of El Litoral.

Later I moved on from puppets to flesh-and-blood actors, directing the first university theater group at the Universidad Nacional del Litoral. My goal as director remained the same: to reach the broadest possible audience within the popular sector. This concern explains, in part, why I was to turn eventually to filmmaking.

My deepest creative roots, however, are in poetry. I began writing poetry as a child, and continue to do so; it is the foundation of all my work. As a puppeteer, as a theater director, as a filmmaker—what has guided my steps is nothing other than the search for and expression of a poetics.

I come from a generation that was practically born with the movies. From early childhood, I went to the movies almost daily. I remember seeing Al Jolson's *The Jazz Singer* while sitting on my father's lap. When, at the height of my success as a theater director, I opted for filmmaking as a career, it was because I realized that neither poetry nor theater could offer me access to audiences larger than those I was already reaching.

The Roots of Political Awareness

Logically enough, this eagerness to reach the broadest possible audience, which characterizes all my work, has a lot to do with my own background and class consciousness. My popular roots are still fresh. I'm a typical Argentine because I am the second generation of an immigrant family. Hard times and intrusive *carabinieri* prompted my anarchist grandfather, a farmer and miller from northern Italy, to emigrate to Argentina around 1880. Many years later, similar circumstances would force me to make the same journey,

Julianne Burton interviewed Fernando Birri at the First International Festival of the New Latin American Cinema, held in Havana in December 1979. The interview was revised and expanded at the Second Havana Festival, held the following year, and was first published in Italian as "Fernando Birri: Pioniere e Pellegrino," in Lino Micciché, ed., *Fernando Birri e la escuela documental de Santa Fe*, 17th Mostra Internazionale del Nuovo Cinema, Pesaro, Italy (June 1981). This slightly edited version omits the section on the feature film *Los inundados* (*Flooded Out*, 1962).

but in reverse.

Once in Argentina, my grandparents moved from the rural to the urban proletariat. My father "moved up in the world" one step more, earning his doctoral degree in social and political sciences at the Universidad Nacional del Litoral. Despite his rise in status, however, he never abandoned his father's political convictions.

I read Georgi Plekhanov's *Art and Society* in my father's library at the age of eleven. From a relatively tender age, I was aware of the social class I belonged to and in the act of becoming class conscious, I also became conscious of my own determination to dedicate all my energies to opposing the value system of my class, the ascendant petite bourgeoisie.

It would have been more gratifying to identify myself with the peasantry or the working class, but it would have also been a falsification and a grave ideological error, leading me to seek my reflection in a mirror that held another image. It was only through the process of recognizing my own bourgeois roots that I could marshal all my intellectual arms to undermine the bourgeois values within my personality and transform them into the values of the popular classes.

But this is not a purely intellectual process; there's an emotional component as well. On a gut level, I have always been on the side of the underdogs, the injured and degraded, the wretched of the earth. As soon as I disowned my bourgeois privilege and took on the responsibilities of an intellectual who belongs to a revolutionary class, I became a part of the injured and degraded. So my class position was a conscious choice.

To Learn to Make Movies

Along with Mexico and Brazil, Argentina has traditionally been one of the great film centers in Latin America. During the early fifties, when I decided to become a filmmaker, the regime of Gen. Juan Perón had diminished and debased the national film industry. Despite this, I decided to leave my native Santa Fe and journey to Buenos Aires to learn to make movies.

I began looking for work as an assistant producer, but I soon learned to lower my sights until, finally, I offered myself to Argentina Sono Film Studios as a janitor. Nothing doing. It seems that all jobs in the film industry were controlled by a kind of mafia. For the likes of me, all doors were closed.

I decided that I would learn filmmaking wherever it was taught and found out about the two leading European film schools—L'IDHEC in Paris and the Centro Sperimentale di Cinematografia in Rome.

Like film fans anywhere in that period, I was most informed about (and most "deformed" by) Hollywood films. I had seen only a limited number of European films—French, Swedish, German—at the film society we had founded in Santa Fe. But at the time I was deciding on a career, postwar Italian Neorealism was taking movie houses around the world by storm.

Bicycle Thief, Rome, Open City, and *La terra trema* had all appeared in the late forties. For me, the great revelation of the Neorealist movement was that, contrary to Hollywood's tenets and example, it was possible to make movies on the same artistic level as a play, a novel, or a poem.

I enrolled in the Centro Sperimentale because it enabled me to be at the center of that important film movement and because it provided practical as well as theoretical training. While studying for my degree, I made several documentaries, worked as assistant to Zavattini and De Sica on *Il tetto*, and acted in Francesco Maselli's first film. I tried to study the filmmaking process from every angle, to master it as a totality.

The Return to Argentina

In 1955 Perón was overthrown, to be replaced by the famous "Liberating Revolution," which would find its most effective leader in Gen. Pedro Aramburu. In 1956 I decided to return to Argentina to pursue my life and work on my own soil. The prospect of having to leave again was unthinkable.

Cartoonists have always depicted Argentina as a dwarf with a giant's head: the oversized head is the capital, Buenos Aires, and the tiny body symbolizes the rest of the country. Film production had always been located in the giant's head. It was clear to me from the first that I was going to have trouble striking any bargains there to do what I thought was necessary to create a new Argentine cinema.

So I decided to give up on Buenos Aires and return to my native Santa Fe, prepared to see if there, starting from zero, I could begin to produce a kind of filmmaking that had nothing to do with the mercantile-industrial setup in the capital. What I wanted was to discover the face of an invisible Argentina—invisible not because it couldn't be seen, but because no one *wanted* to see it.

In Santa Fe, I returned once again to the Universidad Nacional del Litoral, where I had studied law, since, in Argentina as in so many other Latin American countries, the university is a kind of "free zone" that offers its shelter to a lot of "unconventional" activities. The Institute of Sociology asked me to organize a four-day seminar on filmmaking. The fervid enthusiasm of the dozens of young people who attended ensured that the seminar was only a beginning.

Photodocumentaries

After briefly situating the problem in theoretical terms, I immediately confronted my students with a practical task: making photodocumentaries. The idea was simply to venture forth with a still camera and any available tape recorder in search of one's own environment—to converse with and photograph people, places, animals, plants, but mainly *problems* of one's surroundings. One hundred and twenty eager photographers scattered themselves around the city and its outskirts in search of potential topics for a future national cinema.

The experiment produced a rich harvest of themes, all of them informed by an explicit social awareness and concern. *Tire dié*, about the children begging along the railroad trestles, would provide the basis for the first filmed social survey [*encuestra social*] in Latin America. Others included *El conventillo*, on overcrowded housing; *Nuncia*, about a street vendor; *Mercado de abasto* [*Public Market*]; *Un boliche* [*A Tavern*]; and *A la cola* [*Get in Line*], about the consequences of the lack of modern sanitation facilities.

As a result of this seminar, the Institute of Sociology decided to establish an Institute of Cinematography, which would, eventually, assume independence and its own name: La Escuela Documental de Santa Fe [The Documentary School of Santa Fe].

Theory and Practice

My work has always been shaped by a refusal to separate theory from practice. Each film I've made—from *Tire dié*, where I had 120 assistants, through *Los inundados*, where I had nearly 80, to my most recent film, *Org*, where I had only 1—has been a film/school. I do not believe in "formal" education; I believe in learning by doing. Theory and practice must go hand in hand. I would say—without bias and without hesitation—that practice has to be the key, with theory as its guide and interpreter. This is the foundation on which the first school of documentary filmmaking in Latin America was built.

I returned from Europe with the idea of founding a film school modeled after the Centro Sperimentale, where directors, actors, cinematographers, scenographers, sound technicians, and so on, would all receive their training—in short, a school that would produce *fiction* filmmakers. Back in Santa Fe, once I saw the actual conditions of the city and the country, I realized that such a school would be premature. What was needed was a school that would combine the basics of filmmaking with the basics of sociology, history, geography, and politics. Because the real undertaking at hand was a quest for national identity, an identity that had been lost or alienated by a system of economic and political as well as cultural hegemony established by the dominant classes in concert first with Spanish colonizers, later with British investors, and most recently with agents of the United States.

This need to seek out a national identity was what prompted me to pose the problem in strictly *documentary* terms. It is my belief that the first step to be taken by an aspiring national film industry is to document national reality. And so the Escuela Documental concentrated on developing the three major types of cineasts necessary to the documentary: directors, cinematographers, and producers. The organization of the school evolved day by day, on a hit-or-miss basis, guided by our ongoing self-criticism.

Tire dié: Genesis of the First Filmed Social Survey

An exhibition of the original photodocumentaries toured not only the Santa Fe region and Buenos Aires, but other parts of the country as well, ranging as far as Montevideo, at the invitation of the organizers of the SODRE film festival.[1] Our first film project was an outgrowth of that initial experiment with photodocumentaries. From among them we chose the one that seemed to have the most rigor and the greatest impact, the one that offered the fullest opportunity for denouncing a deplorable set of social conditions.

After two years' work and innumerable obstacles, *Tire dié* was transformed from a photodocumentary into a film. We had very few resources. We shot with two borrowed cameras and film stock that was either donated or wangled out of the university. Our tape recorder was not exactly up to professional standards. I remember how we would go every afternoon to those often-flooded lowlands where the film was shot, carrying our modest cameras and the tape recorder's giant battery in a strongbox. The weight of those batteries would sink us up to our knees in mud.

The eighty people who participated in the shooting were divided into groups, each of which concentrated on a specific individual from that shanty community where children daily risked their lives running across the railroad trestle begging coins from passengers of the passing trains. With the exception of the actual photography, which was done by only two people, all tasks were virtually interchangeable. Decisions were made collectively. *Tire dié* was the product of constant, ongoing discussion. During that two-year period, we went almost every afternoon to the river flats to film. We went to observe and understand and exchange ideas with the people who lived there, but we ended up sharing their lives. The film became secondary to the interpersonal relationships that developed between us.

The premier of *Tire dié* in the Great Hall of the Universidad Nacional del Litoral was an event unparalleled in the annals of Argentine university history. The auditorium was filled to capacity with people from the most varied social backgrounds—from august university professors to the little street kids who appear in the film, all dressed up in their cleanest shirt, but barefoot as always, since they had no shoes. We had to screen the film three times. At one o'clock in the morning it was still rolling.

That first version was about an hour long. We showed it to everyone who appeared in it, taking it around the slums of Santa Fe and discussing it with people. Film students made up hundreds of questionnaires inquiring about which parts were effective, which were not, and why. All these data were compiled before cutting the definitive, thirty-three-minute version.

Given the poor quality of our tape recorder, the original soundtrack was virtually unintelligible. But because it was a survey film, it was essential that the audience be able to understand what the interviewees said. So when we made the final cut, we had to do something with the soundtrack as well. We laid on an additional soundtrack in which a leading Argentine actor and actress repeat the key information, serving as intermediaries between the subjects of the film and the audience.

Inspired by my then-remote experiences with the traveling puppet theater, we continued to distribute *Tire dié* and our subsequent films with a primitive "mobile cinema," which consisted of a truck and a projector. Years later, when I made my first trip to Cuba, the first thing I asked to see was a mobile cinema unit. I was taken to the Zapata Swamp to see the screening of a Charlie Chaplin film. It was enormously moving and gratifying to see that what we had attempted with such modest means was being implemented with all the resources a new socialist state could offer.

After *Tire dié*, we made numerous other documentaries, among them *La inundación de Santa Fe* [*The Flooding of Santa Fe*], *El palanquero* [*The Pile Driver*], *El puente de papel* [*The Paper Bridge*], and *Los 40 cuartos* [*The Forty Rooms*]. The photodocumentary and the interviews continued to serve as a first step to the filmed documentary.

The End of an Experiment

A handful of other films were the product of a different approach. *La pampa gringa* [1962], a historical film whose purpose was to commemorate the role played by European immigrants in opening up the Argentine pampa, was constructed from old family photographs. The word *gringo* in this context refers to Europeans of many different nationalities, but principally to the Italians. The film reconstructs the history of the town called Esperanza [hope]—telling name—a colony founded near Santa Fe in the mid-nineteenth century. *La primera fundación de Buenos Aires* [*The First Founding of Buenos Aires*, 1959] was another composite film, based not on photographs but on the cartoon drawings of a popular humorist, Oski.

Commercial distribution of documentary shorts was problematic at best. The new film legislation passed after Perón's ouster decreed that every feature-length film in commercial release had to be accompanied by a short, but in fact the law was not consistently enforced. To overcome this problem, I hit on a solution that was later to be used in several other Latin American countries as well: I strung several thematically related shorts together and distributed them as a feature-length film. *Che, Buenos Aires* [1961] combined two documentary shorts of mine with two by other filmmakers; all four had the capital city as their theme.

These compilation documentaries were "innocent" enough, but the work of the Escuela Documental on contemporary themes was beginning to draw official disapproval and, eventually, censure. From an official standpoint, the definitive proof of the school's subversive nature was the film called *The Forty Rooms* [1962], our second filmed survey, about conditions in an overcrowded tenement called El Conventillo. After being shown as part of the Annual Short Film Showcase organized by the National Board of Culture, the film was confiscated and banned. No amount of public pressure succeeded in obtaining either the film's release or an explanation.

This and other serious problems made it clear to me that I would not long be able to continue as director of the school, which was being labeled a "center for subversive activities." Let's be frank: in fact, it *was*. What kind of subversion? Artistic subversion because we questioned *everything*; political and professional subversion because we were training people different from those who controlled the rest of the Argentine film industry. Our subjects, our goals, our methodology—everything was different.

My last act as director of the Escuela Documental was to assemble a documentary history of our experience from 1956 to 1963. For anyone who has lived through such tumultuous years, ardently involved in political struggle, it would have been all too easy and all too human to subjectivize and thus distort one's account. To avoid this danger, I decided to limit myself to compiling the most relevant materials produced over that seven-year period and publishing them in book form.[2] I was careful to document all the films we made and all the people who worked on them. Many people whose names appear there—Gerardo Vallejo, Diego Bonacina, Jorge Goldenberg, Manuel Horacio Giménez, for example—subsequently spread their filmmaking skills over the length and breadth of Latin America. Others, like Raymundo Gleyzer and Jorge Cedrón, don't appear at all because, during my tenure at least, their ties to the school were more indirect.

The Roads of Exile

With the fall of the Frondizi government and the installation of a military regime, I knew I had to leave. But I did not go alone. Five of us left together as a kind of "scouting party" to investigate what was going on elsewhere in Latin America and, eventually, to create alternative possibilities for those who had stayed behind. In late 1963 we crossed the northern border in semiclandestine fashion. To have left through Buenos Aires would have meant leaving our films behind.

For what seemed like endless days and nights we traveled in an infernal little train across the Brazilian state of Rio Grande do Sul before finally arriving at São Paulo, where we had a number of contacts, among them two former students—Vlado Herzog and Maurice Capovilla.[3] Those filmmakers introduced us to others, including future director Sérgio Muniz and future producer Thomaz Farkas, historian and critic Paulo Emílio Salles Gomes, and Rudá Andrade, director of the Cinemathèque at the Museum of Modern Art in São Paulo.

Andrade organized a retrospective of our work at the museum, which led to other invitations for lectures and screenings and, eventually, to a plan for aseries of documentaries. We began with four short films. Instead of planning them in the conventional way, to be produced one after the other, we decided to produce them all simultaneously. This would not have been possible without the generous financial backing provided by Thomaz Farkas and the unsurpassed production skills of one of the Escuela Documental's most outstanding students, Edgardo Pallero, who had left Argentina with me. The four documentaries—Gerardo Sarno's *Viramundo*, Paulo Gil Soares's *Memória do cangaço* [*Memory of the Cangaço*], Manuel Horacio Giménez's *Nossa escola do samba* [*Our Samba School*], and Maurice Capovilla's *Subterrâneos do futebol* [*Soccer Underground*]—are now landmarks in Brazilian film history, the first examples of an unparalleled series of documentaries on Brazilian culture produced by Thomaz Farkas over a period of several years.

Our experience with the group in São Paulo led to contacts with filmmakers in Rio de Janeiro and then to my own plans for a feature film based on a book on Brazilian popular culture, *Jõao Boa Morte* by Ferreira Gullar.

The political situation in Brazil at this time [early 1964] was very volatile. Jõao Goulart, a progressive, was president. Many sectors of the population were mobilized, among them the peasantry. I remember standing in a public square with some fellow filmmakers while endless truckloads of machete-bearing campesinos arrived to hear Goulart decree Brazil's first land reform.

A short time later, as in Argentina under Frondizi, the colonels decided to let Goulart's head roll.[4] With the military coup of 1 April 1964, I stood by powerless for the second time while my prospects for pursuing the kind of filmmaking to which I was committed were shut down in my face. As a militant who has struggled his whole life long to avoid the separation of personal history and public history, I have had to pay the high price of subordinating my work and my opportunities as a filmmaker to historical circumstances.

Although the Brazilian situation still held some possibilities for my friends and collaborators, it was clear that the kind of feature-length films I had hoped to make there had become impossible. We all agreed that I had to detach myself from our little group and go off to see what alternatives existed in other Latin American territories.

I traveled to Mexico, where I spoke with Emilio García Riera, leading film historian and critic, and with Gabriel García Márquez, who was at that time a frustrated screenwriter in Mexico. Despite sporadic attempts at a "new Mexican cinema," the situation there was quite bleak.

In mid-1964, I arrived in Cuba, where I was greeted with great affection and solidarity. But there, too, the situation was difficult. Cuban filmmakers had to confront grave problems, including severe shortages of equipment and foreign exchange. After some disastrous experiments in coproduction with other countries, it was clear that the first priority was consolidating the internal organization of the Cuban Film Institute. It was not the moment for me to propose another kind of collaboration.

It was only after this long pilgrimage in search of filmmaking opportunities within Latin America, having left no possible stone unturned, that I decided to return to Italy. It was neither a wished for nor a voluntary decision, but one reached out of desperation. I returned to the place where I had been trained and had practiced as a filmmaker in the belief that it might offer opportunities to pursue work that I could not undertake in Latin America at that particular time.

We militant filmmakers are dependent on the "permissiveness," however limited, of bourgeois democratic governments. When the dark night of fascism constricts the room for maneuver offered by more "liberal" regimes, which have a stake, at least, in keeping up appearances, we all face the same range of options: to try to pursue our work in our own country, despite the heightened repression; to "lie low" and wait until circumstances improve; to emigrate to another country in Latin America; or to abandon the continent. Any one of these options might be valid, depending on the particular circumstances, and they must be taken into account when judging the work of any filmmaker.

From Nationalistic to Cosmic, from Realistic to Raving, from Popular to Lumpen

My experience as a filmmaker begins with a manifesto entitled "For a Nationalist, Realist and Popular Cinema" and culminates in another manifesto, entitled "For a Cosmic Cinema, Raving and Lumpen." The breadth of the trajectory is a product of expansion rather than of negation.

This latest manifesto, a poem published in conjunction with the screening at the Venice film festival of my latest film, *Org*, is proof of the fact that I am more than ever a "foreign element" in the country where I have lived now for fifteen years. Consistent with one of the attitudes that has shaped my entire life and work, my years in Italy have been marked by the conscious decision *not* to become a part of Italian life. However painful it may be, I cannot disguise my own condition; I cannot cease to be an uprooted Latin American trying to build a life in exile. Naturally, I take part in the life around me—I attend demonstrations, I participate in debates—but always with the awareness that I am a "marginal" being in the Italian context, and that my "marginalization" has been a conscious choice.

The film I have just completed, *Org*, is also a "marginal" film. Slowly, like a snail that leaves behind a silvery trail, I've assembled the film as I've gone about living my daily life, until the two have become indistinguishable to me. The film is a poem, a fantasy, a Rorschach test for the spectator, more visceral than rational, aimed less at the conscious mind than at the subconscious.

Although it grows out of my filmmaking experiences in Latin America, I don't believe that *Org* belongs with what I call my "Latin American cycle"; but, if pressed, I have to concede that in a sense the film participates in and even anticipates the difficulties and contradictions that countless Latin American filmmakers have been compelled to face, given the tragic historical events that have plagued Latin American political life since the Bolivian coup of 1971 and the overthrow of the Popular Unity government in Chile in 1973.

Evaluation of an Experience

I occasionally hear about other filmmakers who, years later and in relatively distant countries, have developed an approach similar to the one we evolved at the Escuela Documental de Santa Fe. A relatively recent example would be the work of the Colombian documentarists Marta Rodríguez and Jorge Silva. If our experiences parallel each other, the links need not be direct ones. I believe that, on the one hand, the need to confront one's national reality and, on the other, the scarcity of resources endemic to politically committed filmmaking in Latin America, mean that basically unrelated experiences converge in necessity. Our efforts in Santa Fe grew out of a real and vital necessity. Ours was a pilot experience that later took wings throughout the continent, not because of the creative impulse of a single individual but because of the needs and imperatives of a social, political, and historical reality that was bound to find many spokespeople.

There are basically two kinds of filmmakers: one invents an imaginary reality; the other confronts an existing reality and attempts to understand it, analyze it, criticize it, judge it, and, finally, translate it into film. In the latter case, the lasting validity of the work can only be corroborated in space and time, that is, by history and geography. The New Latin American Cinema movement, as it has evolved and spread over the length and breadth of Latin America during the past twenty years, has somehow justified those of us who decided so many years ago to seek out our own national reality and try to communicate it. Not to invent it, but to *re-invent* it: to interpret and transform it.

This First International Festival of New Latin American Cinema here in Havana has given us the opportunity to survey and evaluate the work of the past decade. We stand now on a summit from which we can also make out some of the contours that lie ahead. I believe that the time is ripe for renewal, because the only true revolution is a permanent revolution.

Notes

1. Sponsored by Uruguay's Radio-Electric Broadcasting Society (SODRE) from the early fifties through the late sixties (with a hiatus from 1962 to 1965), this short-film festival gave impetus and visibility to the incipient movement of politically committed documentaries, particularly in the Southern Cone.

2. Fernando Birri, *La Escuela Documental de Santa Fe* (Santa Fe, Argentina: Editorial Documento del Instituto de Cinematografía de la Universidad Nacional del Litoral, 1964).

3. Vladimir Herzog, filmmaker and prominent television journalist in São Paulo, was arrested in 1975 and died in detention shortly thereafter. His death sparked a massive wave of protest around the country. Maurice Capovilla continues to work in film and television in Brazil.

4. This expression is purely metaphorical, since the ousted Goulart fled to the safety of his Uruguayan ranch rather than confront the military.

Chapter 2

Mario Handler
(Uruguay)

Starting from Scratch: Artisanship and Agitprop

Plate 2. Mario Handler at the Second International Festival of the New Latin American Cinema, Havana, 1980. Photo by Julianne Burton.

Though Mario Handler's documentary shorts have not been distributed in North America, his trajectory is of particular interest because of his intellectual familiarity with worldwide developments in documentary, on the one hand, and because of the extreme practical limitations imposed on him by circumstances within his native country, on the other. Handler's resolution of these disparities combined contemporary conceptual advances with primitive technology to produce a new kind of *cine urgente* (urgent cinema), which would exert considerable impact in Uruguay and elsewhere in Latin America.

Julianne Burton interviewed Mario Handler at the First International Festival of the

In the early sixties, on the eve of a political and cultural transformation that would last for a decade, I was an engineering student in Montevideo who had participated in film clubs since the age of fifteen. I was interested in the technical aspects of photography as was one of my teachers, Plácido Añón—epistemologist, philosopher, technical perfectionist—who was making scientific films before his premature death at the age of thirty-three. Añón became my mentor; he furnished me with bibliography and guided my reading in the technical aspects of photography.

In 1963 I was sent to Europe on scholarship to study scientific filmmaking. I spent several months at the Institute for Scientific Cinema in Göttingen, Germany, but I grew impatient with what seemed to me an overly mechanical approach to reality. I wanted to find a point of equilibrium between the detached depiction of existing reality, scientific or otherwise, and artistic expression. I went to Holland, where I developed contacts with a number of documentarists, and from there to Prague, where I made my first film, a fifteen-minute documentary called *En Praga* [*In Prague*, 1964], a kind of critique of Europe as experienced by a young Latin American who had, until that time, been unaware of the existence of cultural colonization. All my alienation just happened to spill over in Czechoslovakia, though it could have happened in Holland or Germany or any other European country I might have been visiting at the time.

Before leaving for Europe, I had been named to fill the post that Añón's death had left vacant at the Film Institute of the University of the Republic [ICUR]. When I returned, I was all ready to put together a million-dollar production setup. I knew exactly where to go and what to buy. But at the institute, they simply said, "No. Here's your salary: $100 a month."

Our existing equipment was minimal and so were the laboratories. Film stock was five times as expensive as in neighboring Argentina. Against the wishes of ICUR's director, I arranged for the purchase of the first Nagra sound recorder, but it was two years in transit. There was simply no infrastructure. Film production began to seem like an impossible dream.

My own particular trajectory as a filmmaker is only meaningful when placed within the context of Latin American—and particularly Uruguayan—social, political, and cultural history. The entire New Latin American Cinema movement can only be understood in light of this broader contextualization. Within Latin America, Uruguay is a somewhat special case—socially, historically, culturally, and in terms of the role it played in film as well.

New Latin American Cinema, held in Havana in December 1979. The interview was revised and expanded at the Second Havana Festival, held the following year. The editor is grateful to Walter Achugar and Danilo Trelles for providing corroborating and supplementary information on the Uruguayan experience in Madrid in summer 1981.

For more than a decade, from 1957 until the end of the sixties, Uruguay played a key role in the diffusion and, to a lesser degree, the production of the New Latin American Cinema. A series of film festivals and a gradual but steady politicization combined to offer a forum for the new cinema, and particularly the social documentary, which did not exist at the time in any other part of the continent. Uruguay became a kind of crossroads for members of the New Latin American Cinema movement and their works. The first systematic attempts at exhibition and distribution on a national and even on an international scale were made in Uruguay during this period. As a result of these efforts, Uruguayan filmgoers enjoyed broader access to politically committed Latin American cinema than their counterparts in any other country in the Americas—with the possible exception of Cuba. The country's growing socioeconomic crisis, combined with the increasingly repressive policies of the government, eventually produced a kind of diaspora, as Uruguayan filmmakers were compelled to emigrate to various Latin American and European countries.

Uruguay had been, until the mid-fifties, one of the most prosperous, progressive, and peaceful countries in Latin America, but in the mid-fifties the country entered a period of convulsive change. The international demand for Uruguayan beef and wool, fueled by World War II and the Korean War, declined with the resolution of these conflicts, bringing about the demise of the great era of national prosperity. Over the next thirty years, the country's economic condition would continue to deteriorate. The "Switzerland of the Americas" would become only a memory. By the late fifties, we were entering a period of manifest social struggle, led by worker and student organizations. In social and political as well as cultural life, a highly critical attitude prevailed, which singled out two primary targets as responsible for the country's woes: the current president of the republic, Luis Batlle Berres, and the United States as a neocolonial power.

The political crisis naturally exerted an impact on cultural activity. The country's traditional "cosmopolitanism," its identification with Europe in general—and France in particular—as the sole source of culture, began to be challenged as musicians, fiction writers, journalists, and filmmakers started redirecting their energies toward national rather than adopted concerns.

We Uruguayans display a tendency toward a kind of "hypercultivation" when it comes to the arts: we try to overcompensate for our distance from the traditional centers of cultural production by being more *au courant* than the Parisians. Film was no exception. Uruguayans tended to be primarily interested in "prestige" cinema. The International Film Festival at Punta del Este was a leading exponent of this bias, emphasizing films by consecrated masters like Ingmar Bergman and Vittorio De Sica.

My countrymen began founding film societies and archives relatively early on—in the late forties and early fifties. The most important of these are the Cine-Club del Uruguay, the Cine-Club Universitario, and the Cinemateca Uruguaya. It wasn't until my generation, which came of age a decade later, that there was a sustained impetus to *create* a film culture of our own rather than merely *appreciate* the film cultures of other countries. But we all began as *cine-clubistas* [film society members]. We had the privilege of being exposed to a broader range of international film culture than anywhere else in Latin America. We saw the best of French, Soviet, Italian, German, British, and American output, as well as more commercial fare and some extremely specialized technical and scientific production. We would watch absolutely anything. We were "filmaniacs."

During the period of national prosperity, an occasional feature film was produced in Uruguay, but this always sporadic activity was definitely curtailed by the worsening economic situation. There was never the kind of infrastructure necessary for a national film industry, since our country simply does not have enough inhabitants to guarantee a return on the investment in film production. The spread of television in the 1950s further reduced exhibition revenues at the movie theaters. Where once Uruguay had boasted one of the highest per capita movie-going rates in the world (fifteen to twenty film viewings per capita per year), we had by the late sixties declined to between six and eight.

If commercial film activity was virtually nil, the possibilities for amateur filmmaking were not much better. Film societies occasionally sponsored "lightning contests," a kind of movie-making marathon in which every contestant was allotted a limited amount of film to be shot in a single day and screened without editing. A number of our future directors got their first filmmaking experience in such contests—Ugo Ulive, Miguel Castro, Walter Dassori, and Alberto Mantarás, among others.

Before detailing the events and circumstances that began to transform this rather dismal panorama, converting a consumer-oriented, contemplative stance into a more active, participatory one, I should summarize the state of Latin American and international film production. The 1950s saw both a postwar resurgence of Hollywood cinema and a challenge to its worldwide hegemony. This challenge was posed by the Italian Neorealist movement, which was stylistically and philosophically antithetical to the Hollywood model. In particular, the Italians' incorporation of certain documentarylike conventions and techniques to portray intimate aspects of the everyday lives of ordinary people had a great impact on us. At the same time, we continued to admire certain Hollywood directors, people like William Wyler and George Stevens. We were less influenced by contemporary French filmmakers than by the French critic and theorist André Bazin, founder of the influential journal *Cahiers du Cinéma*. We were also familiar with the Anglo-American documentary movement led by John Grierson. Among the American documentarists, we were particularly impressed by Robert

Flaherty. We admired Swedish documentarist Arne Sucksdorff. We were also favorably impressed by the Dutch documentary movement, in particular the work of Bert Hanstra, Herman Van der Horstz, and Joris Ivens. This was the period when the development of direct sound technology was transforming documentary pictures through the work of Frenchmen like Jean Rouch and Chris Marker and the American variant of *cinéma vérité* practiced by Richard Leacock and Donn Pennebaker.

In Latin America at the time, there were only two national film traditions: the Argentine and the Mexican. Though the technical level of each was relatively high, the style and content were so excessively formulaic and vacuous that only a bare handful of directors seemed to have anything to offer—people like Lucas Demaré and Hugo del Carril in Argentina, and Fernando de Fuentes in Mexico. In the decade following World War II, both the Mexican and the Argentine film industries began to fall into decline as U.S. companies reasserted their control over Latin American markets. (It wasn't until some years later that we learned of the impressive history of national film production in Brazil, and in particular about the pioneering work of the great realist and fiction filmmaker Humberto Mauro.)

Countries like Colombia and Venezuela managed to produce an occasional feature film, but always with a high percentage of foreign participation. In Cuba, CMQ-TV, the most advanced television network in Latin America at the time, seemed of much greater interest than the sporadic and generally mediocre film production generated on the island. In the remaining countries, we knew of no national filmmaking activity whatsoever.

The International Festival of Documentary and Experimental Film held in Montevideo was founded in 1954 by Danilo Trelles, head of the Cine Arte section of an extraordinary and unique cultural institution called SODRE. This organization enjoyed enormous prestige throughout the continent because of its commitment to gathering, sponsoring, and transmitting the most advanced work in music, ballet, opera, drama, and, later, film. The SODRE film festivals of 1957 and 1958 marked the takeoff of the documentary film movement in Latin America. For the first time documentarists from throughout South America met and shared their work: Fernando Birri and his students from Santa Fe, Argentina; Patricio Kaulen from Chile; Jorge Ruiz from Bolivia; Manuel Chambi from Peru; and Nelson Pereira dos Santos from Brazil, whose fictional films in the Neorealist mode would mark the inception of the Cinema Novo movement. Pereira dos Santos's use of location settings and nonprofessional actors, and his commitment to depicting sectors of the society generally excluded from conventional feature filmmaking, made his work highly respected and influential among documentarists.

The 1958 SODRE festival, with John Grierson as the guest of honor, included Pereira dos Santos's *Rio zona norte* [*Rio Northern Zone*, 1957], the second and last film of the unfinished trilogy begun in 1955 with *Rio cuarenta graus* [*Rio Forty Degrees*]; Ruiz's *Vuelve Sebastiana* [*Come Back, Sebastiana*, 1956], a color treatment of an indigenous theme; Chambi's *Carnaval de Kanas* [1957] on Quechua festivals in the Cuzco region; and the photo-reportages from the Documentary School of Santa Fe, which constituted the first stage of what would become *Tire dié* [*Throw Me a Dime*, 1958/1960]. The cumulative effect of these films was a revelation: we were seeing facets of Latin American social reality that had never been captured for the screen before. We realized that in far-flung corners of the continent, people were pursuing unique and yet remarkably similar kinds of projects.

That same year saw the release of the first important Uruguayan contribution to this burgeoning New Latin American Cinema movement: Alberto Miller's *Cantegriles* [1958]. The originality of this eight-minute documentary lies in its directness and total lack of pretension. With a sober and dispassionate air, it contrasts the luxurious housing of the Cantegril Country Club at Punta del Este with the urban slums of the marginal population, popularly referred to with acid irony as the "cantegriles" of the poor. This film marked a sharp departure from other amateur efforts and the all-too-pervasive imitations of European models. It simply set out to capture an existing social reality and, in doing so, made a great impact on a number of actual and aspiring filmmakers.

Ugo Ulive, who would later be recognized as the most talented member of this generation of filmmakers, made his debut the following year, 1959, with a medium-length feature, *Un vintén Pa'l Judas*. The title refers to the traditional Holy Week custom according to which children construct an effigy of Judas and stuff it with firecrackers. The importance of this film has been recognized only in retrospect, but Ulive's subsequent film, a documentary financed by a national political leader, was widely recognized even at the time of its release as a major step forward for Uruguayan filmmaking. No one had ever seen anything like it before. *Como el Uruguay no hay* [*There's No Place Like Uruguay*, 1960] was an eight-minute collage that combined contemporary and archival footage with primitive animation and other unconventional devices to create the first effective political satire in Latin American film history. Those eight brief minutes were so impressive that even our super-sophisticated Uruguayan critics, always so quick to disparage local efforts for failing to meet their Europe-oriented standards, had to admit that "here at last is evidence of high-quality national filmmaking."

On the strength of this film, the newly founded Cuban Film Institute invited Ulive to Havana. During the years he lived in Cuba, he continued theatrical directing (which had been his principal activity in Uruguay), coscripted Tomás Gutiérrez Alea's second feature, a comedy called *Las doce sillas* [*The Twelve Chairs*, 1962], and eventually directed a feature-length fictional film of his own, *Crónica cubana* [*Cuban Chronicle*, 1963], which was never commercially released. Ulive's return from Cuba roughly coincided with my return from Europe.

With my newly acquired technical expertise and my elaborate plans for launching national film production, I found the lack of local resources and support discouraging, to say the least. When faced with such obstacles, you have to be creative. You join forces with your friends; you invent things. At the Film Institute, I discovered a pile of film stock donated by UNESCO, which had gone unused because of bureaucratic red tape. I took those rolls and said to myself, "This is all I need to make a film."

With my camera, I began to explore the area around the Humanities Building and the port, an old and interesting part of Montevideo. I discovered a *bichicome* [vagabond] who kindled my interest. He called himself a *caminante* [walker] and understood his profession to be a very ancient one. I began to film him. People offered to lend me books about the *clochards* of Paris, but I was fed up with *clochards* and with books. I just wanted to make a modest little film, an *Uruguayan* film, which would approach a particular facet of national reality very directly. I wanted to present a portrait of a society through the study of a single individual, to arrive at the social through the personal. I set aside all my scientific training and worked intuitively. In this case, the research and the creative process were one and the same.

I spent a lot of time with that man, Carlos. We became friends. We would drink beer and talk or we'd walk together for hours on end without saying a word. Gradually I got him accustomed to the camera. I did the sound recording separately after all the shooting was done. In a session that lasted three hours, I asked him questions about life, education, society, himself— sometimes cajoling him and other times treating him quite forcefully.

During the six months I spent working on the film, I had to conceal the fact from the director of the institute. The shooting was slow, exhausting work, and so was the editing, which had to be done with a viewfinder and a projector because there was no moviola in Uruguay at the time. I made all the cuts on the original negative, since I had no money to pay for a work print. The whole experience was a brutal apprenticeship, one I would never wish to repeat.

The finished film was thirty-one minutes long. I called it *Carlos: Cine-retrato de un caminante* [*Carlos: Cine-Portrait of a Vagabond*]. It was premiered at a film festival sponsored by the prestigious Uruguayan news-weekly *Marcha* in 1965—a festival that, until then, had only featured foreign films. I was not at all prepared for the impact that this experiment in direct cinema would have. The audience was enthusiastic, and the next issue of *Marcha* devoted an entire page to the film. One critic wrote, "Fresh start

[*Punto y aparte*]. Uruguayan cinema begins here." At the Festival de Cine Independiente del Cono Sur, which was held in Montevideo that same year, *Carlos* won first prize in the experimental film category, along with Brazilian Geraldo Sarno's *Viramundo* [1965] in the documentary division.

Despite its success, the film had no chance of getting commercial distribution. It was an anomaly. One distributor told me, "Come back when you have more and then we'll see." *Carlos* received wider distribution outside the country. Cosme Alves, director of Cinemateca of Rio's Museum of Modern Art, circulated it throughout Brazil. It was also shown in Argentina, Venezuela, and Chile, where it won a special mention at the 1967 international film festival at Viña del Mar.

It was at this point that Ulive returned from his five-year stay in Cuba, and we decided to collaborate. We intended to make a barbed, analytical documentary about the upcoming national elections. There was no precedent for such an undertaking; not even our long line of fine political commentators had produced an analysis of the Uruguayan electoral process. Since we knew that the director of the University Film Institute, my boss, would never provide support for a critical or satirical effort, we submitted a very bland treatment. We filmed from May through November in the capital and in the interior, concentrating primarily on two candidates in particular, a man and a woman. Our approach was essentially observational, leaving a lot of room for improvisation. We used light, portable equipment and filmed in a very fluid, modernist style, often honing in on telling details of gesture or expression by means of a "choker" close-up, rack focus, extreme angles, and the fragmentation of the image. The editing style we used was equally dynamic and aggressive. Ulive and I alternated doing camera, and we often had a third person assisting on sound. Ulive was very bold. Despite his caustic wit, he could be very ingratiating when necessary. He got us into all sorts of places. In addition, he had a quick, penetrating intelligence that made him a pleasure to work with.

Elecciones [*Elections*, 1965], as the film was called, premiered at the *Marcha* Festival in 1967, where it was very favorably received. It has the distinction of being the first Uruguayan documentary to enjoy commercial release in its own country. Producer and distributor Walter Achugar was embarking on an exhibition venture at that time, and his first billing, which ran for four weeks, paired the Argentine feature *El romance del Aniceto y la Francisca* [*The Ballad of Aniceto and Francisca*, Leonardo Favio, 1966] with *Elections*. The film also enjoyed another, more dubious distinction: it was the first film ever barred from the SODRE festival. Uruguay prided itself on absolute freedom of expression, but with the first attempt at a critical appraisal of the carnivalesque side of the national electoral process, we suddenly had to confront censorship. We raised a great hue and cry, but the decision was not reversed. Ulive decided to leave the country once more, this time for good. He went to Venezuela, where he continues to work as a filmmaker.

Those of us who stayed behind were faced with a burgeoning bureaucracy, a rapidly deteriorating economic situation, and increasing political polarization. I was desperately searching for the means to finance a film on the Conference of American Heads of State at Punta del Este in April of 1967. Lyndon Johnson would be present, along with "liberal" Latin American political leaders like Díaz Ordaz of Mexico, Chile's Eduardo Frei, and Venezuela's Raúl Leoni, as well as blatantly repressive military dictators like Juan Carlos Onganía from Argentina, Alfredo Stroessner from Paraguay, and Brazil's Arturo Costa e Silva.

Montevideo erupted with student demonstrations in response to the conference, and I went out to film them with my Bolex, until one day I was attacked by a policeman, who wrecked my camera. For the sequence shot in Punta del Este, I had no choice but to use a borrowed camera, which would have been notably inferior to the Bolex even *without* the leaky diaphragm. There was thus quite a discrepancy in technical quality between the student footage and that of the heads of state.

Since I had no money for editing or processing, that footage just sat around for several months. Every once in a while I'd work on the editing a bit by hand, intercutting scenes with students and police in the streets with shots of politicians meeting in sedate luxury behind closed doors. Walter Achugar suggested that I try to finish it in time for the 1968 *Marcha* Festival, and the organizers provided me with the minimum amount of cash necessary to do the job.

I was working by myself since I really had to economize. I drew the title by hand right on the negative, one syllable per frame. I decided to do without commentary and just use music. There was already a tremendous disparity between the footage shot in Montevideo and Punta del Este, so I decided to exaggerate that contrast even more by adding music to the student sequences and leaving the footage of the heads of state silent. I asked the Uruguayan folk singer Daniel Viglietti to record something for me. We chose Violeta Parra's "Me gustan los estudiantes" ["I Like Students"] and "Vamos, estudiantes" ["Onward, Students"], a march that Viglietti composed especially for the film.

Without proper equipment, the synchronization process was a nightmare. I worked all night on the eve of the premiere to finish the film in time. Since it was so technically crude, I assumed it would not be very well received, and made only one optical-sound print.

Walter Achugar and José Wainer of *Marcha* were just as nervous as I was at the screening in the Plaza Theater, the largest in Montevideo. They were afraid that the audience would think the sound lapses were a technical defect, so one of them sat in the first row of the theater and the other in the last, and at every lapse in the soundtrack they would yell out, "Right on! Right on!" [¡Así es!]

I had intended to call the film *Violencia en Montevideo* because the gunshots I had filmed were in fact a first in disciplined, democratic Uruguay, and I wanted to draw attention to the fact that there *was* police violence in Montevideo. The members of the audience were so indignant at the visual proof of official violence in their enlightened country that they rushed out of the theater and staged a spontaneous demonstration in the Plaza de la Libertad across the street. *La Nación*, Argentina's leading newspaper, ran a headline that read, "Uruguayan Film Provokes Tumult." The event became famous as a classic case of *agitación directa* (direct agitation). It was, after all, just after May 1968 and student activism was a burning issue around the world.

I was a bit embarrassed to take the film to the Mérida festival in Venezuela because it was so technically imperfect, and I prefer to do things as they should be done. But the response there was just as enthusiastic. The audience went crazy and didn't calm down until the film had been screened three times over.

In the end Viglietti's recording gave its title to the film. *I Like Students* enjoyed enormous success, thanks in large part to Achugar's international connections. It opened in Paris with the Bolivian feature *Blood of the Condor*. Several European countries showed it on television. It was the first Latin American film requested by the Vietnamese. We kept receiving requests for prints, though many people just pirated copies on their own—an expedient that seemed perfectly in keeping with the way the film was made. It never occurred to us to try to make money from it. I remember that eventually I was able to pay Daniel Viglietti one hundred dollars for his collaboration. It was a purely symbolic recompense, since the film's reward was clearly not monetary. *I Like Students* turned out to be a kind of swan song for that early phase of the international student movement, so animated and joyous, because with the seventies came a much more difficult and somber stage in the struggle.

The country's economic situation continued to decline, provoking a steady intensification of both political activism and governmental repression. People had less and less room to maneuvre within conventional, legal limits. Responding to these social, economic, and political pressures, Uruguay became the site of the most successful urban guerrilla movement on the continent, the National Liberation movement (MLN), or Tupamaros. Large street demonstrations were increasingly frequent, but there seemed to be a certain unwritten protocol that restrained the government troops. Though the police often responded violently to the demonstrators, up to this point no one had been killed. Then, in 1969, a student named Liber Arce was killed by the police. Another sign that same year of the escalation of the conflict was the strike in the meat-packing industry, Uruguay's largest industry, which lasted longer than any strike in national history. I made a film called *Uruguay 1969: El problema de la carne* [*Uruguay 1969: The Meat Problem*], which attempted to provide the necessary background to the strike through research into the history of the industry and interviews with union leaders. I see now that because of our reluctance to get embroiled in sectarian issues and interparty conflicts, we held ourselves back from really getting to the root of the political issues and from exploring how the union worked. I originally envisioned a simple newsreel, but, as always, the final product bore little resemblance to the original intent. The film is a kind of essay, didactic and polemical, bearing the influence of *La hora de los hornos* [*The Hour of the Furnaces*, 1968], the three-part documentary epic produced clandestinely in Argentina the preceding year.

In 1970 I made my last film in Uruguay. On the first anniversary of Liber Arce's death, I put together a tribute called *Liber Arce, Liberarse* [a play on words: *liberarse* means "to liberate oneself"]—silent, with intertitles and a lot of quick cutting, a kind of return to the style of *I Like Students*. I expanded the film's frame of reference by inserting still photographs of the three Tupamaro guerrillas killed in the raid on Pando, archival footage of the conflict in Vietnam, and a quote from Che Guevara. The film won the Joris Ivens prize at the Leipzig festival that year.

Repression and political polarization increased during the 1970s. In 1972 the Cinemateca del Tercer Mundo was shut down,[1] its prints and equipment confiscated, and two of its organizers jailed. In June of 1973, the military staged a coup d'état and suppressed all democratic institutions. Thousands of Uruguayans were imprisoned or made to "disappear"; thousands more left the country. I was fortunate to be in the latter group. I have lived for the past decade in Venezuela, where I continue to work as a filmmaker and teacher of film production and to watch with interest the slow but inevitable process of redemocratization in Uruguay.

Note

1. See pages 229 and 231 for a description and history of the organization.

Chapter 3

Jorge Silva and Marta Rodríguez
(Colombia)

Cine-Sociology and Social Change

Plate 3. Marta Rodríguez and Jorge Silva. Photo courtesy the filmmakers.

Marta Rodríguez, a sociologist by training, and Jorge Silva, originally a still photographer, have been collaborating on politically committed documentaries in Colombia since the late sixties. Their first film, *Chircales* (*The Brickmakers*), had its debut at the Second Encounter of Latin American Filmmakers in Mérida, Venezuela, in 1968. Their second, *Planas: Testimony about an Ethnocide*, was released in 1973. Part I of *Campesinos* (*Peasants*) won awards at several European documentary festivals in 1975 and 1976. The fact that each of these films deals with a different sector of Colombia's "lower" classes—unskilled urban workers on the margin of the national economy, the indigenous population completely outside it, and

Q: How did the idea for *The Brickmakers* originate?

Rodríguez: The idea grew out of a sociological study begun in 1958 in the neighborhood of Tunjuelito in the southern suburbs of Bogotá, under the direction of Father Camilo Torres.[1] I was part of a group of students who worked there with Camilo over a three-year period. Through the project, we became familiar with the brickyards and made contacts with the brickmaking families. But the actual production work on the film did not begin until 1967, after I returned from studying in France and after Camilo had left to join the guerrillas.

The film grows out of the need to demonstrate in graphic terms the level of exploitation of the working class. Originally, a different quote from Camilo ended the film: "The people are desperate, ready to fight in order that the next generation shall not be enslaved." Eventually we chose instead, "The struggle is a long one; let us begin." The tremendously constraining material and political circumstances under which the film was made helped us develop a whole new methodology, a different approach to filmmaking.

Q: Can you describe the conditions in the community when you began to do your field observation and prepare for shooting?

Silva: Above all, the community was characterized by its rudimentary political level. They were people in transition. No longer fully part of the peasantry because of the social decomposition that resulted from the decade of *La violencia*,[2] they had migrated to the city but were still not completely integrated into the capitalist production routine. They continued trying to insert a whole series of rural values, however peripheral, into their new urban environment.

Rodríguez: All the structures of country life carry over. The brickyard is analogous to the farm. The overseer is there, as are the geographically dispersed dwellings.

At the beginning, communication was a bit difficult because the peasant finds a lot of resentment in the city, a lot of competition. They had trouble communicating even among themselves. There were rivalries. We were often asked, "Why did you choose these people to make your documentary with and not us?"

Q: Why *did* you choose that particular family, the Castañedas?

Rodríguez: The family whom we initially chose had to leave the brickyards

---

semi-inscribed rural agricultural workers, respectively—is an indication of the social concern and analytical precision that characterizes the work of this filmmaking team. Their most recent documentary, *Nuestra voz de tierra, memoria, y futuro* (*Our Voice of Earth, Memory and Future*), was completed in 1981. Julianne Burton excerpted and translated the Silva/Rodríguez interview from the one by Andrés Caicedo and Luis Ospina which appeared in *Ojo al cine* (Cali, Colombia), no. 1 (1974). The interview has been supplemented by the editor's conversations with the filmmakers in Bogotá in early 1976.

after the first screen tests had been made. Afterwards we tried to find another family whose members also spanned several age levels. The Castañedas' eldest child was about twenty at the time and their youngest was two. We felt that we could establish an excellent rapport with them, and this was an essential prerequisite for becoming a part of their world and being able to convey their situation.

Q: How long did the actual shooting take?

Rodríguez: We continued to film over a five-year period. The process took that long because we were constantly evaluating our work and discovering, through discussions with the participants or our own research, that we had to reevaluate our entire theoretical framework, that our preconceptions were irrelevant in practice, or that we had omitted important aspects.

Silva: The first take wasn't shot until after many months of preparation. We began with a series of informal taped interviews, which also helped us establish a good personal relationship with the people involved. After these interviews had been transcribed, synthesized, and analyzed, they began to indicate a possible structure for the film.

Then we worked with a still camera, and only after that stage did we actually begin to film. But by that time we were no longer a foreign element in the community, no longer the wizards with their weird machines.

Rodríguez: We lived with the film's subjects for almost a year, spending every day in the brickyards and returning to Bogotá only to sleep. In the first stage, we had absolutely no equipment; we just went, the two of us, to talk to them. Later, when we had access to equipment, we would be there with the camera loaded and ready, prepared for whatever might occur. We confined ourselves to following everyday events—stages in the brickmaking process, a first communion ceremony, a worker's funeral.

Silva: Because we had become part of their lives, it was possible for them to assume a very casual, unaffected stance in front of the camera, which neither determined nor modified their behavior.

Q: Are any sequences in *The Brickmakers* staged?

Rodríguez: Well, rather than "staged sequences," I would use the term "reconstructions." Aside from the fact that reconstructions are accepted as a legitimate component of documentary cinema, we had to resort to them because of technical limitations. For example, the day of the first communion we borrowed a camera that turned out to be defective, so we had to observe everything in great detail to reconstruct it when we could obtain reliable equipment. The same thing happened with the final sequence, when the family is expelled from the brickyard. We were unable to obtain a camera that day. All we could do was take still photographs.

Q: Could you describe the first screening for the members of that community?

Rodríguez: We had two screenings. The first was not very satisfactory because it followed a union assembly to elect a new governing board, three theatrical performances, and a group singing protest songs. When the film was finally screened at nearly one o'clock in the morning, people were completely exhausted. This is a concrete example of the distribution problems independent political filmmakers face. You have to consider what this kind of a program attempts to do and to evaluate whether or not it succeeds.

Silva: The most important thing is to be familiar with the milieu. Once you become familiar with the environment and the people, you have the opportunity—which for us was totally unexpected—of evaluating the film while you're making it, with the people you're filming. They themselves decide how the sequences should be ordered, for example.

We started work on *The Brickmakers* in 1967, but because of lack of funds and equipment, we didn't manage to produce a final print until March of 1972. What seemed in the beginning to be an enormous handicap—not being able to finish the film quickly—turned out to be extremely useful in terms of the final structure of the film and our methodology.

One of our primary goals was to break with traditional documentary methods, which allow the filmmaker to manipulate reality according to personal whim. This is an elitist approach, since it does not acknowledge the possibility of collaboration with the people who are being filmed. What might be viewed as a work of art is, above all, *their own situation*. With traditional production methods and timetables, we never would have been able to achieve the degree of popular participation we sought. After all, any corrections in a finished film, like re-recording the soundtrack, involve a series of expenses that, due to our economic limitations, we could never have managed.

The discoveries we made during the lengthy process of putting the film together weren't only practical. Every day we had to question ourselves and our way of seeing the world.

Rodríguez: After the disappointment of our first screening for the brickmakers, we scheduled a second screening as part of another union assembly, but this time things were much better organized because between the two screenings, enormous progress had been made. At the first screening, people had been preoccupied with identifying themselves and each other. "There's so-and-so on the screen!" they would shout. By the second screening, people were able to assume a more critical attitude.

Silva: They began to identify certain mechanisms of domination and exploitation, like *compadrazgo*.[3] They saw themselves listening to soap operas on the radio and they began to understand what those soap operas represent. The audience not only was able to identify particular phenomena, it was able to understand their interrelationship.

We did not moderate because we believe that it should be the subjects themselves who lead the discussion, since this raises both their level of participation and their level of political awareness. Actually, since *The Brickmakers* was made, this brickmaking community has taken great strides in ideological awareness and political organization. They now have a union, for example, and the union has expressed interest in filming a kind of epilogue, which would show the level of organization they have achieved. This really signifies a whole new range of communications possibilities for them.

Here's where the issue of coherency in distribution comes in. An audience is not going to raise its political awareness on the basis of one single film, nor can a film like this be separated effectively from its context. The film is just an auxiliary part of a whole formative process.

Q: What exactly do you mean by "coherent distribution policy"? Are you saying that some preliminary political research is necessary to determine the social conditions and receptivity of each particular audience?

Silva: Yes, that's the idea. Our work is not exclusively confined to sending the film out. Instead, we aim to establish a direct working relationship with the communities where it is shown. All too often we see cases of groups who come to perform a play and never return, failing to establish ongoing contact with the community. We believe that politically committed cultural workers always have to ask, "What happens to these people two hours after seeing that particular performance?"

Q: Once the film was finally completed and demand began to expand, what new distribution problems developed and how did you solve them?

Silva: As we have said, economic problems deferred "normal distribution" for a long time, but we were able to use these limitations creatively. The print's initial distribution without a soundtrack provided the opportunity for an audience with some political sophistication to participate *during* the screening. This enabled us to evaluate and enrich the structure of the film on the basis of reactions from many different audiences. Our audiences, in turn, acquired a richer appreciation of the nature and the importance of this kind of documentary.

But to answer your question fully, I think it is necessary to go back to the very beginning of this kind of filmmaking in Colombia. We have always been very aware that, as independent, politically committed filmmakers, we had to start from scratch. Under any circumstances—as part of an established film industry or as an independent—it is difficult to make the kind of cinema that does not make concessions.

At the beginning of the militant film movement, it was said that the essential thing was to capture reality and nothing more, to make reality manifest. Later, this formulation began to seem insufficient. Then the theory of an "imperfect cinema" began to be put forth in Latin America: a kind of cinema that rejects the quest for technical excellence for its own sake inasmuch as it acknowledges that the artist's conception reproduces very definite class interests. One began to oppose a well-made but basically reactionary cinema and to favor a kind of filmmaking that neglects form and technique for the benefit of content.

But then we began to see more clearly that alternative cinema must have not only high technical quality, but also high formal quality, because the popular viewer—worker or peasant—has been formed or deformed by consumer cinema. A kind of filmmaking that sets out to convey the people's reality should not be at a creative disadvantage in either the quality of its formal expression or its ability to reach people.

All these concepts began to develop and evolve as filmmakers continued to confront their own work critically, becoming less and less "directors" and more and more involved in the social and political process of the masses. Their own intellectual process ceased to be central because the problem was no longer defined as either film for its own sake or a simple "reproduction" of reality. Paradoxically, however, the process of self-criticism became increasingly complex once it was recognized that the key to a more "open," "direct" cinema lay in contact with mass organizations and shared experience in popular struggles. Then the problem that initially seemed very simple—to make films that reflect reality—became increasingly complex, since it was no longer a matter of simply "revealing" reality, but of documenting, penetrating, and analyzing it.

It is to be expected that certain kinds of difficulties arise and it is understandable that we haven't yet found solutions, because where would we be if we had already resolved everything? Difficulties keep cropping up in the area of distribution, and these are among the hardest to solve. Filmmakers cannot disconnect themselves from the process of distribution; that is where our work is submitted to the most important criticism. But neither can we be "traveling minstrels," going from place to place indefinitely with film cans under our arms.

There comes a time when a film no longer belongs to anyone, when everyone wants to see it and things go out of control. That's when the need to ensure that each screening situation occurs in the context of an ongoing political process becomes so important; otherwise, the film loses its effectiveness.

We've abandoned the traditional film society setup in order to avoid the type of audience that analyzes films in exclusively (and often falsely) "aesthetic" terms because this kind of snobbery is not particularly useful to us. The most useful responses we have received have been from other kinds of audiences.

This doesn't mean that we pretend to a false populism, believing that only "the people" are the final judge. In a country like ours, where the dominant class controls the means of information as well as the means of production, it is able to manipulate culture according to its interests with one primary objective: the ideological domination of the exploited classes. This explains why sometimes certain sectors of the exploited public reproduce the ideology of the exploiter and are thus prevented from making a critical analysis of their own situation. Fortunately, this is not universal; there are already certain sectors with highly developed levels of consciousness and organization.

Rodríguez: We showed *The Brickmakers* to a group of construction workers, who later commented on how the exploitative mechanisms shown in the film resemble the ones they face under the "contractor" system. They observed that even though their level of organization is higher than that of the brickmakers, their situation is very similar, and they concluded that it is their responsibility to work with them, "to show our solidarity as a union organization and to share our experience." Rather than compassion or analysis in the abstract, this is a very constructive kind of response.

Q: What possibilities exist for recouping the money invested in your films?

Rodríguez: When we made *The Brickmakers*, we never even thought about how we would go about recouping our investment. If we had tried to solve that problem, the film would never have been finished. Does anyone who tries to make films independently in Colombia know how to break even? We believe that all audiences should be charged for film screenings in keeping with their means. This does not mean that the investment can be recovered, however.

Silva: It's virtually impossible to sell prints in Colombia because very few individuals or organizations have access to 16mm projectors.

Q: You have been invited to screen your films at many foreign film festivals.

Rodríguez: We think it is very important for films to be shown outside the country, which is why we participate in international film festivals. The kind of filmmaking that critically examines itself and its environment is not a Colombian invention. Many groups in Europe, Africa, Latin America, and, interestingly enough, even in the United States, make a very critical cinema and distribute it internationally. Cuban documentarist Santiago Alvarez says, "Filmmakers, when they put their work to the service of their people through a coherent understanding of their country's problems, put it to the service of all other peoples as well."

Q: What is the most important practical result of combining sociology or anthropology and filmmaking?

Rodríguez: When you combine the social sciences with a mass medium like film, you are challenging the uses to which both are put by the privileged class while simultaneously putting them at the service of the working class. In contrast to the kind of hermetic treatise that only five initiates can read, this is a way to use anthropology or sociology so that the working class can put it to use analyzing their particular situation.

With *The Brickmakers*, participatory observation, becoming part of the community, was a major influence. But after the whole process was over, we began to reevaluate certain anthropological concepts—"culture" and "acculturation," for example. In practice, you must reevaluate them all. You find that you're dealing with something else. They are no longer valid because in a university the anthropologist is given training that is totally independent of reality and that, above all, serves a particular system, a dominant ideology.

Silva: But the most important thing about applying the social sciences or "scientific" analysis to reality is the need for analytical tools to perform that operation. One must somehow bring a theoretical framework capable of analyzing and apprehending concrete reality and the mechanisms of exploitation. Then the data have to be systematized on the basis of a theoretical analysis based on prior research. It is the classical chicken-and-egg problem: which comes first, the practical research or the underlying theory? In fact, they are dialectically linked.

Rodríguez: The text from Marx that opens *The Brickmakers* explains that a low level of relations of production and technology is reflected in an equally primitive ideological level: "Technology shows man's attitude toward nature, the direct process of production of his life, as well as the conditions of his social life and the ideas and relations that derive from it." The aim of the film is to demonstrate this, and its final structure is in large part a function of this concept.

Q: Did the fact that the film ends in flight and defeat motivate you to put the quote from Camilo Torres—"The struggle is a long one; let us begin"—at the end? Did you want to counter that final sequence where the family is expelled?

Rodríguez: No, it wasn't done with that in mind; what we were reacting against were certain oversimplifications in the political work being done among such marginal groups.

Silva: People are not going to organize themselves just because some film tells them to. They organize themselves because they find, based on their own analysis of their concrete situation, that it is necessary to get organized. This has to be something that comes from them; it does not depend on someone else's inclination.

Rodríguez: We were not interested in making a kind of "triumphalist" cinema, which claims victories where they have not yet been won. What we wanted to do was investigate the level of one group's political awareness to clarify certain ideas about tactics in working-class organizing.

Silva: We wanted to find out just where the community was so that political cadres would not arbitrarily lay on concepts that the people, given their political level, could not understand. One film does not make a revolution. That attitude is just another form of mysticism. Each film is just a small part, but an important one, of the larger task to be accomplished with the collaboration of the people themselves.

Plate 4. One of the Castañeda children carries unfired bricks to the kiln in a scene from *The Brickmakers*. Photo courtesy the filmmakers.

Notes

1. A priest from the Colombian upper class who studied sociology in Europe and returned to found the country's first university-level sociology program. Gradually politicized, and eventually defrocked for his political activity, he joined the rural guerrillas in 1967. Pursued by the Colombian military he was shot upon capture a few months later.

2. The expression designates more than a decade of internecine rural warfare between "conservative" and "liberal" factions of the peasantry and petite bourgeoisie, characterized by horrifyingly brutal feuds between families, villages, regions. Generally dated from the 1949 assassination of popular political leader Jorge Eliecer Gaitán, *La violencia* lasted into the sixties, first manipulated by national political leaders in their own interests, later raging beyond their control.

3. In this sense, an institution of patronage.

Chapter 4

Jorge Sanjinés
(Bolivia)

Revolutionary Cinema:
The Bolivian Experience

Plate 5. Jorge Sanjinés at the time of *Blood of the Condor*. Photo courtesy Unifilm.

After studying philosophy and filmmaking in Chile in the late 1950s, Jorge Sanjinés returned to his native Bolivia and teamed up with scriptwriter Oscar Soria to found a number of institutions in the early 1960s—a film society, a movie magazine, a film school—that were designed to provide greater public awareness of the local possibilities of the medium. Under the name Kollasuyo Films, the pair made its first short, a publicity vehicle for the national lottery. The expanding group was commissioned to make a number of other promotional shorts before undertaking its first independent film, a ten-minute black and white montage called *Revolución* (1964), which won the Joris Ivens Prize at the Leipzig Festival. Sanjinés began working with "natural" rather than professional actors during the production of the medium-length *Aysa!* (*Landslide!* 1965), shot in the mining region, and in the

Bolivia originates and evolves in two opposing directions, the one in favor of and the other against the people. Artistic currents also follow these two opposing paths, which are typical of the entire political history of Bolivia, where the ongoing struggle between nationalist and antinationalist interests has defined and determined the destiny of the country.

All artistic expression that identifies with the country and touches on social problems is branded "political." Conservative critics and intellectuals, anxious to preserve the status quo, give this word a pejorative connotation that acts as a kind of scarecrow, fending off many young poets, writers, and painters. Others realize what is going on and become radicalized. But isn't the political a fundamental part of all human activity? Participation in the political life of a country does not imply membership in a political party. What is important is *concern*, one's attitude regarding the destiny of a people. Militancy, then, should be understood as that activity that surrenders the best of one's talents and strengths to the cause of the masses. All human behavior entails a political position. There can be no dichotomy or inconsistency between what one believes and what one expresses. Artistic expression always ends up being a profound revelation of the beliefs of its author.

The roots of the Ukamau group go back to 1961, to a time when there was no revolutionary filmmaking in Latin America. Bolivia suffered severe cultural isolation. It is difficult to pinpoint the moment that people commit

---

feature-length *Ukamau* (*That's the Way It Is*, 1966), shot among Aymara-speaking peasants. Renaming themselves in commemoration of the latter film, the group subsequently produced its most famous work, *Yawar Mallku* (*Blood of the Condor*, 1969), the last of their scripted efforts. *El coraje del pueblo* (*The Courage of the People*, 1971) is the first example of the kind of on-site reconstruction of historical events in collaboration with actual participants that characterizes Sanjinés's mature work. Despite the dislocation and hardships of political exile (Sanjinés was compelled to live outside Bolivia between 1971 and 1979), he maintained his collaborative engagement with the "popular memory" of the Andean peasantry: *El enemigo principal* (*The Principal Enemy*, 1973) was shot in Peru; ¡*Fuera de aquí!* (*Get Out of Here!* 1976), in Ecuador; and ¡*Basta ya!* (*That's Enough!* 1979), in Colombia and Venezuela. *Las banderas del amanecer* (*The Banners of the Dawn*, 1984), a feature-length documentary, chronicles political events in Bolivia in 1983.

Excerpted and translated by Julianne Burton from Jorge Sanjinés, "Cine revolucionario: la experiencia boliviana" (*Cine Cubano*, no. 76/77 [1977]), this is the only selection in the present collection that derives from an essay rather than an interview. In his twenty-year career, Sanjinés has granted few interviews; none captures the pivotal point in this filmmaker's unique trajectory as well as this essay does. Nancy Folbré assisted in the initial translation of this essay several years ago, when the editor first began assembling materials for this book. The present translation, which has been approved by Sanjinés, is the product of a substantial reworking and condensation of the original version.

themselves to revolutionary change; it is a process. In Bolivia, death and misery assault the eyes and ears every minute, and those uneasy men who begin to formulate tentative questions are answered with shouts. Slowly the idea of the role that a national cinema should play in a poor country began to take shape. The goals were not initially as well defined as they are today. They were gradually extracted from the direct experience of objective reality and, inevitably, they turned out to be linked to the interests of the dispossessed masses. What began as a petulant, complaining, paternalistic kind of filmmaking became aggressive and capable of dealing serious blows to the enemy. How did this revolutionary cinema move from the *defensive* to the *offensive*? My purpose here is to reflect on that process in the evolution of the Ukamau group.

Some background on the history of filmmaking in Bolivia is relevant here. The first feature-length silent film—*Wara Wara*, based on an Inca legend—was not made in Bolivia until 1929. It was followed by a few other attempts at fictional filmmaking and many silent documentaries, all processed within the country. With the spread of sound, the technology became more complicated and the equipment more expensive, forcing a halt to this incipient activity. There were almost twenty years of silence in Bolivian film. Not until 1950 did a small group of pioneers, led by Jorge Ruiz, produce the first Bolivian sound film, a documentary. Ruiz's group worked for many years and produced valuable documentaries that were not lacking in beauty and technical quality. Their extraordinary *Vuelve Sebastiana* [*Come Back Sebastiana*, 1953], which was shot in color and dealt with the life of an ancient Indian tribe of the *altiplano*, won first prize at the Uruguayan SODRE festival in 1956.[1] Later, they made what could be considered the country's first feature-length talkie, *La vertiente* [*The Watershed*, 1958]. Shot in 35mm, with direct sound, this film had much to recommend it, despite certain flaws in structure and acting. It was an important step forward, though it did not receive sufficient recognition at the time.

Economic problems, lack of government aid, difficulties in importing film stock, high tariffs on equipment, all created a very difficult situation for people who wanted to make films, and slowly they began to turn their talents to producing films commissioned by the United States Information Agency and the U.S. embassy. There came a time when the only films being made in Bolivia were being financed by the Yankees. These filmmakers fell victim to preachings of objectivity and apoliticism, and to their own lack of ideological clarity, as well as to their love of their profession. Only one of them, screenwriter Oscar Soria, split off in 1961 to follow a path more faithful to the interests of his country. With Soria's departure, a new group of filmmakers was born, which only later would adopt the name Ukamau, after the title of their first film.[2]

The first films made by the Ukamau Group documented the poverty and misery of certain strata of the population.[3] These films, initially considered very useful, in fact served no other purpose than to remind bourgeois and petit bourgeois audiences that another class of people existed—in the city itself, in the mines, in the countryside—who constantly fought against incredible misery in a quiet and stoic manner.

We also screened our early documentaries in the mines and marginal barrios, and these popular performances opened our eyes and set us on a different track. We realized that our kind of filmmaking was incomplete, insufficient, limited. In addition to its technical defects, its basic content, its very conception was also defective. The common people themselves made us realize these defects when they said that they knew cases of poverty and suffering much worse than those shown in our films. In other words, such films had nothing new to show them. We began to realize that the people were not interested in seeing films that did not contribute anything, films that merely satisfied their curiosity to see themselves reflected on the screen. We realized that the people knew much more about misery than any filmmaker who might aspire to show it to them. Those workers, miners, and peasants were and are the protagonists of misery in Bolivia. Except for bringing tears to the eyes of a few pious liberals, the kind of films we had been making were good for nothing.

And so the question arose: Given that we want to direct our efforts toward the people, what do they want to see? The answer was clear. The people are more interested in knowing *how* and *why* misery is produced; they want to know *who* causes it and *how* they can oppose them. The people are interested in getting to know the names and faces of the henchmen, assassins, exploiters. They want to learn about the system of exploitation and its inner workings, since undistorted historical truth has been systematically denied them. In short, the people want to be exposed to the *causes* rather than the *effects*. Our future plans were reoriented toward a new goal, based on the key idea of what was the popular interest, and thus we embarked on the *offensive* phase.

We offered our films as weapons against the two-headed enemy that had been identified in Bolivia: the ruling class and Yankee imperialism. The former served as a tool for the latter, collaborating—without a thought for the fate of its country—on North American projects and programs intent on liquidating domestic industrialization to maintain Bolivia as a reliable source of raw materials. It was also important to explain why these people found the annihilation of their country convenient, and how their own cultural sterilization permitted the physical sterilization of the Bolivian people, their genocide through hunger, and the surrender of national resources. It was important to explain the mechanism that converts the national army into a "foreign" one, capable of massacring its own people.

We established a series of themes that could clarify historical events and help nullify the huge blanket of misinformation that has been spread over the people to impede the formation of political consciousness. The most important work that a revolutionary cinema could engage in was to provide liberating knowledge toward the formation of a revolutionary consciousness. Our work began to evolve along these lines with increasing clarity. Although it is true that *Ukamau*, our first feature, could not be considered an effective film weapon due to its structural limitations and its concessions to a still prominent tendency to privilege aesthetic considerations, it did spur people to realize that their struggle against their exploiters had to become a deliberately violent one. This conclusion, clearly expressed at the end of the film, frightened General Barrientos's military regime, which not only expelled us from the Bolivian Film Institute but also immediately shut down that institution.[4]

The government could not prevent the exhibition and distribution of the film, however, and *Ukamau* broke all box office records. Because *Ukamau* had been produced by a state agency, the Instituto Cinematográfico, which was tied directly to the president, the premiere had been attended by the highest authorities. General Ovando, under pressure from the obvious public enthusiasm, made an elegiacal statement that rather compromised the official position. Meanwhile, the prime minister, congratulating us heartily in front of the press, was saying between clenched teeth, "This is a betrayal! This film has nothing to do with the outline you submitted!" Though censorship and repression were unleashed behind the scenes, government officials could not publicly reverse their stance on an official film, so *Ukamau* was shown simultaneously in several cities, enjoying a nine-week run in the capital. Later, all existing prints of the film were ordered destroyed, but by that time more than three hundred thousand people had seen it. (The negative was later burned in Buenos Aires because the Bolivian government refused to pay a small debt that the defunct Film Institute had with a laboratory there.)

The expectations and the immense real and potential audience that *Ukamau* created called for more responsible answers to the questions being pondered by our group. Being able to count on such massive public response was a grave responsibility. The next time, we must deal with only the most essential issues. That hour and a half of unconditional surrender that the Bolivian people offered to the incipient national cinema could not be lost on topics that skirted what it was most urgent to expose and denounce: imperialist penetration.

The most alarming among the numerous activities that North American imperialism had unleashed in Bolivia during those years of cynical collaboration was the criminal campaign of forced sterilization—not only because the infant mortality rate in Bolivia is 40 percent greater than average (which means that there are areas with rates as high as 90 percent in a country that, consequently, has a negative rate of demographic growth), but, more important, because the methods used in sterilizing peasant women without their consent revealed the essentially fascist character of Yankee imperialism. In addition, this theme contained a whole gamut of allegorical possibilities, allowing for a wider vision of the predatory designs of capitalism, which corrupts the very thing it exploits and aspires to the physical and cultural destruction of our people. Denunciation was not sufficient unless it was based on an explanation of the existing social framework, including social stratification and the contradictions involved. The theme also provided an opportunity for giving substance to the notion of imperialism, which our people saw only as an incomprehensible abstraction.

The story of *Blood of the Condor*, inspired by real events, was written with these considerations in mind while faithfully observing the theoretical postulates of aggressive cinema. The results were encouraging. Despite the American Embassy's attempt to suppress the film, attendance exceeded that for *Ukamau*. On the basis of the film's denunciation of involuntary sterilization of indigenous women by members of the Yankee "Progress Corps," groups of university professors, journalists, doctors, and politicians began to investigate the activities of the Peace Corps in Bolivia, giving rise to a genuine national protest campaign against this organization. It can be justly claimed that as an immediate result of the film's distribution, the North Americans suspended their mass distribution of contraceptives, recalled all the members of the organization who had been working in the three sterilization centers, and received several staff members' resignations. They never took the trouble to deny the accusations made against them by even such conservative publications as *Presencia*. Later it became known that a group of peasants accused three Peace Corps volunteers of being sterilizers and were on the verge of lynching them. *Blood of the Condor* had been shown in their area the week before. The film affected other areas in an indirect way. Two peasant communities on the *altiplano* refused access to the Peace Corps, alleging that they had learned of their practices through radio reports about the film. In 1971, in the face of documented evidence of diverse antinational activities, and in view of growing public pressure, the Bolivian government expelled the Peace Corps.

Blood of the Condor proved that revolutionary film could be an effective political weapon. The objective and subjective conditions in Bolivia at the time were admittedly unique; they made it possible for a politically committed film to mobilize public opinion, using the same channels of distribution and exhibition that in other countries were used exclusively by the ruling classes. Still, one cannot ignore the fact that this result would not have been possible had our group, pursuing the goal of "communicability," not consciously set out to produce films that would attract popular interest. This communicability, if structured by a dialectical concept of the relationship between the film and the people, would avoid the twin stumbling blocks of paternalism and elitism. It was a matter of deepening the perception and representation of reality, for clarity of language could not derive from mere simplification but had to come from a lucid synthesis of reality.

Despite the fact that *Blood of the Condor* had attracted a huge audience, and despite its extraordinary success in terms of the objectives we had set for it, it still had not succeeded in fully establishing the possibility of communication through active participation. The structure of the plot, appropriate to a fictional film, made the denunciation seem dangerously unrealistic. This limitation had to be overcome. It was necessary to achieve a people's cinema, which would address real events with irrefutable evidence.

Since ours was a kind of filmmaking that sought to develop parallel to historical evolution, but that also sought to influence the historical process and to extract its constituent elements, it could no longer confine itself to conventional forms and structures. The content demanded a complementary form, which would break with traditional molds, since the results we sought needed to go beyond applause and approval. We did not seek passive results, but dynamic, transcendental ones. If it was absolutely necessary to work with reality and the truth, manipulating live, everyday history, then it was for the same reasons absolutely necessary to find forms that would not undermine or betray their content, as had occurred with *Blood of the Condor*, which employed fictional forms to portray historical facts and thus, because of this formal limitation, was unable to document its own truth.

Subsequent experiences sharpened our awareness of this problem. *Los caminos de la muerte* [*The Roads of Death*, 1970], a film that never saw the light of day, having been sabotaged when it was 70 percent complete, and *The Courage of the People* are two of the Ukamau Group's attempts to create a truly revolutionary cinema.[5] In these two films, a reconstructive method was used based on the equivalent of a law in dialectics: the notion that quantitative changes become qualitative ones. By means of a series of leaps from one historical situation to another, the secret connection, the internal logic, the interrelationships of historical phenomena are elucidated. These interrelationships had previously been deformed by the superimposition of anecdotal elements; these were eliminated in the synthesis. This accumulative structure, which overcame the limitations and disadvantages of a plot, was in turn supported by the active participation of the real protagonists and witnesses to the historical events, who gave their own interpretation of the experience, providing in this way a touch of irrefutable documentation. We thus eliminated "actors" in favor of collective mass participation, and this step, in turn, made possible a more horizontally structured filmmaking process. Social actors, performing spontaneously as the film was being shot, had a very high level of input in the creative process.

The human and political experiences of the people are moving, vital, creative forces. The level of political consciousness of the Bolivian miners, for example, is so high that the possibilities for their participation are immeasurable. There on home ground, close to those people who spontaneously relayed their experience in genuine performances, the form of the people's cinema we were looking for began to emerge. By eliminating the hierarchical structure of a priori filmmaking, where everything is planned by the filmmakers in advance, we took steps toward permitting genuine popular participation in the creative process of a film dealing with the history and destiny of the miners with whom we were working.

Dialogues from reconstructed situations were recorded on the spot. They were discussed there, on the very site of the historical event, with the actual participants in that event. Several times, members of the production crew looked on dumbfounded at a performance that could not be halted. The camera itself was forced into the role of protagonist; it had to interact as yet another participant. The opening massacre scene in *The Courage of the People*, for instance, was filmed in a single take from the time the people descend from the hills to the point on the plain when the army's bullets reach them. The cameramen felt as if they were photographing a real massacre. A large number of simultaneous scenes had to be captured on the spot, very quickly, in order not to lose them, since, like reality itself, they could never be repeated. The psychic climate had been unleashed, and it would only be present once.

What we saw on the editing table convinced us that we were treading solid ground. Those images had not been conjured up by some scriptwriter. They had not been set up or invented by a director who gave precise instructions on how to shout, how to move, how to speak. No, these were images created—or rather, remembered—by the people. They were situations created on the spot by people who, amid the turbulence and explosions, were reliving their past. An incredible capacity for expression had developed among those who collectively reenacted the massacre. If anybody fell short, it was the members of the film crew—victims of the tremendous excitement of that collective pathos that had been unleashed—who lost some of the best moments by shooting without any film in their cameras. Among the onlookers, there were some who wept, unable to distinguish reality from its reenactment. Not even the troop of technicians, cameramen, and soundmen who were spread out among the people signaling to one another and sometimes shouting back and forth, could impair the authenticity of the experience.

This perception forced the group to discuss another problem: emotionalism. We came to the conclusion that not only should we *not* reject the power of affective excitement that film can produce in the viewer, but that we should use that power to awaken a deep concern, a concern that would be generated out of the emotional conflict but that would climb to a self-aware, reflective level. This kind of emotional involvement would not desert spectators when the curtain fell, but would follow them, prodding them toward analysis and self-criticism. We realize that our idea stood in direct opposition to the concept of a cinema that tries to create "distance" between the viewer and the work to avoid impairing the rational, reflective process. We concluded that emotions not only were not an obstacle but could, in fact, be a means of provoking a higher consciousness. We believed that once the trap of "identification" with the actor, with whom spectators tend to associate themselves to escape from their own frustrations, was successfully eliminated, identification with a social group could be fostered. That old atavistic instinct of group solidarity, which survives in the collective subconscious and to which the species owes its survival, could be put into play. Since it is individualistic alienation that corrupts and subverts that impulse, we wanted to replace the individual protagonist with a collective protagonist.

Revolutionary content that is conceived with a revolutionary attitude finds forms to complement it, and these cannot but obey the need for communicability. If the content is not a pretext for individual quests or exclusively personal fulfillment, it will be expressed in a communicable form because it will have meaning only in its relationship to the people. Here is the fundamental problem of revolutionary cinema. The invention of forms cannot be understood in terms of paternalistic simplicity or the "renunciation" of creative powers. (Egocentric aspirations are what needs to be renounced.) The quest for effective language necessarily poses a challenge to the deepest and most genuine creative forces. It must be fueled by a grasp of the mental structures and internal rhythms of the people, rather than by a calculated and vindictive opposition to the language of the oppressor.

There is an essential point of departure for thinking about a cinema directed toward the Bolivian people: the majority of our people do not deal with one another in a manipulative way, as does the dominant westernized majority, but rather through integrated and reciprocal cultural and mental structures. The behavioral patterns of the majority are infused with the idea of the group, of the collective. It is logical that such people will be more effectively mobilized when spurred on by identification with a social group rather than with an individual protagonist. Therefore, a cinema that draws its inspiration from individualist principles or attitudes is not the most appropriate one for this majority.

The members of the Ukamau Group failed to realize this soon enough, causing some alarming conflicts between us and the peasant majority with whom we were attempting to work. Because in the end our mistaken assumptions enabled us to better understand the reality before us, it is useful to recount an incident that occurred at the beginning of the filming of *Blood of the Condor*.

At the end of 1968, our crew of nine arrived at the remote mountain community of Kaata, four hundred kilometers from La Paz. The last fifteen of these could be traveled only on foot because of the steepness of the precipices. Part of the equipment traveled on pack animals, the rest on human carriers. We reached the outskirts of the ancient community sweating and panting, our hearts pounding in our chests. Those who had not visited the village before had their first taste of the exertion required to travel this path, which we would have to do many times, often on stormy nights when the temperature was ten or twelve degrees below zero.

For the inhabitants of Kaata, the arrival of the film crew was incomprehensible. They were filled with anxiety. Who were these unfamiliar people, these strangers with their odd appearance and weird machines? Who were these white men who claimed to be Bolivian but didn't even speak Quechua? Who were these women wearing fur caps and trousers?

These Bolivian "gringos," grinning obsequiously while violating the centuries-old tranquillity of the village, found only one source of hospitality: Marcelino Yanahuaya, Leader of the Community (though his term was to expire within three days). The rest of the villagers, including Marcelino's wife, showed us only suspicion and reserve. As he had promised, Marcelino Yanahuaya provided room and protection in his house for our rather disconcerted band. We had all quickly perceived the indifference and animosity with which the inhabitants of Kaata regarded us.

We had met Marcelino in La Paz, where he had seen *Ukamau*. Subsequently, I had visited him three times and proposed making a movie in his community, going so far as to express the wish that he would participate as one of the actors. Marcelino had always seemed very interested in the project, and this interest never faded, but now he gave the impression that he didn't have much control over the community. When we asked him about the aloofness of his fellow villagers, he shrugged his shoulders. The problem, as will become clear, lay elsewhere.

The script was completely finished by the time we arrived. The shooting locations were selected. The only task remaining was the selection of the remainder of the local cast. This was scheduled to begin the day after our arrival. That night, we started up our generator, and its frightening racket persisted until three o'clock in the morning, no doubt depriving more than one villager of sleep.

At five, the peasants left their homes and climbed up the mountain to their garden plots or their pastures, all above four thousand meters. Our production head had taken care to spread the word that the filming would begin that afternoon, inviting those who were interested to present themselves at the camp. The wages we offered were ten times higher than those generally paid by the exploitative middlemen of the area. He also made it known that we had brought medicines and would tend the sick at no cost. When no one appeared, he began going desperately from house to house, and though he was the only member of our group who had mastered Quechua, he didn't get a single response. During that entire first day, which we had scheduled for filming, we saw only a handful of women who fled questions and hid their faces from our cameras.

Perplexed by this general indifference, we kept asking ourselves what was wrong, what could have provoked this contemptuous disinterest. Marcelino explained nothing; he kept silent or smiled enigmatically in response to our guesses.

The situation was even worse the next day. An official from Charazani, a neighboring community composed of middlemen who live off the petty disputes that they themselves provoke between the peasants and the former landholders who now own mines or trucks, came to warn the villagers that the filmmakers were dangerous Communists intent on robbery and murder. (Like the rest of the inhabitants of Charazani, he was not at all pleased by our presence and even less by the high wages we were offering.) The peasants, he said, should expel the outsiders and rid themselves of their evil threat. For his part, he promised to convince the authorities to dispatch policemen to help with the expulsion. All this transpired at an assembly held at six o'clock in the morning, as previously arranged, while the unsuspecting filmmakers were just opening their eyes to a day full of unpleasant surprises. By seven, the community was up in arms. We heard Marcelino arguing with a group of men. The initial apathy had turned into open hostility, especially on the part of the women, who were more taken in by the official's self-serving intrigues.

Naturally, we didn't get any work done that day, either. At night we heard threatening shouts telling us to clear out, and several stones hit the front door of Marcelino's house. He was accused of having sold himself to the Communists.

We realized that we wouldn't be able to proceed at all if this situation persisted, and that we were endangering Marcelino's prestige. The prudent thing to do was to leave the village. However, we decided to make one last effort to find a solution. We analyzed all the steps taken since the first contact initiated six months before, attempting to decipher the mistakes that had undermined our relationship to the community. At one point in this self-criticism session, someone—I think it was Ricardo Rada—said, despairing of any rational explanation, "¡Esto no se ve ni en coca!" [Even the coca leaves don't have the answer to this one!] This is a very Bolivian way of conveying an absolute negation, a powerless surrender in the face of something that seems impossible to understand.

The phrase hung in the air, and then there was an exchange of significant glances. We spoke with Marcelino: "We think that we should consult the yatiri.[6] We would like to offer a jaiwaco[7] so that the fate of our group can be read in the coca leaves."

Marcelino liked the idea. We were prepared to leave if the yatiri determined, through the complicated ceremony of the jaiwaco, that our intentions were wrongful or inspired by impure motives. We had come to the conclusion that we needed to demonstrate humility commensurate with the condescension, paternalism, and disruption that we had been demonstrating up to that morning. We were, after all, in an environment where respect for people and traditions was essential. For this reason, we accepted the possibility of losing, since we had no chance of winning that did not involve following the rules of a game that, though unfamiliar to us, was inherent to the particular part of the world to which we were trying to establish a connection.

Basically, what had happened was that we had judged the community by the same standards we would have used to analyze people and groups within bourgeois society. We had thought that by mobilizing one man who was powerful and influential, we could mobilize the rest of the group, whom we assumed to be vertically dependent on their leader. We had not understood, until that moment, that the indigenous people gave priority to collective over individual interests. We had failed to understand that, for them, as for their ancestors, what was not good for all of them could not be good for a single one. As René Zavaleta puts it, the Indians think of themselves first as a collective and only afterwards as individuals.

Submitting ourselves and our undertaking to the verdict of the *jaiwaco* ceremony, which takes place in the presence and under the supervision of all the inhabitants of Kaata, was the best way not only to proffer an apology to the entire community, but also to successfully stimulate collective participation in the decision regarding how the film would be made if indeed it were to be made at all. If the ceremony turned out badly and there was nothing for us to do but leave, we would have at least learned something that would give us a better chance of success in our work with subsequent groups, without having to subject ourselves again to a risky game of chance.

That night, after six hours of enormous tension in which all distractions, even sleep, were impossible because three hundred pairs of eyes, sensitive to any sign of weakness, were fixed on each and every member of our group, the *yatiri* examined the coca leaves and declared emphatically that our presence was inspired by good, not evil. Neither the intrigues and threats of the neighboring official, nor the Indians' traditional distrust of whites and mestizos could overrule this verdict.

Our group was accepted and we soon felt the old barriers to communication disappearing in embraces and genuine signs of cordiality. The camp filled up with volunteers and also with sick people—terribly undernourished children, mothers without milk, youngsters with tuberculosis. No doctor had ever shown his face in Kaata.

Some time later, when we were discussing how to create a vital and authentic revolutionary cinema, free of fictions and melodramatic characters, with the people as the protagonists in acts of creative participation, so that we might achieve films that would be passed from town to town, we decided that there in Kaata, at that unique moment, we should have thrown away our prepared script and shot a movie about that experience instead. In light of this and other experiences, we began to question all the films we had made and were planning to make. We began to understand the ways in which our cinematic style was and is impregnated by the concepts of life and reality inherent to our own social class. We also began to understand the distance that Bolivian cinema would have to travel to carry implicit within it the cultural spirit and worldview of its people. We wanted to integrate ourselves with that eager spirit, to purge ourselves of all useless trivia, of all the contradictions of a culture imposed by force, a culture that was and is the vehicle for the deformation of our national identity and the negation of our authentic culture.

It is reasonable to believe that a new language—liberated and liberating—cannot be born except through the exploration of and integration with the people's culture, which is living and dynamic. A revolutionary process does not exist, nor is it ever realized, *except* through the mobilization and dynamic participation of the people. Likewise with revolutionary cinema. If it does not happen, it is because there is no reciprocity. And if there is no reciprocity, it means that there is opposition, ideological conflict. Because what the artist gives to the people should be nothing less than what he or she receives from them.

Everything is interrelated. Isolated phenomena do not exist. The search for a popular cinema is also the search for a more coherent social consciousness. If one admits that it is only right and necessary that all individuals fully realize themselves, one has to understand that this self-realization is only coherently and harmonically possible as a result of the realization of the entire society. From this it follows that everything that an individual does would have some positive meaning for the rest of the society; only in this way could it have a positive meaning for the individual. In a socialist society, toward which a revolutionary cinema projects itself, one cannot conceive of any kind of personal realization that is not expressed in terms of collective fulfillment. If this is understood, creative practice will bring about the birth of genuinely popular art, in which artists and intellectuals will no longer serve as their society's end but as its means.[8]

Notes

1. See chap. 2 for background on the SODRE festival.

2. The core of the Ukamau Group (the term means "That's the way it is" in the Aymara language) was made up of director Jorge Sanjinés, scriptwriter Oscar Soria, cameraman Antonio Eguino, and producer Ricardo Rada. The 1971 military coup that brought General Banzer to power split the group. Sanjinés and Rada, in Italy doing postproduction on *The Courage of the People*, knew they would place themselves in danger if they returned to their country, so they opted to continue their work elsewhere in the Andes. Eguino and Soria, reluctant to leave Bolivia, decided to remain behind to manage as best they could under the repressive conditions. Their films—*Pueblo chico* (*Small Town*, 1974), *Chuquiago* (1977), *Amargo Mar* (*Bitter Sea*, 1984)—also bore the name Grupo Ukamau.

3. Here Sanjinés is probably referring to *Revolución* (*Revolution*, 1964) and *¡Aysa!* (*Landslide!* 1965).

4. When General Barrientos took over the Bolivian presidency in a coup d'état in 1964, one of his first acts was to shut down the Instituto Cinematográfico Boliviano. Unexpectedly, he decided to reopen it the following year, naming Jorge Sanjinés as technical director, a post he held for two years.

5. See chap. 17 for Walter Achugar's account of the production of *The Courage of the People*.

6. A ceremonial figure.

7. A nocturnal ceremony, performed by the *yatiri* in the presence of the entire community, which involves the reading of the coca leaves. Such a ceremony is depicted in *Blood of the Condor*.

8. See Jorge Sanjinés and Grupo Ukamau, *Teoría y práctica de un cine junto al pueblo* (Mexico City: Siglo XXI, 1979).

Chapter 5

Patricio Guzmán
(Chile)

Politics and the Documentary
in People's Chile

Plate 6. Patricio Guzmán during the Parisian release of *The Battle of Chile Part II: The Struggle of a People without Arms*. Photo courtesy Patricio Guzmán.

Patricio Guzmán, founder of the Equipo Tercer Año, the team that made the monumental three-part documentary *La batalla de Chile* (*The Battle of Chile,* 1975-1979), studied filmmaking in Spain before returning to his native Chile with the electoral victory of the Popular Unity coalition in 1970. He directed two other documentaries, *El primer año* (*The First Year,* 1971) and *La respuesta de octubre* (*October's Answer,* 1972) before undertaking *The Battle of Chile*. Since the Chilean coup, he has lived in France, Cuba, and Spain.

Julianne Burton interviewed Patricio Guzmán in Havana in January 1977. The editor is grateful to Equipo Tercer Año member Federico Elton for comments and

Q: How would you describe *The Battle of Chile* to audiences who have not seen the film?
A: The film is an attempt to convey in as much detail as possible the nature and consequences of political events in Chile during the last year of the Allende government. What was happening was of great interest outside as well as inside of Chile, not just for other Latin Americans, but for the workers' movement on an international scale. What Chile represented, after all, was a sort of twentieth-century Paris Commune.

What was going on was of such intense interest that we realized that our camera should encompass as much as possible. We needed to use a wide-angle lens and to situate ourselves at as great a distance as possible from events while still being able to record them. We needed to make sure that the entire process was contained in the film—and not from a narrowly partisan point of view. We realized that it would be a mistake to analyze events from a single perspective, because the interesting thing was to represent *all* points of view within the Left. The same ideological battle then going on in Chile could occur in France or in Italy, for example, in a very similar way. And it will also occur in Mexico or in Venezuela when things enter a more critical phase. The far-reaching relevance of the political model then being tried in Chile was one of the factors that motivated us to make the film.

Q: How do the three parts of the film differ?
A: Part I, *The Insurrection of the Bourgeoisie*, tries to shed light on a fundamental aspect of the problem in Chile: the mass uprising of the middle and upper sectors of the population, in collaboration with foreign interests, and the actions taken by the government and by the Left as a whole to curb this right-wing insurrectionary escalation.

The primary contradiction in the first film is thus between fascism/imperialism/bourgeoisie on the one hand and the working masses on the other. The masses are only present in Part I as a point of reference, since the major focus of this segment is to demonstrate how the Right, through its use of the mass media, and financed by imperialist interests, succeeded in mobilizing the middle class "masses," thus preparing the way for the coup d'état. This is, of course, the most unique aspect of the Chilean coup: the right succeeded in arousing massive resistance among all sectors of the bourgeoisie and in the armed forces, as well as among one sector of the proletariat, the copper miners of El Teniente mine.

Part II, *The Coup d'état*, centers around the same contradiction. It continues to show the mass agitation of the bourgeoisie in opposition to the

clarifications provided in Santa Cruz, California, in March of the same year. The interview first appeared in *Socialist Revolution* (now *Socialist Review*) (Oakland, Ca.), no. 35 (September-October 1977) and was subsequently reprinted in pamphlet form by the New England Free Press, Somerville, Massachusetts.

democratic popular forces, but it adds a third dimension: the diverse and competing strategies that existed within the various groups on the left. This is why the second film is much more difficult than the first. Our decision to maintain the same dialectical style of narration (the voice-over narrator provides only the most essential background information; the bulk of the analysis is given directly by those who participated in the events the film records) means that the viewers have to grasp this triple contradiction for themselves.

Part III, *Popular Power*, is the simplest of the three. It is a very affectionate evocation of the mass organizations during the Popular Unity government, and in particular during 1973. These were very practical organizations that answered concrete needs like how to get food and supplies to the population, how to get a greater yield from a plot of land, how to organize a peoples' supply store [*almacén popular*], how to set up a production committee in the factory.

There were many times during the struggle in Chile that the popular forces would distance themselves temporarily from the action to discuss the nature of the socialist state that was then in the early stages of construction. This was a very calm and measured process, very touching at times. This theoretical development of the workers and peasants—always based on their practical experience—was extremely impressive. The footage we have of these occasions is the most convincing proof of the enormous level of awareness among the Chilean people. Yet if we had inserted these sequences along with the rest of the footage, such discussions would have appeared unreal in the midst of pre-civil war conditions. So, as we edited the first and second parts of the film, we set aside all these sequences that depicted the incipient stages of people's power in Chile for a third segment, which would complement but be different from the first two.

Q: How many people set out to make the film, and how did you decide to go about it?

A: The film was made by a team of five people. We began filming in February of 1973. But before starting the actual shooting, we had frequent meetings to decide on the approach we would use.

From the very beginning, our idea was to make an analytical film, not an agitational one. Naturally, we thought our audience would be Chilean. Three possible roads seemed open to our country at that time: a fascist coup d'état like the one that actually occurred, or a civil war that offered two alternatives—the victory or the defeat of the popular forces. None of us believed at that juncture that the existing situation could sustain itself for long.

We all thought that, in the event of a civil war, the popular forces would eventually win. We expected there to be a split in the armed forces, which never actually occurred, given that the soldiers and sailors who were loyal to Allende were identified and purged before the September 11 military coup.

If the civil war were to result in a victory for the popular forces, we reasoned, our footage would be of great use to the workers, the peasantry, and the Chilean Left as a whole because in the first stage of constructing a new socialist state, it is very important to analyze what has gone before. If there were to be a coup d'état, we knew that we had all the more reason to do what we were doing, since our footage would be a sort of commemoration and tribute to all that the Chilean people had accomplished in those years of democratic peoples' government. And so the coup, though it certainly succeeded in preventing the screening of the film in Chile (for the time being at least) did not really alter either our purpose or our approach. These have been invariable.

The members of the group got together in December of 1972 and agreed that the most important thing to do in Chile at that particular moment was to make a film about what was going on in the country from day to day. Any fictional screenplay, any film structured around a plot—no matter how good—seemed to us to be completely upstaged by contemporary events.

There was another consideration as well. Since the organization of the state was still holding together, it was actually possible to film the events of the class struggle with relative calm. You could record what was going on as easily as you could film a landscape. It was possible to capture the different sectors involved in the class struggle as if in cross-section. It's true that a certain daring was required, since we infiltrated the Right sometimes at great physical risk, but certain guarantees still existed, and we took advantage of them. We also devised our own safeguards, carrying multiple sets of press credentials at all times. One day we claimed to be filming for Chilean television, the next day for French or Swiss TV.

Q: Were there particular films or filmmakers to whom you looked for models in the project you were about to undertake?

A: When we started to debate the methods we would use to make the film, we didn't have any instruction manual to indicate how to go about documenting our own reality. There are very few documentary theorists anywhere on whom we could rely. We had access to all of Cuban documentary cinema, and it was through repeated viewings of these films that we extracted what were for us the essential elements. Julio García Espinosa's *Tercer mundo, tercera guerra mundial* [*Third World, Third World War*, Cuba, 1970] seemed to us to offer a particularly important model.

The Cuban film magazine *Cine cubano* carried translations of the writings of the Russian revolutionary filmmaker Dziga Vertov. Julio García Espinosa's essay "For an Imperfect Cinema" was also an important theoretical source. We also read some unpublished pieces by the contemporary French documentarist Chris Marker,[1] who began to correspond with us, and several articles by other French filmmakers, including Louis Malle on the filming of *Calcutta* [1969].

Next we put together a sort of manifesto listing various approaches that we might follow—what to do, how to do it, when to do it, and why. We tried to develop a system of classification for all the kinds of documentary with which we were familiar: simple exposition, like the film I mentioned by Louis Malle, for example; the agitational documentary, like almost all the films that were being made in Chile at that time, and like the majority of the Cuban documentaries; and the analytical documentary, which didn't really exist in Chile, although many Chilean films had some analytical sequences. The closest thing to what we had in mind was Julio García Espinosa's *Third World, Third World War*. We were not familiar with Pastor Vega's *¡Viva la república!* [*Long Live the Republic!* Cuba, 1972] or with other films that were made later on.

Q: What about the influence of other Latin American films? For example, those that had been shown at the Viña del Mar Festivals in Chile in 1967 and 1969?

A: According to the criteria we developed, *La hora de los hornos* [*The Hour of the Furnaces*, Argentina, Fernando Solanas and Octavio Getino, 1968] might be classified as an analytical film. But it never had the same grip on us as *Third World, Third World War*, for example. *Vidas secas* [*Barren Lives*, Brazil, Nelson Pereira dos Santos, 1963] although it is a fiction film, uses a kind of expository documentary style. There were a few documentaries by the Brazilian filmmaker Leon Hirszman that we liked a lot. Of the Uruguayan films, we were only familiar with one, Mario Handler's *I Like Students*, but it seemed to be pure agitprop. We also considered all the documentaries that had been made under the Popular Unity government in Chile, by the Left as a whole and in particular by those who worked in experimental filmmaking with Pedro Chaskel. But we perceived all of these as being either denunciations of particular problems, or examples of agitprop or of partisan filmmaking, without any real analysis of what was about to happen.

Our next step was to write out various work methods. The first one we analyzed was the chronological one, that is, the attempt to film what is going on around you day by day or week by week, in sequence. We discovered that, although this might be very interesting, many events occur only as the result of a long process—a process that, in the last analysis, often seems invisible. What you are able to film is the culmination of the process, the final, visible event: the workers taking over a factory, for example. But to film this culminating point is to leave out a whole series of important considerations: Why did they take over the factory? What does the government think of the occupation? Who are the leaders of the takeover?

How do the workers perceive their interests in this situation? What solutions to their problems do they seek via this route? All this occurs *before* the takeover. So we concluded that a chronological structuration was too incomplete and superficial. We had already used a similar approach in an earlier film, *The First Year*, and had no desire to repeat it.

Later we realized that if, for example, you are going to film a factory takeover the moment that it occurs, you must initiate a whole series of inquiries to find out why, when, where, how, who, and for whom. You begin to realize that by delving deep enough into a single problem you touch on many different aspects of the larger situation. It is like the expanding waves, which keep growing outward after you throw a stone into a pool. We called this approach "the nucleus method" because it involves locating a nucleus of conflict within the panorama of the class struggle. In the process of filming a single event, you begin to touch on other related ones.

We then looked at another approach, that of analyzing reality chapter by chapter, section by section. For example: education, the social sector of the economy, the conflict between Allende and the bourgeois Parliament, the mass insurrection that the forces of imperialism were instituting in Chile with the help of the bourgeoisie. Each of these is a sample chapter. If you take one, then another, and then another, with five or six you will have the key segments. But then you realize that the chapters have no firm boundaries to separate one from the other. They are all interrelated, and you are not able, for example, to isolate the conflict between Allende and the Parliament because it is in some way connected to all the other issues. This is the reason why we abandoned this approach.

But the other approach, the nucleus method, also involves substantial risks, because sometimes you can confuse a single problem, especially one at the base level (part of the workers' movement), so that you begin to think that the entire revolutionary process is tied to this one phenomenon. This is not really the case, since there is always a dialectical relationship between the superstructure and the base—between the political parties and the masses, for example. There is a tendency to get off the track a bit and to conclude that the revolution is equivalent to the creation of a peoples' supply store or the government's institution of the Food and Price Control Boards. So you conclude that the revolution is purely a workers' phenomenon in which the workers and the peasantry are the center and the heart. Naturally, this is a sector of key importance, absolutely essential, but it is not itself the complete picture. This nucleus-by-nucleus approach leads you to over-emphasize particular sectors. You confuse small representative and symbolic elements, when what one is attempting to do is to encompass the entire picture.

Q: It sounds like there was no ready-made approach sufficient to your analytical needs. How were you able to get around this impasse?

A: After carrying out a sustained critique of other approaches, we came to the conclusion that what we were after was the dialectical sum of all of them. We also concluded that the important thing is not so much to settle on a single fixed methodology as to single out theoretically the key points at which the Chilean class struggle intersects. Which are the key points through which the proletariat and the peasantry must pass in the conquest of state power? And which are the key points through which the bourgeoisie and its imperialist allies must pass to reappropriate that power? If you locate these fifteen or twenty battlegrounds within the larger conflict and you pin them down one by one, you're going to have a dialectical vision of what is going on. This was the approach we finally agreed to use.

The theoretical outline we developed divided Chilean reality into three major areas: ideological, political, and economic. Our point of departure was a Marxist analysis of reality, which we then applied in small chapters that accounted for the seventy-odd divisions in the outline. All the members of the group took part in the process of developing this outline, with the help of the editorial team from the magazine *Chile Hoy* and in particular Marta Harnecker.

The "screenplay" thus took on the form of a map that we hung on the wall. On one side of the room, we listed the key points of the revolutionary struggle as we saw them. On the other side, we would list what we had already filmed. For example, if the problem of education appeared on one wall, on the other we noted what schools or universities we had gone to and what specific sequences corresponded to the theoretical section. So, we had the theoretical outline on one side and the practical outline of what we had actually filmed on the other.

Q: In addition to the complex theoretical and methodological decisions you describe, did you face practical obstacles as well?

A: Definitely, since at the time we began to film there was no raw film stock in Chile. It was one of the many commodities kept out by the economic blockade imposed by the United States. (The blockade also produced a shortage of American and European theatrical films.)

To try to import raw film stock through official channels could have taken a year or more. So I wrote a letter to Chris Marker explaining our projected film and our desperate need for film stock. Within two weeks, we got a package containing the film we needed.

Of course, the major practical obstacle was the nature of the project itself. What we were setting out to do was extremely ambitious, overwhelmingly so. As Chris wrote in his letters, "What you are trying to do is insane, it's impossible, it's just too big." And I would write back saying, "You may be right, but it doesn't matter. We're going to make the effort, no matter what." All the members of the group started out from the same shared realization: that what we were about to attempt was impossible, but that we were determined to undertake it anyway.

We began to film almost every day, on an average of twenty to twenty-five days per month. Our equipment was very limited: one Eclair camera, one Nagra sound recorder, two vehicles. We worked without ever giving any public notice of what we were doing. We didn't grant a single interview or press conference. We didn't tell anyone except the absolutely indispensable people what we were about. These precautions enabled us to engage in a kind of semiclandestine filmmaking, allowing us to infiltrate the Right with a good deal of confidence and, at the same time, to film our own forces without the cumbersome and disruptive presence of a huge team of filmmakers.

Since the workers knew and trusted us, and since we always tried to be as unobtrusive as possible, we could work among them very much at ease. We would arrive at a given meeting hall and immediately set up the key light, but we would try not to distract people with a lot of cables and loud conversations. We almost never spoke among ourselves in anything but a whisper. We came to be so in tune with one another that, in the final months of the filming, the process was almost automatic and communication between us on the shoot was reduced to an exchange of glances.

We went out to film almost every day. We had a clearly defined work plan. We usually ate in the same factories where we were filming. Often we would sleep in the truck. There was a great sense of fraternity generated by this process, not just because we were all very fond of one another but also because we knew that what we were doing together was of crucial importance. We were all convinced of the relevance of the project, and that was extremely important in binding us together and in helping us to develop a smooth work process.

The film was a collective undertaking, but within the collective a certain division of labor was always preserved. That's why the film has a director. In other words, we did not confuse our idea of a collective with the kind of idealist notion of a group in which everyone is responsible for everything and for nothing. Instead, each of us was responsible for a particular aspect.

Federico Elton was in charge of fund raising and production. Jorge Muller was the cameraman and director of photography. Bernardo Menz was the sound technician. José Pino was the assistant director and handled the lighting. Marta Harnecker collaborated in the developing of the shooting script, and occasionally joined us on the shoots.

There was no contradiction between my role as director and the rest of the collective, and there isn't to this day. That would be absurd. The director's role is to give direction to the collective, taking advantage of all the opportunities that arise for a dialectical analysis of the existing situation. As a group, we had many heavy ideological debates because our members were from different political parties. But I would continually warn the group against getting mired down in partisan disputes, because that's where we would have to trade in our wide-angle lens for a narrow point of view. That was the main role I played as director within the collective.

Since the film project was semiclandestine, as I said before, and we had specific divisions of labor, none of us, except me and my *compañera*, knew where the film was stored. After each shooting session, I would collect the cans of film. I'd store the magnetic sound tape in one place and the film footage in another. Only the two of us knew where this material was kept because in critical situations, the less known the better.

Q: Could you describe how the group worked together during the actual shooting process?

A: Our method was not to disperse the crew, but always to stay close together. I would stand next to Jorge Muller, the cameraman, surveying the action and trying to anticipate what was to come. Whenever what was being filmed reached a climax—as soon as I'd see, for example, that the workers and the fascist groups had hit a high point in their street battle—I would say to Jorge, "Now you need to climb up on this box here, but don't look at it. Keep on filming. I'll steady you while you climb up. Now you have the best possible angle on the whole thing. Stay there until I tell you, because to the left a troop of police whom you can't see yet are about to come into view. As soon as they come into range, close in on them."

This kind of interaction accounts for the *mise en scène* of the film. Since I tried to anticipate for him what was about to happen, I could tell him to pan, to lower the camera, to raise it, instructing him to make certain movements that are much more readily identified with fictional than with documentary filmmaking. But why shouldn't they be used in documentary films if they enrich the medium?

We had hand signals that we used to communicate with one another. That is how I would give instructions to Bernardo Menz, the soundman. The assistant director was in charge of turning on the lights. Sometimes I would be whispering directions to the cameraman when the assistant director, at some distance from us, would flash the lights. That was a signal to be on the alert, that something important was about to happen.

Q: What prior training did you have as a filmmaker?

A: I studied film in Spain, at the Escuela de Cine in Madrid, in the late sixties. My major interest then was fictional filmmaking, not documentaries.

I returned to Chile in 1970, with the triumph of the Popular Unity coalition in the national elections. I was all set to make fiction films. I had various screenplays in hand, and even some possibilities for financial backing. But I soon realized that my ideas were completely outstripped by reality. When you see a workers' demonstration pass by your window, and you listen to the rhymed slogans they are shouting, it is much more appealing simply to follow that demonstration. They go to the government palace and call for Allende; Allende comes out and speaks to them; meanwhile, the right wing is organizing on the other side of the square with the intention of provoking an incident; a street fight ensues. What is going on is amazing because the class struggle is so visible and so compelling.

A whole people waking up after having been dormant for several decades—peasants organizing land takeovers, workers occupying factories, the government nationalizing industry, and the Right withdrawing, closing in on itself for the time being. At last the possibility of a real revolution exists. To bear witness to this is so absorbing and so marvelous that I began to feel that to make a film with actors, makeup, costumes, and dialogue written by someone else didn't make any sense at all. It was completely outstripped by what we were all living through.

And so, in 1971 I got very wrapped up in making *The First Year*. It is a very sensuous film, full of affection but without analysis, a kind of commemoration of what was going on at the time. The film was very well received in Chile and abroad. Many said that it was precisely the kind of filmmaking that we should be developing at that time. Chris Marker was very taken with it. He took a print back to France with him and had it dubbed into French. Many leading French actors and actresses—Françoise Arnoul, Yves Montand, Simone Signoret—participated in the dubbing, and they produced an excellent version.

In 1972 I began work on a fiction film called *Manuel Rodríguez*, based on the life of a guerrilla hero of the Chilean war for independence. He was the one who prepared the way for San Martín to come and free Chile from the Spanish. The film has a lot in common with Manuel Octavio Gómez's *The First Charge of the Machete* [Cuba, 1969], since it is a kind of post-facto historical documentary, which exposes and attempts to take apart the means through which it is told. We hadn't seen *The First Charge*, nor had we met Manuel Octavio, but the projects were extremely similar, as I realized later when I came to Cuba. We only managed to film two or three sequences. We had to stop work because of the truck owners' work stoppage of October 1972. The film was suddenly left without funding, and we had to abandon the project.

The truckers' "strike" was the first coordinated offensive by the middle class as a whole against the forces of the Left. The result was an incredible shortage of goods and resources. Although the country continued to move forward, because of extraordinary efforts on the part of the workers and the peasants along with other allied segments of the Popular Unity coalition, we suffered an incredible drain of funds. Our balance of payments was thrown completely off: all imported goods stopped coming in; there were no bank credits; stockpiles of spare parts were used up and could not be replaced.

Raw film stock was one of the very last priorities. Chile Films, the national film production company under whose auspices we were making *Manuel Rodríguez*, ceased being a production company in the broad sense and was only able to produce newsreels. We realized that through Chile Films we weren't going to obtain anything, so we left the organization and began trying to figure out solutions on our own.

We made a film called *October's Answer*, which is about sixty minutes long. It simply attests to how the working class, particularly the *cordones industriales* [industrial belts made up of factories that have been taken over by their workers] in Santiago, managed to keep production going in spite of the boycott organized by the Right. The factories continued to function even though the engineers and technicians refused to come to work, because the workers realized that with one engineer "borrowed" from somewhere else, they could coordinate production and keep the factory going. They began to get together with the workers of neighboring factories, thus developing territorial concentrations of factories under workers' control. Theoretically, these *cordones industriales* also had a higher level of organization, called the *comando comunal*, which also included students, housewives, and middle-level professionals. But this level of organization was only implemented among the workers of Barrancas, and in a rather embryonic stage at that. As soon as we finished shooting, we gave the film over for agitational use. Shot in 16mm, it was destined exclusively for use in the mobile circuits organized by Chile Films to bring relevant cinema into factories, schools, and neighborhoods.

It was at this point that we definitively decided that all fictional options were completely overruled and that what was necessary was a great analytical film. We decided to dedicate all our energies to this end and wrote to Chris Marker requesting film stock. We organized the collective, got hold of an Eclair and a Nagra, and threw ourselves into the filming, which lasted a year.

Q: How many members of the collective had prior filmmaking experience?

A: It is interesting that the collective was almost completely made up of people without prior experience. It was the soundman's first film. The production chief, an architect by training, was also without previous film experience. The assistant director was a sociologist and an economist; it was the first time he had worked on a film. Marta Harnecker, one of Chile's leading political theorists, had worked on *The First Year*. (We had been friends for several years. I met her when she was studying Marxism in Paris with Althusser in 1967. She returned to Chile at the same time I did, when Allende came into power.) Jorge Muller virtually shot his first film with *The Battle of Chile*, since the work which he'd done prior to this film—with Raúl Ruiz, for example—failed to reveal his extraordinary talent. You can see that the potential is there, but it was in our group that he began to realize his creative capacity fully.

The Battle of Chile was also a completely new experience for me, since the blueprint for making such a film does not exist. I'm the member of the group with the most formal training, but in such circumstances, though preparation is important, the most crucial thing is a clear political vision. And this was where we all coincided.

Q: You have alluded more than once to Chile Films. Could you elaborate on the organization and function of this state film enterprise during the Allende years?

A: I spent two years as part of Chile Films. During the first year I worked under Miguel Littín as head of the Documentary Film Studios division. There were five divisions in all: fictional film, documentary, animation, childrens' films, and educational films. Miguel was head of the entire concern, though he only remained about a year, until the end of 1971. When he resigned, we all resigned en masse along with him.

Q: Can you specify what motivated all of you to leave Chile Films?

A: Well, the first thing to keep in mind is that the issue of film in Chile is not a separate question, but is tied to the issue of the means of communication in general. Film was not prey to a unique set of problems; its problems were shared by the other mass media as well. It's just that the crisis was more apparent and more pronounced in the film industry.

What happened is that the ideological struggle going on within the Left played itself out in microcosm within Chile Films. There were always two blocs within the Popular Unity coalition: one sector favored following the "peaceful road to socialism" to its final consequences; the other sector, supported from outside the party by the MIR [Movement of the Revolutionary Left], argued that the potential for progress within the existing state apparatus was limited, since that apparatus could be expected to break down as soon as the class struggle reached a critical point.

Both these factions wanted to control Chile Films, so the struggle that developed within the organization was a political and, in the final analysis, an ideological one: What kind of cinema did we want? How was it to be made? To whom was it to be directed? What forms would it adopt? The two factions were in head-on conflict over these questions because the former favored an agitational, analytical cinema with the goal of maintaining the existing organization of the state and never giving the right wing any indication that we had any intention of abandoning the law; the latter faction, likewise in favor of an agitational and analytical kind of filmmaking, saw the cinema as a vehicle for preparing the masses for a more or less imminent civil war.

These are roughly the outlines of the struggle waged within Chile Films. Both Miguel and I were part of the group that foresaw the breakdown of the state apparatus. Chile Films found itself without film stock at a particular juncture because the Popular Unity government decided that there was such internal chaos within the organization as to make it functionally inoperative. They would only supply the necessary raw film stock after some sort of political accord had been reached. Miguel finally said, "OK, I'm no longer going to take responsibility for this. I prefer to leave, to make my own films independently and to keep working for film and for the revolution on other fronts but not as an administrator or a bureaucratic functionary."

That was more or less how we all saw things at the time. Our goal was to take action, to make films—no matter how—because there is always going to be an ongoing ideological struggle. Since the historical period was so intense, almost everyone left Chile Films to form small working collectives. The avalanche of events was so overpowering that no one could remain behind closed doors saying, "Well, as long as the ideological struggle isn't resolved, I'm not going to do anything." Instead, people continued to make films despite the ideological debates, reasoning more or less as follows: "If Chile Films is shut down or its activities curtailed, it really doesn't matter. Let the people involved solve the problem. We'll just go on making films." That's what we did, and so did Miguel Littín, Sergio and Patricio Castilla, Pedro Chaskel with his Experimental Film group, and others, making films from their particular work base.

In 1972, the second year of the Popular Unity government, there was an institutional reorganization of Chile Films with the goal of giving a certain degree of economic coherence to its film production, something that we had not done. We had tried to spark a kind of broad and nonsectarian creative drive. The subsequent stage was certainly, from an administrative point of view, the most coherent period for that state film enterprise. But it was sterile in creative terms. Even though what Chile Films was about had at last been defined in political terms, the majority of the filmmakers were no longer part of the organization, having already decided to work outside it. And they were not about to return, because Chile Films really had nothing to offer them except the rental of cameras, lighting equipment, and so on.

Q: How would you go about placing the conflict within Chile Films in the context of the intense ideological battle being waged in other sectors of the communications media at the time?

A: The process that occurred in Chile Films was similar to what was happening in television, newspapers, and radio stations. The difference is that the radio stations, for example, were in private hands. If you own a radio station, then you determine the ideological slant that characterizes that particular station. If the station is controlled by a particular party, it carries that particular line, and there is no internal conflict. Likewise with the press: different publications express different points of view according to the interests that control them. The ideological struggle between different sectors of the Left, for example, is resolved at the level of the individual reader, who might read several different newspapers corresponding to various leftist groups and then develop a personal synthesis of the issues.

The struggle in the sphere of television was also a tense one, since all political lines had to coexist on a single channel. But at least the image of the enemy was clearer in this medium. There were no right-wing filmmakers in Chile; the people who formed part of Chile Films were all on the left, so we struggled among ourselves. More than half of the television sector, on the other hand, was controlled by technicians and directors who belonged to the right wing or to the Christian Democrats. Therefore the ideological struggle related to TV always had an attenuating factor: "We can debate all we want among ourselves, but we can't forget that the enemy is right here in our midst." The issues became clearer at an earlier stage.

Generally speaking, the Right consistently won the ideological battle because it had greater means at its disposal, including 70 percent of the radio stations and 80 percent of the press. Consequently, we were always at a disadvantage. But the problem was intensified by the fact that we on the Left were always divided by at least two or three competing strategies. One sector, for example, felt that television should be calm, cautious, and objective, because the majority of those who own TV sets belong to the petite bourgeoisie and the majority of the petite bourgeoisie support the Christian Democrats. Therefore, they argued, if you were to produce a militant, combative kind of programming with the aim of mobilizing people, you would offend those sectors of the population who would then object vociferously, claiming that the government was trying to manipulate people, to persuade them by force, and you would have yet another conflict on your hands. Another sector argued that no matter how cautious, calm, and persuasive you are in your programming, the petite bourgeoisie is still going to accuse you of being biased and manipulative. Since you'll always be at a disadvantage, they reasoned, it is better to make no concessions and instead to dedicate all one's energy to developing a militant, combative kind of programming, consistently on the offensive, aimed at mobilizing the workers and peasants.

This debate about what was to be done in the communications sector is simply another version of the debate about what was to be done in the Chilean revolutionary process as a whole, since the media are not independent or isolated but are part of the larger struggle for political power. The two poles—peoples' power, and the strategy of the antifascist front— were fighting and debating among themselves up until the very day of the coup.

Although it is true that imperialist interests, international reaction, and the national bourgeoisie are responsible for the coup, the defeat is also due to the lack of a unified political direction among the forces of the Left, to a permanent vacillation between two conflicting strategies, and to a Byzantine ideological debate about what needed to be done.

Q: Did all work on *The Battle of Chile* come to an immediate halt when the coup of 11 September 1973 occurred?

A: Actually, we continued to film in the aftermath of the coup, as long as our raw film stock lasted—but in the relative safety of our living rooms, from the television set. No one in the world except us thought to film the first televised communiqué of the junta, for example, on the very evening of the coup. We have other footage as well—the swearing in of the junta, the bombing of the national palace from the army's point of view. It seems unbelievable now that they actually televised such things. It shows their lack of judgment, their ignorance of the media.

Q: Did the coup place members of the collective in imminent danger? How many of you left the country?

A: All the members of the production team—with one crucial exception— left Chile after the coup. We managed to escape in an orderly and staggered fashion, without having to take asylum in any of the embassies, because we decided that there were many others who were more important. We camouflaged ourselves so that no one there would discover that we were filmmakers, and we were allowed to leave the country. The assistant director was the first to leave. He was a Spaniard who, like all foreigners, was in great danger because of the xenophobia of the military junta. I was the next to leave, followed by the producer, and, after him, the soundman.

It was decided that Jorge Muller, our cameraman, should be last. He managed to find work as a technician in advertising, but in November of 1974, more than a year after the coup, he and his *compañera*, Carmen Bueno, were arrested and imprisoned. It was a totally unexpected move. There was no evidence against them, and no charges were ever made. They were simply made to disappear. The families were never notified. Carmen was almost certainly murdered by the junta, but to date we have not received any confirmation of Jorge's death. The Swedish and French governments made high-level appeals for Jorge's release and an international campaign was mounted, but Pinochet's government continues to deny that he was ever arrested.

I was arrested shortly after the coup, and spent two weeks in the National Stadium. One of my neighbors denounced me. My house was searched five times. They learned that I was a technician, a teacher of communications, but nothing else; they never found out that I was a filmmaker.

While I was under arrest, the other members of the group got together and prepared themselves for the contingency of being arrested as a group. They assumed that, since I had already been taken, all the military would have to do is pull the thread, and they would all be arrested. They had to decide whether to begin to get the material out, or to hide it even more. They met with my *compañera* and decided to get the footage out of the country, formulating a plan for doing this. At this stage, it was not just the group's problem, but a concern of the entire Chilean resistance movement. Everyone carried out his or her part. No one broke down at any moment.

They managed to stay calm. Little by little, the footage began to leave the country. Amazingly enough, not a single meter of the twenty hours of footage was lost, not even a fragment of the magnetic sound track, but it took us six months to recover it all.

Of the five of us, four spent time in jail after the coup. Federico Elton, the chief of production, had his house searched and sacked twice; they took him to the Escuela Militar. While Bernardo Menz, the soundman, had the footage in his possession, the building he lived in was searched from top to bottom—except for his apartment. This was pure chance, a reflection of the chaos and total arbitrariness that existed at that time. Under those circumstances, with a little luck, you could pass undetected in a whole range of situations. That period of arbitrary repression lasted about six months. In the subsequent period—once the DINA [Chilean secret police] was organized and all intelligence agencies centralized—the repression became more selective and it became much harder to leave.

Q: Did you attempt to find support for finishing the film in Europe before deciding to come to Cuba?

A: Yes, we asked Chris Marker for financial help, since he had been very involved throughout. Chris spoke with Simone Signoret, Yves Montand, Frédéric Rossif, and others. But I began to realize that the film was enormous, that it was not one film but several, and that it was necessary to have the security to edit the footage calmly. It was not to be subjected to a standard production schedule—three months for the editing, three months for the sound mixing, and so on. It would be impossible to do it that way.

And so I began to tell Chris that we really needed a great deal of money, because we had to support the members of the group and their families, we had to contract new people to work on assembling the film, and above all, it had to be done at a leisurely pace. Other films would be coming out for the purpose of agitation and solidarity, but this film was a treatise, and had to be made at its own pace. A year, two years—it didn't matter, because ten years from now the film will still be relevant. Chris understood this reasoning, but we were unable to raise sufficient funds. Time was going by, and we kept meeting with various people, but getting nowhere.

That was when we met in Paris with Alfredo Guevara and Saúl Yelín of the Cuban Film Institute. "We would like to invite you to come to Havana to finish the film," Saúl and Alfredo said to us. "You'll have access to all that you need. It's up to you as a group to decide." We talked it over, and we agreed. We all came to Cuba. And here we had the good fortune to be reunited with Marta Harnecker, who got here two months before we did.

We also got back together with our editor, Pedro Chaskel, here in Cuba. He had not taken part in the filming nor had he been directly associated with the group in Chile, though we were certainly close friends. When I left Chile, I asked my *compañera* to tell Pedro that he was the person I wanted to edit the film, if he were willing to do it. He agreed, and it was for that reason that he decided to leave Chile, because he had a concrete task to do. Had that not been the case, he would have stayed.

Q: How would you characterize the editing style used in the film?

A: Pedro is an extraordinary editor because he respects the integrity of the material. He uses a "low-profile" style of montage so that the editing is barely noticeable. This was *very* important. I don't think that the job could have been done with another editor.

Once in Cuba, we entered into a marvelous sustained dialogue with Julio García Espinosa, who served as the Cuban Film Institute's adviser on the film. We already felt a great affinity with him, because of our debts to "For an Imperfect Cinema" and *Third World, Third World War*. We all grew in many ways—politically, ideologically, cinematographically—through our work with him. Julio helped us distance ourselves from the experience we had so recently and so intensely lived through. We were still traumatized when we arrived in Cuba, asking ourselves, "How did this happen? How is it possible?" It was Julio who helped us situate ourselves theoretically with regard to what had happened in Chile and to adopt a historical perspective, which was essential in enabling us to deal with the material calmly.

Julio's role was to facilitate the contributions of others. When no one had anything to contribute, when the group was going through a crisis, that was when Julio came in to make concrete suggestions. But when we knew exactly where we were going, the role he played was to stimulate our own creative process, questioning every aspect of what we proposed to do. This challenged us to be very clear about what we were doing and why, to examine every decision continually. Julio also made an important contribution on the ideological level, promoting unity rather than exclusivity while the footage was being edited. He realized the historical importance of the material and urged us to keep the film as broad as possible, but within the margins that seemed tolerable to us, and without ever dictating to us the political perspective that the material should adopt.

Finally, Julio never put the film on a fixed production schedule. On the contrary, we were the ones to promise that we would be finished in a given span of time. But every time we said six months would do it, it turned out to be eight, then ten, then a year. Each part of the film has taken us a year to edit.

Q: What is there about this particular film that makes the process so time-consuming?

A: It's not just the editing that's involved, but the underlying analysis on which the editing is based. For instance, we put together a chronological chart of the events in Chile that is probably one of the most exact chronologies of the period to be assembled anywhere.

Q: Were you surprised at the international acclaim the film received on release?

A: Yes, it was a total surprise. I thought that the film was a brick—a heavy and difficult movie that makes no concessions to the spectator. But in spite of this, the film began to be invited to all the European film festivals, and judging from the response, its importance for Latin America and the world at large continues to grow. In certain European countries where there are particular political parallels with what was attempted in Chile—France and Italy, for example, or Spain and Portugal—it has had a great impact.

Q: How would you evaluate the film's overall impact?

A: It is not a film whose primary motive is the quest for international solidarity or an agitational work whose value depends on a certain set of historical circumstances. It is not a sentimental appeal for people to give money to the Chilean cause. Instead, the film nakedly reveals our lack of direction, the massive offensive organized by the Right, the internal disagreements on the Left, but without mystifying the situation. It removes the veils and shows things as they were.

In this sense, I think it is an optimistic film—because it shows what happened. And to the extent that it does this, people will learn from it, draw lessons from it, and continue to fight. The film neither mystifies particular historical figures nor ceases to recognize what they represented, as is the case with Allende, for example.

The criteria we used to make the film were not apartisan or "objective" in the traditional sense. This is not a film made by journalists or reporters who go to Chile, make their movie, and go away again. Instead, each one of us, as Chileans, had a personal commitment to what we were filming. Our objectivity was based on a militant position *within* the struggle. This is the essence of the film, and it was something we anticipated before we even began to shoot.

The film was an incomparably intense experience for all involved, not just in its historical dimension or for whatever virtues it may have as film, or because of the fact that we managed to rescue it from the chaos and devastation which followed the coup. Through the lived experience of the film, we all came to understand what it means to live through a revolutionary process—what ideological struggle really means, what fascism looks and feels like, what it means for the enraged middle class to rise up against the workers, how invisible imperialism can be. The experience of making the film marked us for the rest of our lives. Everything else is merely a figure of speech.

Plate 7. From the final sequence of *The Battle of Chile, Part I:* An Argentine cameraman films his own execution. Photo courtesy the filmmaker.

Note

1. Chris Marker is a leading French documentarist, best known in this country for *Sunday in Peking* (1955), *Letter from Siberia* (1958), *La Jetée* (1963), and *The Battle of the Ten Million* (Cuba, 1970).

Chapter 6

Emilio Rodríguez Vázquez and Carlos Vicente Ibarra
(Puerto Rico and Nicaragua)

Filmmaking in Nicaragua: From Insurrection to INCINE

Plate 8. Carlos Vicente Ibarra at the First Havana Festival, 1979. Photo by Julianne Burton.

Emilio Rodríguez Vázquez is a Puerto Rican who lived for several years in New York before going to Nicaragua in the spring of 1979 to join the Correspondents' Corps of the Sandinista Liberation Front. When the Sandinistas came to power in July of that year, Rodríguez Vázquez stayed on to work with the newly founded National Film Institute, INCINE. Carlos Vicente Ibarra, a Nicaraguan, is one of the leaders of that organization.

Julianne Burton interviewed Emilio Rodríguez Vázquez via long distance telephone (New York to California) in fall 1979. She interviewed Carlos Vicente Ibarra in person at the First International Festival of the New Latin American Cinema, held in Havana in December 1979. For the sake of clarity and continuity,

Q: The central question that immediately poses itself is why turn to film in a country like Nicaragua—a country with no film-producing tradition and with limited financial and technical resources, particularly in a time of insurrectionary war, when precious resources were too limited for even immediate needs like food, medicine, and arms?

Ibarra: Although there were one or two film-production companies in Nicaragua under Somoza, it is true that there was no tradition of national filmmaking. The existence of 150 movie theaters around the country cannot be overlooked, however, since it accounts for a substantial tradition of film viewing—however we may criticize the kinds of films viewed.

Rodríguez: During the insurrectionary struggle, people from a number of countries came to film in Nicaragua, but the FSLN [Sandinista National Liberation Front] only became directly involved in the production of one of these films, *Patria libre o morir* [*Free Homeland or Death*]. A Costa Rican group called Istmo Films, sympathetic to the cause of Nicaraguan liberation and convinced of the need to create a Central American film industry, began developing a funding structure and took the initiative in presenting a film proposal to the FSLN leadership. With a concrete proposal in hand, members of the Frente got excited, daring for the first time to believe that it was actually possible to make a film about their struggle. The filming itself took about two months. Only toward the end of that period did the crew begin to go into combat situations. Though they wanted to continue filming, they realized that the film had to come out.

Though no Nicaraguans were members of the production crew, many were involved in writing the screenplay, in the organizing, fund raising, and subsequent distribution. At the time, the utility of such a film was seen primarily in terms of its potential for raising money to purchase arms. The film could not be viewed widely inside Nicaragua until after the liberation, but the process by which it was produced and its effectiveness in generating international solidarity convinced the FSLN leadership of the need to get more directly involved in filmmaking.

The need to document the involvement of the masses during the process of liberation—a mobilization without precedent in Nicaraguan history since Augusto César Sandino's resistence to the U.S.-sponsored invasion in the late twenties and early thirties—suddenly became a priority, although the various uses to which this material might be put could not be fully formulated at that time.

In April of 1979, the FSLN decided to begin to develop its own

the two interviews were subsequently edited together to create the impression of a simultaneous exchange. The interview first appeared in *Cineaste* 10, no. 2 (Spring 1980). Portions were translated and reprinted in *Les deux écrans* (Algiers), no. 25 (Summer 1980), and in *Jeune/Young Cinema et Theatre* (Prague), no. 3/80 (Fall 1980).

filmmaking and information infrastructure. It organized two offices: the Office of Information to the Exterior, and the War Correspondents' Corps, the first composed primarily of journalists, the second of photographers and filmmakers. I joined the Correspondents' Corps, working from April to July on the Southern Front (called Benjamin Zeledón), which borders on Costa Rica. About nine other people had assignments similar to mine in other parts of the country, including the Northern Front and certain key cities. We came from various parts of Latin America—from Mexico, Colombia, Bolivia, Ecuador, Peru, Uruguay, and, in my case, Puerto Rico—in response to an international appeal from the FSLN. The idea was to coalesce the kind of talents, experience, and resources that the Nicaraguans could not assemble by themselves, given the exigencies of the war effort and the fact that media expertise had previously been monopolized by the Somoza government. INCINE has its early roots in that volunteer corps.

Q: What previous experience did you bring with you to Nicaragua and what motivated you to make that decision?

Rodríguez: I was born in Cayey, Puerto Rico, in 1949. After studying Latin American literature at the university in San Juan and working in still photography, I moved to New York City in 1969 to work in film on a more professional level. I ended up having to take many kinds of non-film-related jobs, experimenting with different life-styles and eventually moving to the country, but always "keeping my hand in" with still photography and experimental filmmaking. I studied animation techniques and developed different kinds of multimedia presentations, all with the aim of using media in community organizing and political education.

Eventually I decided that I wanted to work full-time as a filmmaker. I developed a proposal for a series of nine documentaries comparing the daily life of nine Puerto Rican families with that of similar families in Cuba. I spent six months trying to raise money for that idea, but without success.

About the time I began working on a film about Puerto Ricans in New York directed by a North American filmmaker, I had occasion to see *Free Homeland or Death*. The film confirmed Cuban theorist Julio García Espinosa's ideas about "imperfect cinema"; despite its technical shortcomings, it moved me deeply. Not too long afterwards, one of the Nicaraguan *compañeros* informed me of the search for skilled media people. Two days later, I was on my way to Costa Rica. It was what you'd call a lightning decision, motivated by a unique opportunity to combine my professional interests and my political ideals.

Q: Are there specific incidents or perhaps a more general description you would like to give from your experience on the Southern Front?

Rodríguez: Very few of the international volunteers had ever received military training. I had refused to join the U.S. Army. Most of the other *compañeros* were also basically pacifists, involved with media rather than armed struggle as the agent of change. Upon arriving in Nicaragua, we all went through two weeks of intensive military training. When we went into the Naranjo offensive on May 20, things were pretty tense. The whole thing seemed like fiction: fifteen hundred "actors" all landing on the beach, unloaded from cattle trucks at 2 a.m. We had to keep very close to the *compañero* in front so as not to lose our way in the thick darkness. For hours an infinite line of invisible bodies moved slowly forward. When day broke we were spotted by a gunboat offshore, which began to attack. A few minutes later, a push-and-pull airplane began firing air-to-land rockets. At first, we didn't know how to react. Those of us who had never been in that kind of spot before stuck very close to those who had. By the end of that first day under fire, we had overcome our panic and learned how to position ourselves to avoid being hit.

My mission was to take both stills and moving footage. I was equipped with two Nikons (with 24mm, 35mm, and 80-200mm zoom lenses) as well as a 16mm Bolex. I was very surprised to see how "objective" one could be, even in the trauma of battle or the exhaustion of its aftermath. I remember a time when we were ambushed. I was part of a cadre that was advancing up a hill, down into a valley, and up another incline. As soon as we reached our destination, Somoza's troops opened fire. We rushed to find cover, but even under the onslaught of a surprise attack I found myself still fully cognizant of the details of exposure time and composition, able to make sure that the material was professional-looking.

Another time we had been marching for several hours before finally coming to a resting place. The others began to relax, but I had to remain on guard—ready to capture spontaneous shots that could not be repeated. We had climbed a steep hill, dodging airplanes, and just as we reached the shelter of the top, it began to rain. Parched and exhausted, all the combatants lay down with their mouths open, trying to catch some drops of water. The rain stopped, but the sky remained dark and low. A young woman suddenly sat up, gazing out into the distance, as if into the future. Behind her, the horizon seemed to open and the sunlight began to filter through the heavy clouds. In front of her, the sky also began to clear, leaving only a thick blanket of clouds just above her head and producing a rare magenta-toned light. That photograph later appeared in *Time* magazine.

Comparing experiences and impressions with cameramen and photographers from other fronts after victory was won, we remarked on that unexpected sense of clarity that possessed us all, on the drive to survive and to turn that experience into a creative rather than a destructive one.

Q: Carlos Vicente, what is the history of your involvement with film before and during the insurrectionary struggle?

Ibarra: My interest in film began in 1960 or 1961, when I was nine or ten years old. Where I grew up, in León, the Coca-Cola trucks would circulate through the poor neighborhoods on Sundays, peddling their product. As a kind of promotional gimmick, they would show movies against the walls of a building. I saw a film by Charlie Chaplin, which etched itself on my brain, and so it began . . .

When I was about thirteen or fourteen, I began to do still photography. I continued to go to the movies often, sometimes two or three times a day. Later I began to do independent reading about film, but it wasn't until three or four years ago that I decided to go into filmmaking. I was in Panama doing political work for the Frente Sandinista, and I took advantage of any free time I had to get involved with the University Experimental Film Group [GECU], directed by Pedro Rivera.

During the insurrection of September 1978 I was doing photographic work on the Southern Front. In the final insurrection, I was not working in either film or still photography, but with Radio Sandino, a clandestine organization.

When the revolution came to power and we all arrived in Managua, I decided that I wanted to work in the film sector. The leadership of the Frente invited me and two other *compañeros*, Franklin Caldera and Ramiro Lacayo, to head up the newly founded film institute. Caldera is an impassioned "film freak"; he is steeped in film history and is a fine critic. Lacayo, who headed the Press and Information Corps [Equipo de Prensa y Propaganda] on the Southern Front during the war, is the director of the first INCINE newsreel.

Q: Did any of the foreign volunteers remain to become part of INCINE? Rodríguez: Only myself and one young Colombian cameraman, Carlos Jiménez. Within a few days of the victory, we all got together and began to confer on what the organization and aims of the Nicaraguan Film Institute would be. The Ministry of Culture, of which we are a part, invited many people to confer with us in the organization process. Many representatives from international organizations concerned about the country's filmmaking plans were also in Managua during those hectic early days. We spent countless hours in meetings.

We were authorized to set up operations at Somoza's film production company, Producine. We found only an empty shell. We began trying to locate the missing equipment. We managed to retrieve what we found at the airport in crates, ready to leave the country, but a great deal had already left with Somoza.

Q: Was any of the footage taken by the Somocistas retrieved? Ibarra: Some 750,000 feet of newsreel footage, equivalent to well over three hundred hours of viewing time. Even though this material was shot by Somocistas, we are confident of being able to put it to good use in future films in which we will explore and assess the long years of rule by the Somoza dynasty.

Q: How much footage was assembled by the liberation forces during the war?

Rodríguez: We estimate that we produced about sixty thousand feet of 16mm color film from 1978 on (no black and white film was shot) and approximately four thousand black and white still photos and three thousand color slides. Many of these photographs were distributed to newspapers throughout Latin America and the Caribbean during the war, and we also intend to incorporate them into future films.

Q: Had there been any alternative cinema activity in Nicaragua prior to Somoza's fall—if not in terms of actual production, at least a familiarity with the kind of politically engaged cinema being produced throughout Latin America and in several European countries during the sixties and seventies?

Ibarra: Before the revolution, film production in Nicaragua was virtually nil—with the sole exception of the Producine Studios, Somoza's private film company, which specialized in "family albums" for Somoza, training films for the National Guard, and some commercial publicity. Certainly, there was no militant cinema movement like those that existed in many other Latin American countries beginning in the late 1950s.

There were, however, some attempts at alternative exhibition while Somoza was still in power. In the early sixties, a *cineclub* movement began in some of the Catholic high schools, supported by progressive political tendencies within the church. It was unusual to program films with an obvious political dimension, but many of the films offered certain implicit parallels to the Latin American political situation. Given the impact of the triumph of the Cuban revolution in 1959, which reverberated throughout Latin America, raising expectations and mobilizing whole sectors of the population, an interest in social transformation existed that, in Nicaragua at least, had few possible outlets. Film forums sponsored by film societies in the schools provided one of the few opportunities for public discussion of political issues.

University film societies offered two different kinds of programming. One group was much more concerned with historical and aesthetic approaches to film than with the political potential of the medium. The Departments of Language and of Literature obtained most of their films from the Alliance Française. Discussions usually centered on whether or not the image was properly framed, what angles were used, how the film was structured, and so on. Occasionally, a film with political implications—Jean Renoir's *La Marseillaise*, for example—would sneak through.

The other group, with more explicitly political concerns, sometimes organized clandestine screenings. I especially remember the showing of Santiago Alvarez's famous documentary *Hanoi, Tuesday April 13th* in 1971 or 1972. Some forty people attended the screening, but all of us had to enter separately to avoid being spotted by Somoza's National Guardsmen.

Later, in 1977 and 1978, a group of people attempted to offer an alternative in the commercial sector. They opened a screening room in downtown Managua called the Chaplin with a commitment to programming films of both high artistic quality and some political resonance. Given the strict control that the Somoza dictatorship exercised over film imports, this was an extraordinarily difficult undertaking. Any political message had to be effectively veiled. Not surprisingly, the attempt was a failure because the competition was too stiff and the aspirations too high.

Q: Can you describe the organization and future plans of INCINE?

Ibarra: Currently the Film Institute is made up of two departments: Production numbers about twenty-five people, about half of them technical personnel (including six camera operators, three film editors, a sound technician, and a screenwriter) and the remainder in charge of equipment maintenance; another twenty people are working in the Distribution Department.

Rodríguez: For its first year INCINE has a production goal of one fifteen to twenty minute newsreel [noticiero] per month. By July of 1980, we hope to double that output.[1] In addition, we have projected four feature-length documentaries per year, 16mm in color.

We see the newsreel as a way of deepening the news coverage provided by television and newspapers as well as a means of filling theater time and easing our dependence on some of the alienating material that has up to now formed the bulk of national film programming. Because of the particular discipline required in newsreel production, we also see this undertaking as crucial to the development of technical skills among our filmmakers.

Q: Is the Noticiero Latinoamericano, the weekly newsreel produced in Cuba under the direction of Santiago Alvarez, a potential model for your work?

Ibarra: It is to the degree that, like those responsible for the Cuban newsreel, we see the form as more than simply a vehicle for fragments of unconnected information. We conceive of each newsreel as having a unity of theme and structure—more like a documentary film than a standard newsreel.

For example, our first newsreel, which had its international premier the opening night of the First International Festival of the New Latin American Cinema in Havana in December of 1979, deals with nationalization of the Nicaraguan gold mines, but the film is structured around the presence of an old veteran who fought with Sandino in the early thirties. Dressed in the uniform of the original Sandinistas, but interviewed and photographed in the context of today's post-Somoza Nicaragua, he symbolically summarizes the evolution of our national history throughout most of this century.

The four projected documentaries, which will be feature length and in color rather than black and white, will take on broader themes than those of the newsreel, but their development and range will clearly be built on the experience that we progressively acquire on the newsreel project. It must be recognized that our technical preparation as professional filmmakers has barely begun. The wartime experience was just a small introduction—predominantly practical without being totally removed from theoretical considerations—to the phenomenon of filmmaking.

Q: Have you already been approached by people from other countries with proposals for coproductions?

Rodríguez: Coproductions offer the obvious advantage of additional resources to bring projects that are beyond our current means into the realm of the possible. The Cuban Film Institute has expressed interest in some kind of coproduction. A film on Sandino would be an obvious priority. Peter Lillienthal, who belongs to the group of new German filmmakers, is currently filming a feature on a Nicaraguan family. A Yugoslav crew is also filming now, and Mexican filmmaker Berta Navarro is in Cuba doing postproduction on her second documentary about Nicaragua. The Cubans have already produced a short called *Monimbó es Nicaragua*, about a particularly militant population in the Maysaya area. Cuban director Jesús Díaz was in the country in November to finish shooting footage for an ambitious four-part, feature-length documentary on Nicaragua. North American filmmaker Barbara Kopple also paid us a visit. It is clear that international interest is high.

In terms of distribution, our priority is the establishment of an effective mobile cinema program. Currently, we are not exactly well equipped for this undertaking. What is generally involved is a single print, a projector, a take-up reel, and a dedicated *compañero* who travels from town to town by bus. This operation will be greatly enhanced when we receive two Land Rovers equipped with projectors, screens, and power speakers promised by the Dutch solidarity committees.

Q: What kind of films are being distributed in this way?

Ibarra: Initially, the mobile cinema units had only about five or six titles to work with. Recently, an alternative distribution company called Zafra, with headquarters in Mexico, has begun providing us with a number of Latin American and European films. The donations we have received from the participants in the First International Festival of the New Latin American Cinema will increase our collection manyfold. In addition to a number of Cuban films, we have been given prints of feature-length documentaries like Patricio Guzmán's *The Battle of Chile* and Barbara Kopple's *Harlan County, U.S.A.* as well as documentary shorts from Argentina, Brazil, Colombia, Mexico, Peru, and Venezuela. Several European socialist countries have also expressed their intention of donating films and equipment.

The idea behind the mobile cinema project is to bring films to the most remote sections of the country, to people who have had little if any prior exposure to the medium. The national leadership has identified two priority areas: the Atlantic coast, and the northern region. The coastal zone has until now been completely isolated from the economic and political development of the rest of the country. It is the area that has been most thoroughly exploited by both the Somoza dynasty and North American business interests, because of its mineral wealth and the richness of its forests and fishing grounds. In the sixties, the northern region was the scene of brutal massacres carried out by Somoza's National Guard with the cooperation of North American advisers and mercenaries from various countries. It is estimated that thirty-five thousand *campesinos* lost their lives during that decade.

Commerical theatrical circuits are the other area of concern. Traditionally, only the most alienating and dehumanizing examples of international film production reached our screens. The task of finding more constructive products for popular entertainment is as difficult as it is urgent. Here again, the Cubans have given us generous assistance, offering 35mm prints of films made in that country and elsewhere.

Q: What kind of equipment do you currently have to work with?

Ibarra: So far, INCINE has only a small studio, an editing room, a darkroom for developing stills, and a recording studio. There is no film laboratory or sound studio because Producine had this kind of work done in Mexico.

Rodríguez: By the middle of next year, we hope to have processing and transfer equipment of our own. Currently, we have to send everything out for processing. It goes either to Mexico or to Cuba, with some peculiar strings attached, namely, that it be done for free, since we have no dollars for foreign exchange.

Our camera equipment consists of two Arriflexes and an old Mitchell, and, in 16mm, one CP16, which is in pretty bad shape, since it was used on the front lines, and a Bolex.

I have made two short trips to the United States and Canada recently, with multiple purposes in mind: to organize solidarity groups to channel resources in support of our efforts; to approach churches and ecumenical groups; to make contact with both organized groups like the National Film Board of Canada and individual filmmakers—not only independents but also those who work in "the industry." We are particularly anxious to secure the institutional support of the various film-related technical unions, though we recognize that this may not be an easy task.

Q: Have any other films been produced to date by INCINE, in addition to the first newsreel?

Rodríguez: I wish that we had been able to do more filming in the days immediately following the revolutionary takeover, but the planning process required a great deal of attention. We managed to begin shooting the first serious documentary in early August, despite great difficulties in getting the equipment to work right and a severe shortage of film stock. Consequently, that first documentary was produced in video.

It is a forty-five-minute film called *La educación no se interrumpió* [*Education Was Not Interrupted*]. It deals with the six weeks prior to the formal reopening of the schools, a period when parents, students, and teachers met together to define their new, postrevolutionary roles, redefining their relationships to one another, and coming to grips with the fact that they all had more responsibility than ever before. The film records the cultural activities—music, plays—as well as the meetings, conferences, and discussions associated with this period.

Q: Do you intend to continue work in video even when you have adequate resources for 16mm and 35mm production?

Ibarra: No, I think that video is more of a short-term strategy. In the early months of the revolutionary government, there was quite a vacuum in television programming. Those in charge sought collaboration from other sectors. Given our shortage of material resources, and our own lack of expertise, even in the film medium, we decided to make the education documentary in video. But I doubt that this will continue to be a constant in our activity, since we prefer to work in 35 or even 16mm.

Q: You have referred to the alienating nature of the kinds of movies traditionally shown in Nicaragua, suggesting that they enforce the passivity rather than the participation of the spectators. It seems to me that the portability and relative inexpensiveness of video might facilitate a more participatory and collaborative kind of filmmaking.

As the experience of the New Latin American Cinema has repeatedly verified, the visual media have a unique potential to catalyze critical consciousness among large groups of people. The very process of having formative input in a film that depicts one's own situation often provides that person or group of people with the necessary distance or "objectivity" to spark a great leap in awareness and determination to effect change.

This interactive or reciprocal process has been most marked precisely when the filmmakers' resources have been most limited, necessitating greater reliance on popular participation and input. This was the case, for example, with *The Brickmakers* by Colombian filmmakers Jorge Silva and Marta Rodríguez, with *The Jackal of Nahueltoro* by Chilean director Miguel Littín, with *The Courage of the People* by Jorge Sanjinés and the Bolivian Grupo Ukamau, and even in Cuba with a film like Sara Gómez's *One Way or Another*. Julio García Espinosa, in the influential essay that Emilio already mentioned, "For an Imperfect Cinema," identifies the need to discover the condition that will enable spectators to transform themselves into agents, into genuine coauthors. He calls for the "liberation of the private means of artistic production" and looks forward to the day when "art will not disappear into nothingness but into everything."

Ibarra: I agree that there has to be interaction between the creators themselves and the people, and that everyone does, in fact, participate in the process of creating culture; but that interaction has to be limited to certain moments in the creative process. What I'm unsure about is to what degree filmmaking can offer a continuity of creative process, given the technical requirements of the medium. I see the principal interaction developing in the initial planning stages, as the filmmaker investigates his or her chosen topic and speaks directly with the people concerned. Afterwards, during the shooting, he or she records the concerns of those people as faithfully as possible and later, in the finished film, returns those concerns to the people involved—but in a carefully elaborated, analytical form, with concrete proposals, wherever possible, for resolution of the problems addressed. Technical requirements would seem to limit popular participation in any but that early stage of production.

In Nicaragua, as in any revolutionary situation, the expression of individual creativity is always conditioned by the interests of broader sectors of the population, since the divorce between the interests of the creative artist and the interests of the people as a whole no longer exists. For one thing, creative artists' membership in political organizations prevents them from losing themselves in idealistic interpretations of reality. I believe that we in Latin America have gone beyond the stage when our goal was merely to document those problems that plague us. We are now at a stage at which events and issues are recorded, reformulated in a revolutionary way, and returned to the people in analytical form, as a project for action, a revolutionary solution.

Note

1. Only one *noticiero* was produced in 1979. Between 1980 and 1983, newsreel production averaged ten per year.

Chapter 7

Helena Solberg-Ladd
(Brazil and United States)

The View from the United States

Plate 9. Helena Solberg-Ladd, 1985. Photo by Dolores Newman.

Helena Solberg-Ladd is a Brazilian-born documentarist who, since 1971, has made her career in the United States. Her work has maintained a dual focus: Latin America in general and women's roles in particular. Her early films—*A entrevista* (*The Interview*, 1966), *The Emerging Woman* (1975), *The Double Day* (1975), *Simplemente Jenny* (1977)—emphasize the latter concern. Since winning an Emmy in 1983 for *From the Ashes . . . Nicaragua Today* (1982), she has concentrated on production for television.

Julianne Burton interviewed Helena Solberg-Ladd via long distance telephone (New York to California) on two occasions in late 1983. The editor is grateful to Melanie Maholik for comments and background information.

I never went to film school. I never expected to become a filmmaker. For me it all started in 1958, when I enrolled at the Catholic University of Rio de Janeiro to study Romance languages. Because I was female, my family had no particular expectations regarding my education. They expected my brothers to become doctors, lawyers, or engineers, but I was just supposed to learn French and read literature and be prepared to be a good wife with a little veneer of culture. I decided to go to the university on my own; it was a big step for me and a big change.

It just happened that my generation at the university was to produce a number of the pioneers of the Cinema Novo movement. I became friends with Carlos (Cacá) Diegues, David Neves, and Arnaldo Jabor. Arnaldo was doing theater and I believe Cacá was studying law. We all worked on a weekly newspaper called *O Metropolitano*, which was sponsored by the National Union of Students and distributed as a Sunday supplement to the *Jornal do Brasil*, a major national newspaper. Cacá was the director; I think Arnaldo wrote literary criticism; David Neves was the film critic; I was a reporter. I loved my job there. I got to interview people like Aldous Huxley, Graham Greene, Jean-Paul Sartre, Simone de Beauvoir. Had we been doing what we were doing in England or France, I doubt that we would have had such extraordinary access to these people, but in a country like Brazil, they were at our disposition.

After spending our afternoons at the newspaper office, our group would often go in the evenings to the Cinemateca at the Museum of Modern Art, which was nearby, or to the Higher Institute of Brazilian Studies, an important center for students and intellectuals of our generation. There was definitely a different quality to the intellectual life of that 1950s generation, formed before the military coup of 1 April 1964, which would end democratic rule by ushering in two decades of dictatorship. There was a different quality to what we were living and how we went about it and what our interests were. The youth were much more politicized, much more interested in social issues than the subsequent generation, formed under the military dictatorship.

Between my job at *Metropolitano* and my decision to make my first film, I got married—a "Big Event." Two or three years passed before I went back to any sort of professional development, since I immediately had a child. I found that being a housewife and mother was not enough; I started feeling bored and restless. I decided I wanted to do a film about myself, to explore the personal crisis I was experiencing as I began to realize that, because I was a woman, my life was going to go differently than if I had been a man. Many of my filmmaker friends got married the same time I did, but they didn't stop working. Of course, their wives *did*. I was the only woman in our group and the only one who dropped out because of marriage and family.

That personal crisis provoked my first film, a documentary called *A entrevista* [*The Interview*, 1966]. I interviewed between seventy and eighty women who had the same upper-middle-class background as I did, and who were educated in the same secondary school as I had been—a French nuns' school, Le Sacre Coeur de Jesu. I had a Nagra recorder with me day and night. I went around to different houses with a questionnaire. I asked about their aspirations during adolescence and about their attitudes toward two critical decisions: whether to go to the university, and whether to get married. Several of the women were already married, and their interviews were often quite shocking. I discovered that, despite their comfortable economic and social situation, these women were very, very unhappy. Though they were quite bright, they weren't able to envision much of a future for themselves. Their lack of options left them with a sense of hopelessness and futility.

Mário Carneiro, a very talented cameraman who had worked with Paulo César Saraceni and Joaquim Pedro de Andrade, shot the film. Rogério Sganzerla did the editing. The central image is a bride being prepared for the wedding—being dressed, having her hair combed and her makeup applied. A familiar ritual. The interviews are heard in voice over. Their impact is to totally undermine the image, which of itself is very beautiful. The sense of schizophrenia is intentional. As you watch the images, you are not sure where the voices are coming from. At the end of the film, I am shown on camera interviewing the bride. The idea is to rupture the dream imagery of the wedding preparation ritual by asking the real person about her marriage.

I ended *The Interview* in a rather strange way. Many people, including Jean Claude Bernardet, one of the foremost critics associated with the Cinema Novo movement, have criticized the ending as having no bearing on the rest of the film, but I still like it very much. I cut from the hesitations of this woman trying to explain her personal problems and ambivalences in front of the camera, using a very abstract, intellectual vocabulary, to the images of the military coup. Middle-class women had in fact played a significant role in that military takeover, which occurred while I was doing the interviewing for this film. When they took to the streets claiming that the family and traditional values were being endangered by the progressive direction of national politics, much of the rest of the population was moved to support the reactionary elements that orchestrated the coup d'état. I was shocked and disgusted by the fact that women would capitalize on their image as pure and disinterested souls defending "eternal values" when in fact what they were defending were the economic interests of their husbands. In my interviews for the documentary, I made a point of asking women about their political beliefs, and most of them replied that they didn't like or understand politics, that they simply deferred to their husband's political opinions. But when the coup came, they went out into the streets. The film ends with still photographs of masses of women carrying placards.

Perhaps one always has a special attachment to one's first film, but I can see in *The Interview* many of the elements of what I always wanted to do and in fact have ended up doing: to reach out from the individual and the personal to the larger sociopolitical context. My first film started out as a very personal exploration, provoked by a crisis in my own life, but even at that early stage I saw that you could not offer any meaningful analysis without amplifying the context in which you were posing the questions, without analyzing the implications of individual decisions within society as a whole. Even at this early stage, I saw that these self-contained women who focus on their religious concerns or their sexual problems and profess ignorance of broader social and political questions are not in fact innocent, or if they are "innocent" in the sense of being uninformed, then they have to pay the price for that choice.

When I decided to do the film in 1963, I went to talk with Glauber Rocha. We arranged to meet on the beach, where we spent two or three hours discussing my ideas. He was extremely helpful. He wrote a letter of support for my grant application to CAIC [Commissão de Auxílio à Indústria Cinematográfica, Commission to Aid the Film Industry], and I believe he ws the decisive factor in my getting that first grant. Occasionally you hear allegations that the members of the Cinema Novo group were *machista* or antifemale, but my experience was totally to the contrary. I think that male chauvinist tendencies undeniably existed in the society as a whole at that time, and that as feminism developed its own momentum as a social force, there was in reaction an increase in male aggression. But in the early sixties, nobody was talking about feminism, and I never felt discriminated against by the Cinema Novo people because I was a woman. Who knows? Perhaps there *was* a degree of paternalism: "Helena wants to do a film; she's just a woman; let's give her a helping hand." Maybe there was a little of that, but if so, I didn't object to it; I took advantage of it. Today there are many more women involved in filmmaking in Brazil, including two excellent feature filmmakers, Tizuka Yamasaki and Ana Carolina.

I had no illusions about making money with the film. There is no such thing as a 16mm documentary market in Brazil. *The Interview* was viewed by a lot of people in *cinemateca* [film society] showings. It went abroad to film festivals in Krakow, Poland, and Populi, Italy, where it received honorable mentions. I never distributed it, though I still occasionally think about doing something with it—perhaps dubbing it into English. I showed it in Washington, D.C., not long ago, and some Latin American women in the audience told me that they thought it was still extremely current.

I was pregnant with my second child while I was making *The Interview*, and it's interesting that the pregnancy didn't curtail my activity in the least, whereas with the first one I had just sat at home, paralyzed and terrified, watching my belly grow.

My only "training" in filmmaking at that early stage was purely observational. I remember watching Cacá shoot his first "experimental" film in the corridors of the university. When Joaquim Pedro de Andrade was filming *O padre e a moça* [*The Priest and the Girl*, 1965], I wrote to him for permission to come and observe the filming and spent some time in the interior of Minas Gerais observing. Later I worked as script girl on a film by Paulo César Saraceni called *Capitú* [1968]. Then I worked with Rogério Sganzerla as an assistant director on another feature called *A mulher de todos* [*Everybody's Woman*, 1969].

These experiences inspired a rather crazy project, a ten-minute fictional short called *Meio dia* [*Noon*, 1970], which I shot in 35mm with professional actors, just to have the experience. The film, inspired in Jean Vigo's *Zéro de conduite*, involves a rebellion in a classroom during which the children kill their teacher. I financed it myself with my own money and private contributions. The soundtrack consisted of only one song: Caetano Veloso's "É prohibido prohibir" ["It's Forbidden to Forbid"], which was itself banned in Brazil at the time. The film was screened at the Museum of Modern Art while I was out of the country, but the reports I got indicated that audience reaction was quite polarized, which pleased me.

After these two initial efforts, I left Brazil and went with my two children to live in Cambridge, Massachusetts, for two years while my husband, an American, went to business school. After we returned to Brazil, there was a long period when I wasn't very active. The children were growing, and they occupied a lot of my time. I participated peripherally in some film productions, and then, in 1971, we moved back to the States.

At that time, the feminist movement in the United States was really taking off. My first film here was *The Emerging Woman* [1975]. I didn't know anything about the women's movement when I arrived, but I read Betty Friedan's *The Feminine Mystique*, which had quite an impact on me. She goes from house to house interviewing women in the suburbs, much as I had done in my first film. Some of the things she recounts are absolutely devastating—like the housewife who hanged herself in her basement, but only after washing and ironing the week's laundry. I decided I wanted to know more about the feminist movement, and that a good way to go about it would be to do a film on the topic.

The Emerging Woman is a very modest film, done primarily with stills. I got a grant from the National Endowment for the Humanities, and I don't think the film cost more than twenty thousand dollars. I didn't know a soul in Washington, D.C., where we were living. I needed to get in touch with other filmmakers, but I didn't know how to go about it. The only thing that occurred to me was to go to the Biograph, a repertoire film house in Georgetown, and ask to talk to the owner. I explained that I was newly arrived from Brazil and asked if he could put me in contact with any local film people. This was something of a long shot, but David Levy turned out to be a wonderful person and introduced me to a number of local filmmakers. Through Grady Watts (who recently completed a television documentary about censorship called *Books on Fire*, which was nominated for an Emmy this year), I met Roberto Faenza, an Italian filmmaker working at Federal City College. In Italy, he had been associated with Bellochio and Bertolucci, but he split off from them for political reasons and came to the United States to learn video technology. He eventually returned to Emilia Romana, where he did a lot of video work for the local Communist party. At the time I met him, in addition to teaching at Federal City College, he was working with an independent video group. I was a total novice, but I joined the group.

The first project we did together was May Day, 1971, the last big antiwar demonstration of the Vietnam era, when the organizers and protestors promised to shut the nation's capital down, and almost succeeded. Demonstrators came from all over the United States; so did video crews. Ten or twelve of these groups got together with the May Day Collective, the organizers of the event, to decide how we were going to cover the action. We did a considerable amount of advance planning, including making minitapes to inform protestors about the organization of the march and familiarize them with the Washington street plan. In keeping with the style of those times, we decided to pool all the May Day material from these separate crews into a single film.

May Day was an incredible experience. I was fresh from Brazil, and I simply couldn't believe my eyes. What an introduction to life in America! Our crew spent the night at the same house, so we could get up at 4 A.M. and be out on the street by 5 A.M.. By 7 A.M., we had all been arrested. The beauty of this was that they never confiscated our equipment, so we were able to shoot inside of the stadium where all those arrested were temporarily housed. But we needed to find some way of getting the tapes out, since ours was the only footage shot there. Some congressmen came to the stadium to survey the situation firsthand. We would interview them, and while they were on camera, we would ask them point-blank, "Will you take this tape out for us?" Finally, one congressman agreed.

Abbie Hoffman was walking around the stadium with his nose broken. I remember trying to focus the camera on a very distinguished old man, dressed in a suit and tie, who looked a bit anomalous in that crowd. I approached him and inquired, "Sir, may I interview you? What is your name?" He replied, "My name is Dr. Spock." I almost dropped the camera. I had used his books in rearing my children. It was amazing to me to be thrown in with all these American public personalities.

Despite the tanks in the streets, despite the heavily armed police and paramilitary groups, despite the massive illegal arrests, there was still an air of festivity. People on the street would dance and throw flowers as the police came to arrest them. There were people in the stadium singing and smoking dope. Compared with what I had seen in Brazil in 1964, where demonstrators were actually being shot by the police, all this seemed strangely mild. People here could afford to be more arrogant, or more assertive, because they knew they were protected by the law. Imagine suing the government for illegal arrest in Brazil! Yet here thousands of the people who were detained in the stadium brought suit and eventually won their case against the government. Coming out of a Latin American tradition, where there are no cracks in the repressive powers of the government, I was amazed.

Once we had been fingerprinted and released, we met with the other video crews to decide how we were going to edit the film. A group from New York, the Video Freaks, invited everyone to their studio, which they claimed was the only one large enough to accommodate all the groups. Their "studio" turned out to be an enormous loft, totally bare except for pillows on the floor and ten video monitors. The idea was for all of us (we were twenty or more) to lie on the floor and watch all the hours and hours of footage shot by the various groups. At the end, by some kind of spontaneous consensus, we were supposed to come up with a script. It seemed preposterous to me, but being a foreigner, I didn't want to betray my ignorance by asking too many questions. Of course, it turned out to be impossible for us to come to any agreement.

One day we arrived at the loft for another go-round, only to discover that all the tapes had disappeared. In their place we found a little note: "I stole the tapes so that we can all love each other again." Can you imagine the furious pursuit through the streets of New York City trying to find the woman who had stolen everybody's tapes? People were out for blood. Finally she reappeared and gave everyone back their tapes. But by that point, our group had decided that we wanted to be out of it. We realized that the vision the Video Freaks had of May Day was very different from ours. Faenza felt that our tape needed a very clear political message and structure, one that could only be provided by the people who had organized the event. The Video Freaks' vision, on the other hand, was a totally surrealistic one. To make a long story short, two tapes were finally produced: one by each group. Ours was a very specific analysis of May Day's importance as a political action; the Video Freaks' was a kind of celebration of May Day as a cultural event. Both are good in their own way, but they fulfill very different functions.

The idea with *The Emerging Woman* was to do a short didactic film that would explain the genesis and nature of the women's movement. Through a notice posted at a local women's commune, I located two George Washington University students, Roberta Haber and Melanie Maholick, who were willing to assist with research for the film and could arrange to receive independent study credit for their work. (Melanie continues to work with me to this day.) During May Day, I had also met Lorraine Grey, at the time a still photographer who would later direct the award-winning *With Babies and Banners*. I invited her to work with us on *The Emerging Woman*. I knew more about filmmaking, but the other women knew more about the American women's movement, so we worked pretty collectively to share knowledge and skills.

That was the first time in my life I worked with an all-female crew. It was not a conscious decision; it just happened that way. The subject matter of the film required female participation, but I never thought of myself as taking a political position in putting the film together without male participation.

The woman whose photograph is used for the opening of the film, and again in the publicity brochure, is in fact a Brazilian. Years earlier, when I was working on *Capitú* with Saraceni, someone brought an old photograph in a little silver frame to be used as part of the decor for one of the sets. I thought the woman in the photograph had an absolutely amazing expression of determination tempered with sensuality, a rare combination for a Brazilian woman in the 1800s. I fell in love with the photograph, and had a blowup made. This is the image we used in the film, and for the publicity poster, which was widely used by women's groups around the United States. Eventually I heard from the Brazilian friend who had lent the photograph: "What do you think you're doing making an American feminist out of my grandmother?"

The Emerging Woman offers a history of the women's movement from the 1800s through the 1970s, focusing on working women and women of color as well as on the middle class. All that in forty minutes! Though somewhat amateurish, the film is very spirited and proved extremely useful, particularly for classroom situations, because of its chronological organization.

Today when I undertake a film project, I analyze what the potential market might be, how many films on the topic already exist, and so forth. With *The Emerging Woman*, these practical considerations never entered my mind. As it turned out, there was no other film on the market quite like it. Ours was the first to attempt such a broad overview. We ended up selling more than four hundred prints. It's still a "best seller." It became an official film of the American Bicentennial Commission. We were invited to the White House—Nixon's White House! Ironically, my first film in the United States, made before I really "knew the ropes," is still the most successful in terms of the return it has generated.

All the interest sparked by *The Emerging Woman* made me wonder what it would be like to do a parallel film about women in Latin America. What would the other side of the coin look like? As a Latin American woman, I saw several things in the North American women's movement that I disagreed with or that I felt overlooked other kinds of equally valid concerns. That's what *The Double Day* [1975] is about.

Once again, I began by forming a group to research the idea for the film. I made contact with a French woman and an Argentinian woman who were living in Washington and interested in the project. Along with Melanie Maholick, we decided to incorporate as a nonprofit corporation for the production and distribution of educational films. Because of our varied nationalities, we chose to call ourselves the International Women's Film Project. In this instance I was quite conscious of wanting a female crew because I believed that this would make the Latin American women we intended to interview more comfortable. I also thought that seeing women working as technicians might have a notable impact, as in fact it did. Our crew traveled through Latin America for three months; there were five women and only one man—Brazilian cinematographer Affonso Beato, who had shot several important Latin American feature films, including works by the Brazilian director Glauber Rocha and the Chilean Miguel Littin. The other cameraperson was Christine Burrill. I remember women in the factories in Argentina telling us that they had never seen such a sight—a group of women handling all that technical equipment.

We received funding from the Inter-American Foundation, an organization funded by Congress to do projects in Latin America, which was not at that time as controversial as it is today. Later on, it came under criticism for having a rather paternalistic attitude, but our experience with it was excellent. The foundation never tried to intervene in determining the content of the film, though I think it was a little dismayed by the final project. In one of its internal documents, *The Double Day* is described as promoting a Marxist analysis of the situation of women in Latin America, and it proceeded to question the wisdom of funding such films in the future.

The film's title comes from a Bolivian Indian woman we interviewed who says, "Nosotras las mujeres trabajamos una doble jornada...": "We women work a double shift, one in the factory and another in the home." I thought this was very well put, and decided that it would be the title for the film. Other people criticized me, saying that no one would know what "double day" meant, but the interesting thing is that the phrase and the concept have taken on a life of their own.

Setting up the shooting for *The Double Day* was a tremendous amount of work. First, I went by myself to a month-long seminar on women in Latin America organized by Helen Safa, an American political scientist, and held in Cuernavaca, Mexico, in 1975. Since women came from all over Latin America to attend, it provided me with bibliographical sources, including a number of studies that had not even come into print yet, and personal contacts as well. From there, I proceeded to the various countries in which I intended to film—Bolivia, Argentina, and Venezuela, in addition to Mexico—to meet people and make production arrangements. The third phase was the actual shooting with the whole crew. We traveled together for three months, spending almost a month in Argentina at the end. I also intended to shoot in Brazil, but when we arrived there, the government forbade me to shoot and confiscated my raw film stock.

We shot a lot of footage that we couldn't include in the film. For example, we interviewed a *montonera* [Argentine guerrilla group] activist, María Antonia, who was later killed. We accumulated an enormous amount of material, but in the editing we had to be ruthlessly selective, basically concentrating on a single theme, that of women's work. Even so, the film has too many ideas. It is quite dense.

One of the structural mechanisms involves the progression from most underdeveloped to most developed, from the situation in the Bolivian mines to the much superior conditions in the Argentine factories. Exploitation exists in both cases, but the contrast between the two is enormous. The section shot in Venezuela features a group of middle-class women discussing the structure of marriage and the family. In each of these situations, women perceive their oppression to be located in different zones. But the film's overall structure is circular, because it returns in the end to a Bolivian miner's wife, Domitila Barrios de Chungara, who says that Latin American women are no longer afraid to speak out.

We wanted to release the film at the inaugural conference of the United Nations–sponsored International Women's Year, which was held in Mexico City in 1975. When we were shooting in the Bolivian mining region, I had mentioned the upcoming Mexico City Conference to Domitila, an outspoken leader of the Housewives' Organization, and asked if she would be willing to attend. Many people had promised to arrange things for her that had never come through, so she was understandably skeptical, but we managed to get the United Nations to pay her way and send her a plane ticket. She recounts all this in her book, *Let Me Speak! Testimony of a Woman of the Mines of Bolivia* [Monthly Review Press, 1978]. Her presence at the conference was extremely important. Because she is so outspoken, I was very afraid for her safety, particularly in a country like Mexico. She was also under considerable pressure from different groups of Bolivian exiles who wanted her to take this or that position on a given political issue. It was potentially very confusing for someone who was traveling abroad for the first time.

I remember trying to prepare her the day before she would have her chance to speak to the assembly: "Domi, do you know that you will have to speak to several hundred delegates and journalists from all over the world? That you'll be standing on a platform in front of a battery of microphones?" I was afraid she might be intimidated. "Are the police going to be there?" she asked me. "Will there be tear gas?" "Of course not!" I told her, surprised. "Then what is there to be afraid of?" she asked, equally amazed. This woman, who had seldom been outside her little company mining town in

Bolivia, stood up in front of that huge crowd, one of dozens of speakers. Each speaker was allotted only ten minutes, but when her time was up, the whole audience started spontaneously shouting, "Let her speak! Let her speak!" the phrase that became the English title of her book.

I had mixed feelings about having brought her to the conference. I wondered whether it had been a good thing to take this person out of her own milieu, where she was so effective and so needed, because from then on she became an international figure. But she went back and continued to be just as active as before. Moema Viezzer, a Brazilian journalist, followed her back to Bolivia and taped the long series of interviews that were then edited into the book *Let Me Speak* [*Si me permiten hablar* in Spanish]. At one point, Domitila was even named as candidate to the presidency of Bolivia by the miners' group. Later she was forced into exile by a military coup that threatened her life. She lived in Sweden for a few years, but now she is back again in Bolivia.

The response to *The Double Day* at the conference was very good. What particularly pleased me was the reaction of the poor and working-class women whom the Mexican government had trucked in from all over the country to show that the conference was including poor women. They were very moved by the film. I had been afraid that it was too intellectual, but there were obviously sections in which these women could see their own lives reflected. In the United States and elsewhere, audiences expressed surprise at the outspokenness of the Latin American women, at their willingness and ability to express themselves publicly. They were apparently used to films that portrayed Latin American women as timid and silent.

The Double Day is widely used in Latin America, despite the limited access there to 16mm projection facilities. Here in the United States, every church and school and neighborhood group has its own 16mm projector, but in Latin America, such equipment is very rare and the problems of distribution are enormous. Still, the film gets used, particularly in Mexico, Bolivia, Venezuela, and Colombia.

I recently returned from another trip to Bolivia, where I was shooting part of a film on Indians of the Americas. In the middle of an interview with Lucila Morales, an Indian woman who was part of the Second Peasant Congress, she said, "Well, you know, just like they say in *The Double Day*." I wasn't sure I had heard her right, so I finished the interview, and then I asked her to repeat what she had said. "I was referring to that women's film," she told me, and I realized that she meant *our* film. She had seen it. There are only two or three copies in Bolivia, but it is very gratifying to know that they continue to circulate in the Indian communities even now, ten years later.

In a sense it's true what people say, that filmmakers simply remake the same film their whole life long, that we just move on to different aspects of the same themes. When I shot *The Double Day*, I was also shooting my next film, *Simplemente Jenny* [1977], though at the time my intention was that they be a single film. *Jenny* has a central fantasy image of women being dressed for marriage, and it also uses shots of mannequins to express the irrelevance of "ideal" femininity to the actual daily lives of these young Bolivian women. *The Double Day* has a more analytical tone; it proposes a thesis about women in the work force. Originally, I had hoped to combine both these approaches—the poetic and the analytical—but the time pressure we were under to have the film ready in time for the inaugural session of International Women's Year made it impossible to weave together the two strands, as I had wanted to, and so my editors, Christine Burrill and Suzanne Fenn, had to eliminate a lot of valuable footage.

From the outtakes of *The Double Day*, we constructed *Simplemente Jenny*. *Jenny* seems to me to be a more accessible film than its counterpart. My hope was always that they would be shown together, since I see them as complementary. Here again, one of the people being interviewed gives the film its title. Jenny is one of three adolescent girls whose lives and dreams and prospects are presented in the film. At one point she says, "I just want to be Jenny" ["Simplemente Jenny," an echo of the most popular Spanish-language soap opera of all time, *Simplemente María*]. When I asked this thirteen-year-old girl, who was raped at an early age and forced into prostitution, about her image of happiness, she invoked a very traditional, middle-class vision of marriage. This is why I decided to include a section on the Spanish conquest, colonialism, the inculcation of Western religious values, and how this process continues now through *fotonovelas* and other mass media. When, I wondered as we were shooting and editing this footage, does a woman reach the point that the disjunction between imposed "ideals" and the realities of her own life drives her to refuse these ideals, to rebel, to develop a revolutionary consciousness? I think this is only possible in the relative collectivity of a work situation, because women within the family are too isolated to see their situation clearly and objectively.

After *The Double Day* and *Simplemente Jenny*, I felt I might be running the risk of becoming a feminist filmmaker in an exclusionary sense. I *am* a feminist filmmaker, but I didn't want to limit myself to making only films about women. A relatively long time passed before I started work on another film. I was having tremendous difficulties raising money. I also got more involved in the process of distribution for *The Double Day* and *Jenny*. I was asked to give a lot of talks, participate in conferences, and so on. I spent a year or more essentially doing promotional and follow-up work on those two films.

This is not work that I really enjoy, but I don't think independent filmmakers have any alternative. The distribution problem is still a big obstacle. If you go with an established distributor, the terms of the contract are often outrageous (25 percent of the gross, for example, is considered good). If you decide to do your own distribution, you have taken on a full-time job, which prevents you from working on other films. Since the demise of Unifilm, all my films have been picked up by The Cinema Guild. I am glad to have them in one place. They continue to circulate, and from time to time we sell a print, though with the economic crisis, schools and libraries have had to cut back on film purchasing and rentals. What happens to most independents is that from time to time you end up in debt, and it takes you years to repay your debts on a particular film.

The idea for *From the Ashes . . . Nicaragua Today* [1982] arose out of a certain conviction I have that the media have an anesthetizing effect. Despite thousands of hours of news reports on the conflicts in Central America, the different situations in Nicaragua, El Salvador, Guatemala, and Honduras all end up looking alike. The public remains unclear about who's who and what's going on, about which sides the U.S. government supports and why.

I wanted to make a film that would give a human face to Nicaragua, a film with a dramatic structure that would touch people emotionally. I concluded that this emotional linkage, or empathy, could best be achieved through mechanisms of identification. I had the idea of using a family in which there was something of a generational split, with the children enthusiastically participating in the revolutionary process and the parents more questioning, but eventually deciding to lend their support. I also wanted the film to have an accurate historical base because I don't believe in manipulating the public and I think that, in general, the viewers are much more intelligent than the networks give them credit for being.

To make the film, I had to get permission from the Nicaraguan government. I had several preliminary conversations with people at INCINE [The Nicaraguan Film Institute], especially Ramiro Lacayo. We discussed what role INCINE should have in making this film, or whether it should even *have* a role. I didn't think it knew what the American audience would respond to; I felt that should be for me to determine. I didn't want to do a coproduction, or even to submit the film to INCINE's scrutiny. Basically, I wanted carte blanche, and that's exactly what I got. I made all the decisions about whom I would shoot, when, where, and how. Nobody interfered. I was very impressed by how open the Nicaraguan officials were, at least at that stage. I'm sure they cannot afford the same openness today. Given the attacks against them, they would have to be much more rigid about screening and supervising who is coming to their country to do what. But in my case, they imposed no controls; they never even asked to see footage.

I asked the Nicaraguan Women's Organization for orientation concerning the various neighborhoods, and they suggested certain general areas. I spent four or five afternoons walking around one neighborhood, going from door to door, meeting and talking with people. Some people were suspicious, but most were very open and friendly, as Nicaraguans tend to be. They would invite me to have coffee, and we'd sit outside the house to talk. Gradually, the neighbors would filter over to find out who you were and what was going on. That's how I met Clara Chavarría.

I was looking for interesting, expressive, articulate people, and I was drawn to Clara. I had explained that I wanted to make a film in Nicaragua, but I had not indicated that I was trying to choose a specific family as the focus of my film. Clara invited me to her house, where I met her husband, José, a shoemaker who works at home. Then their eldest daughter—Elís, nineteen years old—arrived. Originally, I thought of using her as the narrator of the film, but I could not, because her language was so highly rhetorical that I knew it would never work with an American audience. I preferred talking to the parents, who said things plainly and directly and who were less caught up in national politics. Perhaps their caution made them a little more reflective. They were not prone to jargon, and they had a lot of life experience behind them, so they could think in a more personal, mature way about what was happening around them. I like the fact that there were some splits within the family—between the parents and their daughters, and between the eldest and the younger girls. Some of the Chavarrías' values could be middle-class American values. They were concerned about the risks of indoctrination through the literacy campaign; they were concerned for their children's physical and moral welfare. I made at least five trips to Nicaragua during the course of the filming, to record the family's response to various events and to monitor how their lives were being affected.

I would have made a much more personal film if it weren't for the fact that, when you are doing a film about Latin America for a North American audience, you always have to start from scratch. You can't assume any knowledge on the part of your viewers. You have to lay out the location and history of the country, what language people speak, and so forth. In a one-hour film, that takes up a tremendous proportion of your time. I always find myself wishing, "If I just could do this film for a Latin American audience . . . " In that case, I could have allowed myself to get much closer to my subjects than I did. For example, some of my footage explores tensions between the husband and wife, but I was compelled to eliminate these sections.

There are certain modes of being characteristic of Latin Americans that cannot be easily apprehended by North American audiences. Elís, the same daughter whose language is permeated with political jargon, said to me at one point, "Do you know what they found in Somoza's prisons? The prisoners' beards reached the floor and their fingernails had grown into claws, and when they brought them out into the light of day, they disintegrated into a pile of ashes!" Can you imagine putting this kind of language into a film for an American audience? What she was saying was that Somoza's prisons were a horror, and for that she unconsciously chose poetic imagery, but no one from as rationalist a tradition as that of the United States is going to understand such a thing. They'd say the girl should be sent to a mental hospital. With a Latin American audience, on the contrary, one could even use this speech or others like it to reflect on the phenomenon of more permeable boundaries between the imaginary and the real.

It wasn't until the middle of the editing process that I discovered I was making a film for television. (We ran out of funds at that point, and the Corporation for Public Broadcasting [CPB] stepped in with a completion grant.) This narrowed the film's approach even further in some ways. I had wanted to do a film that was both more poetic and more political. I wanted to examine the process of politicization itself, to look at how a shoemaker like José or a housewife like Clara, who had absolutely no prior history of political involvement, decide to actively support a revolutionary government. The war politicized a lot of people, but not in depth. No one was really prepared for the difficulties that would come after the overthrow of the dictator whose hated presence had unified virtually the entire population. Poverty and unemployment were not going to be eliminated overnight. Somoza's overthrow was not an end but a beginning. I think that the Sandinistas themselves underestimated the need to prepare people for this much longer and more difficult process. This would have been my focus if I had been able to make the film for a Latin American audience: What are the problems a country faces after that first enthusiastic affirmation of "Yes, we want to rule ourselves at last"? Because that's the question facing a lot of Latin American countries right now, particularly as a number of South American military dictatorships are giving government power back to civilians.

The first funding grant for the project (three thousand dollars) came from the Swedish Development Agency [SIDA], an organization that had also contributed to *The Double Day* and *Simplemente Jenny*. Then the Wisconsin Committee for the Humanities gave us a grant, and a guarantee of additional matching funds. The total cost of the film was around two hundred thousand dollars. Through a program set up in the days of the Alliance for Progress, Wisconsin is the "sister state" of Nicaragua. My coproducer, Glenn Silber, was a graduate of the University of Wisconsin at Madison.

Once it was aired on public television, *From the Ashes* became the target of the most vicious attacks made against any independent film in recent years. It was used as a scapegoat, as a means of telling independents, "Watch out, the rules of the game have changed, and you cannot go on making this kind of film." William Bennett, chairman of the National Endowment for the Humanities and a Reagan appointee, personally led the campaign.

One morning in April 1982, I was awakened by a phone call about 7 A.M.: "Have you seen the front page of the *New York Times*? Take a look." And sure enough, there was the Bennett attack on the film. He called it "unabashed socialist realism propaganda" [*sic*]. He claimed he never knew the Wisconsin NEH affiliate was providing funding.

The coverage went on for several days, and the controversy went on for weeks with such sensationalist headlines as "Leftists Feed at Public Trough" and "How Radical Filmmakers Get Your Tax Dollars." A piece in the Sunday television column of *The New York Times* was titled, "Swan Song for Independents?" My first response was panic. I didn't know what to do. A few people called me to say, "Congratulations! All the commotion is terrific publicity for your film." I thought at the time that this was a peculiarly American way of seeing things, but in fact they were right. In that sense, Bennett made a big mistake. The controversy prompted a lot more people to see the film.

The attacks always took a rather paternalistic tone. They would acknowledge that the film was well done, but deplore the fact that it was hopelessly "naïve." My question is, if the film is so naïve, why did it provoke such ferocious attacks? I think the answer has to do with the film's success at reaching people emotionally. If you wish to wage a war against another country, you prefer that its citizens remain faceless. *From the Ashes* put faces on the Nicaraguans.

The independent filmmaking community was not prepared for the extent or the virulence of the attack, and we were unable to react in any unified way. I had to respond as an individual. Some independents felt that if I made too much of a fuss, I was going to jeopardize their chances for funding and contracts. There was the danger that I would be thrown to the wolves, so to speak, blacklisted, with even my fellow independents refusing to associate with me. Others would call me and advise me not to respond at all, just to let things blow over. The AIVF [Association of Independent Video and Filmmakers] was not ready to respond to this kind of situation at that time. I believe that they are more organized today and would probably take a more aggressive position to defend independent filmmakers under similar attack. Throughout the whole thing, PBS [Public Broadcasting Service] and CPB behaved very honorably. They responded to Bennett by saying that they aired the film because they thought it was good, and because they thought there was a place for such points of view.

It took a lot of time and energy to respond to the attacks against the film, and I began to fear that my career as a filmmaker was at an end. I was afraid that I would not be able to shake Bennett's labels. I decided that the only thing to do was to try to make another film immediately, rather than sitting back and waiting. More than a year later, in November 1983, *From the Ashes . . . Nicaragua Today* won the Emmy for outstanding background analysis of a current story.

I have not returned to Nicaragua since the shooting of *From the Ashes*, so I don't know what response the film has had there. Unfortunately, we did not have sufficient funds to make a Spanish-language version; the film only exists in English. I haven't given up on the idea, but we were twenty thousand dollars in debt when we finished the film, and are still paying lab bills. Gary Crowdus, our distributor, tells us that the film is being widely used, and so we are optimistic that we will soon be able to pay off our debts, and then we hope to do a Spanish version. The film is so tailored to an American audience, however, that I don't know how useful it would be in Nicaragua. At one point, PBS approached me about going back to locate the Chavarrías and make a sequel to the film, "The Chavarrías Revisited." I thought it was a terrific idea, until I realized that they would only be interested in such an up-date if the Chavarrías had changed their position from one of support to one of disaffection toward the Sandinistas. I refused.

Still, that kind of idea always has an immense appeal. One day I would like to go back to Bolivia, find Jenny, and follow up on what has happened to her. I would like to film the Chavarrías again, though perhaps not until three or four more years have passed, to see what has happened to their children, and how their perception of the political issues has changed.

These are things we independent producers can seldom do without an infrastructure of support. Otherwise, we are always too busy scrambling to finance each film on an ad hoc basis. In fact, there's no such thing as an "independent" filmmaker—fully independent—since where the money comes from always determines to some degree what the film will be like.

This is sometimes frustrating, but it also can be very interesting. For instance, *The Brazilian Connection* [1982] and *Chile: By Reason or by Force* [1983] were completely different from my previous experiences as a filmmaker. Both were made in collaboration with David Meyer, a former ABC producer who has since joined the ranks of the independents. We went to the News and Current Events section of PBS to propose a film on Brazil. They are interested in what they call "hard news"—very current material that can compete with network news coverage, though their budget is only a fraction of the networks' news budgets. They give you only one month to shoot, and another to edit before they expect to air the program. I had never worked on such a tight schedule. It was excellent training. I learned that it is actually possible to put a film together in that amount of time. You might just about kill yourself in the process, but it can be done. Maybe we independents indulge ourselves when we take a whole year to do a film. Doing hard news films for PBS is not lucrative, since the budgets are low, but the experience posed a challenge and also allowed me to examine two current situations in Latin American that are extremely important, and to provide coverage of them as they happened.

The Brazilian Connection deals with Brazil's foreign debt crisis, but as it turned out, we were shooting during the first national election after eighteen years of military dictatorship. The upcoming elections were what enabled us finally to sell the idea to PBS. The electoral activity gave a lot of dynamism and energy to the film—a good thing, since the external debt is not very photogenic.

Our film goes back to the military coup of April 1964 and explores the role of the United States. We have an interview with Lincoln Gordon, American ambassador to Brazil at the time, who now officially works for the CIA. We try to analyze what was behind the subsequent so-called economic miracle and how the external debt crisis is an outgrowth of those economic policies. We predict that Brazil might ask for a moratorium on the debt. People thought that this was alarmist, irresponsible, and just plain crazy at the time, but it turns out that we were on the right track, and now a debt moratorium is being discussed openly in a number of countries as Third World nations begin to realize that they can use their external debt as a weapon against the developed countries.

The film also discusses models of development. Third World countries were told that if they followed the economic policies promoted by the United States, they would eventually be able to join the developed nations, but the Brazilian case proves that there is no room at the top. The gap between the industrialized countries and the so-called developing countries only grows larger.

Maybe one of the characteristics of my films is that they try to go beyond information to provide an analysis, a theoretical perspective from which to understand the issues. This is true of *The Emerging Woman* as well as of *The Double Day* and *The Brazilian Connection*. At the same time, I try to find ways to simplify the issues so that they can be easily grasped and digested. I try to familiarize myself with a topic without immersing myself in it to a degree that would prevent me from having to ask very basic questions—the kind of questions the audience would ask. Otherwise, I might as well write a book rather than make a film.

As Brazilians, both Affonso Beato (my cameraman on *The Double Day* and *The Brazilian Connection*) and I took great satisfaction in being able to do a film in Brazil—particularly one that had a significant impact. After all these years, going back to film in Brazil was an incredible high. We saw a wonderful resurgence of vitality and energy after so many years when the country seemed dead. It was delightful to see it turned upside down, back again to what it used to be—everyone discussing politics and arguing among themselves with a kind of crazy energy that resembles carnival.

We had a five-person crew—Affonso, David, myself, and two additional crew members whom we hired in Brazil. We shot in 16mm and then transferred to tape for the airing. We don't even have prints in 16mm, since we didn't have the money for them. *The Brazilian Connection* is in distribution now, but only on videotape. We would like to make both films available in 16mm, if the market warrants and if we can afford it. The only problem is that this film, like our subsequent *Chile: By Reason or by Force*, has a strictly news format: both films have a "host"—Warren Hoge, Brazilian correspondent for the *New York Times*, and former *Washington Post* and *Time* magazine reporter John Dinges for the Chile film.

I told PBS that I think they are making a mistake in trying to compete with the commercial networks, that their attempt to be just as up-to-the-minute is almost an impossible task because their financial and technical resources are much more limited. The strength of PBS lies in its opportunity to provide an analysis of the news. This naturally takes more time. I think they should consider making their format much more flexible and eliminating the host, who is only there because the network news shows have hosts.

As if to prove my point, *The Brazilian Connection* really scooped the networks. Two months after it was aired, I had people from ABC calling to ask me for contacts in Brazil. They sent a crew down to make essentially the same film we had done. They had finally discovered that there was a story there.

We subsequently approached PBS with the idea of a film based on the tenth anniversary of the coup that overthrew Allende. The film examines the pressure being put on the government through massive public demonstrations to return to a more democratic form of government. We also looked at the results of the economic policies imposed by the "Chicago Boys," Milton Friedman and his disciples. I think we got tear gassed every morning we went there. We were always running from the police, but we got absolutely great footage. We did the shooting in October, and the film was aired on 2 November 1983.

Here again, we used a small, five-person crew: David Meyer and I codirected; Adrian Cooper, an Englishman who had worked in Chile under the Allende regime, did the camera; the rest of the crew was Chilean. We filmed mainly in Santiago, with a side trip to Temuco. We emphasized how Chile seems divided into two different worlds, depending on whether you're talking to the middle-class people in the cities or to the people of the *poblaciones* [squatters' settlements] and the rural areas. The people in the *poblaciones* don't even accept the concept of the Democratic Alliance because they think that establishing a dialogue with the military government is a form of betrayal of democratic principles, lending spurious legitimacy to a basically fascist regime. Unless the pro-democratic forces can convince this sector to join them, there is no hope in Chile for a peaceful solution. We visited the coal mines and interviewed striking copper miners. We also interviewed Onofre Arpa, the minister of the interior, whom many view as a likely successor to Pinochet. Like *The Brazilian Connection, Chile: By Reason or by Force* was aired during prime-time to a massive audience.

I'm currently working on a film called *The Home of the Brave*, not an anthropological but a political film provoked by the internationalization of the Indian question. I went to Geneva to film the Second World Conference on Racism and Racial Discrimination, in August 1983. The conference looked at the Palestinian problem, the question of race in South Africa, and so on. One topic had to do with Indians, and there were representatives from Indian populations from throughout the Americas.

What the Indians have been arguing for a long time—the need for human beings to live in harmony with the environment—has now become a major political question worldwide. The film deals with issues of class and ethnicity, and the relationship between them. It deals with the issue of trying to inscribe peoples from traditional cultures into modern society, including the kind of civil warfare currently going on in a country like Guatemala against the indigenous population.

We filmed some exceptional footage of the Bolivian peasant leader Genaro Flores and of the Second National Campesino Conference in that country. What the Bolivian Indians are seeking is political power through union organization—a strategy that is completely different from those being pursued in any other country. In Brazil, unfortunately, the "Indian question" is almost as pathetic as in the United States, since the Indians make up less than 2 percent of the population and consequently have no real power base. But then there are other countries like Peru or Guatemala or Ecuador, where no political solution is possible without the participation of the indigenous peoples. It is no longer a question of paternalism or protectionism. Many of these indigenous populations now have a level of political organization and articulateness that would astonish you. It is not a question of "bringing them back into the mainstream of history." The fact is, there is no possibility of history *without* their participation.

I often think of going back to Latin America to live and work on a permanent basis, but I hesitate to be put in a position where I have to compete for jobs and funding with Latin American filmmakers who have neither, particularly since I have been fortunate enough to keep my career going in the United States. I also have to be realistic about the fact that I can be more effective doing what I do from here. I have a rare opportunity to present an "insider's" view of Latin America to North American audiences, and few people in Latin America would underestimate the tremendous impact-making potential of the North American media, particularly television. Because I have lived for so many years now in the United States, I have a good sense of the culture and the social environment. I know a lot about how American audiences respond, and about what they respond to. Yet I still have close ties with Latin America. When I film in Spanish-speaking countries, I am neither a local nor an outsider. Though my Spanish has a marked Portuguese accent, I am always accepted as a member of the larger cultural community that is Latin America. This gives me a degree of access that few if any North Americans or Europeans can attain.

Yet my situation is not without its strains and contradictions. It is essential for me to maintain contact with Latin American filmmakers and to be able to see their work. Despite its cosmopolitanism, New York does not offer the possibility of viewing the work of even the best Latin American directors on a regular basis. German, French, and Australian cinema have received much more attention here in the last few years. Despite my nostalgia, my desire to go back to Latin America to live, I think I have finally come to grips with the fact that there is important work to be done from here, and that it would be foolish to drop it now for sentimental reasons. Besides, distances are shorter in today's world. And part of Latin America, a substantial part, lives today inside the United States, which is now the sixth largest Spanish-speaking country in the world. We Latin Americans who have made our home here must leave our mark; we have to make a statement.

Compared to the economic situation of most Latin American documentarists, North American independents have had it very good. This is why I make a point of hiring as many Latin Americans as possible every time I film in Latin America—to provide both salaries and training.

Yet, Latin American filmmakers have some things to offer their North American counterparts, particularly in these critical times when funding seems to be drying up, when television programmers fall prey to intimidation tactics, and filmmakers fear a return to the blacklist. We go to meetings and conferences and debate how we can be more effective, what kind of film language we should use, how we can counter the "oversaturation" of our public. We discuss the "death" of documentary. I think this is absurd, since there is still so much that needs to be done. It's just a question of being genuinely creative, and of finding—or creating—spaces in which to work. Maybe the solution is to approach certain topics less directly, to find other ways of saying things. This is where Latin American filmmakers offer a particularly useful set of examples, having developed ways of communicating under the harshest kinds of censorship and repression.

We recently received a research and development grant for a series of interrelated documentaries on Latin America. It is a joint effort involving the Press and the Public Project and Terra Productions as well as David Meyer and myself. We have formed a new entity called the Latin American Project and are currently seeking production grants from CPB and PBS to begin work on eight hour-long programs. We are optimistic about obtaining the necessary funding, but one never knows . . . For me, it will be a new and challenging experience. As executive director, I will oversee production on all the films and guarantee the unity and coherence of the series.

One of my contacts at PBS has advised me to diversify to avoid being perceived as limited to a single geographical region. This might be sound advice, but Latin America is the region I love most, where I have the deepest ties and the greatest interest. I'm not saying that it would be impossible for me to do a film on an unrelated topic. (In fact, the International Women's Film Project is currently producing a film on New York's Chelsea Hotel, though my work on the *The Home of the Brave* project has prevented me from having a high degree of participation in the Chelsea film.) But there is still so much about Latin America that needs to be said, so much we haven't even touched on that is urgent and vital, that I would love to continue doing what I'm doing for as long as I'm able.

Part II

FICTIONAL FILMMAKING
The Reality of Drama

Glauber Rocha
(Brazil)

Cinema Novo and the Dialectics of Popular Culture

Plate 10. Glauber Rocha, 1970. Photo by Robert Phillip Kolker.

Glauber Rocha was the guiding genius of the Cinema Novo movement, its most prominent—and polemical—advocate, theorist, and practitioner. "The Aesthetics of Hunger" (sometimes called "The Aesthetics of Violence"), his powerful essay on cinema and underdevelopment, has circulated widely. He made his first feature film, *Barravento* (*Turning Wind*, 1962) in his native Bahia before his twentieth birthday. Three other major films followed before the close of the decade, focusing worldwide attention on Brazilian and Latin American cinema. Unable to work effectively in the repressive political climate prevailing in Brazil, Rocha spent most of the 1970s outside the country. His last feature film, *A idade da terra* (*The Age of the Earth*, 1980) was completed after his return. Rocha died unexpectedly after a brief illness

Q: I would like you to tell me how you view *Antônio das Mortes* [1969] in relation to your previous work. Does it represent the pursuit of a new line of development in your work or the continuation of the theme of the *cangaçeiro* [bandit associated with the Northeast]?

A: I made *Antônio das Mortes* for various reasons. First, I wanted to address the problems of the Brazilian Northeast again, from a different point of view than that of *Deus e o diabo na terra do sol* [*Black God, White Devil*, 1963], because the latter now seems very romantic in theme. I wanted to offer a more reflexive vision of the problems of the Northeast and above all of the social and political contradictions of mysticism, the most vital social force in the region. Although mysticism is a negative phenomenon in sociological terms, I think that it is very positive from a subjective and unconscious point of view, because it signifies a permanent rebellion of the people against the kinds of oppression they have traditionally suffered.

I chose the character of Antônio because he had been extremely successful in *Black God, White Devil*. This character, wedged between the powerful and the oppressed, goes through a kind of moral crisis. He is a unifying element. And since he is also typical of the region, I wanted to use him again as the means to a political discussion.

The other reason was my personal need to make a film that would allow me to increase my skill as a filmmaker. That's why I chose a treatment that was less complex than those of *Black God, White Devil* and *Terra em transe* [*Land in Anguish*, 1967], one that would allow me to develop my own cinematic language to a greater degree, and that was also more accessible to the public, more communicative—especially to Brazilians.

Antônio das Mortes was a great success in Brazil, much more so than *Black God, White Devil* and *Land in Anguish*. The latter was well received in the cities, but not in the interior. *Black God, White Devil* was well received in both places, but its run was nothing out of the ordinary. The structure of *Antônio das Mortes*, like *Black God, White Devil*, is very close to the *romanceiro* [collection of popular oral ballads], but since it is colder, more direct, and technically superior, it has drawn a larger audience. This is a stance that I and other Brazilian directors have defended: Joaquim Pedro de Andrade, for example, with *Macunaíma* [1969] . . . or Carlos Diegues with *Os herdeiros* [*The Heirs*, 1968]. After our first experiences with Cinema Novo, we decided that it was necessary to purify our language more in order to enhance the level of communication with the public.

Let me explain what I mean when I say "we." Brazilian cinema began

---

the following year, at the age of forty-three.

The interview with Glauber Rocha, conducted by Cuban filmmaker Miguel Torres and translated by Julianne Burton, appeared in *Cine Cubano*, no. 60/61/62 (1970) as "Entrevista con Glauber Rocha sobre *Antônio das Mortes*."

with eleven directors and today we have fifty. There is still the original nucleus of the Cinema Novo filmmakers, but there are many others as well who produce their work in affiliation with the Cinema Novo or as independents.[1]

We know that the problem of communicating with the Brazilian public is a very difficult one because it is very alienated and unaware. It is enslaved by the language of foreign films—particularly North American movies. Film distribution in Brazil is controlled by North American companies. Even though a Brazilian film might enjoy great popularity, it will never attain the same level of success as foreign films because it is unable to secure a long run for itself.[2]

We tried to alleviate this situation a bit. We had already overcome certain crises, such as when they said that our films were not genuinely popular in the sense of deriving from the people. We were not interested in making films to praise the people, nor were we interested in making demagogical films. We didn't want to borrow forms from traditional commercial filmmaking to reach our public, either, because we could not use the forms traditionally employed to transmit imperialist ideology to convey a different kind. We feel that language and idea, form and content, are organically linked. That poses a great problem for us. *Antônio das Mortes* was an experiment in this sense, and it was relatively successful. Although the film has its flaws, I think it is more important than *Land in Anguish* because it proposes a more general and open kind of political discourse on the problems of Latin America.

I think that as a filmmaker I grew a great deal with *Antônio*. It was like the conclusion of a specific phase that had begun with the two previous films. It allowed me to free myself of certain cinematic and aesthetic concerns and go on to other things.

Q: It seems that one of your major goals in the film was to use a new kind of language to enhance the degree of communication with the audience without resorting to commercial formulas.

A: Of course. This is what my fellow filmmakers and I have been working on in Brazil. The problem is that we don't believe that there are certain films that the public understands and others that they do not. What happens, in fact, is that the public is educated in a certain kind of language. It's as if they had been taught to read in German and someone showed them a book written in English. It would be impossible for them to understand it because they had been educated in the structure of another language. Like Godard said, there is an economic and aesthetic dictatorship of American filmmaking, which produces an ideological-linguistic complex. We cannot make films to express Brazilian or Latin American content using North American language. This is a very great contradiction, because the cultural forms themselves, which are tied to the problem, must also be freed from alienation.

I'm particularly interested in the question of Brazilian popular culture, since we also have, as you do here in Cuba, a very strong tradition of popular theater. Other filmmakers are more interested in urban themes, seeking to develop their cinematic language on the basis of their search for authentic cultural forms in that sector. Various roads are open to us. We have the Brazilian *romanceiro*, which I have used in two of my films and which represents the most direct route. And we also recently discovered the meaning of Brazilian comedy—and not simply the innocuous comedy of manners.

We rediscovered the whole tradition of the modernist movement in the 1920s, a very aggressive and anarchistic surrealist movement, which is known in Brazil as Tropicalismo. We did some research on Brazilian literary and musical traditions and we discovered that the Tropicalist style had an infinite range of possibilities for communicating with the public through a very violent, very aggressive language that derives from a kind of picaresque urban comedy. We are now trying to pursue the line that Diegues used in *The Heirs*, where he made extensive use of popular music and urban popular theater. [Joaquim Pedro de Andrade's *Macunaíma* (1969) is considered the foremost example of the Tropicalist approach. Rocha's own *Land in Anguish* was the leading forerunner of this style.]

We are currently researching the popular forms that are tied to the people through theater, music, dance, and literature. In extracting certain forms that can still be used today, we are searching for a means of communicating with the public through a language already familiar to them, one that uses many elements created by the people themselves. Though the process will be a long one, we believe we can achieve a genuinely Brazilian cinema that, since the structures are very similar, can also be a genuinely Latin American one. This naturally leads to a new acting style, a new way of using music, new uses of color and forms of montage.

This is obviously not the product of a priori theorizing, because we feel that, since we are beginning at zero filmically, we cannot develop a theory and then attempt to illustrate it. So it is better to make films, though they may contain mistakes and contradictions, as a way of arriving at a more defined and representative language with which the people can identify directly, rather than use the alienating elements of imported commercial cinema to accomplish our goals.

Besides, I believe that the public is not stupid, that it has a substantial capacity for discussion and criticism. Even though it may be ignorant or alienated, it still has this sensitivity. We do not want to patronize the public; we want the public to participate a great deal in our films, to debate among themselves. We believe that when a film's message is hermetic, the audience leaves the theater and promptly forgets about the film and the problems it presented. This is why we feel that film should have a dialectical relationship to its audience, meaning that the issues should be openly posed to the public in a way that allows for debate between the audience and the film. If the film poses a question that the audience supports or opposes, it is stimulated intellectually and indicates its opinion. It is not a matter of trying to provoke a gratuitous clash, like avant-garde European or North American art, which seeks only the psychological shock—a very bourgeois way of exerting an impact on the audience. For us, the violent elements typical of Brazilian films are a means of provoking the public out of its alienation.

Q: From this point of view, how would you analyze the final massacre in *Antônio das Mortes*, which so shocked the audience at Cannes?

A: The European film-going audience sees war films and other commercial movies where many people are massacred, and everyone applauds. In a Latin American film, human life has great value, and death is not shown superficially, but in a very dramatic form. Audiences are shocked when, in *Antônio das Mortes*, the whole thrust of the film is directed toward the definition of a firm stance, and when there is a violent action that transforms the situation in the town. The film is not symbolic theater.

For a Brazilian audience, the scene is quite effective. The audience follows the itinerary of Antônio das Mortes and the professor, and it arrives at the final scene tied to the characters. . . . I intended that explosion of violence to have a symbolic dimension to give the scene more meaning. If the audience leaves the theater discussing the violence of the last scene, that is a good sign because it indicates that the film stimulated discussion and that other issues will also be raised.

I always maintain that in filmmaking, as in art in general, there is not just a single method. As a matter of fact, I don't believe in formulas. I think that each film should always invent its own forms, its own methods. When things convey a kind of formulaic sense, they tend to exert a fascistic control over the audience. This is why the only way to guarantee public participation is always to maintain a very dialectical procedure. Almost all Brazilian films deal with political and social problems. Each has a definite stance, but they use very different forms. I think that systematization in art is very dangerous. In Brazil, we search for ways to systematize production and distribution. But how do we do this? If you see ten Brazilian films, you will notice the constant presence of a political issue, but each is dealt with in a different way. Since society is very complex and has various levels of alienation, we believe that we should use different styles even though we are dealing with the same themes in varying degree. This is an important element in the development of our national cinema.

In my case, I have a particular preference for violent films because I like the epic genre. I lack the inclination to make subjective or psychological films, although I believe that such films are valid. I acknowledge that one can make a very violent political film on a very intimate theme. But to do this, it is necessary to have a well-defined method or else the film becomes an abstraction or a meditation on aesthetics. Besides, it's much more difficult to make a political film with a personal theme than with an epic one. I have neither the education nor the temperament for this. Though some Brazilian filmmakers have attempted this kind of film, I think that it is a very difficult thing to achieve in a Latin American country, since our political and cultural tradition is not a subjective one.

A people who have suffered centuries of oppression have many violent aspects: problems of hunger and psychological neuroses that derive from social and economic circumstances. This is why it's a mistake to make Latin American films in which the characters behave like Europeans. The result rings false because the same personal problems in Latin America do not resemble those of people in France or Italy. This is an old issue. If an imitation of Antonioni is made in Argentina or Brazil, it's a cultural error, because European existential anguish is caused by another social and political system. In Latin America, as I said, these problems are caused by hunger, oppression, and the frustrations of daily life. If this type of neurosis and alienation comes from other kinds of problems, it is clear that the language the film uses also has to be different. It has to be capable of revealing the causes of these inequities.

There are certain directors who don't share this critical vision and who believe they are making avant-garde art when, in fact, they are only making an imitation, a "pastiche" devoid of meaning. When these works are presented in Europe, European audiences are not interested in them because they realize that they are products of cultural colonization.

I believe that the cinema is a great instrument for communication, and that it is also a great tool for learning about humanity and society. This is why I feel that film must be used in all its potential—for education and information, for political propaganda, for dramatic, poetic, and philosophic ends—since film is a tool that is capable of increasingly clarifying reality and man's relationship to it. But it is always necessary to examine the issues with a dialectical methodology. One thing that is apparent now, especially in Europe, where political films are much discussed, is that these films lack a dialectical method for studying reality. This accounts for their superficiality. Even though the theme may be revolutionary, the film is meaningless. Marxism's great contribution is precisely the revelation of the possibilities for the development and application of dialectical thought. This is essential in the arts, because art can only develop through a rigorous and permanent application of the dialectical method.

Q: What made you decide to make *Antônio das Mortes* in color?

A: I decided to film it in color for two very practical reasons. The first was technical. Color films are increasingly common, whereas black and white movies are practically disappearing. We also reached the conclusion that we should make color films in Brazil because a production study indicated that they aren't much more expensive than black and white. Besides, this is one means of doing away with the Brazilian public's sense that national films are "inferior" to foreign ones—a very complicated, very Brazilian phenomenon. The colors used in the film are the natural colors of the region, since the city where we filmed is, in fact, a real city built by real people and not a movie set. All the clothes worn by Antônio das Mortes derive from popular theatrical tradition. I wanted to display the wealth of popular culture as a kind of challenge to oppressive cultural forms, since I'm also interested in showing how the economically and politically oppressed have great creative strength in their music, clothing, and choreography. The local people contributed a great deal to parts of *Antônio das Mortes*. For example, the duel between Antônio and the *cangaçeiro* was a traditional event in the region. The positioning of the actors, the music, the dancing were practically all the work of the local people. I explained what I wanted to do, they discussed it among themselves and set it up, and then I filmed it.

Brazil is a very colorful country. We have a tradition called the *reisados* in which the people dress up as Nativity figures; we have the tradition of popular engravings and the rural circuses. Since I believe that film is also linked to painting, I'm interested in that kind of visual integration of color with music and dance. In *Antônio das Mortes*, the color is totally unsophisticated. I didn't even use artificial illumination or filters on the camera. It was filmed with a very documentary vision, but it has real impact because the colors are strong ones. I don't have anything against films in black and white, but if I can make a movie in color, I prefer it. . . . Since there is now a good color laboratory in Brazil, one can free oneself of technological competition with imported films to compete on a purely cultural and political level.

Q: What can you tell me about your future plans, and how they are related to the immediate future of Brazilian cinema?

A: One of the most serious problems that Brazilian cinema faces is financial, since the market is dominated by American films. Although Brazilian cinema has produced a great deal recently and its audience has grown, above all because we have struggled to organize a strong national distribution network, the competition with Hollywood cinema is tremendous. The truth is that Brazilian cinema has survived through a limited but carefully organized international distribution campaign. We have to work a great deal to get sufficient financial return to allow us to continue making films. But censorship is very strong in Brazil, and every film must go through its own epic struggle with the censors. This explains why anything one might say about the future of Brazilian cinema is very vague, since the fate of our national cinema is directly linked to the country's economic and political problems.

However, there are certain objective facts about Brazilian cinema that can be cited. The movement didn't even exist as a cultural phenomenon at the beginning of 1960, and today it is an important cultural, political, and economic reality. We have succeeded in creating a new mentality in opposition to commercial cinema, even to the extent that we have eliminated the traditional concept of the film producer. Now all Brazilian directors are the producers of their own films. Many commercial films are still made, but the attitude that the cinema should be a cultural and political instrument and not merely a means of economic gain is very prevalent today in Brazil. I can say this about the future: many new directors have come forth who can now make films much more easily than we could, that is, with more technical and financial ease—not with fewer restrictions due to censorship. This is the current situation; the future of the cinema depends on the political future of the country, which is very contradictory and impossible to predict.

I personally have worked for ten years making films in Brazil as a distributor, producer, director, and publicist. I did everything with the same enthusiasm. Since I have some ideas about a genuine tricontinental or Third World cinema, I now want to get involved in another type of activity in the Third World—partly in Africa, partly in Latin America. I want to make some films connected to this concept as well as to develop some of the ideas from my other films. And now, after *Antônio das Mortes*, I feel more prepared to confront this new phase, though I'm not sure what the outcome will be. I intend to make a film on the anti-imperialist revolution in Africa.[3] Afterwards, if I'm granted permission, I would like to make a film in Spain because the cultural origins of Latin America lie in Spain and Portugal.[4] I'd like to make a film that would differ in both style and theme from the African film, but that would remain tied to the theme of the Third World from a Hispanic point of view.

After that, I would like to make a film in Latin America. I have an old project in mind, but one that would be very difficult to bring about because it would be very expensive. It is another project that will take time to shape, because after the two films I've just mentioned, I intend to go to a Latin American country to film a kind of sequel to *Land in Anguish*. I still haven't finished the screenplay, though I have tried to write it many times, but the exact idea still eludes me.

So this is the general plan. . . . After all this, I always intend to return to Brazil, but at least for the time being I do not want to live permanently in any Latin American country. I would like to participate in the debates that are now taking place in many national film industries. I don't want only to make films; I also want to debate, to try to organize things. It is a program that I will have to carry out, since I will not be able to continue making films within the structures that now exist in Brazil.

Q: Does this mean that you have left behind the theme of the *cangaceiro*, which made you famous?

A: No, I can still return to that theme.

Q: But in *Antônio das Mortes*, one senses that the end has been reached . . .

A: I will come back to that theme, but much later. That is another thing I would like to do, a film about Lampião, a *cangaceiro* whom I've mentioned a lot in my films but who has never appeared in them. He was the most important *cangaceiro* and dominated the Northeast for twenty-five years during a genuine guerrilla war. This film about Lampião interests me a great deal, but not for the time being, because it demands a great deal of historical investigation for which I have neither the time nor the patience right now. And besides, I believe that this is not the proper time to do it.

Brazil will always continue to produce *cangaceiro* films, since the theme is very tied to the country, like the samurai in Japan or the westerns in the United States. The *cangaceiros* have a great bond with the people, since they are the true heroes of Brazilian folk mythology.

Notes

1. In an interview with Raquel Gerber in 1973, Rocha named seven original members of the Cinema Novo: Nelson Pereira dos Santos, Carlos Diegues, Joaquim Pedro de Andrade, Leon Hirszman, Ruy Guerra, Paulo César Saraceni, and himself. Though several others were also involved, the figure of fifty may be a typical Galuberian hyperbole.

2. By law theater owners are required to show Brazilian-made films a certain number of days per year. Because they tend to get a better return from foreign films, exhibitors oppose this legislation and resist compliance.

3. *Der leone have sept cabeças* (*The Lion Has Seven Heads*, Brazzaville, Congo, 1970).

4. *Cabeças cortadas* (*Severed Heads*, Spain, 1971).

Chapter 9

Tomás Gutiérrez Alea
(Cuba)

Beyond the Reflection of Reality

Plate 11. Tomás Gutiérrez Alea, 1980. Photo courtesy ICAIC.

Tomás Gutiérrez Alea, or Titón, as he is familiarly called, is Cuba's most acclaimed director. Upon their return from film study at Italy's Centro Sperimentale, he and Julio García Espinosa collaborated on a medium-length, documentary-style feature called *El mégano* (*The Charcoal Worker*, 1955), which was suppressed by the Batista regime. Since Batista's overthrow and the founding of ICAIC, the Cuban Institute for Cinematic Art and Industry, Gutiérrez Alea has made numerous documentaries and nine feature films, the most acclaimed of which is *Memories of Underdevelopment* (1968). In 1982 he published a collection of theoretical essays reflecting upon his experience, *Dialéctica del espectador*.

Julianne Burton interviewed Tomás Gutiérrez Alea in Havana in January 1977. This version is excerpted from "Individual Fulfillment and Collective Achievement: An Interview with Tomás Gutiérrez Alea," *Cineaste* 8, no. 1 (Summer 1977).

Q: *Memories of Underdevelopment* met with great success on its theatrical release in the U.S. in 1973. How would you evaluate U.S. film critics' response to the film?

A: I am not fully informed of critical response to the film in the United States, because the only thing I can base my assessment on is a file of clippings that the film's U.S. distributor, Tricontinental Film Center, has sent me. Naturally, the reviews range from good to mediocre to bad, but in general, I would say that several of them are extremely interesting. The tendency to interpret the film as a subversive act was not as manifest in the United States as, for example, in England. *Sight & Sound* published an absolutely sinister article, which began by comparing the film to Buñuel's

Plate 12. Actor Sergio Corrieri reflects on fame, suicide, and the politics of culture on a visit to Hemingway's Cuban residence in *Memories of Underdevelopment*. Photo courtesy ICAIC.

Viridiana—made under Franco's very nose and proceeding to blow up in his face—and ended up comparing me to Solzhenitsyn. It was obvious that the intention was to misconstrue both the film and the circumstances under which it was produced, for the actual situation had nothing in common with the version put forth in the review.

It seems to me that *Memories* was in general much better understood and evaluated in the United States because people perceived the attempt to criticize a bourgeois mentality that, understandably, persists in our society despite the many changes we've gone through.

Q: It also seems, however, that there were many critics who articulated that critique much less vociferously than what they perceived in the film as a critique of the revolution itself.

A: Yes, of course, such a critique is also implicit in the film. But what was the nature of that critique? What I'm saying is that most of the U.S. critics were on target in that they realized that in contrast to the bourgeois mentality represented by the protagonist, the film reveals an entire people in the process of being born—with all the problems and difficulties that involves, but with enormous vitality as well. This new world devours the protagonist in the end. That is the image we wanted to convey with the film, and judging from the reviews I read, it seems to me that U.S. critics grasped it more clearly than their counterparts in other countries.

Q: I have shown and discussed the film with many audiences in the United States, and one striking thing is the tremendous urgency and persistence with which they search for a shred of optimism regarding Sergio's fate. Because they identify so completely with him, they desperately want to believe that he is somehow "saved" at the end. Surely Cuban audiences view the end of the film very differently?

A: Yes, they do. The film had a very good response here, relatively speaking. In fact, something happened with this movie that I had never seen with either my own films or anyone else's: many people went to see *Memories* more than once, and some returned as many as four or five times. That makes me think that the film hit its mark, which was, first and foremost, to communicate with the Cuban public—not with audiences from other countries. It achieved its goal in the sense that it disturbed and unsettled its audience; it forced people to think. When they return to see the film again, it means that it has kept on churning around inside them even after they leave the theater. As far as I'm concerned, this is the most important thing.

Q: The particular process by which *Memories* was adapted from the novel of the same name has always struck me as somewhat unique. Would you comment on the collaboration of novelist Edmundo Desnoes on the production of the film? To what degree was he involved in the actual filmmaking process?

A: My work with him involved an extremely flexible creative process. We did not attempt to "translate" the novel into cinema. For me this kind of loose adaptation turned out to be much easier, but for Desnoes it perhaps demanded a much higher level of violence against his own work and against himself, because at a certain point his novel was to be betrayed, negated, transformed into something else. He was fully conscious of this and worked over his novel as if it were raw material, not like something already fully achieved, which was going to be "translated" into cinema. Because he maintained this attitude, which is, of course, the only one to have if you are going to do this kind of thing, our work together was very fruitful. He often attended our shooting sessions and made many excellent suggestions.

The original screenplay, which we worked out together, kept being transformed in the actual shooting process. There are even several scenes—and this is very significant—that carry great weight in the film but that were never anticipated in the original screenplay. There were also details. The telescope, for instance, which becomes a very important image, a symbol of Sergio's alienation from his environment, didn't occur to us until we had started shooting, almost at the last moment. Or scenes like the one where Sergio is returning home and comes across a group of people marching in the opposite direction on their way to a political gathering. The scene is very significant, because Sergio is always heading in the other direction from everyone else. As an image it functions very well. The sequence was filmed almost coincidentally, at Desnoes's suggestion, because we just happened to come across a group that was preparing for a May Day demonstration or some such celebration. It was his idea that we take advantage of that situation, and I think that it turned out very well because we were able to film it very spontaneously. We simply had the actor begin walking through that group of people. There were no extras involved, no preliminary preparations.

Q: What about entire sequences that did not appear in the original version of the novel, like the one that takes place in the Hemingway museum? Were these developed at your initiative and only later incorporated by Desnoes in the subsequent English version of the novel, *Inconsolable Memories*?

A: Yes, he later included these scenes in the revised version of the novel on his own initiative. The fact was that I felt the need to say things other than those included in the original novel, and thus he would write something at my request, which I would later expand and rework. But I think that even the second version of the novel is quite different from the film.

In my view, the Sergio character is very complex. On one hand, he incarnates all the bourgeois ideology that has marked our people right up until the triumph of the Revolution and still has carryovers, an ideology that even permeates the proletarian strata. In one sense Sergio represents the ideal of what every man with that particular kind of mentality would like to have been: rich, good-looking, intelligent, with access to the upper social strata and to beautiful women who are very willing to go to bed with him. That is to say, identify to a certain degree with him as a character. The film plays with this identification, trying to ensure that the viewer at first identifies with the character, despite his conventionality and his commitment to bourgeois ideology.

But then what happens? As the film progresses, one begins to perceive not only the vision that Sergio has of himself but also the vision that reality gives to *us*, the people who made the film. This is the reason for the documentary sequences and other kinds of confrontation situations that appear in the film. They correspond to our vision of reality and also to our critical view of the protagonist. Little by little, the character begins to destroy himself precisely because reality begins to overwhelm him, for he is unable to act. At the end of the film, the protagonist ends up like a cockroach—squashed by his fear, by his impotence, by everything.

So then what happens to the spectator? Why does it trouble him or her to such a degree that she or he feels compelled to see the film again? Because the spectators feel caught in a trap since they have identified with a character who proceeds to destroy himself and is reduced to ... nothing. The spectators then have to re-examine themselves and all those values, consciously or unconsciously held, that have motivated them to identify with Sergio. They realize that those values are questioned by a reality that is much stronger, much more potent and vital.

I feel that it is in this sense that the film carries out an operation that is the most revolutionary, so to speak, the most dialectical with regard to the spectator. The film does not humor its audience; it does not permit them to leave the theater feeling self-satisfied. The importance of this phenomenon lies in the fact that it is the precondition for any kind of transformation.

Q: It is interesting to observe how well the character of the film's protagonist corresponds to a whole stratum of not just Cuban, but Latin American intellectuals from the haute bourgeoisie. What has been the response to the film among Latin American audiences?

A: Unfortunately, it has not been widely shown, but it has enjoyed great success in the countries where it has been seen, according to the news I've received. For example, it was shown in Chile during the Allende period, and I received very positive responses by word of mouth. Unfortunately, before the reviews could be assembled and sent to Cuba, the coup occurred and they were lost.

Q: Speaking of the need that the audience feels to see *Memories* more than once, in your latest film, *The Last Supper* [1976] and in other recent films, it seems that the narrative line has become flatter, more chronological, more *linear*. Do you see this change from a more narratively fragmented and "deconstructed" kind of filmmaking to more linear narration as a current tendency within Cuban cinema?

A: It's not really a matter of identifying a tendency, since it seems a little risky and potentially premature to draw such conclusions. I believe that we are guilty of having overindulged our interest in historical topics, despite their great importance at this state in our national development. We are very much involved in re-evaluating our past. All of us feel the need to clarify a whole series of historical problems because that is a way of also reaffirming our present reality. It is a genuine necessity. It has, however, led us to neglect our contemporary situation a bit. Clearly the challenge that we now confront is to develop a penetrating vision of our contemporary situation and to make more films dealing with current problems.

Q: At the Pesaro Festival in Italy in September 1975, I was able to see Sarita Gómez's *De cierta manera* [*One Way or Another*], a film on which you served as consultant, and which you completed after her premature death.[1] The film was extremely interesting to me precisely because of its exploration and treatment of contemporary Cuban reality.

A: I see that film as a kind of model; I think it is quite extraordinary. Unfortunately, there have been some problems in getting a final print. The one you saw in Pesaro was somewhat deficient with regard to technical standards. It was filmed in 16mm, and the laboratory had many technical problems with it. We had to send it to Sweden to be restored. It's now back in Cuba and they're in the process of reassembling the film for release here.

Q: Related to this, there is a criticism of Cuban cinema, quite common abroad, that holds that in Cuba the only topics that are permissible in the work of art, and film in particular, are those that confine themselves to the more or less remote historical past.

Your own *Death of a Bureaucrat*, Manuel Octavio Gómez's *Ustedes tienen la palabra* [*Now It's Up to You*], and most recently Sarita Gómez's film counter that criticism. Unfortunately, none of them as yet have been widely seen in the United States. There is the possibility of certain political problems with *One Way or Another* because of the incredible frankness with which it looks at problems of race and sex and class marginalization in Cuba, because of the candid and critical way in which it challenges certain still incomplete aspects of Cuban social transformation.

A: I can't predict what the response would be, how the film would be handled, because, as you know, everything is manipulable in one sense or another. This is particularly true with films, because whatever "reality" is captured on film is capable of lending itself to tendentious uses. So in the ideological struggle in which we're involved, we have to cover ourselves, we have to refrain from giving ammunition to our enemies.

Personally, I think that *One Way or Another* is not such a case. In my view, that film, like many others that examine our present reality, merely registers a lived situation, that is to say, one in which the contradictions are manifest and in the process of being resolved. Because the only way to eliminate the contradictions is to have a sincere and open attitude toward them and to try to resolve the conflicts. I believe that this, in the long run, is absolutely and undeniably positive.

However, I'm not always sure how this should be dealt with in distributing films abroad. For example, when *Death of a Bureaucrat* was made, someone from the United States, I don't remember now exactly who, requested a print of it for exhibition there. At that time, the people here at ICAIC—and I was in complete agreement with them—decided that *Death of a Bureaucrat* was not the best film to show in the United States before any other Cuban film had been seen there. That decision seemed to me at the time a very wise one.

I think that now it would be perfectly possible to show it; I don't think that there would be any problem. But these things depend on particular circumstances and thus must be treated with care. We cannot remain removed from the political questions or retain a liberal mode of thinking or anything of the sort. We have to be fully conscious of what our films mean and how they are viewed in a particular setting and at a particular historical moment.

On the other hand, *Death of a Bureaucrat* in our own context—aside from the fact that it was a great success with the public—was very healthy because it revitalized the entire discussion, the whole polemic about the risks of bureaucratization in our incipient socialist society. It was very positive.

Q: Returning to the question of the relation of the form to the content of the film—more precisely, the way in which the audience is incorporated into the experience of the film—it seems that there is an enormous difference between a film like *Memories*, for example, or even *One Way or Another*, and a film like *The Last Supper*. In the latter, with its traditional story line, the audience does not need to involve itself as actively in the film. Whereas in a film like *Memories*, there is a level of active intellectual involvement required of the viewer because of either an intentional "deconstruction" of the narrative line or because of a self-conscious effort to constantly expose, subvert, or call into question the filmic forms that are being used.

I've seen the same phenomenon in other films as well—in *Bay of Pigs* [1972], in *The First Charge of the Machete* [1969], in *The Other Francisco* [1975], and most recently in *Mella* [1975]—but in the most recent films it is much less apparent. Do you see this as characteristic of current film production?

A: I think it is determined, in *The Last Supper* at least, by the theme itself, which is very linear, based as it is on a very simple anecdote. There is no reason to make it more complicated, to restructure it in any but a very natural and organic way according to the central concern of the theme itself. In historical films in general, it seems to me that this is more or less the case, because things can be seen more clearly.

Q: What about a historical film like *The First Charge of the Machete*?

Despite its flaws, despite the exaggerated use of high contrast, it is a historical film that operates as a presentation of a historical event, but always reminding the spectator that she or he is viewing not history itself, but an act of historical *interpretation*. To accomplish this, the director had to forsake traditional narrative devices for a much more disruptive presentation of events.

A: As I see it, *The First Charge* is an extremely significant and important film—very revealing in its way of approaching history. I agree with you that it is flawed, especially at the end. That is, the Charge of the Machete, the actual battle, is so overworked that it almost remains unseen, or unseeable. It's a shame, since it is a film that is developed out of a very important idea. Its means of approaching the historical event are brilliant, as far as I'm concerned.

Q: What is interesting about Cuban cinema in this regard is that it is committed not only to exploring and reclaiming the historical event, but also to constantly revealing a self-conscious awareness about the process of historical interpretation. I regret having been unable so far to see your film *A Cuban Struggle against the Demons* [1971], because I am very curious to see exactly how it deals with these issues.

A: Aside from the fact that the film in and of itself is very confused because it is too overladen with various layers of meaning, and with excessively difficult metaphors, I also made a fundamental mistake in the editing. Because it turned out to be too weighty for the viewing public, I tried to lighten it up a bit by editing out some of the narrative. Afterwards, I realized that I had only confused matters further.

I'm afraid that right now there are no complete copies. The last time I saw the film—a few months ago on television—the copy was damaged in many places with crucial portions of some scenes missing. The copies that exist are the ones that were shown in the theaters, and since it was not a film that enjoyed a great deal of success with the public, there has been no interest in making new copies to replace the worn and damaged ones.

Q: *The Last Supper* is the first feature film you have made in color. Have you found any significant differences between working in black and white and working in color?

A: It seems much more interesting to work in color, as long as it is handled in a disciplined way. Color is, after all, yet one more expressive resource, and as such, it has great attractions for me. I think that we did an extraordinary job with color in *The Last Supper*, thanks primarily to the director of photography, Mario García Joya, who worked out a very intensive and precise color analysis.

Q: Would you have made the film differently had you been working in black and white?

A: I never really thought about it in those terms, but I think I would have had to look for other solutions to create a similar atmosphere in black and white. For example, the supper sequence, which has an ochre color, a kind of illumination that corresponds to candlelight, would have been very difficult to create in black and white.

Q: Since you have been so involved in the development of Cuban cinema, even before the revolution with the filming of *El mégano* [1955], I would like to ask how you see the evolution of the Cuban cinematic process in the last decade. What do you see as the major influences on Cuban film activity—not only in thematic and stylistic terms, but in terms of the mode of production as well, that is, the process by which Cuban filmmakers organize their filmmaking activity?

I know, for instance, that the influence of Italian Neorealism in the early years was substantial, and you are in an excellent position to evaluate its impact since you studied in Italy and have subsequently witnessed the whole evolution of Cuban filmmaking first-hand. Then, of course, there are other influences as well—early Soviet cinema, the French New Wave, Hollywood films, other films from Latin America . . .

A: Perhaps I won't be able to answer your question with as much depth and precision as I would like because I am not very clear about the most recent years. As a matter of fact, at this particular time I am in the process of researching the various factors influencing this situation, but I have not as yet developed a full analysis.

However, one thing is obvious. From the beginning of the Revolution, our artistic foundation was in fact essentially Italian Neorealism. Very obvious considerations account for this, and not only the fact that Julio García Espinosa and I had studied in Italy during that period and were pretty permeated with that mode of approaching filmmaking.

I have to say that when we returned we continued to hold a very positive estimation of that experience in a historical perspective, but when it came to our evaluation of Neorealism as an aesthetic we were no longer so positive, because we had conclusively seen all its potential limitations. What we were looking for was something else. However, Neorealism was our origin, and we couldn't deny it even if we wanted to.

Q: Could you be more specific about the aesthetic limitations you mentioned?

A: At the time it appeared, Neorealism reflected a very confusing reality—that of postwar Italy. To the degree that it did this accurately and honestly, it was, of course, very constructive, because it allowed the essence of that reality to be shown. It was a very transparent kind of reality, since such convulsive historical moments virtually express themselves. Because everything seems so apparent at such times, the requisite analysis turns out to be much easier. Since film is a good medium for capturing apparent realities, the Neorealist experience is a very constructive one. That reality perceived by the camera in and of itself conveyed a situation full of contradictions; the act of documenting that historical moment could not in fact avoid bringing them to the forefront.

In our view, as that particular reality began to evolve and to change, Neorealism began to lose its early driving force. It did not evolve in a parallel or proportionate way, but instead began to deteriorate, to accommodate itself to a commercialized concept of film as simply merchandise. Thus only those spectacular elements of Neorealism that were capable of maintaining a hold on the public continued to be exploited. We saw this very clearly.

What happened to us, then? We date the beginning of our filmmaking here from after the Revolution took power in 1959, since *El mégano* is nothing more than a forerunner that, if you like, reveals our concerns but without yet integrating them. So when we began to make films in a postrevolutionary situation, that Neorealist mode of approaching reality was very useful to us because in that early stage we needed little more. First of all, we were not developed enough as filmmakers to posit other approaches. Second, our own national situation at that juncture was convulsive, very transparent, very clear. All we had to do was set up a camera in the street and we were able to capture a reality that was spectacular in and of itself, extremely absorbing, and laden with meaning. That kind of filmmaking was perfectly valid for that particular historical moment.

But our revolution also began to undergo a process of change. Though certainly not the same as that which occurred in postwar Italy, the meaning of external events began to become less obvious, less apparent, much deeper and more profound. That process forced us to adopt an analytical attitude toward the reality that surrounded us. A greater discipline, a much more exact theoretical criterion was then required of us to be able to properly analyze and interpret what we were living through. We, of course, retained the clear intention of projecting ourselves toward the future, of fulfilling the social function of cinema in the most effective way possible.

I should add that subsequently we have had access to the entire gamut of world film production. We have obviously been influenced by the French New Wave. Naturally this produced a few flawed efforts, since the concerns of the New Wave filmmakers had in fact very little to do with our own reality and with our own approach to it.

Godard, for example, has exerted an inescapable influence. Since he is such a brilliant destroyer of the cinema, he offers many challenges. From this distance, I think that the Godard phenomenon can begin to be properly evaluated, noting his limitations as well as his successes. His intention was clearly to make the revolution in the realm of the cinema before making the revolution in reality. However, his endeavor has been a very constructive force because he succeeds to a certain extent in making us see, in making us question the degree to which we might be at the rear of the revolutionary process rather than in the vanguard.

Our role is to be united with the revolutionary process. Thus our language as filmmakers has to evolve parallel with the revolution. It is important to be conscious of this, because one can accommodate oneself very easily to stereotypes, to comfortable ways of doing things. Let's face it, there is a tendency sometimes to resist change, don't you think? So that I think Godard's work has been useful to us in this sense. What condemns Godardian cinema in the last analysis is its own incommunicability. If it doesn't reach the people, it is of no use. For us, genuine communication is absolutely fundamental, so we must avoid falling into this syndrome at all costs. However, as I've been saying, to the degree that Godard provoked the destruction of an entire series of models of bourgeois cinema, his work has been very valuable.

What other influences have we felt? There's the "marginal cinema," with which we are only partially familiar. We have seen very little of the North American underground cinema, for example, so I am unable to evaluate it. We are familiar, though, with the kind of alternative cinema that is being produced in several Latin American countries: a militant cinema that aims at the poorest sectors of the country and seeks to spark a *toma de conciencia* about the social and political problems that those people face. It is a valuable and necessary kind of cinema, but one that must not forget that the cultural struggle must also be waged and won on the commercial screens. In making that kind of "marginal" or alternative cinema, you can obviously not compete with the kind of Hollywood spectacles shown in commercial theaters, the kinds of films that attract, among others, that very section of the population that the militant filmmakers are trying to reach. It is thus also necessary to try to reach the commercial screens with a kind of cinema that is essentially different from, for example, *Jaws*.

Q: Your emphasis on the importance of a commercially viable alternative cinema makes me think of the Brazilian Cinema Novo movement, because of the effort Brazilian filmmakers made throughout the sixties to ensure and expand their access to a broad national public in commercial theaters. Has the Cinema Novo movement exerted any influence on Cuban cinema?

A: Yes, Brazilian cinema also had an impact here. It was a kind of revelation for us, primarily the early works of Glauber Rocha, although a great deal of Brazilian cinema has been shown in Cuba.

In fact, we see an extremely broad range of films here. Of course, our situation is very different from that of most film-producing countries because in addition to controlling production, we also control the movie screens. That is, what we see is in fact what we choose to see. This is another way to educate the public.

This process of training the public taste is very interesting. Obviously, we made a revolution here, we won, and that revolution developed and was radicalized quite rapidly; in the process we became conscious of what socialism was. All this happened very fast, at an almost dizzying pace. But during this very fervid time, the Cuban public continued to see Hollywood and Mexican films. When the United States imposed the blockade [1961], it was no longer possible to continue to see the new Hollywood films, though the older ones continued to be shown with great success. Mexican movies also stopped coming, even though diplomatic relations with Mexico were never severed, once the Mexican film enterprises that existed in Cuba had been nationalized by the revolutionary government.

Initially it seemed that this cutting off of the feature film supply was a disaster. Our public was thoroughly accustomed to those films. But I think it was actually a great boon for us. Traditional Mexican cinema—apart from a few exceptions and some interesting things that are currently being done—is absolutely dismal. It conditions the public to respond to the worst commercial motives and devices, just as Hollywood films do to a very large extent. (I don't mean to say that every Hollywood film functions this way, but certainly the vast majority do.)

So what happened when the supply was so abruptly cut off? The film-going public, despite being at that time in full support of socialism, ready in fact to give their lives to preserve the revolutionary system of government that was being implemented here, was reluctant to go to the movies to see the films that we were able to show at that time—Soviet films, Czech films, in short, what was then accessible to us—because these films represented a new kind of film language for them, one that was too alien.

There's another thing that should be noted. Because of the film shortage, we were compelled to import films rather indiscriminately, without a careful selection process to determine which films were more adaptable to the taste and needs of our people. Instead, it was necessary to bring in whatever we could because we had to fill the screens of our theaters. So, many things that were in fact quite mediocre (because mediocre films are produced everywhere) were brought in. Subsequently, film exhibition became much more diversified. A great deal of European production was brought in. All the films imported from the socialist camp were subjected to more of a selection process. Currently, the film-going public in Cuba is massive, and very impressive. They have come to accept and understand other film languages, other approaches to filmmaking. I think it's very interesting that the evolution in the awareness and sophistication of our viewing public, though it was forced upon us by circumstances beyond our control, turned out to be very positive.

Q: Have there been studies here in Cuba of audience response to various kinds of films?

A: It's an area that we've just begun to work in. Personally, I think it is of cardinal importance. It grows out of something we were discussing before, the necessity that all of us feel to delve deeper into the theoretical criteria with which we confront our cinematic task. As I've said, up until now these have been quite spontaneous and circumstantially imposed, but now—in our current stage of institutionalization[2]—theoretical inquiry must acquire a new level and a new dimension.

Q: Do you think it's possible to identify specific characteristics of Cuban cinema—not so much of the production process but on the level of the films themselves?

A: I take it that you're asking whether there is an identifiably Cuban film "language." Well, let's see. Since our entire initial stage was marked by improvisation and an emphasis on what was feasible, it may have been somewhat slow in its utilization of expressive resources, but it certainly manifested itself in a very fresh and direct way. It has continued to consolidate a certain style, which seems to mark each of us equally. This has been to our advantage. At this stage, the idea is not to abandon that style, but rather to take advantage of it—of its popular, authentic, organic elements. I think the formation of a certain style, a tendency or direction that marks us all, is inevitable. But still there is a certain dispersion as well; many different styles and concepts continue to exist. We're still in a period of quest.

When it comes to trying to generalize as to the nature of this style, it is clear that our Neorealist foundation has not totally disappeared. Despite all of its ideological and political limitations, despite our own evolution, which has gone in a different direction, one thing is sure and continues to condition us: our film production must of necessity be inexpensive. We do not have the means to undertake superproductions. So the kind of cinema that adapts itself to our interests, fortunately, is a kind of light, agile cinema, one that is very directly founded on our own reality. We have never lost sight of this. In fact, I think that the best of our cinema, the most fully realized works, are achieved through a very direct link with our particular circumstances. You must have seen this in *One Way or Another*, for example. The film seems a bit careless, a little awkward, almost as if it had been let loose on its own, but it also succeeds in penetrating our reality to an uncommon degree, producing an impact somehow charged with poetry. I think that it is there above all that our reality is shaped.

Q: Is it a policy at ICAIC to give the opportunity to make feature-length films to younger people who are still very much in the process of artistic development?

A: This is clearly a necessity. What happens is that not all of the young directors are sufficiently trained. Many have reached the stage of making feature films without a solid enough background. This happens with shorts as well. We have gone about learning to make films through the practical, concrete experience of making them. This method naturally carries with it a great deal of imbalance and notable shortcomings in some cases.

Q: With regard to your future plans, will assisting in the development of younger directors be your primary activity?

A: In fact, my intention is to keep alternating between making films myself and assisting developing filmmakers. I am also extremely interested in continuing to develop a level of theoretical activity. This is one of the things that most concerns us, because now, at this particular stage, we realize that we must dedicate much more attention to theoretical work, to formulating our concerns on a much more profound level. We have to analyze all that we have done to plan for the future with a greater awareness instead of leaving everything to spontaneous solutions, which is more or less what we have been doing up to now.

I should clarify that our work was never totally improvised; there have always been theoretical investigations, but never with the degree of discipline or insistence that we should now be able to achieve. It is not that this work is just beginning now. In fact, it began some time ago, but these theoretical inquiries have to continue to expand. I think that now we will see increasing emphasis on this kind of work.

This is not likely to produce immediate results, but I'm committed to it even though I know it's a long-term process. I'd like to define more clearly all that we have done here at ICAIC. I've begun to work on the question of the relationship between the film as spectacle and the audience.[3] Specifically, what are the different levels of relation between film as pure spectacle and a cinema of ideas? Clearly, these are not mutually exclusive poles, but rather both kinds of filmmaking must be employed simultaneously because each fulfills an important social function. I'm interested in how audience response is produced and in the uses to which this knowledge can be put. My aim would be to achieve an even greater effectiveness in the socially committed, revolutionary propositions that can be presented through film.

Q: Exactly what form does this theoretical work take? Is it primarily confined to group discussions within the organization, or do you intend for your theoretical work to reach a broader audience?

A: For some time now all the film directors and camera people have been having weekly meetings. We almost always view and discuss a film made by one of us, or a foreign film of general interest. Then we have open discussion about the film. But in addition to this practice, there is still the need to do more directed theoretical work.

My intention with my own theoretical work is to ensure the widest exposure possible. Julio García Espinosa is also continuing his theoretical writing and will soon publish a new essay on mass communications in the magazine *Casa de las Americas*.[4]

Cine Cubano is obviously another outlet for this kind of work. As you know, the magazine ceased to appear for a time due to a vast reorganization here at ICAIC, which is only now assuming its final form. But it will soon reappear, and, we hope, with much greater regularity.

Q: As a final area of discussion, I'd like to ask what you see as the personal advantages of the kind of state-owned film production system that currently exists in Cuba, in contrast to the Hollywood system, for example, or to the conditions in Italy when you studied filmmaking there in the early fifties.

A: I imagine that this is a very difficult thing for the majority of people in a nonsocialist country to understand. They find the idea of giving up certain limited bourgeois freedoms to be a very painful one because they are unable to conceive of freedom in any other terms. For me, their point of view has very grave limitations.

To the extent that we are part of our revolutionary process, to the extent that we believe in it and realize that for the first time we are in control of what we're doing, of our own actions, we are exercising a much greater freedom than that which can be exercised in any country where conflict between different classes continues to exist. For a social system based on unequal exercise of power and influence *always* works in favor of the most powerful, who sometimes grant some scraps of apparent freedom to those whose lives they dominate. However, these always turn out to be more illusory than real.

In contrast, the freedom that we feel here—I'm sorry if this sounds a little abstract, but it's hard to express—derives from the fact that we are very aware of working together toward a common goal. We feel united around an idea and involved in implementing it together. This freedom we feel in working together is a completely different experience from the purely individual creative freedom so precious to people in capitalist society.

We, too, have to undergo certain contradictions. We discover things that we feel we have to fight against. But it is on another level. For example, the struggle against bureaucratization is one we know we will win. It is not that despairing fight that reduces you to a state of frustration. On the contrary, we here have to be optimists. Not because anyone requires us to be, but because our real-life situation imposes that optimism on us in indicating to us that we are on the right track.

A state-owned, centralized production system like the one that we have is very different from what an "independent" private company, for instance, might be. I put "independent" in quotation marks because under such a system one is always dependent to some extent on those in power. When you attempt to free yourself from that dependence, you are reduced either to impotence or to total incommunication. So you see that there is really no means of comparison.

Q: I remember in 1973 when there was all the commotion about the U.S. State Department's refusal to allow you to attend the National Society of Film Critics' awards ceremonies, where you were to receive a special award for *Memories of Underdevelopment*. I think it was in the speech that Andrew Sarris gave as president of the organization where he lamented that you had not been allowed to make another film here in Cuba subsequent to *Memories*. Even though the assertion was false—you had already made *A Cuban Struggle against the Demons*—it is typical of strong desire abroad to view you as a prisoner of the Cuban regime. Their idea is that you are a great director who should be putting out a film a year. If you are not, it must be because you are not allowed to.

A: That was in fact the most unfortunate statement to be found in all the articles I read, because it is evident that the man had a personal stake in giving his own interpretation, despite the fact that it had no connection with the actual situation. His lack of information was such that one suspects a kind of tendentious ignorance. It's hard to know in such cases where ignorance leaves off and malice begins.

The fact is that I have been dedicating a lot of my time to the kind of work I was describing to you before—the process of acting as adviser for other *compañeros*—which I view as being just as important as my own personal achievement as a director. For someone like Andrew Sarris it must be extremely difficult to understand, but I have to say that for me what I might achieve as an individual director is no more important than what the whole group of us here at ICAIC achieves together. I have no desire to stand out more than the other simply to fulfill my own creative needs at the expense of my fellow filmmakers. Individual fulfillment is not everything. In a situation like ours, the collective achievement is just as important as the personal one. This assertion does not grow out of any attempt to appear more generous or less egotistical, but rather from my firm belief in what we as a group are doing. For me to fulfill my individual creative needs as a director, I need for there to be a Cuban cinema. To find my own personal fulfillment, I need the existence of the entire Cuban film movement as well. Without such a movement, my work might appear as a kind of "accident" within a given artistic tendency. Under such circumstances, one might enjoy some degree of importance, but without ever achieving the level of self-realization to which you really aspire. This is not measured by the level of recognition you might achieve, but rather by the knowledge that you are giving all you can and that the environment you work in guarantees you that possibility.

Notes

1. Sara Gómez died of acute asthma in 1974 at the age of thirty-one, just short of completing her first feature film.

2. This process of making governmental institutions more permanent was uppermost on the national agenda in 1977, the Year of Institutionalization. The First Party Congress, the inauguration of Popular Power elections, and the founding of the Ministry of Culture are examples of attempts to "institutionalize" the revolutionary regime.

3. Gutiérrez Alea's *La dialéctica del espectador* was published in Havana in 1982 (UNEAC). See *Jump/Cut: A Review of Contemporary Media*, nos. 29, 30, and 31, for an English translation by Julia Lesage, "The Viewer's Dialectic."

4. Julio García Espinosa published a volume of collected essays, *Una imagen recorre el mundo*, in Havana in 1979 (Letras Cubanas).

Chapter 10

Nelson Pereira dos Santos
(Brazil)
Toward a Popular Cinema

Plate 13. Nelson Pereira dos Santos. Photo courtesy ICAIC.

No other filmmaker exemplifies the evolution of Cinema Novo as well as Nelson Pereira dos Santos. None has been more prolific. With *Rio 40 graus* (*Rio 40 Degrees*, 1955), he helped introduce Neorealist techniques to Brazilian cinema, and his *Vidas secas* (*Barren Lives*, 1963) is the high point of the initial phase of Cinema Novo (1960-1964). With *Fome de amor* (*Hunger for Love*, 1968), he participated in the anguished self-criticism of the second phase (1964-1968) as well as in the incipient underground film movement. *Azyllo muito louco* (*The Alienist*, 1970) exemplifies the third or "Tropicalist" phase (1968-1972), with its allegorized discussion of the repressive nature of ideology. Since the mid-1970s his work has initiated a renewed concern with the nature of popular culture and with cinema's distance from or proximity to that culture in films like *O amuleto de Ogum* (*The*

Q: Many observers say that Cinema Novo, which began in the late 1950s, was severely weakened by the coup d'état of 1964 and destroyed in 1968 with the implementation of the repressive Institutional Act No. Five. What has happened since 1968? How has Cinema Novo evolved?
A: Initially, production was extremely difficult. Filmmakers associated with Cinema Novo were blacklisted; they could not find producers. Joaquim Pedro de Andrade turned to Italy for coproduction funding for *Os inconfidentes* [*The Conspirators*, 1971]. I made *Quem é Beta?* [*Who Is Beta?*1973], a French coproduction. Glauber Rocha was traveling in Europe, Africa, and the United States, compelled to make his films outside Brazil. For a few years we were very hard-pressed. I was able to continue making films because of support from abroad. I managed to secure local financing for *How Tasty Was My Little Frenchman*, thanks to a law that stipulates that the income tax on imported films could be waived if the importer also produced films in Brazil.

We all did our best to survive individually by making films with scarce and sometimes nonexistent resources. In Brazil, as in other underdeveloped countries, national cinema cannot survive without state intervention. Embrafilme, the government film enterprise set up in the early 1970s, now provides financing, production assistance, and distribution for a significant portion of the films made in Brazil. Starting with *The Amulet of Ogum*, I received assistance from Embrafilme.
Q: Was the earlier economic isolation politically motivated?
A: Yes, it was. Now the political climate has begun to change, and under the new program initiated in 1973 everyone was back in action, making one film after another. Our approach has become less ideological and more anthropological. We are more restrained in our use of the camera. We have also learned to turn the government's interest in historical themes to our own purposes, expanding the official parameters, which equate historical subjects with our heroic founding fathers and other grade school pieties. The historical dimension of *How Tasty Was My Little Frenchman* went largely unrecognized in official circles. It was viewed as a fiction—as if official history were not itself a fiction!

Amulet of Ogum, 1974), *Tenda dos milagres* (*Tent of Miracles*, 1977), and *Estrada da vida* (*The Road of Life*, 1980). His *Como era gostoso o meu francês* (*How Tasty Was My Little Frenchman*, 1971) remains one of his most original contributions. Dos Santos's acclaimed *Memórias do cárcere* (*Prison Memoirs*, 1984) returns to the writings of Graciliano Ramos, which, twenty years earlier, inspired his memorable *Barren Lives*.

Randal Johnson's interview with Nelson Pereira dos Santos was conducted in Portuguese in New York. What appears here in revised form was originally published in *Studies in Latin American Popular Culture* 1 (1982).

Embrafilme's policies displayed certain blatant contradictions. You had the government financing pornographic films, for example.

Q: You allude to this in *Tent of Miracles*, in the scene where Fausto Pena, seated in front of a poster advertising a porno-detective film, tries unsuccessfully to call Embrafilme.

A: Exactly. Imagine the credits: "The Ministry of Education and Culture presents *The Virgin Widow* or *The Woman Who Does I Don't Know What.*" In light of the moralism espoused by the Brazilian military government, this was a violent contradiction. Filmmakers, musicians, and theater people who considered ourselves on the left joined forces with independent producers to combat such policies and propose alternatives. We succeeded in placing Roberto Farias, himself a filmmaker, as head of Embrafilme.

Cinema in Brazil today is thus a kind of popular front activity. Those of us who were affiliated with Cinema Novo are considered to be on the far left of the spectrum, though in fact the documentarists are more radical than we are. Though we do not participate directly in Embrafilme's decision-making process, we have considerable influence in determining the makeup of the organization. About a third of our proposals have now been implemented. We continue to struggle to implement the rest.

Now another major change is under way. The coming elections have marginalized us again, because nobody wants to have anything to do with the Left. We are bad company. Once more, every film we make involves a struggle. We have begun making common cause with actors and technicians, trying to organize unions to secure more equitable working conditions and remuneration. If output continues at its present high level, filmmakers should be able to support themselves.

Q: Isn't that possible now?

A: No, it isn't. I practice two other professions, professor and journalist. Film directing does not provide me with enough income to live on.

Q: When *The Amulet of Ogum* was released in Brazil in 1975, you also published "The Manifesto for a Popular Cinema." Could you explain how this manifesto relates to that particular film and to the general situation of Brazilian cinema at that time?

A: The idea of a popular cinema was born in the period I was just referring to, when auteurs and independent producers were engaged in a common effort on behalf of a genuinely national cinema. In this context, I argued that each film had to be effective in reaching the Brazilian public and ensuring its own success in the home market. The idea is not merely to make lucrative movies, but rather to affirm the principles of Brazilian popular culture through our films.

Popular culture is different from other more superficial, elitist cultural forms that follow antiquated, colonized models. My idea also involved defending popular political ideas, the legitimate claims of the masses, which have been hidden from view until now and which our films should somehow reflect. It is true that the expression of the most urgent of these demands is prohibited in the political arena as well as in film and other art forms. But the deepest forms of cultural expression, those that come from the roots—like the expression of religious sentiment among the marginal sectors, for example—have always been suppressed and repressed within Brazilian culture. Religious expression has always had to conform to the needs of the colonizer. I proposed to use popular response to this repression of "deviant" spirituality as my point of departure, since it gave me a global vision, a way of thinking in relation to all of Brazilian society rather than to a small component.

With *The Amulet of Ogum*, I was careful to situate the point of view *within* this marginalized universe, criticizing the dominant society from this internal perspective rather than maintaining the distance that a more standard, sociological approach imposes.

Q: So you're now trying to avoid the "sociological distance" of the early years of Cinema Novo?

A: Yes, though I can't speak for all of my fellow filmmakers. I can only speak of my own experience as an auteur and of what I propose to my colleagues. Cinema Novo is a group of auteurs whose cultural politics involve a collective practice. With regard to principles and methods of filmmaking, however, each director has his own domain. We do not subscribe to a common aesthetic. Each of us enjoys freedom of subject matter and means of expression.

What I propose is a popular cinema in the sense I just described. Commercial success comes later. I think we have to begin with the integration of the auteur and the audience. Yet I recognize that all this is somewhat naïve on my part. The audience to whom we direct our films too often lacks the minimal conditions that would enable it to attend the movies. In Brazil the exhibitors largely predetermine their audience. Fifteen years ago, for example, men without neckties were not permitted in movie houses. Blacks had to be very well dressed and could not sit beside the "regular" clientele. This illustrates how thoroughly the spectacle of motion pictures was directed toward specific sectors—the middle and upper classes. Ticket prices and geographical location guarantee the desired audience, but many exhibitors are not above policing their theaters if necessary.

Q: Did these problems prevent *The Amulet of Ogum* from reaching the goals spelled out in the Manifesto?

A: Of course, initially. As I have said, the theater owners have the power to select their films. *The Amulet of Ogum* was initially categorized as an "art" film for intellectual audiences, so it was exhibited only in small theaters to a limited public.

Q: Didn't it play in working-class areas?

A: That only came later, but once it happened I was pleased to see that the film established a completely different relationship to its audience, especially among practitioners of the *umbanda* religion, because they felt that the film legitimated their beliefs and practices. *Umbanda* is not officially recognized as a religion in Brazil, though there are a lot of middle-class citizens who lead a "double life"—nominal Catholics who worship *umbanda* saints. *The Amulet of Ogum* gave a lot of people the courage to say, "I'm an *umbandista*. I believe in *umbanda*." It was very satisfying to see how cinema can have an immediate effect on social relations.

Q: Is *Tent of Miracles* a continuation of the program you outlined in your manifesto?

A: It's a little more ambitious. It deals with the process of the formation of African-derived culture in Brazil and its integration into Brazilian society. It denounces antiquated, racist ideas that still exist and it also criticizes the entire mass communications system and the way it functions today in Brazil. The modern media are much more refined than the instruments used at the turn of the century by the faculty members of the School of Medicine who are portrayed in *Tent of Miracles*, yet modern-day television maintains the same stance, discriminating against blacks, indigenous peoples, and representations of popular culture.

Q: How does your treatment of Afro-Brazilian religion differ in the two films?

A: *The Amulet of Ogum* deals with *umbanda*, a more open religion in which Indian and Portuguese Catholic influences are superimposed on an African base. Each *umbanda* sect develops its own theology. *Candomblé*, on the other hand, the religion depicted in *Tent of Miracles*, perpetuates the heritage of Africans who conserved their religion during and after slavery. It is much more specific and bound by tradition. As in all African religions, initiation rites are very severe. Centuries of harsh repression taught the different African groups in Bahia to practice their religion clandestinely. As a result, the most traditional sects are still very difficult to join.

Q: Jorge Amado is a novelist who seems to be much in vogue these days. *Gabriela, Clove and Cinnamon* has been made into a television serial. Bruno Bareto filmed *Doña Flor and Her Two Husbands* [1976]. Even the French director Marcel Camus, who made *Black Orpheus* [1958], has recently made a film based on an Amado novel. What drew you to *Tent of Miracles*?

A: This novel confronts racial and cultural questions that interested me. Amado wrote *Tent of Miracles* after *Doña Flor* and *Gabriela*, but it seems to be atypical of him at that stage of his career. It's a book that harks back to an earlier phase of his writing, when he was closer to the life of the people. (He is from Bahia and has profound ties to *candomblé* and other popular regional customs.) To me the novel synthesizes all his work up to that time, though the style is less ornamental, drier. In *Tent of Miracles*, the heroes and villains are ideas, not people. The propagation of racist ideas by the medical school faculty, the repressive actions taken by the dominant classes, the links between the police and the power structure that force the former to take action against the people—all this is readily apparent. I had no need to write my own story; the book was made to order.

Q: How did you approach the adaptation process?

A: On a formal level, I tried to maintain the flavor of Amado's narrative style. The novel has several narrators and multiple narrative threads. One of the more important is Fausto Pena, a poet who begins to investigate the life of the mulatto Pedro Archanjo, though his motives are limited—he merely wants to get ahead, earn some money, and hang on to his woman. I converted this character into a composite of the young Brazilian intellectual (well, maybe not so young)—sociologist-playwright-filmmaker-poet—who, when faced with the limited opportunities for artists and intellectuals in Brazil, is obligated to do things that he would not ordinarily do. A negative hero who yet undertakes and achieves the rediscovery of Pedro Archanjo. The novel makes free use of all sorts of different narrative devices; my film resembles a television spectacle.

Q: The film opens, before the credits, with a brief shot of a TV weather forecaster, who says, "In Bahia, the weather is good." So *Tent of Miracles* is a film-within-a-film-within-a-TV show?

A: Exactly.

Q: The narrative structure seems to have confused some viewers. Why did you keep it so complex?

A: The book and the film deal with how, today, we are suddenly beginning to concern ourselves with the phenomenon of popular culture, with African religions, with the integration of blacks into society. We Brazilian intellectuals are influenced by all sorts of pressures and contradictions. We filmmakers take government money to finance our films, but we do not support that government. In fact, we are viscerally opposed to such regimes. In our efforts to realize our projects, we find government censors waiting for us around the corner. Filmmakers are not the only victims of this type of contradiction; all creative artists in Brazil are subject to it. Artists and intellectuals are particularly conscious of this because we are trained to reflect upon our situation, but I think that the same existential experience is common to all Brazilians. *Tent of Miracles* is about the moment we are living through, and about how new, humanistic ideas are obstructed and diluted. To perpetuate this situation is to ensure intellectual stagnation.

Q: Characters in the film often seem very camera-conscious and there are many self-referential moments. What motivates these distancing devices?

A: That's difficult to say. I didn't want to make a closed film that would permit only one reading. The means we filmmakers have at our disposal are in fact very powerful. The spectator is seated, isolated, captive to begin with and becomes even more so if I construct my film in a way that requires a certain reading. The greatest problems in terms of the average spectator are that he or she is already accustomed to just this kind of film. I think that the distancing effects, the breaks in the actors' characterizations, convey the possibility of multiple readings. This is one way to play with ideas, to say, "Look, here's a chance to think differently than you're used to thinking."

Q: Your film seems to criticize those intellectuals who maintain an orthodox Marxist position. I'm referring in particular to the young professor who defends his thesis.

A: He represents the orthodox Marxist who throughout the years has been just as colonizing as the non-Marxist colonizer because he has not been able to transfer the mode of thought but has instead merely transferred the observations achieved through that method. Our society does not fit within these formulations because they originated in and pertain to another context. It's easier to insist on the validity of the dogma than to change the reality of the situation. This attitude has a long history in Brazil.

I am criticizing myself as well, because I have fallen into the same trap. It's part of my being—this attitude that we call sociological, distanced, elitist, professorial, removed from the reality of the people and their interests. An intellectual like the professor you refer to envisions the transformation of society. He is sincere about this, but his life of social mobility—first he becomes a professor, then director of the institute—is a contradiction. His background, class, and position prevent him from including truly popular manifestations—specifically religion—in his cultural universe. His thought is very positivistic. He is unable to reconcile thinking and action.

Today, for example, it is clearer than ever that the indigenous tribes are an integral part of our history, yet there are Marxist thinkers in Brazil who ignore the existence of Indian culture and its influence on national culture. There are those who still maintain that the history of Brazil begins with European colonization. According to that view, social history dates from 1500. The Indian disappears, as if he has had nothing to offer.

Q: You explored this theme in *How Tasty Was My Little Frenchman*.

A: Yes, and it's also alluded to in *Tent of Miracles*, which ends with the commemoration of Brazilian independence. In reality, there were two moments of independence: the official proclamation in Rio de Janeiro in 1822, when Dom Pedro declared, "As the son of the King of Portugal, Brazil no longer has anything to do with Portugal. I am Emperor of Brazil"; and the defeat of loyalist Portuguese troops the following year at the hands of a popular militia composed of blacks, Indians, and poor Brazilians who went to war to expel the Portuguese from Bahia. The end of my film commemorates the 1823 event because it was the only real war for independence. Indians played an important role in this struggle. In Bahia the Indians are revered; many *umbanda* figures, for example, derive from Indian cultures.

Because our situation is complex and unique, I think we must be very wary when analyzing any social or political phenomenon. We have to ask whether we are merely reproducing observations appropriate to another context or if we are applying Marxist methodology in terms of our own society and arriving at a new interpretation.

Q: There is a widely accepted myth that there is no racism in Brazil. *Tent of Miracles* and Carlos Diegues's *Xica da Silva*, among others, show just the opposite.

A: Racism still exists in Brazil, but the forms and rationale behind it do not correspond to what you have here in the United States. In the late nineteenth century, a theory was developed about blacks in Brazil. Sociologists like Nina Rodrigues, who is quoted by Professor Nilo Argolo in my film, studied African culture in depth because of their concern with how former slaves, human commodities who with emancipation became legal citizens of Brazil, were to be incorporated into society. The social model these thinkers wanted to perpetuate was the same model imposed from the origins of the colony. Brazil had to be a Europeanized society, following European models in everything, because Brazilians like Rodrigues were ashamed of being colonized and anxious to deny their colonial condition. But this "European-ness" was contingent on one race's being capable of gaining world hegemony—a "pure" white race. Once blacks became incorporated into society, according to these thinkers, the complexion of Brazilian society would inevitably darken, and tribal forms of social organization would presumably become the models for the organization of the Brazilian state. This prejudice in favor of whiteness persists in Brazil.

Q: The historian Thomas Skidmore discusses "whitening" as a social policy, citing governmental preference for European immigration, for example.

A: The *café com leite* theory: add more cream and the coffee will become white. An extremely racist ideology.

Q: Does *Tent of Miracles* attempt to demystify this attitude?

A: The film states that racism persists, merely that. In the end, the newspaper publisher and the whole financial elite no longer discuss the issue directly, as did the professor of legal medicine; they simply try to make it disappear. They co-opt the figure of Pedro Archanjo not as a black but as a "great man" with a "white" soul. The fact that *one* black managed to hold a chair of medicine helps them maintain the whole structure of oppression and discrimination. Not just any black can become professor of medicine; he must be superqualified to differentiate himself from his fellow blacks, who are condemned to a life of cheap labor. In short, blacks either mix and become "white" or they do not have a place in society.

Q: I think that one of the strong points of Tent of Miracles, in contrast to other films on the topic, is that it goes beyond denunciation to a more constructive cultural affirmation.

A: I tried to make the hero a winner. I think that when we create a hero who succumbs at the hands of the powerful, we are in fact taking the side of the powerful. Giuliano Montaldo's Giordano Bruno [1973], a film about a marvelous Renaissance figure who fell into the hands of the Inquisition and was burned at the stake, made me see this clearly. Though its makers were in favor of freedom and revolutionary change, the movie was contributing to the perpetuation of the repression of the masses by the dominant classes. Whoever does certain things is going to burn at the stake. That's both a warning and a threat, isn't it? I wanted the hero of Tent of Miracles to be a survivor.

Q: Does this appreciation of and alliance with the popular sectors represent a new, optimistic phase of Cinema Novo?

A: This goal is optimistic because it makes everyone begin to study their culture and to locate themselves more precisely within the Brazilian social spectrum. On the other hand, the road we have chosen is not without detours. Certain critics accuse us of making populist rather than popular cinema, arguing that a genuinely popular cinema must engage the people on a political level, furthering the cause of popular revolution. Yet I prefer our present path to the one we had been following before, which grew out of deep political and theoretical convictions but conveyed these in a language destined only for initiates. Like the figure of Pedro Archanjo, this type of filmmaking was also co-optable and co-opted by the dominant classes, the mass media; it was construed as intellectual fare for limited audiences or the international festival circuit.

Brazilian cinema has only one hope for survival: generating a genuine response from the public. I don't mean the kind of response elicited by imported movies, the local pornographic film industry, or other kinds of purely commercial cinema favored by local exhibitors. In competitive terms, we are at a real disadvantage. Last year's one hundred nationally produced films had to compete against twelve hundred imported films. When we include series, documentaries, and films for television, this number jumps to three thousand. Only by establishing a special relationship with our audience can those of us interested in producing an autonomous, genuinely national cinema survive. In view of current changes in working conditions, I am optimistic about the future of Brazilian cinema. Our work is going to demand more perspicacity, more combativeness, more energy, but it also promises to be much more enriching.

Chapter 11

Humberto Solás
(Cuba)

Every Point of Arrival Is a Point of Departure

Plate 14. Humberto Solás, 1978. Photo by Mario García Joya.

Humberto Solás joined ICAIC, the Cuban Film Institute, in 1959, the year of its founding, at the age of seventeen. His early films were highly experimental and somewhat hermetic. Only the medium-length feature *Manuela* (1966) hinted at the talent that would produce one of the all-time masterpieces of Latin American filmmaking two years later. The three-part *Lucía* (1968) is remarkable for the dialectical complexity of its independent narratives and the virtuosity of its three different styles. In *Simparele* (1974) and *Cantata de Chile* (1975), Solás worked extensively and effectively with tableaux, choreography, minimal scenography, and expressionistic lighting in an attempt to integrate various modes of popular culture into film. His ambitious adaptation of the nineteenth-century Cuban novel *Cecilia Valdés* (*Cecilia*, 1982) met with a lukewarm reception in Cuba and abroad.

The Early Years

Q: In an interview for *Cine Cubano* magazine [no. 52/53, 1968] you stated that you can no longer identify with any of the films you made before *Manuela* [1966]. Can you explain why?

A: I was referring to all of the early films, especially *Minerva traduce el mar* [*Minerva Translates the Sea*, 1962] because they do not, in my opinion, have any lasting validity. They belong to a very special moment in history, to the beginning of the development of our national cinema.

ICAIC was born out of the victory of the Revolution. The situation was very difficult for the group of *compañeros* who founded it. It is well known that there was no filmmaking tradition worthy of imitation here in Cuba prior to the triumph of the Revolution.

The situation was not the same for writers or musicians, for example, since these fields succeeded in producing expressions of an authentic culture with democratic and even socialist characteristics even before the Revolution. Our leading national poet, Nicolás Guillén, the musician Harold Gramatges, the novelist Alejo Carpentier, and the painter René Portocarrero are examples of this.

Those of us who were about to attempt to found a national film industry from scratch faced a set of problems that we had to resolve immediately. Our problem was a basic cultural dichotomy, as in Lenin's thesis on national cultures. We had an elitist cultural tradition that represented the interests of the dominant class, and a more clandestine culture that, through such examples as Nicolás Guillén, had received wide exposure and already demonstrated extraordinary quality. One had to choose between these two forms of cultural expression.

But in fact the choice was not that simple, because the clandestine culture had been permeated for decades by the influence of elitist forms, and there was a tendency to convert all cultural expression into products of a consumer-oriented culture. There came a point, for example, when you really didn't know the extent to which folklore was still a valid and authentic expression of the "folk," since it was being used in radio soap operas, in toothpaste commercials, and so on. Originally genuine forms of cultural expression had reached a point of total degeneration. To give you a concrete example, the musical form that we know by the name "Guantanamera," originally an authentic folk form developed by the Cuban *guajiros* [peasants], had been adopted by a national radio program, which came to be

Marta Alvear is the pseudonym for Brazilian-born filmmaker Teté Vasconcelos, who interviewed Humberto Solás in Havana in 1978. Julianne Burton helped to translate and edit the transcript. The interview first appeared in Part 1 of a 3-part Special Section on Twenty Years of Revolutionary Cuban Cinema in *Jump/Cut: A Review of Contemporary Cinema*, no. 19 (December 1978).

called the "Red Chronicle," to broadcast the more sensationalist and bloody news items of the day. This kind of program helped to build up an immunity to such forms of popular expression.[1]

Because this phenomenon was so widespread, because elitist culture and this ersatz popular culture were so intimately tied, because petit bourgeois consciousness and influences from Europe and North America were so dominant, our general cultural panorama at the time of the Revolution was in fact a pretty desolate one. So what happened? We either had to make a choice between these two rather decadent cultural tendencies and work to analyze and expose their shortcomings, or passively accept the model that the artistic vanguard of the developed world held out to us. This was during the sixties, when the most important film movement was the French New Wave. Films like Alain Resnais's *Hiroshima, mon amour* [1959] or Michelangelo Antonioni's *L'Avventura* [1959] marked most of the subsequent decade.

The legacy that the imitation of these trends left us here at ICAIC was, to a large degree, a harmful one, first of all, because these influences alienated us from our indigenous cultural forms and from a more serious search for a kind of cultural expression consistent with national life, with the explosive dynamism of the Revolution and its goals for artistic culture. We adopted certain models from the so-called European avant-garde in a very passive way. Yet this was also a path we clearly had to travel, and so in another sense the experience was a very useful one. It allowed us to assess and purify our own criteria. Anyone who picks up the tools of artistic activity for the first time is going to be vulnerable to outside influences. This was almost inevitable for us at that time, especially in light of the inferiority complex stemming from underdevelopment and our related fascination with everything that arrived with a North American or European label.

As it progressed, the Revolution began, through a very natural process, to eliminate the more inauthentic expressions of popular culture. Subsequently, spontaneous movements began to spring up, like popular iconography reflected in the graphic arts or a primitive and genuinely popular theater sometimes enriched by the participation of such first-rate actors as Sergio Corrieri (*Memories of Underdevelopment, The Man from Maisinicú*, etc.). The development of a wide range of activities in all cultural spheres provided the impetus and the frame of reference we needed for our own development as filmmakers. The process was unavoidable. It was not a matter of simply saying, "OK, we'll start right away to make films that are a coherent expression of this new social structure we live in." Instead, we had to go through a long period of experimentation. It was very painful at times, so these early films often represent a good deal of frustration.

To Europe and Back

Q: What happened to resolve this frustration in your own case? You went to

Europe and things changed?

A: Of course. These things happen to the Latin American, the Asian, the African; it's inevitable. I had never been outside my country, so in 1964 I decided to see the entire European continent. I left on a cargo ship without a penny. It was the kind of trip one has to take before turning thirty. It was an attempt at complete demystification. For the most part, I stayed in Italy, though I did visit the major cultural centers in Germany, France, and several other countries.

Q: Did you feel closer to Cuban culture when you returned?

A: Naturally, because such a trip is actually the discovery of your own personality. You go to the premiere of Antonioni's *Red Desert* [1964] and you realize how little the film has to do with the real problems facing Italian society in the sixties. Seeing *Red Desert* in Havana is not the same as seeing it after six months in Italy. You develop a critical perspective.

European society seems drained, culturally crippled. I don't believe that one can escape from the fact of a universal culture. I confess that the early films of Visconti—*La terra trema* [1948], *Ossessione* [1942]—did have a formative effect on me. Of course, I try to maintain a critical perspective on them and to extrapolate only what is consistent with my own particular interests. I can tell you that the later Visconti, from *Vaghe stelle dell'orsa* [*Sandra* in the U.S.; *Sandra of a Thousand Delights* in the U.K., 1965] and his subsequent films, does not interest me in the least. In this sense, one is aware of one's own maturation.

Between 1968 and 1970, I went a bit overboard in my rejection of foreign culture. I was too impassioned, too irrational, not reflexive enough. I think the ideas that the Brazilian filmmaker Glauber Rocha expressed in his essay "The Aesthetics of Violence" had a lot to do with this.[2] I remember being absolutely unable to watch a European film at that time. It seemed degrading, useless, obsolete. I closed my eyes to all forms of artistic expression that came from the developed world, and this definitely limited me. As a continent, we had begun to recognize our own voice, our own image, and though our response to this discovery was somewhat extreme, it was also a necessary stage in our development.

And it was a beautiful time. The whole continent was reasserting itself. It was the time of the big student movements in Latin America and the rest of the world as well; of social upheavals in Mexico and Brazil. It was also a time when Latin American culture reached a high point because of this favorable atmosphere: the "boom" of the contemporary novel, the Cinema Novo movement in Brazil, the Grupo Ukamau [*Blood of the Condor*, 1969] in Bolivia, Miguel Littín and *The Jackal of Nahueltoro* [1969] in Chile. We in Cuba, impregnated with the social transformations at home and throughout the continent, were able to create very vigorous, fresh, and passionate works.

I now think that our attempt at a complete rejection of European culture was obviously immature. In fact, one cannot live detached from the theoretical advances taking place in Europe. The generous allocation of resources there for just such kinds of inquiry enables a large number of intellectuals to pursue serious theoretical research in areas like theater, film, the fine arts, and so on. Political and economic limitations make this kind of research impossible on our continent. So, to summarize, I think that we should strive to preserve our own image and personality while at the same time keeping our eyes open for the achievements of writers and filmmakers who are working in different contexts.

From *Manuela* to *Lucia*

Q: Could you give us some background on the genesis of *Manuela*?
A: It began in 1965. By that time, there were already a substantial number of *compañeros* at ICAIC who were qualified and ready to move from the documentary to the fiction film. But our material base has always been modest and it was thus impossible for everyone to try their wings at once. So someone came up with the idea—actually, I think it was a collective decision—of a contest for the best screenplay based on the theme of guerrilla warfare. It was a theme that had not been particularly developed by Cuban filmmakers up to that time. I submitted my script, was lucky enough to have it chosen, and proceeded to make the film. It's the first picture in which I feel that I'm expressing the interests of the collectivity of which I am a part.
Q: How is *Manuela* a product of the particular social and historical conditions of the period in which it was made?
A: At that time, in 1966, the guerrilla struggle, though still cherished, was past history for us here in Cuba, but it was an immediate reality on the rest of the continent. It was the era of Che in Latin America. So it was very stimulating to make a film about guerrilla warfare; you felt that you were making a film with continental relevance. It was thus a very intense and impassioned activity for me and for the whole crew.

But I was also pursuing another objective in *Manuela*, attempting to meet another kind of challenge. As far as I was concerned, up to that point Cuban cinema had not yet succeeded in expressing the idiosyncrasies of our particular situation. I was most aware of this shortcoming in the handling of dialogue and in the actors' performances. These are a product of a theatrical conception combined with a personal style, in turn the product of the actor's own research and reflection. Let's say that there was a preference for the character actor over the personality actor.

I was extremely interested in making a film in which the Cuban personality would for the first time be conveyed more spontaneously. So I decided, very intuitively, to make improvisation the basis of my work with the actors.

I can't take it when actors recite the script from memory. In the first place, I have little faith in the script, since I've written it myself. Second, it's obvious that their lines have been memorized, so I prefer them to say the same thing in a different, more personal way. In fact, often I won't discuss the actors' suggestions for revising their part; I simply start to film and they start to talk, giving me for the first and only time an original script. And if we have to repeat the take for technical reasons, or because the improvisation has deviated too much from the original concept, then I ask the actors to make up new lines. I give them very little time to do so to force them to practically live the situation. They must think and act at the same time. This sets up a dynamic relationship between the actors and the script.

It is the only way I know to achieve something I strive for in film acting: the moment of truth for each take. Sometimes we miss the mark because the actors lack sufficient imagination, or because my relationship with them didn't make it possible. But my task essentially consists of creating just such a relationship with the actors, providing them with circumstances in which they feel comfortable enough to create a vivid portrayal.

In *Manuela*, there were only two professional actors; the rest were nonprofessionals. Because of this, direction was difficult; I had to proceed in several different ways. Sometimes I would work separately with different actors in a single scene. Often I used techniques that involved surprise, so that the actors—and in particular Adela Legrá, who played the female lead—would express spontaneous personal feelings. It was exhausting.

I worked very hard on this aspect, and one can see it clearly in the film. *Manuela* helped resolve certain conceptual problems of staging, and from that point on one can see more spontaneity in the acting, more freshness in the actors, and more genuinely Cuban forms of expression in the dialogue. The end result was a closer bond of communication with the public, however distant this might seem from the somewhat cold and cerebral concept of *mise en scène*.

Q: To what extent did you employ similar techniques of improvisation in *Lucía* [1968]?

A: Of the three segments of the film, part 1 contains the least amount of improvisation. The cast of *Lucía 1895* was made up of highly professional actors, like Raquel Revuelta, who directs her own theater company. Naturally, she has her own particular work style, yet she was still very helpful in proposing changes in the script that gave great freshness to the work. In this sense, there was a degree of improvisation even in this part of the film.

Q: Do your most recent films continue to depend on such a high degree of improvisation in the acting?

A: Absolutely! It's all improvisation. My most recent film, *Cantata de Chile* [1975] is in fact the one I rehearsed the least before the actual shooting. I really never decided more than an hour before filming how to handle the staging. The actors began with a script because to organize the work you have to have a text.

About 90 percent of the cast were nonprofessionals, Chilean *compañeros* in exile in Cuba who worked on the film as a political activity for the liberation of their country. Under such circumstances, I could never demand that they memorize the script, nor would I have wanted to. In fact it was up to the lead actor, Nelson Villagra, to adjust himself to this rather unusual procedure. The whole film was made in this improvised way, calling for very long shooting sessions, many hours of exhausting work at a stretch, and a great deal of uncertainty. Furthermore, it's just not the same to improvise with one hundred actors as it is with three. Given the size of its cast and the ambitiousness of its *mise en scène*, *Cantata de Chile* is certainly not an example of cost efficiency.

Q: Going back to *Lucía*, you once stated that you personally identify most with the segment that takes place in the thirties. Why is that?

A: Primarily for very personal reasons. *Lucía 1933* is a reflection on a family experience, particularly the story of my father—a man who participated in the insurrection against the dictatorship of Gerardo Machado. He didn't die a violent death then, as the character Aldo does, but he "died" as a vital human being—a sort of death by frustration. When I was born, I was surrounded by all those ghosts, by a failed revolution, by a man whose course in life was interrupted by this collective failure.

That segment of the film grows in part out of the need to express this experience that, though not directly mine, touched me deeply. The fact that I joined the revolutionary insurrection against Batista when I was very young, given my lack of ideological orientation at the time and the spontaneous nature of my actions, must have had a lot to do with my desire to resume my father's interrupted trajectory.

It is also true that the thirties were a very attractive period, a time of extraordinary richness in Cuban ideological life that had not yet been touched on in films. After the war for independence from Spain at the end of the last century and the rise of a revolutionary poet and thinker of the stature of José Martí, there came this second period during which the interaction between political ideology and artistic activity proved extremely fruitful. There were new movements in painting and poetry; Carpentier began to write his first novels. There was a political activist of the stature of Julio Antonio Mella, whose life story has recently been the inspiration for a feature film by Enrique Pineda Barnet [*Mella*, 1975].

We speak of the frustrated revolution of the thirties, but in reality the thirties served as an indispensable foundation on which the Revolution of the fifties was built. Without the previous experience, we would not have been capable of bringing the Revolution to victory in such a short time.

In this sense the thirties were both a step forward and a great setback. They marked the nation's subsequent cultural and political development. I would like to deal with the period again in a film. For instance, there is a theme that I think would be fascinating: the founding of the people's university, which appears in one of the episodes of *Mella*. The creation of a workers' university in the thirties is to me a remarkable accomplishment for that period, and one that anticipates educational policies that have been implemented since the Revolution on a broad scale.

Q: How would you relate the first segment of *Lucía* to the situation in Cuba in 1967 and 1968, when you were making the film?

A: At that time, we were celebrating what we called "The One Hundred Years of Struggle," the century-long search for genuine independence that began with the *Grito de Yara* [the call to secede from Spain] and continued with the Revolution that began in 1959. I wanted to view our history in phases, to show how apparent frustrations and setbacks—such as the decade of the thirties—led us to a higher stage of national life. This was the underlying principle.

But whenever you make a historical film, whether it's set two decades or two centuries ago, you are referring to the present. In *Lucía 1933* as well as in *Lucía 1895* there are aspects of the plot that are tied to the most immediate contemporary realities. For example, in the 1933 segment, there is the whole struggle in the final part between the opportunists and the genuine revolutionaries. This struggle occurs in every revolutionary process. Certain aspects that appear there could be linked to opportunism and sectarianism in certain areas of national life at the time the film was made—problems that were later resolved.

Q: Having chosen to make a film about historical transformation and the revolutionary process, why did you decide to cast a woman as the central figure rather than a man, a couple, or a group?

A: As you well know, women are traditionally the number one victims in all social confrontations. The woman's role always lays bare the contradictions of a period and makes them explicit. There is the problem of *machismo*, especially apparent in the third segment, which undermines a woman's chances for self-fulfillment and at the same time feeds a whole subculture of underdevelopment.

As I've had to argue many times, *Lucía* is not a film about women; it's a film about society. But within that society, I chose the most vulnerable character, the one who is most transcendentally affected at any given moment by contradictions and change.

Q: You also cast a woman as the central figure of *Manuela*.

A: For exactly the same reason. My point of departure was the same premise, that the effects of social transformations on a woman's life are more transparent. Because they are traditionally assigned to a submissive role, women have suffered more from society's contradictions and are thus more sensitive to them and more hungry for change. From this perspective, I feel that the female character has a great deal of dramatic potential through which I can express the entire social phenomenon I want to portray. This is a very personal and a very practical position. It has nothing to do with feminism per se.

Audience Response in Cuba

Q: Have you perceived changes in the Cuban film-going public since you began making films?
A: Certainly, and the more acutely you feel this, the more it demands from you as a filmmaker. You might have noticed that we have the custom of having public discussions of films, in the boarding schools in the countryside, for example. The Cuban public is very sharp, very aware. This does not mean that they are immune to the attractions of purely commercial cinema. But when they see a film like *Jaws*, they view it from a very critical perspective. They can be highly entertained by the movie and recommend it to their friends, but behind their response there is always an intelligent commentary.
Q: Since the Cuban film audience was so thoroughly conditioned to Hollywood standards of film language, how have they received ICAIC's attempts at developing a new film language?
A: There seems to be a very curious phenomenon operating here. Despite the formative, or rather "de-formative" influence Hollywood has had in the past, Cuban cinema is very well received at home. Even very experimental films like *The First Charge of the Machete* [Manuel Octavio Gómez, 1969] have received the kind of broad audience acceptance that would have been absolutely inconceivable in the fifties. It is certainly true that a lot of hard work lies behind this fact: television shows like Enrique Colina's "Twenty-four Times a Second" and José Antonio González's "History of the Cinema"; debates that take place in schools and workplaces after film screenings; and so on. These activities have encouraged our film-going public to become very active and sophisticated.
Q: Do you have a particular kind of audience in mind when you make a film?
A: Absolutely. I think in terms of a very vast audience. Who makes up an audience? It is really a difficult question. Unfortunately, we don't have as scientific a conception as we should of what an audience is, though we have taken the first steps toward a systematic study of this. Unfortunately, we don't have a group of sociologists who can dedicate themselves exclusively

to this kind of inquiry. We know that our film public is heterogeneous and that it contains many diverse interests.

Making revolutionary cinema is very risky. There is no certain way to predict how your work will interact with the audience. For example, I had hoped that *Cantata de Chile* would be more successful in Cuba than it was. The members of the crew were convinced that we were working on a very illuminating film, one that clarified a lot of complex issues. But perhaps because of the high degree of political development of the Cuban film audience, because of the amount of information it has access to and the amount of debate that goes on in schools and work centers, the clarifications the film offered came as no surprise to the Cuban public. The film turned out to be more appropriate for other sectors of Latin America, where the issues raised by the Chilean experience are still confused and distorted.

Those of us who belong to the first generation of Cuban filmmakers, facing the task of creating a new cinema, have had very disconcerting careers. My own is a case in point. *Lucía* was extremely well received by the public. According to conventional expectations, I should have turned this success into a "formula," as a director in a capitalist context would be inclined to do. Instead, after *Lucía* I made *Un día de Noviembre* [*A Day in November*, 1972] in a totally opposite vein, as a kind of antidote.

I haven't been particularly interested in having the film screened in Cuba, because I consider it a failure, and I think that, despite the costs involved, a director should have the right to keep a film more or less under wraps if he wishes. I wasn't able to prevent its exhibition outside the country. It got excellent reviews in Venezuela and in Germany, but I haven't wanted it shown in Havana. I don't want to receive the criticism that I know would come out of its screening here.

I think that the film reflects many of our anxieties during the period between 1969 and 1971, but I expressed them poorly. Some of my *compañeros* warned me that the script was a little green. I think I shot the film prematurely. There was also the problem of my selection of the male lead. He was not an actor but a university professor, and I did not handle him well. All the weight of the film falls on him. I was frustrated because he found it so difficult to work as I like to with actors, encouraging them to enrich the script on their own. And I didn't have the courage to stop the filming. It was a big mess.

Then there's the case of *Cantata de Chile*, an experimental film in all senses, where I sought to achieve a convergence between formal and ideological components. But it seems that again I lost touch a bit with my audience. I expected it to derive tremendous enjoyment from this particular type of visual experimentation, from the allegorical *mise en scène*, not on the basis of the fact that it is my invention, but rather because it derives from a tradition of popular theater and iconography. But it seems that I was not able to bring it all together; I did not achieve the level of communication with the audience that I had hoped for. That caused me to feel that I had reached a crisis point in my work. I had a horrendous sense of failure.

But now I am aware of the valuable role that the film has been able to play in other countries, and I realize that it was an important film to make. We Latin American nations, and other underdeveloped countries as well, all have similar histories, despite secondary differences. I believe that the points I wanted to clarify with *Cantata de Chile* are relevant to any country that has passed through the stages of colonial and neocolonial domination. For example, the film was extraordinarily well received in India, where they have also passed from the colonial to the neocolonial stage.

Q: You experiment a lot with the time factor in *Cantata* in contrast to the much more linear structure of a film like *Lucía*. Do you think that this might have been one of the reasons why the film was not more successful in Cuba?

A: Probably, though I have no doubts about the Cuban audience's capacity to enjoy the film from a formal point of view, for the uniqueness of its language and visual expression. But the play with time and space in *Cantata* did little to enhance this communication. The fact is, however, that I had used the same kind of experimentation in a medium-length film called *Simparele* [1974]. This interpretive documentary about the history of the people's struggle in Haiti was a kind of prelude to *Cantata*. In spite of a similar kind of spatial and temporal experimentation, it was extremely popular. The film was full of constant ruptures. I combined politically committed poetry and song with other popular art forms. I even incorporated and evoked primitive painting, creating a mixture of all these elements. And yet the film met with extraordinary acclaim. So I think that it is somewhat premature for me to make a final judgment on this, because these two experiments were very similar; nevertheless, one was very favorably received and the other was not as successful.

Q: I see what you mean when you say that your career is very disconcerting. Does this explain some of the long intervals between films?

A: After the tremendous success of *Lucía*, a film with great international repercussions, came the disaster of *A Day in November*. Consequently, I went through a crisis. I began to doubt my talent as a filmmaker and attempted to work in other areas. I went through a period of rather utopian theatrical work, which never really amounted to much. There were certain periods when I was totally inactive. I dedicated myself to studying; I wasn't interested in making films. I decided that I had lost the ability to be a filmmaker and that I would have to realize myself politically through other kinds of activity. I wrote some theoretical pieces on film and theater that I don't think are worth much now. I began to study history.

I was free to do these things here, though in another country I would have had to work at something else to survive economically. But here I could allow myself the luxury of taking some time out—until I was ready to make *Simparele*, a highly motivated film that grew out of the desire to concretize some ideas about formal experimentation.

It has consistently taken me a long time to find the proper form to express my ideas, a form that is avant-garde and at the same time not avant-garde. What I found most frustrating with *A Day in November* was that I had made a film that was avant-garde in content but that had a traditional, even archaic form. But I eventually found an answer to that impasse.

On History and Architecture

Q: You mentioned that when you took time off from film work, you began studying history. I thought that you were more interested in architecture as a possible career.

A: I began studying architecture in 1957, but I had to interrupt my studies because of my participation in the insurrectionary struggle against Batista. I was a member of a section of the 26th of July Movement[3] known as Acción y Sabotaje [Action and Sabotage]. I was an urban guerrilla. It was a very unstable time to try to study. Either Batista closed down the university, or we did.

With the triumph of the Revolution, I became interested in film, and I couldn't combine working with studying at the university because at that time there were no night classes in architecture. Filmmaking became a concrete possibility once ICAIC was founded. At the time I didn't have a very rational explanation for why I changed from one profession to the other. Afterwards, when I began to think about it, I realized that as a filmmaker I succeeded in escaping a sense of frustration.

I still feel drawn to both. When I have a little time at home, I design architectural projects or work on my own plan for the restoration of Old Havana or for remodeling the commercial and administrative section of the city.

I think that cinema and architecture have a lot in common. They both require sociological research. They are both industrial arts. You work in groups; you need a substantial budget; your creative concepts do not take shape independently but rather in constant confrontation with those of other people. And you can also link the structure of the film image with architectural spaces and structures. The image isn't everything in film; it is an aspect that you handle in conjunction with content. The same thing happens in architecture, where need corresponds to narrative content in film. But in architecture the image is a more absolute fact; it has a value in and of itself. In film there is a whole series of elements—acting, sound, etc.—that participate more or less at the same level.

My career as a student of history is not an end in itself; it has a real connection with my work as a filmmaker. My study of history has provided me with a bibliography and a set of files. It has taught me to organize my research so that I lose less time when working on a historical theme for a film script. I do not intend to become a full-time researcher, nor a history professor, although I would be interested in teaching history as a political activity, like a lot of *compañeros* who give courses to their fellow workers in the union.

My plan is to get my degree in history within a year and a half.[4] Then I intend to re-enter the School of Architecture, since it now has night sessions. One of my goals in life is to have my plan for the urban renewal of Havana approved. I realize that it's going to be a little difficult. I'm thirty-five now. I'll be thirty-seven when I get my degree in history. Studying architecture in night school will take me at least ten years . . . But this isn't a joke, really. It has been an obsession of mine for years. And I'm going to do it.

Political Cinema, Revolutionary Cinema

Q: Moving from the personal realm to more general issues, how would you define political cinema?
A: I should state first of all that I consider all films to be political, though I certainly don't consider all films to be revolutionary. I have a certain concept of what film is, and it is shared by millions of people around the world. It's not at all original. I think film is a means of cognition, a way of discovering reality. Cinema takes on a revolutionary character to the extent that it becomes a weapon of struggle. As I see it, film offers very concrete possibilities for contributing to social change throughout the world.

I was saying that I believe all films are political: a Walt Disney movie, a film by François Truffaut, a Hollywood musical . . . the kind of film that seems furthest from any sort of ideological debate is always the expression of a political position. It is always defending a certain set of beliefs and privileges, a certain class position. On the basis of this principle, I don't believe that there is such a thing as film for film's sake. That is a hoax. Ideology is the expression of culture's self-awareness; all artistic expression represents an ideology.

While I was in India two months ago, I remember talking a great deal about these things with a student there who insisted, after a trip to the Taj Mahal, that I concede that the monument was devoid of any ideological dimension. She said that it was art for art's sake, a play on forms and a pretext for visual pleasure. I insisted that it had an ideological dimension because a man had built it as a monument to one of his many women, his favorite, and in the construction countless thousands of workers died. If they cut off the architect's hands so that he couldn't duplicate the work, it was certainly not art for art's sake or anything of the sort, but rather an expression of princely prerogative.

Q: How do you differentiate a revolutionary film from a political one, then?
A: A revolutionary film, in my opinion, must begin with a Marxist conception of reality, be it conscious or intuitive. This concept must be expressed in combative terms, with an eye to actually transforming a situation. I believe that the revolutionary is unable simply to bear witness in a passive way; he or she is always trying to find a solution to difficulties, to transform reality.

Since my recent trip to India is still much on my mind, let's take the example of *Calcutta* [1969], the film by Louis Malle. It is a very Manichaean film; there are the evil bourgeois who go to the horse races and spend ten thousand dollars on a single sari, and the vast majority of have-nots with nowhere to live and nothing to eat. When you see *Calcutta*, you're inclined at first to think that it is a revolutionary film, because the director is apparently dissecting the society and showing the way things are. But when you actually see the city itself, you realize that the film is a very passive document, and what's more, a reactionary one. Calcutta is the capital of Bengal, the Indian state with more intense political life than any other, where the left-wing parties continue to make new inroads in the Congress at each election. From an economic point of view, the poverty-stricken sectors of the population are very sensitized to existing social problems.

I found something surprising in Calcutta: a street called Lenin Avenue, which is nothing less than the second major artery in the entire city, with its statue of Lenin in full view. It was at the insistence of the workers of Calcutta that the avenue was named after Lenin and the statue put there. What does this signify? That Louis Malle's *Calcutta* is only a weak, partial, petit bourgeois vision of a society in which people are dying of hunger in the streets. A genuinely revolutionary film would make an analysis of that society, looking for the contradictions, showing the intensity of the ongoing class struggle, exploring all aspects of that reality, demonstrating that it is neither static nor beyond hope of change. On the contrary, if the beginning of a revolutionary process could take place anywhere in India, it is in Bengal.

A film like *Calcutta* is made with a lot of . . . well, glamour. It is technically perfect. It gives you the impression of exposing the real situation, but in fact it does not give any information. Rather than leading to a greater understanding of that reality, it obstructs it. It offers instead a vision of a hopeless society where the rich feed off the poor, and the poor have no will for change. This is both untrue and defeatist, an expression of impotence.

I don't believe that a single movie is going to transform society. I think that this was one of the errors of the first Neorealists, like De Sica, who eventually became terribly frustrated because they overestimated the possibilities of film and its potential for changing society. In the first place, they had no way to transform it. Though their films were very beautiful, at times extraordinary, they were also only passive testimonials to the good and the bad, the rich and the poor—nothing more. They didn't give people the tools that would enable them to use the opportunities offered by political life itself to change society.

Q: This is clearly a problem that you've had to face in your own work. For example, how to end *Cantata de Chile* without being completely defeatist.

A: We ran the risk of becoming inscribed in the defeatist tale of the Chilean drama that you are constantly reading about in the international press. Some intellectuals on the left commit the same mistake. I think that Allende's government was a step to a higher stage of revolution. The situation is very difficult now, but we must try to see things in a historical perspective. We have the tendency to limit the history of humanity to our own life span, which makes us susceptible to such mistakes.

Q: What role do you see for revolutionary film in capitalist and in socialist societies?

A: The question is a bit difficult. I believe that these are two totally different situations. Therefore, the purposes and ways of approaching reality are different. For me, revolutionary political life in a capitalist country is insurrectionary activity. A revolutionary film would thus be one that is capable of becoming the equivalent of an insurrectionary act. If a revolutionary film in the capitalist world becomes an explicit political action, it can be as effective as the action of a guerrilla commando group. Very few films in the capitalist world would meet this criterion. There are prestigious films that offer a leftist analysis, and there are many others that are simply exposés.

In the socialist world, a revolutionary film is no longer the equivalent of a guerrilla action. Instead, it must present the revolution as a permanent fact, an ongoing process that nothing can reverse. Such a film must regard every point of arrival in the revolutionary process as a point of departure. It must use the medium to destroy whatever bourgeois concepts persist on either the administrative or the individual level, for I believe that in a society in transition—as all socialist societies are—many bourgeois traces remain, and the individual can become the personification of all these archaic aspects. I believe that in this context the revolutionary must constantly struggle to destroy all that creates untenable contradictions. It is without doubt a process that tears you apart. Every day you are forced to make choices. You must choose in the knowledge that you may eventually criticize yourself for having made that particular choice.

Historical Reassessment and Issues of Contemporary Life

Q: So you see the role of cinema in a socialist society as pointing out the contradictions that still exist?

A: You have put your finger on an important problem. During the past decade, we at ICAIC have been inclined to deal with historical themes. It is as if we have made a rather clumsy practical division of cinematographic activity, leaving it up to the documentary to deal with all aspects of immediate reality. But the documentary is limited when it comes to approaching problems of a more subtle nature, since it can't determine characters or dialogue.

Because our history has been filtered through a bourgeois lens, we have been compelled to live with terrible distortions. We lacked a coherent, lucid, and dignified appreciation of our national past. This accounts in large part for our decision to take up historical themes. When Enrique Pineda Barnet made *Mella*, he undertook some historical research, which will probably be published. Even though Julio Antonio Mella was an extremely important figure, there wasn't an adequate biography of him available anywhere. If this is the case with Mella, imagine how it is with historical figures and events of lesser importance.

This is the reason there are so many films on the history of slavery. I feel that *The Last Supper* [Tomás Gutiérrez Alea, 1977] is a very important film because it offers a very complex vision of slave society. All sorts of slaves with their contradictions and their particular problems are represented there. We could also say that in the early years of the Revolution, we indulged in a romanticization of the slaves and the dispossessed, which we are now correcting.

In our determination to carry out a rigorous dialectical investigation of all aspects of our history, we have given insufficient attention to contemporary themes. We are now beginning to get closer to concrete issues of contemporary life. There are problems that we have been contending with in our personal lives, in our union activity, in our political life from the local to the national level. But perhaps it is only now that we have begun to deal with these issues on an artistic level.

Originally, perhaps because of the high political content of our daily lives, we did not feel the need to convey contemporary reality through our films and instead felt freed to undertake the historical investigation necessary to discover our roots and to find out who we really are. But there is no doubt that we must also deal with contemporary themes. Currently, of every three projected screenplays, two are linked to issues of contemporary life, and in a very acute and penetrating way.

Q: What do you have to say about freedom of expression as it exists at ICAIC?

A: Freedom is a very subjective thing. Revolutionary freedom involves the freedom to produce revolutionary art, whereas petit bourgeois freedom entails the possibility of presenting an anguished criticism, one that is often arrogant and seldom productive.

We here at ICAIC have had very intense discussions about this with foreign visitors, who usually come with a very liberal concept of what creative freedom is all about. We do not accept such a liberal stance. We accept a certain society, we live within it and belong to it; we defend it and we want to enrich it. Because of this, our critical attitude is very different from that of someone who lives and works in an environment that he or she considers hostile and alienating. These are two totally different situations. I can say that I feel completely free as a filmmaker because my interest lies in making revolutionary cinema, and here in Cuba I have the conditions that enable me to do that.

Plate 15. *Mise-en-scène* in *Lucía III*. Production still courtesy ICAIC.

160 Humberto Solás

Notes

1. Solás reappropriates this improvisational song format and the performer who made it famous, Joseíto Fernández, in part 3 of *Lucía*.
2. This essay was published in *Revista Civilização Brasileira*, no. 3 (July 1965), under the title "A estética da fome" (The Aesthetics of Hunger).
3. The name of Fidel Castro's revolutionary party, in commemoration of the abortive attack on the Moncada Barracks in Santiago on this date in 1953, the event from which the Cubans date their revolution.
4. Solás did in fact receive his degree on schedule, in June 1978.

Chapter 12

Antonio Eguino
(Bolivia)
Neorealism in Bolivia

Plate 16. Antonio Eguino (holding camera) with scriptwriter Oscar Soria (center) and director Jorge Sanjinés (right) during the shooting of *Blood of the Condor*. Photo courtesy Unifilm.

Antonio Eguino spent almost a decade in the United States, studying mechanical engineering, working in commerical photography, going to film school. Back in Bolivia, he served as cameraman on *Yawar Mallku* (*Blood of the Condor*, 1969) and *El coraje del pueblo* (*The Courage of the People*, 1971) under the direction of Jorge Sanjinés. Over the past decade Eguino has directed three major features of his own: *Pueblo chico* (*Small Town* 1974), *Chuquiago* (1977), and *Amargo mar* (*Bitter Sea*, 1984). The second of these, in which four loosely connected dramatic episodes represent different social strata in Bolivia's capital city (La Paz to the Spaniards, Chuquiago to the indigenous population), has been the most commercially

Q: Would you tell us a little about your beginnings as a filmmaker and about the Ukamau Group?

A: The Ukamau Group was formed by Jorge Sanjinés and Oscar Soria back in 1960-61. At that time the Group wasn't called Ukamau. Sanjinés was just beginning his filmmaking career. In 1965 he made the first sound feature made in Bolivia, *Ukamau*, from which the group got its name. In 1966, I returned to Bolivia from New York where I had been studying filmmaking at CCNY, but unfortunately there was no possibility of work. The Film Institute where Sanjinés and his group had been working was shut down by the Barrientos government because it thought *Ukamau* was "subversive." So, Sanjinés, with Soria, the scriptwriter, and Ricardo Rada, named their group Ukamau. I had known Sanjinés from early childhood, and I, too, joined the Group at that time.

We were planning on making a film independently, and we all contributed to the script. We worked on this project with very little money. Then a group of doctors, politically oriented, decided to help us with a contribution—with this, and the money we all chipped in, we managed to start the film. This was *Blood of the Condor*. It was my first work as a cameraman and I gained some very important experience. I had to solve technical problems that I had never thought of. We didn't have the proper equipment and were shooting in an Indian community far from everything, so we had to improvise all the time. This training was extremely valuable to me because I also followed the film to the end. I worked very closely with Sanjinés throughout the editing, the laboratory process, and also in the distribution of the film.

Q: In an interview, Sanjinés said that the complex structure of the film is deliberate, that the audience must grasp a film at the level of the narrative and a simplistic structure prevents didacticism and a real discussion of problems. Do you think that, in terms of the film's distribution, it got its point across and was effective?

A: Frankly, the structure of the film was a disadvantage in terms of getting across to people. Even audiences accustomed to seeing films were somewhat disconcerted by the flashbacks. As far as showing the film among workers and peasants, who do not regularly go to movies, it was even more problematic. We realized that the structure of the film was not an advantage for this type of distribution, and Sanjinés decided to rearrange a linear narrative on the print itself.

Q: Is the film that we see different from the way it was conceived?

A: You see the film almost as it was conceived, although the script had

successful film in Bolivian history.

Udayan Gupta's interview with Antonio Eguino was conducted in English in New York City and originally appeared in *Cineaste* 9, no. 2 (Winter, 1978-79).

many changes along the way. In its early stage, it started somewhat differently, then we came across the denunciation of the birth control practiced by the Peace Corps in the Lake Titicaca area. We investigated further, and this issue was incorporated into the final script. Although many people were skeptical, a conservative newspaper and various religious organizations began a campaign against the official birth control program the Peace Corps had in Bolivia. This helped to focus much attention on the film when it was released. *Blood of the Condor* was a success among people on the left in Bolivia, but it didn't reach regular cinema audiences as much as we expected it would.

Blood of the Condor infuriated many areas of our society—the government, the bourgeoisie, and the military. The film was banned for a few days, but the ban was lifted after the vigorous protest of the press, the unions, students, and intellectuals. Soon afterwards, the film was widely shown in Bolivia, and we still show it occasionally. The radical groups and those who were aware of the issues behind the film liked it very much, but there were a number of people who did not quite grasp the message. By comparison, Sanjinés's first feature, *Ukamau*, was received better as far as the general public was concerned.

Q: You also worked on *The Courage of the People* with Sanjinés.

A: *The Courage of the People* was a film produced and financed by Italian TV for a series entitled "Latin America Viewed by Its Filmmakers." The film was originally conceived as an hour-long documentary, but we ended up making an hour-and-a-half feature. Our group financed the extra half-hour of the film. This was under the Torres regime. We didn't shoot the film openly, nor exactly clandestinely, either, but in a covert sort of way. We hoped that once the film was finished, it would be approved by the Torres regime. During the final stages of editing, however, the rightist coup d'état took place, and all possibilities of showing the film in Bolivia were lost. That film was the last of our radical film culture. Sanjinés left the country, and remained in exile until not too long ago.

Q: After *Courage*, though, you and Oscar Soria stayed behind.

A: After *Blood of the Condor*, and before we began to make *Courage*, our group had grown to about seven people. We had shot about 60 percent of a film that was never finished, which was going to be called *Los caminos de la muerte* [*The Roads of Death*]. In a way, this unfinished film helped us reconceive our idea of teamwork. After the coup, members of the group were forced to leave the country. A few of us stayed behind in a very uncertain fashion, not knowing whether we could continue making films. After a while, only Oscar and I were left. We decided we could still make films, not radical ones, as before, but films with a social, analytical content. And that's how *Pueblo chico*, my first feature as a director, was made.

Q: In talking about a new cinema, we are talking about a cinema that is away from the commercial mainstream strongly influenced by Hollywood, and that looks dialectically at historical and contemporary situations. Do you see your films, *Pueblo chico* and *Chuquiago*, as part of this movement? A: Yes, both *Pueblo chico* and *Chuquiago* have started a new type of filmmaking in Bolivia. I believe these films are a logical continuation of the filmmaking started before. But because we had chosen to remain in Bolivia and work as filmmakers rather than seek asylum abroad, we had to adopt different guidelines. A film that would have directly accused our military government, present or past, or openly criticized the bourgeoisie for its complicity and rapacity, that type of filmmaking would have been condemned and not been permitted to be shown at all.

We feel that to make a revolutionary film, you don't necessarily have to violently attack the forces of the system that holds power; you don't have to pick up guns. We think that the honest purpose of this new cinema should be to contribute to people's enlightenment about the historical and social themes that have influenced our development as a nation, being aware of the class system, the racial prejudices that the Spaniards utilized to introduce feudal-type exploitation, and to finally make films that could contribute to our awareness of what we Bolivians are really like. I feel we have to analyze ourselves—what are we as a country, as a culture? To understand the problems of our dependency and be aware of how our country is exploited. Before we point toward solutions, political or social, we have to know ourselves much better, understand the causes of economic and mental dependency.

In my country, those who speak Spanish and live in the cities know very little about the social structure of the Quechua and Aymara Indians. So *Pueblo chico* is an analysis of the mentality of certain people in this country. *Pueblo chico*, in Spanish, does not only mean small town or village; it can also signify a narrow area of understanding, a small mind. It is a film that is critical of the way middle-class Bolivians are. It was called pessimistic, but by all means true and honest. We use the historical moment of 1962-67, when the country was coming out of the agrarian reform, dictated by the MNR regime back in 1953,[1] to show that the agrarian reform didn't work, that the condition of the peasants did not change as the government propagandized, that the mentality of the landowners was still feudal, and that the lives of the Indians, the Quechuas in that region, did not basically change. We had changed systems of government, but in practice very little was accomplished. The way demagogy was utilized, especially in the countryside, showed us that we were very far from doing justice to the long-oppressed peasants, who today are still manipulated politically.

Pueblo chico is the viewpoint of a landowner's young son, who looks at his country with new eyes. His attitude toward the problems he encounters is shown in the way a sensitive, but somewhat disoriented, young man would feel. We wanted our protagonist to be representative of a new generation, awakening and becoming aware of the ugly reality long hidden by the blindness of the dominant class. He has the normal and honest attitude of someone confronted with injustice, but he is misinformed and politically immature.

Q: How does a film like *Pueblo chico* affect an audience that is basically unconscious and unsympathetic?

A: When we make a film, we have to take into consideration what kind of an audience we are trying to reach. We have to aim for the groups that regularly go to the cinema, which is only 5 percent of Bolivia's population. And to reach these people we have to use the established channels of communication and distribution. We have to move an audience to get our message across. We don't have the means or the organization to create an alternative distribution system, and we do not think that showing a film with a portable 16mm projector to a limited number of people is effective. It is unrealistic to think that we are going to make a film exclusively for the peasants who do not have access to cinema at all—although the Quechuas and Aymaras are the majority of the population—or for the workers, who are only 3 percent of the population.

I don't think our audiences are unconscious or unsympathetic. I would call them misinformed or culturally alienated. Don't forget that fifty years of foreign cinema, basically American, have left an influence. If there were no alternative cinema, our audiences would become culturally defeated. Our experience, however, has shown that we can rescue cultural values through our filmmaking, especially among the young. In the numerous debates we have held with young audiences, the discussion of the film leads into an analysis of the ills of our society, and it is clear that they are fervently concerned about their own country.

Q: What do you ultimately hope to achieve with an audience that has some kind of vested interest in maintaining the existing social and economic structure?

A: First of all, I believe that by representing certain problems of Bolivian life dramatically, the public will identify with what we are showing; they will recognize themselves. People who live in the cities assume certain things about the way the Indians live—somehow it's not their problem, although 98 percent of Bolivians have Indian blood. But when we show them their own middle-class problems, there is a direct identification. Once this is achieved, then other questions are raised. Why aren't things going right? Will the problems always be the same? What is the solution?

Our films do not present a solution; there is no happy ending in the traditional way or the revolutionary way, no attempt to guide the spectator through a predetermined path or solution. That is why we call our cinema *el cine abierto*, open cinema. We are questioning the issues, and it's up to the spectator to think about the solutions. We do not want, and are not going, to tell the audience what to do. The viewers have to examine the issues exposed in the film. Each spectator, I hope, does not leave the theater happy, but carrying the weight of the problems on his or her back. In this way, we might hope for some change in their attitudes.

Q: Where does *Chuquiago* go from there? Does it take this analysis of problems and extend it further?

A: *Pueblo chico* dealt with the middle class after the agrarian reform, people who live in the valley areas of Bolivia. *Chuquiago* deals with the attitude of people within the city, within La Paz. In it, we are trying to analyze the daily problems and attitudes of our four protagonists in the city. Each character is going through a process of illusion and frustration. In some ways, *Chuquiago* is perhaps a continuation of *Pueblo chico*.

Q: Is this where you want to stop, or do you want to reach a more dynamic, more militant stage in your filmmaking?

A: I don't think that the type of filmmaking you may expect to see in our countries is the type of filmmaking I am going to do. We are not going to be the guerrillas of Latin American cinema all the time. It is very romantic for intellectually oriented Europeans and Americans to applaud the filmmaker who carries a camera in one hand and a gun in the other. Militant films are all right when they are backed by an organization, when they have immediate issues to communicate. Nevertheless, they are limited in their distribution.

I want to reach a greater number of people with my films. *Chuquiago* did. Almost five hundred thousand people saw our film, and no other film in Bolivia has achieved this. We can say that we have finally reached that 5 percent of our population that, according to statistics, are regular moviegoers. Step by step, we are creating our own cinema, we are talking to Bolivians in their own language, and what is for us very important, we are gaining screen time by replacing, little by little, the alienating commercial cinema, basically backed by American distribution monopolies, that invades us.

Q: You mentioned before that *Chuquiago* is a disturbing film for your audiences. Could you explain that a little more?

A: Audiences in Bolivia, like in any other country, are accustomed to a commercial cinema—the happy ending, the adventure, the tearjerker, the diabolical film. They are not accustomed to seeing films that question their social reality, and because of it will be bothered internally. Our filmmaking will probably not please the audience in the traditional way, but will trouble them emotionally. We are representing their basic everyday problems in such an honest and true way that they will have to recognize themselves and, when they do, they are going to be troubled. They will start to think about and evaluate their roles in society; political and social questions will be raised.

Through this type of filmmaking we are forcing an audience to examine its own attitudes toward our dependency, to be able to *see*, not just look.

Some people have become apathetic; they begin to believe the official propaganda that the country is overcoming its dependency and underdevelopment, that the economic resources are being used to raise the standard of living of the people. I think *Chuquiago* contradicts this and questions the way our country is going. We are questioning ourselves. The film depicts faithfully four stories representing four persons in their own class stratum. I am aware that the film is bitter—it is a mirror of reality that we often refuse to look at. In a way, *Chuquiago* is portraying what we feel as filmmakers, as witnesses of our reality.

Q: Would you describe either or both of your films as Neorealist in terms of their cinematic roots?

A: The term is suitable to describe our filmmaking. For us, the term means filmmaking with a certain commitment toward the society we are involved in, with little money, shooting with nonactors, mostly outdoors. We don't even have the minimum infrastructure—we wait more than a month to see our dailies, there are no labs, no sound or editing facilities—we are absolutely dependent. Every time we make a film we are deeper in debt. I can't imagine what we would do if our next film fails. We don't have a filmmaking tradition like Argentina, Brazil, or Mexico. Yet we have managed to catch some attention with our cinema. The concern of filmmaking in Bolivia, at least for our group, is to make honest films that we hope will contribute to a better understanding of our country. In that sense, our filmmaking utilizes the same methods as the Neorealists.

Q: Over the last few years, many filmmakers in Latin America—including Sanjinés, Miguel Littín, and Fernando Solanas—have left their countries and have started to work elsewhere. They have given up working in those areas that they were most familiar with and taken up different subjects and different themes. What do you think is the future for this kind of filmmaking?

A: I don't see much of a future for that, because filmmakers work at their most intense capabilities and resources within their own country. Perhaps I am wrong, because many novelists have written their best works outside of their own countries, but let me make a comparison. Glauber Rocha's films in Brazil were very strong and beautiful. When he made films outside of Brazil, they were much weaker. I admire and respect Sanjinés's way of filmmaking—he has remained faithful, outside of Bolivia, to his commitments, making films that deal basically with Indian problems and Indian cultures in the Andean republics, yet I think *Courage of the People* is the most intense film Sanjinés has ever made. Solanas, after leaving Argentina, would seem to have a greater problem because the issues within Argentina are not necessarily applicable in other countries where Solanas can work.

I believe that the way to make a really powerful film depicting the problems of a country is from within the country. Under the present circumstances, however, this is almost impossible in many Latin American countries, so the only alternative is to continue making the same films outside.

Q: Assuming that radical filmmaking is proscribed in Latin America, a certain kind of permissive tolerance allows films to be made at a less militant, less effective level, a level that can easily be contained. Is that all films can be in Latin America today?

A: This permissive tolerance you talk about is not a conscious tolerance, because with our previous films we have built our audience. The authorities have no choice but to let us do the films that we are doing. Supposing they forbid us? We do have sympathizers, both inside and outside of Bolivia, friends who would protest against this repression. Our country is very conscious of criticism of its methods of repression.

They are not *permitting* us to make films; we have won that right. I was put into jail for my participation in *Courage of the People*, but even the bourgeois press protested my arrest. Somehow, within our country, even within the present structure, we are respected. They might not agree with us, but we have made ourselves respected by the role we play. And that is a significant step for us, as filmmakers.

Note

1. The Movimiento Nacional Revolucionario (National Revolutionary Movement), a political coalition founded in the early forties, came to power in the popular revolution of 1952.

Chapter 13
Carlos Diegues
(Brazil)
The Mind of Cinema Novo

Plate 17. Carlos Diegues atop the Holiday Caravan truck used in *Bye Bye Brasil*.
Photo courtesy Randal Johnson.

The success of Carlos Diegues's *Xica da Silva* (1976) and *Bye Bye Brasil* (1980)
inaugurated a new era of national popularity and commercial viability for Brazilian
cinema. His interest in filmmaking dates back to his student days in Rio in the 1950s
and his association with a number of young people who were to form the core of the
Cinema Novo movement. With nine features to his credit between 1963 and 1984,
Diegues's productivity is second only to that of Nelson Pereira dos Santos. Both have
been major spokesmen for Brazilian cinema, particularly in the numerous debates
that have erupted within Brazil during the past decade.

Dan Yakir's interview with Carlos Diegues was conducted in English in New York
City and originally appeared in *Film Comment* 16, no. 5 (September-October
1980).

Q: How would you describe the state of Brazilian cinema today and how has it evolved since its inception as the Cinema Novo?

A: What one calls the Cinema Novo was nothing less than the establishment of modern cinema in Brazil. It wasn't a school or an aesthetic movement, but simply a reunion of certain young filmmakers who decided to make films that deal with Brazilian problems, a revelatory cinema made in a modern way. This is clear now, twenty years later, when you see that each director went his own way, in a very precise direction. Today you can't talk about a Cinema Novo or even of a group of filmmakers, but rather of a Brazilian cinema that produces close to one hundred films a year, by good and bad directors alike.

The history of modern cinema in Brazil can be divided into three periods; the first is the Cinema Novo. There was no Brazilian cinema prior to its birth, only a need to invent an image for Brazil—an audiovisual dimension that it didn't have. You have to understand the cultural colonization of Brazil at the time. Before *Ganga Zumba* [1963], I made a short about a samba school, an organization in the Rio slums that gathers people to dance the samba. It was a complex organization and I wanted to show through it how people organize. I lived with them in the slums for a few months in 1961 while I shot the film. When it was ready, I screened it for them. They said, "This is very nice, but it isn't cinema." Cinema for them was the western, French blondes, the samurai—because the Brazilian image had never appeared on film before. That's the achievement of the Cinema Novo: showing what was happening then, allowing the Brazilian people to look at themselves on the screen for the first time. And each director chose his own way of recording this human and physical geography—be it the baroque, epic films that Glauber Rocha shot in the Northeast or the poetic realism that Nelson Pereira dos Santos applied to urban settings.

The second period begins in 1968, with the coup d'état and the ensuing dictatorship, violence, torture, censorship. From that moment, there started a period that I call "the aesthetic of silence." Toward the end of the first period, we were trying to reflect on the role of the intellectual in Brazilian cinema—in films like Rocha's *Land in Anguish* [1967], Joaquim Pedro de Andrade's *Macunaíma* [1969], my own *The Heirs* [1968]—but this reflection was completely obstructed by the regime. So, we had to express ourselves via metaphors, allegories, and symbols. We said as much as we could. It was one of the most beautiful moments in the history of the *cinéma de résistance* in the world, because we didn't look at things complacently. Nor did we content ourselves with lamenting the situation. We created a language out of this very repression.

This period continued until 1975-1976, when a new political openness began, a certain liberalization of the regime, which isn't the democracy of my dreams but still a step forward. The torture, repression, and censorship are almost entirely gone and films like *Z*, which were banned for many years, are now shown and doing very well.

From 1976 on, Brazilian cinema started regaining its voice. I don't know exactly what will happen, but things are moving. Young directors are making their first pictures and, most importantly, for the first time quality films are finding their audience—and doing well—which is exactly what the Cinema Novo wanted: to be a popular, national cinema. You have to get the people into the theater, not only show them on the screen. So, once again, we have a renaissance of Brazilian cinema.

Q: It seems that the wild, ecstatic rhythms and the nervous energy of the Cinema Novo have now been replaced by a mellower, less urgent mood.
A: In the beginning, there were very few of us, maybe eight or nine. We were always together and each of us served as mouthpiece for the others. Everything we said was exactly what the others thought. Now it's different. There are more of us and I'm no longer speaking for others. I think that it's not that Brazilian cinema has become less energetic—it's still personal and experimental—but now it has its public. The energy that was once found in the formalistic quest is now part of the dialogue between the film and the public.

Q: How was the Cinema Novo born and why did it emerge when it did?
A: It was a coincidence. I asked Louis Malle a similar question about the birth of the New Wave, because there was the Cahiers du Cinéma group, but there were also people who had nothing to do with it, like Malle and Alain Resnais. And he said, "The nouvelle vague is an invention of Arriflex and Dupont, because the former manufactures a lightweight camera and the latter the 3x film, which is very sensitive. Because of these, we could make films cheaply, in the street, with no great compromises." It's amusing, but it makes sense.

In Brazil, I think it's similar. It happened during the regime of Kubitschek, when everyone believed that Brazil was about to take off. Things were easier to do. The explosion of TV took place in the fifties and whatever film industry there was was incorporated by it. So, the time was right.

There were three groups in Rio: the Catholic University group, which included Arnaldo Jabor and myself; the guys from the national university, like Leon Hirszman; and those who came from Bahia, like Glauber Rocha. We all met around the Museum of Modern Art, where we founded the first cinemathèque in Rio. We started to create the Cinema Novo. But the movement was born before the films, unlike the New Wave, which was proclaimed once the films were shown. I was writing for newspapers, as were Glauber and others, and we were already talking about a movement. In 1960, I remember reading an article by Miguel Borges, which declared, "The Cinema Novo is dead!"

Q: How did you actually start making films? And how do you feel you have evolved?
A: When I look back at my films, I'm very proud of them—mostly because each of them, whether good or bad, corresponds to a moment in my and my

country's history. It's a coincidence of biography and history.

I started making films in 1962, with *Ganga Zumba*, while I was a student. It was a fantastic, euphoric period, which corresponded to *prima della rivoluzione*—before the coup d'état. It witnessed the emergence of the new Brazilian music, the bossa nova, the new theater. . . . We were completely sure we were going to change the country with our films, that they had the power to change the world.

But it was a cinema of illusions. In 1968, we realized that this was impossible: we made a revolutionary cinema that went in one direction while society went in another. It made me ill; I was desolate and depressed. And out of my reflection came *The Heirs*, which tries to examine the role of the intellectual and the artist in society, to understand what can be done. I had a "sick" period. Not that I preferred the "sane" one: I was really in love with death, frustration, sadness, and *The Heirs*, like *Quando o carnaval chegar* [*When Carnival Comes*, 1972], corresponded to my feeling that there was nothing left but death.

Now I feel much better. I know that cinema can't change the world, but I still feel that it's the most important means of expression in this century, because it directs itself to the emotions and the subconscious of the people. Cinema has changed not the world, but the way of understanding the world in this century. And I'm convinced that someone like Godard is as important as Sartre. A Godard film is more important than a painting by Monet.

But cinema has played this role when made in a relaxed manner, as a personal manifestation of feelings and ideas. Not films made as theoretical tracts, or as entertainment—these have always been bad. I don't think that the movie theater is a classroom, nor is it a torture chamber. That's why I feel increasingly better about the cinema, more at ease, because I no longer have theories or preconceptions. I try to surprise myself with each film. And I make films because I love it and because I want to know others and allow them to know me by getting to know themselves a little better.

I no longer want to prove anything, just to express how I feel about the world. It's much less "aristocratic," much less repressive in the sense that when you try to prove something you become a leader, a guide—as if you were informing people of what they ought to do. I don't want it anymore. I just want to be one among many. That's what cinema is about.

Q: It's clear from all this that you think of all cinema as political.

A: Absolutely. But what's political is the fact that cinema has changed our way of looking at the world, not the power relationships portrayed in the film. A film like *La fievre monte à El Pao* was about such power relationships and it's very interesting, but Buñuel's less explicitly political presentations are no less illuminating.

Q: Why did you choose to make your first film about a black? Did you, as part of the effort to create a Brazilian screen image, try to shock, to go all the way back to the "roots"?

A: Maybe, yes. I've always been interested in black culture. It's the element that has completely modified Brazil, which otherwise would be a mere cultural colony of Portugal and Spain. Black culture gave us originality. In *Ganga Zumba*, there's a metaphor: black culture, with its sensuality and paganlike religion, is liberating. Instead of one oppressive God, it features many. It chronicles the first popular revolution in Latin America—in fact, in the entire continent—the revolution of the black slaves in Brazil in the seventeenth century.

The principal theme of all my films is freedom and how to exercise it. In *Ganga Zumba*, it's the simplest level: how to escape slavery.

Q: And *Xica da Silva*?

A: *Ganga Zumba* is a film about the love of freedom; *Xica* is about the freedom to love. *Ganga Zumba* is a programmatic, collective vision pertaining to the question of how a group can strive for it. *Xica* shows that every time you try to liberate yourself you fail, because it's not a personal matter for Superman to solve. *Xica* is the true story of a black girl in the eighteenth century who tries to attain her freedom without concern for the others. But she can't; it's not a solitary quest. I don't condemn Xica—I love her—but she made a mistake.

I think that what happened to the hippies in the sixties is a modern tragedy. They were people who tried to create an alternative society—which is impossible, because people won't let you. In all my films there's this kind of statement: there's society and there's you. And at the same time that you shouldn't try to change the regime to get an orgasm, you should always seek pleasure while knowing that you won't get it without help from the others. This is what my films are about—pleasure and complicity with the others.

Q: Where does the operatic tone in some of your films—most notably, *The Heirs*—come from?

A: I don't know anything about opera and I don't really like it. I always have arguments with Bernardo [Bertolucci], who adores it.

I was born in a poor, remote region in the Northeast, Alagoas, and it's there that I acquired a taste for representation—from the dramatic spectacles of the circus. Before the appearance of the acrobats, magicians, and fire-eaters, there was always a short, dramatic play, about twenty minutes long, with overacting and larger-than-life characters. It was somewhat operatic. And then, I've always been moved by Carnival—not the way tourists get to see it, but its true, dramatic, larger-than-life manifestation. The samba always tells a story. The dramatic information I received in my youth came from that.

Q: How did you construct *The Heirs*? It's very complex.

A: Next to *Chuvas de verão* [*Summer Showers*, 1978], it was the most difficult script to write. It's paradoxical, because they couldn't be more dissimilar. But they do have the same construction: that of tableaux. The heroes in both serve as catalysts, as means to explore the other characters. In *The Heirs*, the journalist (played by Jean-Pierre Léaud) was me. It was a way of getting closer to the characters I wanted to explore. The same goes for *Summer Showers*.

For *The Heirs*, I had to do a lot of historical and sociological research, because of the period depicted—the thirties—and then eliminate the unessential and make the character's personal life coincide with the history of Brazil, which engulfed him. But the story is very simple. There's no plot. It's just a look at that man from his youth to his death, and through him, all the characters around him. It was the same with *Summer Showers*, even though it's a "chamber film."

Q: How did you get the idea for *The Heirs* and *Joana Francesa* [*Joanna the Frenchwoman*, 1974]?

A: I never thought of doing *The Heirs*. I wanted to make a film about Getúlio Vargas, the dictator who was to Brazil what Perón was to Argentina. I started preparing the film around him but after the first draft I became afraid and felt I couldn't do it: Vargas changed from a fascist and an early supporter of Nazis to a man who, in 1950, appeared as a socialist leader. It was a crazy story. I felt it wouldn't be understood; it was too arbitrary. He even had Carmen Miranda for a mistress! So I chose instead to make a film about someone who lived in that period.

About *Joanna*, I'll tell you a secret. Everything in it either took place in my family or I had heard my grandfather talk about it. He died when I was fourteen; I was his favorite grandson. One day I just had to make a film about it. I shot the film where I was born. I invented nothing. Even the character of Joanna is based on a real woman: a prostitute from São Paulo, whom one of my cousins met—and had children with, unlike in the film. After World War I, many French and Polish women came to South America and, among those who became prostitutes in São Paulo and Rio, some were very cultivated. In Porto Alegre, the university was founded by a Polish whore. It's fantastic.

Q: The fact that Joanna is a foreigner seems to be more than just an exotic detail.

A: In all my films there's an outsider, a character who doesn't belong. In *Ganga Zumba*, the young prince has nothing to do with the other slaves. *A grande cidade* [*The Big City*, 1966] is about migrants to the city. I don't know why. It's not willed. Only now do I start to understand what I'm doing.

Joanna occurred in the worst moment in my life, and my country's: I had friends who disappeared in broad daylight or were tortured or went into hiding. *Joanna* is one of my favorite films, but it's very "sick." It's about my "sickness" about death. It's a film where each character chooses the moment of his or her death, which is bizarre and hard.

Q: How does using the "road movie" format help you state all these themes in *Bye Bye Brasil* [1980]?

A: I started thinking about *Bye Bye* when I was shooting *Joanna*. It was shot under very difficult conditions in the middle of a very hot summer. Jeanne Moreau wasn't free at any other time, and we had to shoot very quickly because she had to return to Europe. Unfortunately, the production wasn't well organized.

One day, we returned to the tiny village (five thousand inhabitants), where we were staying. I was completely tired and miserable, but my curiosity was aroused when I saw a strange blue light in the village square. It was a television screen and the people—the sugarcane cutter, the small functionary, etc.—were watching a program from Rio that featured elegantly dressed people with modern cars: the emblem of consumerism. I was completely amazed and felt I had to film it. This was the first image of *Bye Bye*, in 1972.

I felt that Brazilian cinema found itself amidst a certain claustrophobia. Gone were the wide open spaces of *Antônio das Mortes, Ganga Zumba, Os fuzis* [*The Guns*, 1964], and *Barren Lives* [1964]. It had become a cinema trapped in apartments and urban malaise, and I felt it was time to shoot out in the open. In Rio, one knows little about the interior: the Amazon or the Nordeste. A film like *Bye Bye Brasil* is a surprise, even a scandal, when shown in the big cities—while in the periphery, they do know about the big centers. I traveled several times across the country, which is enormous, because I realized I didn't know it at all. So, in the film, too, there's a trajectory from the Northeast to the Amazon to Brasília.

Q: And in terms of character development?

A: The three main characters—the black fire-eater Andorinha (Príncipe Nabor), the magician Lord Cigano (José Wilker), and the dancer Salomé (Betty Faria)—are characters from my childhood, from the circus, the *caravana*. The young couple (Fábio Júnior and Zaira Zambelli) is completely invented: they're "normal" people. Salomé and Cigano are always in the process of representing. They wear makeup even when they don't give a show. They're always "on stage" while the young couple watches and observes. These are two ways of responding to reality. I like the pregnant young woman because she's really modern, very objective, with her feet on the ground. Her husband is a romantic, but he's "normal." The magician and the dancer, on the other hand, have no rapport with reality. It's pure fantasy.

It's this dialectic that provides us with the balanced view that we get. I chose these *charactères de spectacle* because I wanted to look at this film with the eyes of an artist rather than of a sociologist or a political scientist.

We shot the picture like the navigators of the sixteenth and seventeenth centuries, who came from Europe to the new continent without knowing what to expect. We tried to give a personal impression of what we saw. We were a tight community. The actors helped a lot, especially José Wilker, who's a playwright, an intellectual, and a friend. It was a discovery for everybody.

Bye Bye Brasil is a film about everything that happens along the way. The peasants, the prostitutes, the Indians, the projectionist are no less important than the principal characters.

Q: If this is a film about discovery, then *Summer Showers* is about letting skeletons out of the closet. How do you see the film in view of the claustrophobic cinema you have discussed?

A: It corresponds to the period, but it's no longer a "sick" film. It's a film of recovery. I made it as a reaction to *Joanna the Frenchwoman*. *Summer Showers* is about a moment of happiness that one has to savor rather than becoming fatalistic and accepting death. What will be will be, but one shouldn't seek it. In that sense, it's an optimistic film, almost Walt Disney—because it tells the story of people who ruined their lives because they attributed too much importance to insignificant details. And at the same time it's about the "doubleness" of life: you never know your parents, friends, neighbors. They're never who you think they are.

Q: Which is why you didn't develop a confrontation between the hero [Jofre Soares] and the terrorist who dies in his house; that's another story.

A: Absolutely.

Q: What was *The Big City* [1966] about?

A: It's about four men who come from the Northeast to Rio. Today São Paulo is the more mythical city, but back then it was Rio; they thought its streets were paved with gold. These outsiders arrive and try to understand what goes on. It's also a film about complicity. It shows that people have to help each other, because otherwise we're completely in the shit—social, economic, but mostly in the sense of lack of affection and tenderness.

Like *Summer Showers*, it's a "chamber film"; it's very simple. It's not pessimistic, but maybe melancholic in the sense of regretting that things aren't what we want them to be. Anyway, two of the characters die, one returns to the Northeast, and the main character, the same black actor who played in *Ganga Zumba* [Antônio Pitanga] decides to stay and the film ends with his dancing.

In a way, it's the birth of *Xica*—because he understands that for all the suffering and derision, he has to survive.

Q: And *When Carnival Comes* [1978]?

A: *When Carnival Comes* wasn't understood at all when it came out. It's one of my least popular films. Today, curiously, it's often shown on TV and people start to get the point. I understand why: it was very difficult to watch it at the time. The three principal characters were popular singers—Chico Buarque, Nara Leão, and Maria Bethânia—and people went to the theater to see a cheerful musical comedy. Instead they got a very sad film about frustration, defiance, and perseverance.

Q: How do you use music in your films? For example, in *Xica da Silva* the title song appears on the soundtrack as the director's comment only to be repeated later by one of the characters humming it as part of the action. It's multilayered.

A: It's evident that music plays a very important role in my films. Sometimes it's born at the same time as the film. It's an inherent part of it. In *The Heirs* there's a song by Villa-Lobos that was written in 1943. I always had it in my head. When I write a script, I see in my mind the images of the actors' faces and hear the songs I'm going to use. Even if I end up not using them, I write thinking about them. I can't write otherwise.

All my films are either musical or have a musical construction. It's never decorative or used to underline the action. It has an important dramatic role, it adds new information. In *The Heirs*, we told the history of Brazilian music of the last forty years on the soundtrack. We used a song to represent each year in that historical tableau, so you could see the film with closed eyes— because the story is repeated on the soundtrack.

Q: Could you trace the influences on your work—and the Cinema Novo— then and now?

A: The New Wave was more an alliance than an influence on us. It was a kind of model. It wasn't the films themselves so much—even though I was always taken with Godard—but the principle.

What influenced us enormously was the American cinema, which we've known since our childhood. Aside from Neorealism, we weren't all that familiar with European cinema.

Personally, I love John Ford and Howard Hawks. I first saw their films and only later went to the library to read about them. It was an education more cinematic than literary. Maybe for the first time there was in Brazil a generation that had a visual culture. We're also influenced by Brazilian writers—especially the modernists of the beginning of the century—but it was an influence after the fact.

I don't know what influences me today. I can trace my influence in the films of Arnaldo Jabor, of Glauber in my films, and of Nelson Pereira dos Santos in those of Joaquim Pedro de Andrade. We influence each other and there's a younger generation that's greatly influenced by the Cinema Novo.

Today, we need to create a Latin cinema—but not in the ethnic or racial sense. Unlike the Europeans, whose culture is petrified, we need to build rather than destroy. And what I envision is a cinematographic body in which Renoir is the head, Rossellini the heart, and Buñuel the gut.

Chapter 14

Raúl Ruiz
(Chile and France)

Between Institutions

Plate 18. Raúl Ruiz. Photo courtesy Ian Christie.

Of all the Latin American filmmakers in European exile, Raúl Ruiz has been the most prolific, completing twenty-eight films for both television and theatrical viewing in his first decade abroad. He has been honored by retrospectives at the British Film Institute (1981), Madrid's *Cinemateca* and *Action République* in Paris (both 1983), and the Toronto Festival of Festivals (1985).

Ian Christie and Malcolm Coad interviewed Raúl Ruiz in London in November 1980. The interview, conducted in English, appeared in *Afterimage*, no. 10 (Fall 1981).

Q: After the London Festival screening of *Des Grands événements et des gens ordinaires: Les élections* [*Of Great Events and Ordinary People: The Elections*, 1979], you described it as your first "Protestant" rather than "Catholic" film. What did you mean by that?

A: For a long time I tried to make films that expressed a concrete tendency, whether that of a party or a political movement, so the films were built around a set of propositions. When I came to make *La Vocation suspendue* [*The Interrupted Vocation*, 1977], I recognized a Catholic tendency in myself to respect institutions, and I tried in that film to explore the relationship between the individual and the organization. And in this last film, I tried to clarify my attitude toward my own work and activity, which is like having a direct relationship with God!

Q: That's a rather theological view.

A: Yes, but it is also a highly appropriate metaphor that arises from the actual terms of the television commission: they asked me to be *me*. For the first time I was able to make "my" film, consciously and without guilt.

Q: So you had to construct a fictional "you" as the alien filmmaker observing French daily life?

A: Yes, and of course it's also not me, since it is not even my voice on the soundtrack, although it is my house and *quartier*. The "I" that is looking and investigating is of course fictional. But you must also remember that the position of the filmmaker in France, even if he is a militant, is very personal and individualistic. What happens in his head is very important to him, and if nothing happens, then it is assumed that he should not be a filmmaker. Before coming to France I had thought that a good filmmaker should have his head empty and be open to influence and experience. I remember during the shooting of *Of Great Events* everyone kept asking me: what are *your* ideas, what do you want? So I was supposed to wait for something to happen inside me.

Q: Surely this is only true within the French art cinema, where the *film d'auteur* is an established convention?

A: No, you find it just as often among militant political filmmakers and even among the makers of commercials and industrial documentaries. The filmmaker is supposed to know completely what he is making—and if he doesn't know he pretends. This is what French common sense requires. In fact, there aren't any real political films in France; there are only films expressing individual attitudes, although the filmmaker is expected to know "what the party wants" or doesn't want. But for my own part I still try to mediate different positions, even though I may have personal or social obsessions that I include in my films.

Q: You have talked elsewhere about the church as the key institution that can serve as a metaphor for all other institutions.

A: It would be more accurate to call it the metainstitution, since its mission was to change the world and to the extent that it succeeded we are no longer conscious of its total impact. It has been assimilated. However, there are other kinds of institutions that are quite different from the church: large factories, for instance.

Q: How did your upbringing and education in Chile influence your view of the church as an institution?

A: I remember from childhood that the worst sin, far worse than murder or fornication, was not to attend mass. It was not until later, when I had some experience of other institutions, that I began to understand this paradox of an institution more concerned with its own destiny than with the morality of its members. I recall being very shocked when I read Gramsci for the first time and found that he compares the [Communist] party with the church, recommending the Jesuits as an example to be followed. And then, of course, there is all that American theory of institutions. But what is not present in this, and what I have come to think of as essential to all institutional behavior, is the symptomatic bad faith that arises from a fascination with the perfection of the institution itself, without any concern about its reasons for existing.

Q: There seems to be a tension running through your work between the demands of militancy and what you have called "irresponsibility," and this relates to the evaluation of institutions as both positive and negative. What do you consider the responsibility of an artist to be?

A: I try to work as an artist, which means to experience feelings and to make connections between what I learn and what I feel—which also involves my militancy—and to express these in artistic form. Sometimes in making these connections, I make metaphors based on the church, rather than talking about personal experience within a party. But it is, of course, a political decision not to work within institutions and there are many instances of this attitude through the centuries, from Christ to Galileo. I am trying not to elude the question about when institutions are negative: I think there is a moment when an institution becomes tautological, it becomes the referent of reality. At this point everything becomes institutionalized, and there is the ambiguity of everything being political, which can be used to fight against the institutional drive.

Q: What do you mean by "irresponsibility"?

A: There are many kinds of artist and many kinds of activity. Artistic activity is very difficult to explain and in relation to politics there has to be an experimental attitude. If you think back to the Renaissance, there was a strong interest in ideal societies, and you can use the aesthetics of experimental fiction to test the limits of tolerance of a society or institution.

Q: At what point then does "irresponsibility" become something negative? I was reading your comments on the film you made with Saul Landau, ¿Qué hacer? [1970].

A: In that case we thought we were making a film to help a movement, but we didn't really know what the movement was about. We were not prepared to say that it was negative or to criticize it. If you are going to talk about artistic integrity, then you must consider how to remain open to the situation in which you are living—open to the reaction I have as a petit bourgeois in the society, assimilating its values and tendencies. I would draw a comparison between the artist, who should be sensitive toward all tendencies, and the militant, who must also remain open to changing conditions. Both are testing reality.

Q: You often invert preconceptions so that you become truer to them than are those who actually hold them. I am thinking of your answer to a question after *Of Great Events*, when you said that it wasn't a political film, but that it was concerned with your moral sense of what was involved in making a film about this subject. This reply obviously challenged the questioner's ideas about what is and what is not a political film. It also reminded me of your position in the debate among filmmakers before the coup in Chile, when there was a move to create a kind of official necrology, with films about national heroes like Balmaceda and Manuel Rodríguez. You argued that it was more important to make films that affirmed a national psyche, that would deal with the ways people represent themselves to each other. In fact, you were arguing that the apparently political films were actually more abstract and *less* political than what you proposed.

A: There is a very strong emotional attraction toward making heroic films. It is very easy to build a mythology and very difficult to destroy it. I think I am now more critical of that kind of filmmaking than I was then. It involves a kind of "status" relation between the spectator and the mythology, instead of a relation between the reality of the film and where it is being shown. I remember the reaction we had to American westerns in Latin America: it was a very direct and intense relationship, much more so than with anything in our own country—I always regarded the Indians as pure invention.

Q: How did your early interests in theater and cinema connect with your political activism?

A: You must remember that there was a generation of young people in Latin America in the sixties who, largely inspired by Cuba, connected Marxism for the first time with Latin American reality. I say "for the first time," because most Latin American Communist parties were small; and even if they were strong, as in Chile, they were almost exclusively working class and closely tied to the Moscow mythology. This was a very curious relationship. I remember feeling very close to Moscow and Stalin because of the anti-Communist propaganda and I knew many who joined the Communist party in reaction to the constant theme of the "evil of Communism" that the government encouraged in books and films, and the radio soap operas that most children followed every day. At a certain moment, there seemed to be a vital connection between Marxism and the social situation and a whole generation felt called to take up the struggle. This movement could not be absorbed by the Communist party, so many joined the Socialist party and a fraction of this formed the MIR [Movement of the Revolutionary Left]. Only a very few conservative members of this generation remained unpolitical, and so I naturally became politically active. In the early seventies, when Allende came to power, there was an attempt to build a Leninist party, which didn't work because it was essentially a popular party, and here I saw the fascination of the party as institution. It was an intensely contradictory movement, yet all the contradictions became elements of cohesion and not of destruction. I had worked in theater during the sixties, but at the point where I became interested in showing [images of] my country, I became a filmmaker.

Q: What kind of theater did you produce? I have heard it said that you were doing theater of the absurd before Ionesco had been heard of in Chile.

A: Perhaps, since there were no translations! But we had our models, in my case Claudel, Calderón, and Gogol, as well as the avant-garde playwrights of that period and the surrealists. Incidentally, I never directed any plays, despite what some biographies claim, although I wrote over a hundred plays between 1956 and 1962.

Q: Were you influenced by the Chilean tradition of popular theater?

A: Not at this time, because I did not yet appreciate kitsch. Although there was very little economic difference between the working class and the petite bourgeoisie in Chile, there was a great cultural gulf. For instance, we never expected to understand the words of songs; they were always in English, never in Spanish (I later discovered that in some parts of Africa, songs are traditionally sung in a kind of imaginary Spanish, as a language not to be understood). So I had no contact with the popular theater that used songs and music; I knew only the very orthodox kind promoted by the Communist party. The first popular songs and poetry I really discovered and learned by heart were Mexican.

Q: What kind of models did you have access to as a filmmaker when you made *Tres tristes tigres* [*Three Sad Tigers*] in 1968?

A: I was influenced by the *nouvelle vague* rather than by Neorealism. The idea was to put the camera not where it would see best, but where it should be, in the normal position. This means that there is always some obstruction and things are not seen from an ideal standpoint. There was also an antidramatic tendency, working against the narrative, favoring privileged moments; the style was anticompositional, using off-screen space, with everything hand-held (except the last fight sequence). But the aim was not just to reproduce the *nouvelle vague* style. There was also an attempt to tackle the embarrassment of Mexican melodrama by a kind of inversion, as if the camera were in the opposite position, showing the secondary characters, extras waiting for the big scene to take place.

Interestingly, when I started to make films in France, I felt thta I had to use elegant framing and beautiful photography, otherwise I would not be accepted as a filmmaker. So I tried to do this in *The Interrupted Vocation*, although sometimes in a kitsch manner as a parody of *"un beau film."* But I still felt guilty because I would have preferred to make a more natural film.

Q: But it is possible to trace a direct line between *Tres tristes tigres* and a recent film like *Of Great Events* through their common concern with the informal institutions of certain social groupings, whether it is the melodramatic subculture of the Chilean petite bourgeoisie, or the attitudes of various professionals to elections in Paris.

A: Yes, I am interested in the formalization of relationships and I remember there was a project to adapt a novel by Jorge Edwards, which dealt with the people's attitude toward time—the famous *peso de la noche* of Portales—which explains the incapacity to act that prevents Chile from becoming a real nation. In *Tres tristes tigres* there is both an expansion and a contraction of time: although the exact time of day is clear, it is difficult to know whether events are taking place over a single day or a week.

Q: What was the reaction of other filmmakers in Chile to *Tres tristes tigres*?

A: There weren't many filmmakers in Chile at that time and most of them were friends; it was almost like a club. Three of the films that all came out at the same time were made with the same camera. I remember it well because when we finished shooting *Tres tristes tigres* around eleven one morning, the people arrived from Valparaíso to take the camera for *Valparaíso mi amor* [Aldo Francia, *Valparaiso My Love*] to start shooting the same day; and after they had finished the same camera was used for *The Jackal of Nahueltoro* [Littín].

Q: Was there much discussion about these films as a group when they appeared at the same time? The others were more clearly influenced by Neorealism, whereas yours dealt with more interior concerns and with language.

A: There were some issues in common, such as the interest in "everyday violence," and we were all trying to assimilate this into a political context.

Q: How widely were these films seen? Like so many other "breakthrough" films elsewhere, were they shown only in specialized cinemas?

A: When *Tres tristes tigres* was first shown in eight cinemas and advertised like a Mexican film, it didn't really work. But when it was at only one cinema, the attendance was quite good, about forty thousand. All three of these films were seen by ordinary filmgoers. Due to new tax laws, it was the first time that Chilean filmmakers had an opportunity. In Chile, Argentina, and elsewhere in Latin America at this time, there was a mixture of avant-gardism and the desire to lay foundations among filmmakers who had long been marginalized. In Chile there was both a feeling of rediscovery and vanguard attitude: filmmakers were excited at the prospect of making real industry films, but lacking the usual technique, they had to adopt an artisanal approach.

Q: In this situation *La colonia penal* [*The Penal Colony*, 1971] seems a surprising departure.

A: I was thinking about that recently and wondering why, at a time when there were so few military dictatorships in Latin America, so many poets and painters (like my friend Sotelo), began to produce antimilitaristic work in 1967-1968. I criticized this tendency at the time, but in 1969 I started to make a film (which has never been shown) called *Militarism and Torture*, a kind of parody lecture/demonstration on how to carry out torture. Then I made *The Penal Colony*, where the action takes place on an island with everyone dressed in military uniform. Chileans are very nationalistic and, although there were military dictatorships at this time in Brazil and Bolivia, it still seems a strange movie to have made, almost a presentiment.

Q: The period 1970-1971 was a crucial moment, when Chilean filmmakers were debating the different kinds of film that should be made. You spoke of different levels—instrumental, investigative, etc.—of filmmaking, but what governed the choice for you at that time?

A: Well, there were many options and I wanted to try them all! There was the situation of Chile and the place of my generation, which was a different matter. I was interested in what was happening in the country and I wanted to do something to help. But no one at the political level ever asked me or anyone else to do anything specific. I was completely free to do what I wanted. At that time I think I had an alibi, but I have since forgotten it!

Q: Why was *La expropriación* (*The Expropriation*) not finished at the time it was shot [late 1971]?

A: Mainly because it was considered more of a provocation than a constructive intervention, which the party did not want to have widely shown, although it was seen by some militants in double-head form. It was made at a time when the MIR had become critical of Popular Unity. I was trying to show what happens when general theory is contradicted by reality and social paradoxes emerge from generalizations. When land is given to the peasants they are supposed to be happy, but often this is not so and great damage can be done, as in La Vendée during the French Revolution, when a general theory is put into practice wholesale. I wanted to show this paradox in action and, as in most of my films, there was a satirical attitude developed by working with the actors. And in my next film, *Realismo socialista* [*Socialist Realism*, 1973], I included what I had observed in the reaction to *The Expropriation*. None of these films were scripted in advance, from *Tres tristes tigres* onwards: they were improvised from day to day during the shooting. I still work this way and the only really scripted film I have made is *The Interrupted Vocation*.

Q: *Diálogo de exilados* [*Dialogue of Exiles*] also provoked controversy among Chilean exiles when it appeared in 1974: some argued that it was the wrong kind of film to make and others that it was the wrong time to make such a film.

A: I saw the film again recently and I felt the same about it as I did about *Socialist Realism*. It was also an improvised film with no dialogue written in advance. I established the ground rules in terms of "You come in and say something like this, then you go out." It is a very bitter film, certainly—it could be seen as negative—but the bitterness has to do with the morale of the exiles. It is not really a psychodrama, since there is a distance between the situations represented and reality; but there are propositions, things that *could* happen. This was the original idea, but the bitterness felt by those involved was so great that it became a very bitter film; and I can see how I tried to manipulate the bitterness, to exacerbate it.

Q: What do you think the controversy over the film tells us about Chilean cinema in exile?

A: It says a lot about the actual model we were building, which was a compulsive model of political activity, almost Stalinist, although I would not want to use that term. I remember that during Popular Unity everyone always asked to be given "the line." All the time that I was film adviser to the Socialist party, half a dozen painters, poets, and artists of all sorts would come every day to be told "the line." They didn't want to write simple poems that might be unconnected with the political situation; they wanted "the line" and they wanted to impose it absolutely on others . . .

Q: While the mass movement, the people themselves, were doing quite the opposite; they were creating *cordones industriales* [industrial areas where workers had assumed control of the factories] and organs of popular power.

A: Yes, it was very open, very creative, and very complex; yet the artists wanted the "line" of a classical Leninist party. I saw that their attitude was like a parody, or maybe a simple imitation, of what they had read about Communists in anti-Communist literature. I could not understand this: if you are an artist and free to do what you want, this is surely a good thing.

Q: But in exile do political positions not become more idealized and abstract?

A: Yes, the parody becomes more extreme. Of course, one must remember that there were some perfectly rational explanations for this behavior. For the first time artists felt they had some importance—normally, they were complete outsiders—and the mark of acceptance was to adopt a militant line.

Q: What was the outcome of the controversy over *Dialogue of Exiles* in 1974?

A: There was no real discussion. The shock was considerable, so we never actually had a discussion. Miguel Littín said that he thought it was not the right moment, but that he liked the film; many others told me the same, although they acted quite differently when together.

Q: Did that make you think that you should change the direction of your career as a filmmaker in exile?

A: Yes, at that time I wanted to make a political intervention, but instead I made *The Interrupted Vocation*.

Q: Which appears at first a totally nonpolitical work and seems to be deliberately a "difficult" film . . .

A: I was only trying to reproduce the instability that exists in the novel. Klossowski's novel is autobiographical, about his leaving the church. He wanted to be more Catholic than the church and so became a kind of dissident. I read the novel for the first time shortly before making the film because I saw the connections with my own experiences in the Party. The story is exactly the same as that of the novel, except that the more political allusions are mine.

Q: How does this connect with your experience?

A: Because I feel very much in harmony with Stalinism in many ways and to fight against this creates many difficulties. This is hard to explain to myself: for instance, I find it impossible not to cry during certain Stalinist films—like the Dovzhenko scene where a man is expelled from his community and the party representative tells his son, "Don't worry, now the party is your father." This moves me and, however horrible it may be in political films, I am not afraid of it; I think the drive involved is very important and meaningful.

Q: Chilean filmmakers in exile have had to tackle a twofold crisis: the crisis of Marxism-Leninism, and the crisis of representation. And this is perhaps why their experience has been watched with such attention by the Left in Europe. Their problems are seen as symptomatic of a crisis in the very idea of political art and cinema—and this would explain why Littín's "*grandes frescos*" have been so poorly received.

A: I became very interested in the *grandes frescos* when I was making *L'Hypothèse du tableau volé* [*The Hypothesis of the Stolen Painting*, 1978], and for the first time I studied the official painting of the nineteenth century, the *peintres pompiers*. This characteristic representation of the rise of democracy and capitalism is common to both France and Britain. I became interested in *all* forms of official art, including socialist realism, and for the first time I saw painting as an actual site of political struggle. This stemmed from my discovery of the First Empire painter Torpinon le Brun, who painted large tableaux like *The Death of Caius Gracchus*. Torpinon was on the far left and he was arrested for this picture because the figures in it were in the same configuration and the knife was the same as that in the attempted assassination of the Emperor Napoleon. Since the painting dated from before the assassination attempt, he was accused of incitation to murder and was executed! This seemed very interesting as an example of "political economy" in a time of struggle, in the sense that perhaps the persecution of artists—or the importance they are given in socialist countries and at times of struggle elsewhere—is a form of economy, concentrating the struggle in a symbolic way. As a result, I became more respectful of such work and its significance.

So there is the question: What kind of official art? Is it to be political art reflecting the aspirations of the state, or is it to be the model of a future state? And there is also the question of dissident art, which is not official and therefore not art. I tried to learn more about official art and this led me to make the *Petit manuel d'histoire de France* [*Handbook of French History*, 1979], which is a two-hour compilation drawn from the very worst of the French television *grandes frescos* dealing with French history. This stereotypic history has three sources in France—Victor Hugo, Alexandre Dumas, and Michelet—and it seems to be the first strong expression of a history that goes from primitive tribes to the perfection of society, with a succession of heroes as the key figures.

Interestingly, the stereotypes are the same as in Latin American history, and the idea of the "invention" of Latin America is not far from the virtual invention of France that occurred in the nineteenth century. Now everyone knows who was good and who was bad, and the films that were made by Communists and right-wingers are exactly the same, with the same themes of unity, the conjunction of power and centralism, nationalism. I think there has been a real drive toward centralization of the Latin American continent, which is analogous to the unification of France. Or perhaps the Latin American movement was a parody, since they even named the battles after European battles: Bolívar called himself Caesar and referred to his battles as Thermopylae, Waterloo, Trafalgar, and the like. But if we call this a parody, we must remember that a parody is a very mysterious thing.

Q: How does this relate to the films being made by Chileans in exile?
A: First, I think there is a version of the "official art" attitude, which sets out to make "history" exist. They start with the history of Latin America, which is a history of betrayals and of imperialism; the massacres are mostly hidden and the record of the peasants' and people's movements is equally unknown. So there is an obvious point in making films to reveal this forgotten history and make known the secret massacres. But this is more difficult to accept when it becomes an imperative duty to follow the political line, showing ever more massacres and creating a vast funeral ceremony.

Q: There seems to be growing obsession among some Latin American filmmakers with the decadence of the enemy, dwelling on the dictatorships and making a great icon of them.
A: Maybe you have to accept this as a personal tendency and a personal

tendency is always a tendency of more than one person. Or perhaps you should regard it as the symptom of a sickness. At any rate, it is true that everyone wants to make films about history; although I am not in touch with many younger filmmakers and I would have thought they were more interested in making films from a documentary standpoint, which has never been easily accepted as a method in Latin America.

Q: Your own methods are quite different, however, although you may be dealing obliquely with the same issues. Your "European" films are ironic, often parodies or pastiches of familiar forms, and their labyrinthine construction inevitably invites comparison—especially for Europeans—with Borges.

A: There are good reasons for working in this way: I am trying to demonstrate that *all* films are necessarily oblique. Even a very simple film about political struggle involves a political calculation and an element of obscenity to make you respond emotionally. Borges is another matter. I think he represents an important position for Latin Americans in relation to culture. If you read the confrontation between Borges and Sábato in *Sobre héroes y tumbas*, Sábato makes some criticisms of Borges that have become standard. One of them is very curious: he speaks of intellectuals for whom it is the same to live in London, Paris, Rome, or Buenos Aires, and he calls them simply European traitors. But he forgets that it is difficult to imagine a Roman, for instance, who would find it the same to live in London or Paris. The Latin American experience is of being outside (or inside) European culture *in general*, whereas the European is within one specific culture or another. This hyperabstraction is typically Latin American, and so Borges is an important key to understanding the invention of Latin America, but for me personally Borges is also an excellent guide to reading and a fine writer.

Q: Do you feel that García Márquez has contributed something more specific with his invention of a Latin American baroque that deals with characteristic attitudes to time, landscape, and psychology?

A: It is true that he has developed the elements of a relationship between these, but he did so by standing outside and considering Latin America in general, as he might consider Europe. Rather like the *man without qualities*, he presents the "continent without qualities" and this view of a heteroclite culture under construction is a positive idea. I feel, however, that others have been more significant than García Márquez. There is Alfonso Reyes, for example, a greater Latin American encyclopedist than Borges, even, who makes connections between very distant and apparently unrelated things, sometimes simply because they begin with the same letter.

Q: In *Of Great Events* you refer to yourself as an exiled Chilean and you ask, no doubt rhetorically, how you can make a political film in France. How restricted do you feel?

A: You feel many things. First you feel estranged from the language: there are some sounds that you know definitively you will never be able to pronounce. Then there is the feeling of a society that is so open that it can accept you—perhaps even eat you—without destroying you, because it has this capacity for abstraction. And then there are all the feelings about being part of the first generation of Chileans to suffer exile on a massive scale. Now we have this Borgesian experience of living in London, or Paris, or Rome. In the *Framework* interview I mentioned the three legendary stereotypes of Latin American intellectuals—Lautaro, Jimmy Button, and Valderomar[1]—and these also relate to the experience of exile. Often now I feel like Lautaro, the Indian who copies the style of fighting of the invaders, as I learn how the European cultural machine works.

Q: You also invoked Montesquieu and the *Lettres persannes* in *Of Grand Events* as the model for oblique political commentary, using the device of foreignness. Can you *use* the circumstance of exile?

A: I think there is a greater opportunity to be both inside and outside in France than there would be in England. Foreigners are not uncommon in French cultural life and many celebrated actors have strong foreign accents, but I cannot imagine an actor with a Spanish accent playing Hamlet in England. I have no general program to communicate, but all the time I have small things to say.

One thing I feel constantly is that exile quickly becomes permanent, and even if I were to go back to Chile I would still be an exile. It is like a triangle: there are always two other points where I feel I should be but am not. When I was in Rome several months ago, I was talking with other Chilean exiles about how the feeling of schizophrenia is becoming stronger after seven years. One recalled that he had seen himself walking down the street; another saw himself drinking a cup of coffee; and I, who normally write the dialogue for my films in a Spanish that can easily be translated into French, saw my own hand writing in French. After that I began to write in French all the time. Another was in a tailor's shop surrounded by mirrors and saw a profile that he could not identify; only after several minutes did he recognize himself.

Q: These anecdotes go some way toward explaining the acute self-awareness and ambivalence of your films during the last five years, but I have the feeling that you have also constructed an eclectic intellectual universe, based on writers like Klossowski and Baudrillard, which underpins all the apparently diverse films.

A: All my films since *Dialogue of Exiles* have been made as commissions of one sort or another, except *The Interrupted Vocation* and *Colloque de chiens* [*Dogs' Dialogue*, 1977]. Even *The Hypothesis of the Stolen Painting* began as a documentary on Klossowski, but what interested me was his concept of the simulacrum, the idea that some kinds of representation or ceremony acquire their own reality in certain moments of great historical change. However, my puritanism made me reject the whole sexual economy in Klossowski that derives from his study of de Sade.

Q: Klossowski is also fascinated by the relationship between words and pictures, the difference between showing and telling, and you use his "exemplary fiction," the painter Tonnerre, in *Hypothesis*.

A: Tonnerre is supposed to have posed *tableaux vivants* for his subject paintings, like many nineteenth-century painters, and I used this as the basis for the exploration of certain ideas about photographic and cinematographic representation. One idea has to do with the "suspension" of the photograph: you can postulate that immediately after a photograph has been taken someone shoots one of the subjects with a gun. . . . Another idea has to do with the "emptiness" of the photograph. You may remember that Alberti speaks of the emptiness of the space between objects in the first chapter of the *Della Pittura*. I discovered that Chinese aesthetics also recognizes this emptiness as a function of the picture surface itself.

In *Hypothesis* and *Dogs' Dialogue* and also in the didactic fiction *Le Jeu de l'oie* [*Snakes and Ladders*, 1980] I have been exploring different kinds of space and the effects of separation between the components of cinematic representation: story, location, commentary, etc. Theory becomes another object to be made visible. In *Of Great Events* the commentary is very difficult to follow even for a French audience (which may explain why it has never been shown on French television); it is like my talking now, full of gaps, hesitations, and mistakes. The aim is to make you "see" the commentary in the same way as you see the film.

Q: Your latest film, *The Territory* [1981], seems to mark a new departure. You have described it as a commercial film with a straightforward narrative.

A: It should work as a story and even as an "exploitation" film, but there are other elements of interest. It is about people who want to isolate themselves without reason and as such it may shed some light on the psychopathology of exile.

Note

1. In an interview with Don Ranvaud (*Framework: A Film Journal*, no. 10 [Spring 1979], p. 17), Ruiz says,

At one stage I wanted to create a series of characters which would typify the Latin American intellectual in relation to the power of culture. In this context I see at least three typifications. . . . In the first place Lautaro, a Chilean Indian who fights against the invasion of foreigners and, understanding that he doesn't have the necessary weapons, copies the style of the invader. He raises his people in revolt and wins, but in a deeper sense the invasion is successful because the Indian culture was penetrated by the foreigner. The second symbolic character is Jimmy [*sic*] Button, [who] belonged to one of the most primitive tribes in the world (whose vocabulary consisted of sixty words, who were cannibals and whose culture was reduced to a minimum) . . . [who] is kidnapped by Fitzroy and in a period of about two months learns English perfectly, as well as other languages, becomes conscious of his identity when he is given a mirror, and in England integrates into the Puritan world, becoming a Protestant. . . . He is then taken back to Chile and the simple contact with his people makes him forget all he has learnt in a very short time. That is, he could only communicate with his people if he forgot all he had learnt. The third is Valderomar, the Oscar Wilde of the Indian, whose relationship with the civilized world is much more usual in our intellectuals. He is the man who is used by the civilized world in order to emphasize their feelings of superiority.

Chapter 15

Marcela Fernández Violante
(Mexico)

Inside the Mexican Film Industry: A Woman's Perspective

Plate 19. Marcela Fernández Violante with cameraman Danny López on the set of *Mystery*. Photo courtesy Marcela Fernández Violante.

A product of CUEC, the film school of Mexico's national university, and appointed its director in 1985, Marcela Fernández Violante is a teacher and lecturer who also has four feature films and numerous awards to her credit. She enjoys the distinction of being the only woman working within the notoriously closed directorial ranks of the official Mexican film industry.

Julianne Burton interviewed Marcela Fernández Violante at Fernández's home in Mexico City in October 1983. John Mraz, who set up the meeting, also participated in the discussion. The editor is responsible for the translation and organization of the piece.

Q: You are often identified as the only woman director in the Mexican film industry. Is that an accurate description?

A: Yes, I am the only female member of our film directors' union, though, in fact, one of our honorary members is also a woman. It happens that I am currently filming a tribute to her for television. She is Matilde Landeta, one of three women pioneers in the Mexican film industry. Landeta made three feature films: *Lola Casanova* in 1948, which dealt with an indigenous theme; *La negra Angustias (Angustias the Black Woman)* in 1949, the story of a female colonel in Zapata's army; and *La Trotacalles* [*Streetwalker*] in 1951. *La negra Angustias* is a marvelous film, unique in Mexican film history because it shows a woman triumphant, a leader of men who maintains her superior position rather than surrendering it. I was startled at how modern the film seems, particularly since strong female figures are so rare in our cinematic mythology. Landeta is now seventy-three years old and has not made a film for over thirty years.

I just finished filming part of the tribute in her house. I arranged to have another of our women film pioneers, Carmen Toscano, there as well. Carmen is the daughter of Salvador Toscano, who is generally regarded as the first Mexican documentarist. In 1950 she released *Memorias de un mexicano* [*Memories of a Mexican*], a compilation documentary with archival footage spanning half a century of Mexican history—from the 1890s through the Revolution and beyond. In 1976 she did a kind of update of her earlier film, but *Ronda revolucionaria* [*Revolutionary Round*] was never released. I would have liked to have arranged to do a tribute to her as well, but she has suffered a series of strokes recently and is not in good health.

There's a third female film pioneer in Mexico, who predates both Toscano and Landeta—Adela Sequeyro, often called "Perlita" [Little Pearl]. She began her film career as an actress [in Fernando de Fuentes's *El prisionero 13*] and subsequently made two features of her own: *La mujer de nadie* [*Nobody's Woman*] in 1937 and *Angeles del arrabal* [*Slum Angels*] in 1939. I haven't been able to trace Sequeyro; she seems to have disappeared. I know that she has a daughter, but since she has a different last name, I haven't been able to find her, either.

Q: Could you describe how your own involvement with film began?

A: I entered the National University in 1964, the same year they opened the film school there—CUEC, the University Center for Film Education. I intended to study philosophy and letters, but several friends suggested that, if I was thinking of becoming a writer, I should consider writing filmscripts. I liked the idea and began taking courses in both programs.

Things were a bit precarious those first few years. There was still some doubt about whether filmmaking was an appropriate pursuit at the university level. We were very short on equipment, and on funds.

I wrote my first screenplay during my second year. One of my fellow students directed it, casting me as one of the actresses. It was a disaster. I decided I needed to direct my own screenplays. My first effort was a rudimentary little experimental film called *Azul* [*Blue*], which ended up winning a Diosa de Plata [Silver Goddess] critics' award in 1967 for best experimental fictional short.

The school encouraged me to keep on directing, and gave me a feature-length film to direct that same year called *Gayoso da descuentos* [*Gayosso Gives Discounts*—Gayosso is the most important chain of funeral homes in Mexico City, almost a monopoly]. The film was to be the story of three old men: one who had fought in the Revolution but never received his pension; another who had been a railroad man during the big rail strikes and had retired with full benefits; and a third who had worked as a petty clerk for the church, which had cast him out into the street with only five hundred pesos to his name.

This was to be CUEC's first feature-length film and almost everyone in the school was involved. We started shooting in 1968, the year of the Mexican Olympics and of student demonstrations that eventually culminated in the government-ordered massacre of an estimated four hundred to six hundred people in the Plaza of Tlatelolco just before the Olympics were scheduled to begin. With the country in such turmoil, nobody wanted to work on a fiction film. Everybody went out to participate and to film what was happening. The project had to be postponed, and by the time I was able to get back to it, one of the old men had already died.

It was during that same period that I got married—to Roberto Jaime Sánchez Martínez, a fellow film student and cameraman. Soon after, pregnant with my first child, I had an accident that provoked a miscarriage.

I went back to the university to complete my thesis, a film on the Mexican painter Frida Kahlo. There has recently been a great burst of interest in her work. In the United States, Hayden Herrera published a major biography in 1983. That same year in Mexico, Raquel Tibol published *Frida Kahlo: una vida abierta*. A major exhibition of her work, along with that of Italian-born photographer Tina Modotti, was staged in London and New York, organized in part by British filmmakers and theorists Laura Mulvey and Peter Wollen, who made a documentary on the two artists called *Frida and Tina*.

But in 1971, Frida was not all that well known. I learned about her at the university, but I already knew who she was from my father, who attended the same preparatory school as Frida at about the same time. My father was a lawyer and historian, with certain Bohemian airs. He loved to sip cognac after dinner with a friend and read poetry by Baudelaire and Rimbaud aloud. My mother also loved to read and exposed her children to a lot of European classics. It was not unusual in our household to discuss the arts.

When I started doing the research for my thesis film, I ran into problems.

Dolores Olmedo, who is in charge of the Frida Kahlo museum—the house where Frida was born and later lived with her twice-husband, the famous muralist Diego Rivera—refused to grant me access to Frida's personal papers or her now-famous diary. Then I realized that Frida's paintings tell the whole story of her life more eloquently than any written words could. I decided to let her images, and the house she lived in, which reflects so much of her personality, speak for themselves. I kept the voice-over narration to a minimum; I resisted getting embroiled in technicalities about this or that school of painting. I didn't want to make an "educational" documentary; I wanted to make a film that would have such an impact on the spectators that it would provoke them to discover more about Frida on their own.

Thanks to *Frida Kahlo* [1971], I began to travel. The film was shown at the Museum of Modern Art in New York; it was shown at festivals in Moscow, Oberhausen, and London. I received another Silver Goddess Award and also an Ariel, the Mexican equivalent of the Oscar, for best documentary.

Based on the success of this short, the university Film Department [Departamento de Actividades Cinematográficas], which had provided the funding for *Frida Kahlo*, offered to finance my first feature film. I wanted to do something set during the Mexican Revolution, but they were afraid that a period film would be too expensive. I ended up arranging to use locations without charge, since part of my father's family still lives in the town of Tulancingo, in the state of Hidalgo. We shot the location footage at my cousin's hacienda, and other relatives—hotel owners—provided eight rooms for the crew free of charge and meals at a reduced rate.

My idea was to view the Revolution, specifically the phase of the Cristero Rebellion of 1926 and 1927 [a conservative counterrevolution led by the clergy with the support of the big rural landowners], through the eyes of a young girl. Though the film has lots of technical problems, I still defend the ideological position it takes. *De todos modos Juan te llamas* [*Whatever You Do, It's No Good*, 1975] was the first film to put the armed forces on the screen. I may not have had the money necessary to make the film as I wanted, but with the university behind me, there was no risk of censorship. I had the freedom to attack two of the most powerful institutions in Latin America, the military and the clergy. I also examine the institution of the family. The film asks what combinations of power lead an apparently idealistic person to betray his or her goals. The anarchist question is also treated in the film through the sympathetic figure of the girl's young uncle, whom her father eventually has killed. I would explore this theme in greater detail in my subsequent film, *Cananea* [1977].

Q: Would you say that your vision of the Revolution is more personal than historical here?

A: I don't believe in the Mexican Revolution as our historians present it to us. I have more faith in the artist's conception than in the historian's. Besides, with the same political party now in office for nearly seventy years, how are we to know what the truth is? *Whatever You Do* was an attempt to demystify the Revolution. How was it possible, for example, that after all the fighting the peasants still followed the priests? It was possible because after the Revolution the generals remained in power, never distributing the land to the peasantry as they had promised, never providing them with seed or financial backing or anything. Contrary to the conventional wisdom, the Revolution was not won. At that point of "consolidation" between 1917 and 1926, it was lost.

Naturally, the film has a lot of problems, beginning with the script, since this was my first trial by fire as a screenwriter. I wanted to emphasize the female points of view more than I did, but as it turned out, the whole film was made on the fly and by the seat of our pants. Take the scene when the stables catch on fire, for example. Since it was a big scene, I had managed to get two cameras, though in Mexico, customarily, we only shoot with one. I told the actress who was playing the little girl not to come out of the stable until the cameras were rolling, but then I realized that the stables had caught fire for real. We had to rescue both the girl and one of the cameras. The scene where the Cristero soldiers and priests blow up the buildings with dynamite was just as real; I never have been able to pay for rebuilding my cousin's wall. I suppose I'm not very welcome in Tulancingo anymore.

The film cost three hundred thousand pesos [about fifty thousand dollars]. It competed that year with Miguel Littín's *Actas de Marusia* [*Letters from Marusia*] and Felipe Cazal's *Canoa*, both big-budget films in Mexican terms, costing twenty-four million and four million pesos, respectively. My film was nominated for almost all categories of the Ariel awards and won two of them for best acting, as well as Silver Goddesses for acting and direction. I was invited to screen it at the Museum of Modern Art in New York as part of the New Directors, New Films series.

At that point, I was invited to join the film directors' union and to make *Cananea* for the industry. Suddenly I woke up to find myself a filmmaker. I never thought things would turn out this way. I thought I would continue my writing and go into teaching, because I was married to a filmmaker, after all, and believed that he would be the one to advance in his career while I remained somewhat on the sidelines. As it turned out, I was the one who got ahead, and this put severe strains on the marriage. We have been divorced now for eight years.

Q: Does *Cananea* also have a historical theme?

A: *Cananea* [1977] is set before the Mexican Revolution. The film is based on a famous historical incident in which a North American mine owner in northern Mexico violently suppressed a strike by calling in the Texas Rangers from across the border. Because Littín's *Letters from Marusia*, set in approximately the same period, had assumed the perspective of the miners, I was told to do something different. I decided to take the point of view of the imperialist entrepeneur, the Yankee mine owner.

Q: This seems to be the film's biggest problem—that it tries to present a vision sympathetic to the striking miners, but through the eyes of their enemy. Since so much of the film is from Green's point of view, the pathos becomes his, not the miners'.

A: What I was trying to do here was to confront two different ideologies, two ways of looking at the world: what it means to be a white, Anglo-Saxon Protestant; and what it means to be a brown-skinned, Catholic Mexican. Protestantism teaches that the rich get rich through God's help. Catholicism teaches that the rich do not get to heaven. Catholics are taught to sacrifice themselves; Protestants strive to succeed.

I wasn't looking for heroes. Green is a cynic, and to deal with one cynic, what you need is another cynic. The two anarchists in the film, Esteban Baca Calderón and Manuel Diéguez, are not the ones who can do away with Green. It takes a bastard to combat a bastard. To fight your enemies, you have to assume their dress and take up their arms. If you can't, you're lost.

In *Cananea*, as in *Whatever You Do, It's No Good*, I wanted to portray anarchists as the conscience of society, but not as the solution to society's problems. Baca Calderón, the intellectual anarchist, is really an emblem for Ricardo Flores Magón, often regarded as the principal ideologue of the Mexican Revolution, who died in jail in the United States, where he had been imprisoned for agitating against U.S. involvement in World War I. For all his theoretical brilliance, Flores Magón could never take action. In the Baca Calderón figure, I also wanted to emphasize the class difference between those restless, idealistic youths of the Mexican haute bourgeoisie, and the popular masses they purport to serve. There are real communication barriers between them, as the figure of the working class anarchist, Diéguez, makes clear.

Green's problem, then, is the arrival of Baca Calderón, which provokes a confrontation of two opposite ideologies. Had he not arrived, Green would have kept on doing what he was doing. This is the history of Mexico writ small. In this game, nobody wins and everybody loses.

Since all the characters are losers in the end, *Cananea* becomes an ambiguous, difficult film for the spectator. I think the main problem with *Cananea* is that it turned out to be too intellectual, too Brechtian, too didactic. The characters are too cold, too distant. There is no emotional involvement.

The theme of vengeance is also prominent in both films. I think this obsession is part of our Mediterranean strain. I don't subscribe to the idea of the Mexicans' indigenous heritage. To me, Mexico is very Spanish. The more I search out our culture's indigenous roots, the more I discover Spanish influence. We are the most Spanish of all the Latin American countries.

Cananea led me to *Misterio* [*Mystery*, 1980]. It was getting toward Christmas time and Margarita López Portillo, sister of the president and head of the national film industry, decided to put people back to work for a change, since so many technical workers had been laid off. They found an old script by Vicente Leñero based on his novel, *Estudio Q*, in a drawer somewhere and dusted it off. They had to call in the author to sell them the rights for the second time, since the first rights, negotiated under the Echeverría regime, had lapsed. Then they began to call in prospective filmmakers, but they all insisted they would need at least six weeks to shoot the thing, and most of them said that they couldn't make head or tails of it, anyway. Eventually they got to the bottom of the list and called me in.

I thought the project was intriguing. The novel is very cinematic in an undirect, unconscious way. It's the story of a soap opera star who cannot leave his role—or his director—behind. Everywhere he goes turns out to be a set; everything he says turns out to be a script. They gave me three weeks to make the film, but I insisted on four.

What a marathon! They did not provide me with videotape, so I had to shoot everything twice in 35mm—one take for the full context shots and another for the parts that would be viewed on the video monitors, the films-within-the-film. We used the same kind of lighting as they use in television. There was no time to wait for them to process the master and do the intercutting. The pace of the shooting was absolutely frantic, but I think that this is what gives the film its rhythm. I learned a lot of camera choreography from that experience. There were several scenes where characters who had not been visible before had to appear within the frame as if they'd been there all along. In the past, most directors would have used a cut, but I wanted to avoid the obvious "trick" of editing, so I used a zoom-out and the characters, at a signal from me, would appear as if by magic, though in fact they had simply emerged from behind a table or a doorway.

Most of the actors were assigned to me without consultation by the director of the state-owned film company, CONACINE. I would have preferred to do my own casting. The major exceptions were Juan Ferrera, who plays the lead, and Beatriz Sheridan, who plays the scriptwriter, Gladys. Víctor Junco, who plays the director, has been acting in films for thirty years. He has appeared in over two hundred movies, but he just won his first Ariel—for his role in *Mystery*.

I discovered that I had to impose a different work method on most of the actors. Mexican actors tend to use their faces only and keep their bodies immobilized. I wanted them to move around. They complained that I kept rehearsing them as if we were doing a play. I compelled them to give me complete scenes, rather than scene fragments, as they're used to doing, because I didn't have time to construct small scenes for subsequent editing and consequently had to edit in the camera. This was one of those times when you make a virtue out of necessity. Some of the actors were rather fatuous, some were just plain bad, but in *Mystery*, I let this work to my advantage.

Mystery is a critique of Televisa, our privately owned television production monopoly. Televisa makes it its business to strangle any attempts at independent production for television. They'll blacklist anyone who tries it. Yet they produce all sorts of films for theatrical release. And their films do well at the box office largely because they are widely promoted on television.

Mystery is a satire, a farce, though a lot of people, including a number of critics, have only read it on a very literal, melodramatic level, without perceiving the subtext. You laugh while you're watching it, but then when the actor finally succeeds in stepping out of his role and shooting the director, it creates such an impact that you begin to see the whole film in a new light. You begin to see its political dimension. I like this play of genres and these changes in tone. *Mystery* combines melodrama with farce, but with an undercurrent of tragedy. This is not common in Mexican film.

I had to fight with Vicente Leñero, the author of the novel and the screenplay (and someone I love and admire) over this ending. In his version, the actor, Alex, commits suicide in the last scene. I told Leñero that he was still stuck in his postwar, Catholic existentialism. *Mystery* is really about oppression, about the total denial of breathing space. There's a real atmosphere of asphyxiation in the film. Alex's house is not his house, but a studio. He tries to escape to the street, but that also turns into a TV set, and the cameras follow him everywhere. It seems to me that if a person is robbing you of your space, sooner or later you are going to kill that person, before he destroys you. Leñero finally told me, "All right, if that's the way you want to do it, but if your ending doesn't work on the screen, I won't assume any responsibility for its failure." I should have gotten credit as co-scriptwriter, but through some oversight I did not. Leñero later tried to correct this by giving me a special acknowledgment in his recent book, *Vivir del teatro*.

Q: How was *Mystery* received?

A: The film ran for only a week in Mexico. CONACINE didn't do much publicity, and they made the mistake of releasing it the same week that the annual International Film Festival opened. Since roughly 90 percent of the films released in Mexico come from the United States, and the other 10 percent are Mexican, people seriously interested in movies are naturally going to take advantage of the all too rare opportunity to catch up with what is happening on the international film scene. Besides, it was December and everyone was running around frantically doing their Christmas shopping. For whatever reason, *Mystery* did so badly at the box office that it was withdrawn after the first week.

With two notable exceptions, the Mexican critics did not like the film much. The irony, of course, is that it completely swept the Ariel awards, winning eight out of the twelve that year, including best male and female actors and supporting actors, best screenplay, and best editing.

In sharp contrast to its lukewarm reception in Mexico, *Mystery* has done quite well abroad. It was shown at the Biarritz Festival, and at the Mystery and Suspense Film Festival in Italy, where it won a special jury prize in 1981. It was shown at FilmEx in Los Angeles in 1983, and in New York and Chicago. Azteca Films distributes it in the United States with English subtitles.

After *Mystery*, I made a children's feature called *En el país de los pies ligeros* [*In the Land of Light Feet*, 1981]. It centers on two young boys—one from Mexico City and the other a Tarahumara Indian. Because it is set in the Tarahumara region, the film reverses the customary movement of the Indians to the city by developing a situation where the city kid tries to adapt among the Indians. I wanted Mexican children to be able to discover the wonders of the Tarahumaran habitat through this film. I wanted to show the remarkable intelligence and competence of the indigenous peoples in their own environment. The Indian boy teaches the white child which plants are medicinal and which can be used as food. When they are stranded in the wild, he teaches him how to defend himself from nocturnal animal attacks by drawing a circle of urine and staying within it. The film turns the "normal" process of acculturation—rural to urban, non-Western to Western—on its head.

Visually, the film is very dynamic. There is a lot of movement, because I believe that the aesthetics of movement is what film is all about. This is a far cry from the "classic" Mexican cinema of Gabriel Figueroa and Emilio Fernández, with their debt to Eisenstein's unfinished *Que viva México*, where the Indians are treated like statues and the emphasis is on still composition within the frame. This kind of rigid formalism just about did away with the film's dramatic potential. I think this kind of "visual nationalism," this hypostatization of one particular visual style, is a thing of the past. It has been associated primarily with the cinematographer Figueroa, but it has never created a school or a following, though it fulfilled a useful function in its time.

The fact is that nobody creates his or her own "school" in Mexico—at least not in film. The film directors' union was closed to new members for thirty years! We skipped a whole generation, so how can we expect there to be any continuity? Emilio Fernández and his generation are now in their eighties. People of my generation are in their forties. There is almost no one in between. In the decade following the Experimental Film Contest of 1965, about forty new directors made their debut. Other countries display greater continuity from one generation to another, but here it is as if we had to start from scratch because the gap is so large. We are the product of professional film schools, while our predecessors went to the empirical school. This creates a certain distrust between us, or at least certain communications barriers. We have a level of film culture that our predecessors did not have. We have been trained in scriptwriting and immersed in auteurist cinema. We have been taught production skills such as how to manage the budget and how to make a shooting schedule.

Our generation has another common trait: all of us have made explicitly political films. When censorship was lifted under Echeverría, and we were encouraged to make films that looked critically at national life, everyone began making explicitly political films. When censorship was reimposed, we went back again to metaphor.

Q: How do you see the current prospects of Mexican film?

A: They are not good. Let's say they're in conflict. Our film studios are currently in the hands of foreigners. De Laurentis has leased Churubusco Studios for the production of *Dune*. Michael Douglas bought the Alatriste Studios outright. The Mexican government, which could finance national production, is in acute financial crisis because of the drop in oil prices, the external debt, high interest rates, the abuse and corruption of its own officials, and the capital drain of funds from the country. It is not in a good position to refuse foreign productions, because these at least provide jobs for the technical crews (although, naturally, all the important technicians are brought in from abroad).

I read recently that *Tootsie* cost thirty million dollars. If those dollars were converted to pesos, that amount would keep all the Mexican directors making movies for the next six years! Our low production costs are naturally very attractive to foreign producers, and we are very close to Hollywood and can offer good laboratories and other advantages. Still, this leaves directors, screenwriters, composers, and camerapeople out of work.

And if the Mexican government is so short of money that it can't even support its own film industry, what business does it have offering to finance half of John Huston's *Under the Volcano*? With 225 million pesos, at least a dozen Mexican directors could be put to work. Huston is a world-class director; he doesn't need to come to us for financing. But our government seems to have a penchant for "world-class" directors. We co-produced *Campanas rojas* [*Red Bells*], Soviet director Sergei Bondarchuk's three-part epic based on the life of John Reed, which was a miserable failure. We also financed Spanish director Carlos Saura's *Antonieta*, based on the life and death of José Vasconcelos's lover, Antonieta Rivas Mercado, another monumental disaster, in my book.

Until the state begins to give its own intellectual workers a hand, we're in bad shape. Unemployment will continue and there will no longer be a Mexican film industry. The first years of López Portillo's presidency were okay, since the momentum of the Echeverría years carried over, but in the last four years of his six-year term, production virtually came to a halt. Now, under Miguel de la Madrid, the country is facing a severe economic crisis.

Production is one thing, but distribution and exhibition are just as bad. I did some research recently for a lecture I had to give. Under the Echeverría regime, we spent nine million dollars to cover royalties for American films. Under López Portillo, we spent sixty million dollars—more than six times as much! The exhibitors say that they prefer American to Mexican films because they bring in more money, but I say that the whole thing smacks of corruption: "Give me your dollars and I'll strangle Mexican cinema." There's something else at work here, too, a certain snobbery on the part of the middle-class audience, which admires the ballet, the symphony, the theater, but thinks that movies, especially Mexican movies, are beneath it. Some of our critics are at least partially responsible. Emilio García Riera now only does criticism of televised films. Imagine a movie critic who refuses to go to the movies!

Margarita López Portillo did a lot to encourage these "aristocratic" airs. Her tenure as head of the film industry is the blackest chapter of Mexican film history. Knowing full well the dangers involved, but preferring to squander a fortune on the Mexican-Soviet co-production of *Red Bells* rather than spend a modest amount building much-needed new film storage facilities, she literally let a time bomb explode. When the old nitrate prints stored "temporarily" in the basement of the Nacional Cineteca [film archive] caught fire, many lives were lost and the entire history of Mexican cinema went up in smoke.

Despite all these problems, I still believe that the film industry can recover. There is a large group of younger directors who now have six or seven feature films under their belts. It seems unthinkable to squander all that talent and all the money invested in their training. Producing for television is not the answer. Some films are aired on the state educational network, channel 13, but Televisa controls the rest and has its own production people. If we can't reach an agreement with the government, we'll have to go independent, producing and distributing our films outside the state-controlled circuits. This is an enormous risk, particularly in a country like Mexico, where the industry has been so rigidly controlled. You can be a genius, but what good does it do if your films sit in cans under your bed? Unless your films get shown, you simply don't exist.

Film could be a very effective weapon in the current "morale-boosting" campaign against government corruption. I wish the officials would recognize its potential. Mexico has already surrendered a huge share of the Latin American film market to U.S. interests, and I doubt that we will be able to win it back. It's a shame and a scandal, particularly since Mexico has enjoyed such favorable circumstances in comparison to most other Latin American countries, where there is no domestic market for national film production, let alone an international one.

Mexico is extremely fortunate to have such a large market for its films in the United States, yet just look at what gets shown there. Ninety-nine percent of it is pure trash! Azteca has five branches in the United States, but they have chosen to "specialize" in *churros* [low-budget "quickies"] and soft-core porn. There is clearly also a potential North American market for more serious Mexican films. Look at what the Brazilians have been able to do in the United States. But Azteca doesn't seem to notice. There has been a great lack of imagination and initiative there, since we could easily put together a package of at least thirty fine films made since the Echeverría administration [1970-1976], which, once subtitled, could open a whole new market in the United States. On a recent visit to Los Angeles as guest of the July 1984 FilmEx, I had the pleasure of discovering that, thanks to the enlightened attitudes of its new director, Esteban de Icaza, Azteca is changing its distribution policies.

Q: Do you have any sense of identification with the new cinema movements that have taken place in many Latin American countries during the past twenty years?

A: I was still a student when Brazilian Cinema Novo came on the scene in the early sixties. I found the movement very exciting, but I also felt very removed from it—not geographically or thematically or stylistically, but because of its rapid development and international recognition.

Yes, I do feel closely identified with the new cinema movements in Latin America. I was a juror for the Fourth Havana Festival of the New Latin American Cinema, in 1982. There I was able to see films and to meet filmmakers from all over the continent. I met Adolfo Aristaraín, the talented Argentine director of the extraordinarily powerful *Tiempo de revancha* [*Time of Revenge*], at the 1983 FilmEx in Los Angeles. I've also met some of the Venezuelan directors. I feel a sense of cultural identification with all of them. We are united by our protest of the treatment of Latin American cinema by North American interests. But the distressing thing is that we seem to remain at this level of protest, rather than moving on to make concrete changes in the situation.

Mexico could take the lead here. We could start exhibiting Cuban films on a large scale, for example. The state controls a huge chain of theaters, but since López Portillo these aren't even used to exhibit Mexican films, let alone films from other Latin American countries. This exclusive focus on movies made in the U.S.A. produces a fatal vicious circle, because the more the Mexican public gets accustomed to this particular type of film style and pacing, the less it will be open to different approaches, even by Mexican filmmakers. Homogenization is a tremendous danger. American films and television series as the dominant media product will sooner or later destroy our sense of national identity.

Though I feel a part of my generation of filmmakers both within Mexico and throughout Latin America, I also need to stress that I try to maintain my independence from all groups. I don't like to have labels put on me. I am not a feminist or a leftist in the sense of belonging to a group or seeing myself as part of a movement. Like most human beings, I like to conserve my complexity, my ambiguity, my ambivalence. I don't want to have to follow anyone else's slogans.

Film critics also have their own groupings, their own cliques. I prefer to go my own way. If they like my work, they can praise it, and if they don't, they won't.

Q: Don't you think that in a country like Mexico, you are also classified if you do not associate yourself with any group?

A: They can only classify you as "crazy," and I interpret that as high praise.

Part III

BEHIND THE SCENES

Chapter 16

Nelson Villagra
(Chile)

The Actor at Home and in Exile

Plate 20. Nelson Villagra in *Cantata de Chile*. Photo courtesy ICAIC.

Because of his exceptional range, Nelson Villagra has established himself as one of the leading Latin American actors. His most notable roles include the leads in *El Chacal de Nahueltoro* (*The Jackal of Nahueltoro*, Miguel Littín, Chile, 1968); *Tres tristes tigres* (*Three Sad Tigers*, Raúl Ruiz, Chile, 1968); *La tierra prometida* (*The Promised Land*, Miguel Littín, Chile, 1973); *Cantata de Chile* (Humberto Solás, Cuba, 1975); *La última cena* (*The Last Supper*, Tomás Gutiérrez Alea, Cuba, 1977); *El recurso del método* (*Reasons of State/Viva el Presidente*, Miguel Littín, Cuba/Mexico/France, 1978); and the cooperatively financed *La viuda de Montiel* (*Montiel's Widow*, Miguel Littín, Mexico, 1979).

Julianne Burton interviewed Nelson Villagra in Havana in June 1978.

I was born and raised in the central region of Chile, in Chillán, an agricultural zone. My father was a doctor's assistant for the state railroad. Though we lived in an urban area, I felt very attached to the country because from the time she was a child, my mother had strong ties to the land and during my childhood she continued to maintain a small farm.

There had never been any artists in my family, or for that matter anyone with any conscious interest in art, though as I think back on it, music played a big role in family life. When I became involved in an amateur theater group at thirteen, my family thought my sudden artistic aspirations surprising and strange. This made it somewhat difficult for me to go to Santiago to study. But I managed, with rather limited financial support from my parents, who would have preferred that I stay to work with them.

After three years of study, I graduated from the University Drama School in Santiago. I had a rather strange reaction: I wanted to withdraw from all artistic activity. I made plans to go into business with my mother in the country. I think that after three years in the big city, I felt the pull of my country roots. My experience in the capital had made me feel somewhat out of my element. The artistic environment didn't correspond to my way of seeing life at the time, my idea of one's relationship to nature and so on. So I went back home to work, convinced that my world and my people were in the country.

What I didn't realize was that I had the theater bug inside me. My poor parents were greatly disappointed once again, because when I got a letter inviting me to join a university theater group in Concepción, I immediately decided to accept. Their proposal interested me precisely because it didn't come from the capital. I had already turned down two invitations from Santiago. The tendency toward the centralization of cultural activity and resources was very pronounced in Chile, as it is in the rest of Latin America, where the capital cities tend to absorb everything. Because my early experience had involved an amateur theater group in the provinces, I was convinced of the need to cultivate provincial theater and decentralize the whole cultural scene.

I spent seven years in Concepción. I would say that the experience there was my most important formative period. In a provincial group at that time in Chile, you didn't have the competitive spirit that was part of theatrical activity in the capital. You could work much more calmly, perfecting your skills. The members of that group worked out a program of exercises and study that proved very beneficial to us all in developing dramatic technique and promoting what we called "cultural integration."

Through our discussions on aesthetics, we became acquainted with Marxism. Our reading of Marxist interpretations of art led us in turn to the study of dialectics, historical materialism, and so on. We arrived at what was for us a new way of looking at the world.

Our practical work developed parallel to our more general theoretical studies. We began with one common goal: to create a regional dramaturgy. We wanted to maintain a Chilean framework, but with the accent on the regional element. We took advantage of the fact that we were located in a rather special region. Concepción province is an industrial zone. The old fighters of the Chilean working class are to be found in the saltpeter mines of the north and the coal mines to the south. The mines in Lota and Coronel are very close to Concepción, so there is a large number of industrial workers. We wanted to create a theater related to the lives and problems of those people.

Our audience was initially made up of the usual sectors of the petite bourgeoisie. But little by little we began to build ties to the more popular sectors. When we analyzed the kinds of plays we were doing—Arthur Miller's *Death of a Salesman* and *All My Sons*, for instance—we realized that the workers were missing a necessary link, which would enable them to understand that kind of theater. We saw that we would have to build that bridge. That was how the idea of a regional dramaturgy arose. We organized a play-writing workshop and began to develop a series of plays that, though they certainly weren't masterpieces, met our objective of trying to connect with the problems of the audience we wanted to reach.

We didn't wait for the working public to come to us; we went to them. Through the university, we made a series of agreements with labor unions. We worked with their amateur theater groups and also staged our own plays. We were thus working on a dual level: improving the general cultural level, and sharing concrete skills. Naturally, while we were teaching them, they were teaching us.

Through the direct experience of presenting these plays to worker and *campesino* audiences, along with the study program we were pursuing, we began to develop and refine a new concept of our goals and our audience. We developed close personal ties, a common aesthetic language, and a kind of theater that actually broke the patterns of cultural centralization. In a short time, we became recognized as the best theater group in the country. For the first time, national critics began to travel to the provinces. They awarded us the National Critics' Prize.

Throughout the whole experience, our developing praxis was becoming increasingly radicalized. Naturally we began to have problems with the university administration. Finally, we could not go on without crossing the boundaries the university had set for us. Our interests had become too different from theirs. I happened to be delegated to act as our group's representative before the Association of University Employees. We lost the fight. The theater was declared "in recess" and we were obliged to find other work.

Some of us—the "academics"—had come from Santiago; others had gotten their training locally, on the boards. When the conflict with the university arose, the ones who came from Santiago were the first to have to withdraw because we were being characterized as "outside agitators." A Santiago theater sent me a contract, and later other *compañeros* also found work there, including some of the people who had gotten all their training in the provinces.

I began working with the Icthus Theater in Santiago, which had a very effective program for reaching a specific kind of audience—primarily petit bourgeois intellectuals and progressive students. Although it was not the kind of audience I was interested in, I still saw this policy of defining a target audience as a positive thing. I didn't believe then, and I don't believe now, in a theater that aspires to universality. Given the conditions of underdevelopment, we need to channel our energies and resources toward specific sectors of the population.

Little by little, I began to get involved in television. At that time, Chilean television still had pretty high cultural standards. All the channels were run by the universities; there was no state-owned television at that point.

During the same period, Chilean cinema began to show new signs of life. Interest in the kind of cinema that would critically examine national reality had been in the air for some time, but after the Viña del Mar film festival of 1967, when militant Latin American filmmakers from all over the continent gathered to view each other's work for the first time, the movement really took off. A whole generation of directors, actors, producers, and technicians suddenly emerged, many from television and the theater.

This movement was in part the product of our shared need to analyze and express what was happening in the struggle between social classes in Chile. In 1964 Allende lost his third bid for the presidency. This produced a series of political readjustments, but the national economic and social crisis persisted. Some of us were more conscious than others, but we were all trying to come to grips with and express this situation. A certain homogeneity of thought, concepts, and standards, only apparently spontaneous, facilitated the artistic dialogue between actors, filmmakers, and technical personnel.

It was tremendously exciting and rewarding to collaborate as an actor in that great unleashing of creative energies that gave rise to the first fruits of a new national cinema. In 1968 I played the lead in two films, both directorial debuts: Miguel Littín's *The Jackal of Nahueltoro*, and Raúl Ruiz's *Three Sad Tigers*. Both films were widely acclaimed in Chile and abroad, and both filmmakers' talents are now internationally recognized. Some countries have to make a hundred films to produce half a dozen good ones, whereas the first half dozen features to come out of Chile in the late sixties were all of remarkable quality.

Some people wonder whether I find film acting more fragmenting than giving theatrical performances. In fact, I find that the fragmented chronology of character development, which is virtually built into film acting, given that scenes are seldom shot in sequence, stimulates my own critical spirit with regard to the character I am trying to create.

My method of character development, partly inspired by Brecht and Stanislavsky, involves several steps.[1] I begin with the director's initial orientation and my first impression upon reading the script through rapidly once or twice. Then I set the script aside and begin to research the sociohistorical context in which the action takes place. I draw certain situations out of my readings, developing certain dramatic exercises for myself and running through them in my mind, without moving from my desk. Later, after more research into the sociohistorical context, I will return to those exercises, filling out each situation in great detail (odors, temperature, etc.) and physically acting them out, but only after I have begun to identify historical or living models for my character. Generally at this stage, the model just looks on in silence, but occasionally I split myself in two so that model and character interact.

After about two weeks spent developing the character in imaginary situations, I go back to the original script and stage a confrontation. In this third stage I have to get the definitive grip on the essence of the character, what I call his "mode." Then I begin to work on the situations that are actually part of the script, deriving from them whatever other improvisations I find necessary.

Once the central model (which must be capable of subsuming other models) and the central "mode" have been determined, I submit them to the proof of "daily life" [actualidad cotidiana]. I ride the bus in character; I speak to my wife and children in character. I become unbearable. In recent years I have played a pious, slave-owning count of colonial times, a Cuban counterrevolutionary, a Latin American dictator, an agent in Pinochet's secret police, and a small town caudillo. Just imagine what the daily routine at home has been like!

Here the most active stage begins. I have got the "essence" attached to the model with safety pins; now I have to integrate and internalize the two. This is the stage when I really begin to see the character. I caress him, I summon him, I leave him sitting in an armchair, I take pity on him and cover him with an overcoat. I feel him cross over and pass through me.

With José del Carmen Valenzuela, alias "The Jackal of Nahueltoro," that "subhuman" peasant who was imprisoned and later executed for murdering a widow and her five children in cold blood, this intermingling was a calm but sorrowful process. How dismal to have to look at the world with a blunted mind, as if through a poorly focused lens, debilitated and stupefied. How else could this man walk, surrounded outside and within by underdevelopment, except so softly that he seemed to be asking permission from the very ground under his feet? I am afraid to step briskly. Perhaps the ground will rise up against me in anger, grab a stick and start to beat me, and send me away howling in pain, hopping on one foot . . .

The images are completely different when I approach the count of *The Last Supper*. I try to grasp his inner world: the arthritis centered in my lower vertebrae is a mild penance that God, in His infinite generosity, has imposed on me to remind me of that pain that He bore out of His love for mankind. He has lodged within me, His humble slave, in a manner both evident and undeserved. The greater one's suffering, the more God's presence reposes within one, the more purely we bear His presence on earth. I will cross these slopes and valleys, trying to hold in check these all too human times. It is necessary that I defile my soul—even with vile money— living and speaking of earthly goods, because this is the only way of knowing whether I am capable of ascending to Your divine dignity, Master.

Or again, the First Magistrate of *Reasons of State/Viva el Presidente*: Aha! Ha, ha! Where do you think you're taking me, you old rogue? Who do you think you're fooling with your acrimony and displays of power? I know too well that behind all your pomp, you have an enormous crater where your soul should be. And it hurts. I take a stethoscope and listen: "Carajo! Won't I ever get to sleep? Maybe I should have stayed under my mother's skirts in the shadow of the fig tree. AAAHHH! The idiocies of insomnia! Peralta! Where's Peralta? Where the hell did you put that rum? You dare to threaten me, you evil-mothered gringos? To hell with your diplomatic nonsense! Tomorrow for sure I'll send a cable direct to Washington: 'Half for you.' Peralta! Peralta! More rum, carajo!"

I think it is significant that during the past five years, I have only been called on to play characters who belong to the dominant classes or those in their service. Times have changed, and today a strong current of counterrevolution runs across Latin America. Current circumstances require us to reflect on these issues and ask why most of us in Latin America (with the exception of Cuba) are worse off than before. On the one hand, monopolistic sectors have increased their domination. On the other, certain deceptive alternatives have emerged that tend to confuse the masses.

Filmmakers want to comprehend and reveal the inner workings of those who wield power over peoples whose incipient revolt has caused more than one dictator to waver. Miguel Littín's *Reasons of State* is an important film because it begins to examine the nature of the enemy. Art must be capable of expressing current phenomena. These new "modernized" dictatorships must be carefully considered.

It is important and necessary to particularize this Latin American who has so illegitimately assumed power, to penetrate this uncharted terrain and break apart the false stereotypes to which we so tenaciously hold. Alejo Carpentier, author of the novel *Reasons of State*, has also written a book called *Tientas y diferencias* in which he asserts, "Our art has always been

Baroque—from the splendid pre-Columbian architecture and the magnificent codices to the best of the contemporary novel, including the colonial monasteries and cathedrals of our continent." I ask myself, then, what connections the old dictator's anxious cultivation of his personal dignity might have to the Baroque, and I venture the following conclusions. The First Magistrate wields his dignity like a defense mechanism on the one hand, whereas on the other it reflects his own image of those who exercise Power, mythically conceived. Thus he finds it expedient to project his sense of dignity to those he dominates. Because his dignity is a programmatic tool of his trade, it is an artificial construct, which he must polish daily like his boots. He would like it to be aseptic; instead his origins have stamped his precious dignity with a comic rusticity. His is a purely ornamental dignity, overelaborate, excessively gaudy, in a word—baroque.

The problem presented in *Reasons of State* is a universal one: illegitimate political power. Those who collaborated on the film felt they were dealing with problems extracted from their own personal experience. That such illegitimate regimes are particularly prevalent in contemporary Latin America does not mean that other parts of the world are innocent of the experience.

In the past, we Latin Americans have had a tendency to produce an excessively rhetorical kind of cinema with an overly apologetic vision of Latin America. Given our progressive perspective, we have been very preoccupied with the dominated classes. The problem is that, with the exception of Cuba, the dominated sectors of Latin America continue to be dominated. The proletarian sector has not yet been able to develop consistently revolutionary positions. In cinema, and to a lesser degree in literature, we have tended to overestimate the political maturity of our continent. Our heroes or antiheroes from the world of the underdogs have always demonstrated attitudes that are too exceptional, too removed from the grayer, sadder, more frustrating facts of actual life. Our attitude has been a bit too "triumphalistic."

As creative artists, everyone, from film technicians to directors, must reconsider our own conceptions and analyze them more deeply. We have to avoid oversimplification. Life keeps teaching us that reality is more complex and less mechanical than we tend to assume. More dialectical. As creative artists, we must think about what we identify with—not merely on a rational, intellectual plane, but on a visceral level. The creative process should be a kind of strainer that retains only what the person truly understands and feels. This is one method for confronting the current situation in Latin America.

Of the films I have appeared in, several have successfully approached this goal. My first film, *The Jackal of Nahueltoro*, had an immediate connection with the audience it was aimed at, and, curiously enough, its connection with a specific sector of the public enabled it to reach other sectors as well. Of those films made in exile, perhaps *The Last Supper* and the more recent *Reasons of State* would be the best examples of films in which there is a clear correspondence between the theme and how it is conveyed, and the goals of those who participated in the process.

Through my experience as a Chilean actor working in exile (in my attempt to solve extremely difficult problems of accent, for example) I have come to realize that phrases like *"la patria grande"* denote a genuine reality. *Reasons of State* combined Chilean, Cuban, and Mexican actors, but the various nationalities are not immediately identifiable on seeing the film. We are all Latin Americans. With a minimum of effort, we can all adapt ourselves to a common accent. But I'm now convinced that what is much more important is the capacity to delve into the inner attitudes and behavior common to us as Latin Americans. This praxis has given me a much more universal vision of my profession.

Note

1. This section has been expanded using Villagra's essay "Un actor y su trabajo," *Cine cubano*, no. 96 (1980).

Chapter 17

Walter Achugar
(Uruguay and Latin America at Large)

Using Movies to Make Movies

Plate 21. Walter Achugar (left) converses with Fernando Birri at the First
International Festival of the New Latin American Cinema, Havana, 1979. Photo by
Julianne Burton.

The promotion and distribution of Latin American cinema have kept Walter
Achugar on the move throughout the Americas, Europe, and beyond since the early
sixties. Political and economic vicissitudes have compelled him to shift his home
base from Uruguay to Argentina, then to Venezuela, and later to Spain, where he
lived for nearly a decade before a more hospitable political climate permitted him to
move back to Montevideo in 1985.

This interview is a composite of taped conversations between Julianne Burton and
Walter Achugar. The first was held in Havana in June 1978 and was followed by
others in December 1980 (Havana), in June 1981 (Madrid), and in December 1985

It's always hard to pinpoint the beginning of a career or a political orientation, but if I had to pick a date, I'd say that 1960 was the watershed year for me. That was when I met the two people who were most crucial to my decision to make film my career, Fernando Birri and Edgardo Pallero. I had always been drawn to the arts. Even as a high school student, I was a devoted theatergoer, and during those years there was an impressive surge of independent theater activity in Uruguay. I acted in two student productions at the Liceo Francés in Montevideo, directed by Ugo Ulive, who would later turn to filmmaking. I began taking acting lessons with him at the Teatro Galpón, still Uruguay's most famous theatrical organization, which has been in exile in Mexico since the mid-seventies.

I also loved movies and had been seeing several films a week ever since I was a little kid. Like many teenagers, I had a phenomenal memory for names, dates, titles, and assorted movie trivia. In 1956, when I was eighteen, I met a girl who belonged to Cine Universitario, one of Montevideo's larger film societies. She had to explain to me what a film society was all about. My only exposure to serious film appreciation had been a national magazine called *Film*, edited by Jaime Francisco Botet and Homero Alsina Thevenet. It featured several of the country's leading writers and critics. I joined the film society and began working in the archival section, classifying clippings.

I got increasingly involved in the film society movement, serving on the board of directors of the Cine Universitario and as treasurer of the Uruguayan Federation of Film Societies. I traveled back and forth between Montevideo and Buenos Aires relatively frequently on film society business and served as liaison and correspondent for *Tiempo de cine*, an Argentine film magazine put out by Cine-club Núcleo, one of the oldest and most respected film societies in Latin America.

I had seen Fernando Birri's *Throw Me a Dime* at the SODRE festival in 1960 [for background on the SODRE festival, see Handler interview, Part I], and it made a big impression on me. The kind of testimonial documentary that Birri and his students were making at the Documentary Film School of Santa Fe in Argentina opened my eyes to social conditions in Latin America that I had never been aware of before. I had led a pretty sheltered existence. Uruguay during the 1950s was a kind of island, a pseudo-paradise of bourgeois democracy—"the Switzerland of Latin America," it was called. It would be years before the country was swept into the vortex of Latin American revolutionary convulsions. My social involvement with the Cine Universitario, my exposure to a broad range of films through the film society and the SODRE documentary festivals, and my friendship with a number of

(Havana). The interview is dedicated to Alfredo Guevara, founding director of the Cuban Film Institute and close friend of Achugar, who helped overcome the reluctance of the interviewee.

people in Montevideo and Buenos Aires, many of them filmmakers, gradually transformed my way of looking at the world. I began to question the conservative political attitudes I had inherited and started moving to the left. Fernando Birri and one of his associates at the Documentary Film School were very instrumental in that process.

I had been anxious to meet Birri, and when I learned that he and his students were working on a Neorealist-style feature, *Los inundados* [*Flooded Out*, 1962], I arranged to interview him for the Montevideo daily *El País*. We met at a cafe in Buenos Aires. Birri brought one of his colleagues from the Film School along with him—Edgardo Pallero, a former student who was to become the foremost producer of the New Latin American Cinema movement. I had no way of knowing at the time that Pallero and I would become close associates. That meeting in 1960 was the beginning of a lifelong friendship.

Around this same time I was asked to serve as secretary for one of the international juries at the Mar del Plata film festival in Argentina. I had to handle press releases, general public relations, and other practical matters, as well as acting as translator for the members of the jury who spoke English, French, and Italian. In 1960 I was also invited to serve as executive producer for a series of documentary shorts sponsored by the National Office of Tourism. The director of this particular project was Armando Matos, an architect by profession, who was one of the craziest, most creative people I knew in Uruguay at the time. He assembled a very talented group of people and, as a result, rather than the typical tourist fluff, several interesting short films were produced: Carlos Maggi, a playwright and humorist, made *La raya amarilla* [*The Yellow Line*], Alberto Mantaras Rogé made *Punta del Este, ciudad sin horas* [*Punta del Este, City without Hours*], and Feruccio Musitelli made *Piriápolis*. There was also a fourth film, by Miguel Castro.

Other members of my generation whose interests ran parallel to mine either wanted to be film directors or critics. Uruguay was very rich in critics, and if we were poor in film directors it was presumably because the country lacked the population and the resources to support sustained film production. I wanted to challenge that assumption. Unlike most of my peers, I didn't feel the call to creativity. I lacked the urgent longing to express my innermost self through art. I guess the demons within just weren't particularly insistent in my case. I perceived another need—for someone to invest his or her energy in trying to resolve the economic problems that kept other people from exercising their creative talents. I believed that there was potential for national film production in Uruguay, and I wanted to see what I could do to make it happen.

My idea has always been to use distribution as the foundation stone for production. Rather than coming *after* the production stage, a coherent distribution policy should precede it and guarantee its continued existence. I have always thought that, in economic terms, *film should nourish film*. Why not use movies to make movies?

In January of 1962, two events occurred that I see in retrospect as marking the end of my youth: I had a serious accident, and my father died. While producing the *Piriápolis* film, I took a headlong fall and suffered a serious concussion. I lost all sense of taste and smell and was confined to a darkened bedroom for four weeks while I gradually recovered. Meanwhile my father was dying of lung cancer in the next room.

I was the eldest of two brothers so it fell to me to take over the family business. I had to drop out of law school in my fourth year. My father was of working-class extraction, but with his furniture factory he had managed to raise the family's economic status to a very comfortable, solidly middle-class level. He had prepared me to take over for him by putting me in charge of sales after school and during vacations, so I already knew a good deal about the business. Still, I was in the process of deciding that I wanted a very different sort of career. For some time I wore both hats; I managed the furniture business I had inherited from my father and dabbled in film distribution on the side.

I knew that there were lots of important films that were not available in Uruguay, so I decided to "get my feet wet" in the film distribution business by purchasing a print. I bought a feature-length collection of four Chaplin shorts and contracted an established firm to distribute it for me. (Uruguay was such a small country that for all practical purposes, distribution was done with a single print.) When that proved to be a good investment, I purchased Hitchcock's *The Lady Vanishes*, then Kobayashi's *Harakiri*, Bellochio's *Fists in the Pocket*, and works by Jacques Tati. Before long, I was able to set up my own distribution company, Renacimiento [Renaissance] Films, named for my father's first shop.

In 1964 I embarked on my first production venture, as associate producer of *Crónica de un niño solo* [*Chronicle of a Boy Alone*], by a promising young Argentine director, Leonardo Favio. I provided some of the financing in the final stages and took charge of international sales and distribution. I also participated in the production of his second film, *El romance de Aniceto y la Francisca* [*Ballad of Aniceto and Francisca*], made the following year.

That was also my first year on the international film festival circuit. Using furniture company business as a pretext, I made my first trip to Europe and Africa via New York. In Italy I attended the Columbianum at Sestri Levante, which had a special *Rassegna del Cinema Latinoamericano* that year. I particularly remember seeing Glauber Rocha's *Black God, White Devil*, which opened my eyes to what was going on in Brazilian film at the time. At the Cannes festival I met Saúl Yelín, chief of international relations for Cuba's ICAIC. Yelín was at Cannes to promote what I thought was a rather delirious coproduction, Armand Gatti's *El otro Cristóbal* [*The Other Christopher*]. That was my first exposure to Cuban filmmaking; there would be much more.

I returned through Brazil, where I was able to meet a number of Cinema Novo directors and see their work. I also witnessed the coup d'état, which removed President João Goulart from power on 1 April 1964.

Inspired by the Brazilian films I'd seen, I decided, with Pallero's support, to expand Renacimiento's holdings, which up to this point had consisted primarily of European offerings, with some titles from Brazil. Between 1967 and 1971, I arranged for the Uruguayan release of Nelson Pereira dos Santos's *Barren Lives*, Glauber Rocha's *Black God, White Devil, Land in Anguish*, and *Antônio das Mortes*; and Joaquim Pedro de Andrade's *Macunaíma*. Renacimiento was one of the first organizations to try to break down the cultural barriers between Brazil and the rest of Latin America. Though the language barrier is a formidable one, it is not insurmountable because there are other ties between Brazil and the rest of Latin America that transcend linguistic boundaries. Film was a powerful means of reconnecting Brazil to the rest of the continent, and Uruguay was the first country where Cinema Novo became available on a significant scale.

By the early 1970s, Renacimiento's emphasis had broadened to include films from all over Latin America. Uruguay was the first Latin American country to screen Cuban films on a significant scale, as Renacimiento released films like Tomás Gutiérrez Alea's *Death of a Bureaucrat*, Humberto Solás's *Lucía*, and Manuel Octavio Gómez's *The First Charge of the Machete*. The company's holdings eventually grew to eighty titles.

Renacimiento Films served a number of purposes: it provided a material base for a series of efforts, including the production of a number of short films; it helped in our efforts to expand the range of films exhibitors would show; it even served as a repository for the semiclandestine films we would later bring in for the *Marcha* festivals that would eventually become part of the Third World Cinemathèque collection. The company continued to function for a time after I was forced to leave the country in September of 1972 for political reasons. In early 1973 it ceased to exist.

I had continued to see Pallero frequently over the years, even though he was working originally in Santa Fe and later, after 1963, in Brazil for several years producing documentaries for Thomaz Farkas out of São Paulo. When we happened to be in Buenos Aires at the same time, we would often meet at the Cine Club Núcleo. Pallero and I jointly founded another, independent Renacimiento Films distribution company in Buenos Aires. Unfortunately, the competition there was stiffer and our venture less successful than in Uruguay. We naïvely took on some pretty stiff competition—the big distributors that represented U.S. interests, as well as smaller concerns, much more professionally run than we were, which also specialized in an *arte y ensayo* [quality cinema] line. We brought out the Cinema Novo films in Argentina as best we could, but they didn't do as well as in Uruguay. The association with Pallero also brought me into contact with film activity in other parts of Latin America, since he was a kind of human clearinghouse for politically committed filmmaking throughout the continent. He invited me to attend the First Encounter of Latin American Filmmakers at Viña del Mar, Chile, in April 1967. This event, which Pallero helped to organize, was the first *continental* meeting of Latin American filmmakers. In terms of political development, cultural exchange, and the evolution of Latin American film language, the importance of Viña 1967 cannot be exaggerated. The burst of filmmaking activity in a number of countries, and particularly in Chile and Brazil, subsequent to Viña testifies to this.

One of the many benefits of Viña 1967 was the opportunity for more sustained contact and collaboration with Cubans Saúl Yelín and Alfredo Guevara, founding head of ICAIC. I would make my first visit to Cuba that year, traveling with Pallero, to select films for Uruguay's *Marcha* festival. Traditionally, this had been a pretty conventional festival, typically eclectic. I returned from Viña del Mar with prints of Santiago Alvarez's *Now* [1965] and Leon Hirszman's *Maioria absoluta* [*Absolute Majority*, 1964], a plan for distributing Cuban cinema, and a new concept for the *Marcha* festival. *Marcha* was a widely respected newsweekly, strong on both political and cultural coverage, and leftist in its orientation. I approached Hugo Alfaro, the editor in charge of the festival. Judging from what transpired at the Viña del Mar festival, and from the outpouring of political cinema in Europe and elsewhere, I argued, there was evidently an explosion of political filmmaking on a worldwide scale, which was not being seen in Uruguay. Given what *Marcha* stood for, given its international focus and its stance toward Latin American issues, I proposed that it would be much more appropriate for its festival to focus on *cine de combate* from around the world. Alfaro was enthusiastic about the idea, and I immediately began working on the organizational aspects with a small group of *compañeros* that included Mario Handler, José Wainer, Mario Jacob, and Alfaro himself.

The 1967 *Marcha* Festival, with its new focus on political filmmaking from Asia, Africa, and Latin America, was such a resounding success that it had to be repeated. Customarily, the festival was held on a Sunday morning in one of the larger commercial movie houses in downtown Montevideo. Thus, even if the program were a sellout, the films were only seen by a small group of people—the two thousand who could fit in the theater. I wanted to see that kind of programming not on a one-shot basis but in a commercial theater in continuous session. The entire *Marcha* Festival could be viewed in a single morning because the practice was to show clips rather than to screen the films in their entirety. I saw that this exhibition strategy effectively turned the fragments into "trailers," kindling the spectators' avid curiosity to see the films in their entirety. In the context of the *Marcha* Festival, this was only possible for the film that won first prize. This was another reason for undertaking a more sustained exhibition effort.

I happened to hear about a centrally located theater that ran B-grade movies. It was doing badly and available for lease. Its name was particularly appropriate to my first venture into exhibition: the Cine Renacimiento. I took it over on a trial basis and we opened on 14 June 1967, with the films from the *Marcha* festival in continuous session. Later I programmed Leonardo Favio's *Ballad of Aniceto and Francisca* with the Uruguayan short *Elecciones [Elections*, 1966] by Ugo Ulive and Mario Handler. A clip from *Elections* had been part of the *Marcha* festival program. This was the first successful documentary satire of the Uruguayan political system, and the first Uruguayan documentary to be released commercially. That double bill did very well, running for more than four weeks.

We had some other modest box office successes—Rocha's *Black God, White Devil*, Lelouch's *A Man and a Woman* [1966], a Jacques Tati–Charlie Chaplin double bill—all films that I distributed through Renacimiento Films. But when we tried to obtain titles from other distributors, we came up against a de facto boycott. Only Artkino Pictures, the distributor for Soviet and Eastern European cinema, would do business with us. Working with Lirio Rodríguez of that office, we premiered one Soviet and one Bulgarian film.

The shortage of films was not the only problem I faced in managing the Cine Renacimiento. From the beginning my idea had been not only to set up the first *teatro de arte y ensayo* in Uruguay, but also to organize complementary or "parallel" activities there—expositions, lectures, seminars. Writers and journalists like Eduardo Galeano, Mario Benedetti, Carlos María Gutiérrez, and Angel Rama would be invited to speak after the last show on Saturday nights.

For a while it had been clear that the employees of the theater did not approve of the new programming. They had organized themselves into a cooperative long before I had arrived on the scene, and this fact had led me to assume—mistakenly—that we shared similar political sympathies. One evening in October 1967 we organized a benefit in support of Che Guevara's guerrilla campaign in Bolivia. Frightened by this step, the officials of the cooperative saw fit to point out to me that the contract stipulated that the theater be used only for film screenings and that they did not wish to be party to "other kinds of activities." And so began another whole series of problems and tensions. The experiment ended before the year was out. The lease had a clause that gave me a right to get out of the contract, and by March of 1968 I had done so.

That decision did not mean that things slowed down. On the contrary, 1968, 1969, and 1970 were years of redoubled activity in exhibition, distribution, and production. It was a volatile time in Europe and the Americas.

In April of 1968, I traveled to Europe to attend the Cannes and Pesaro festivals. I remember being at the Librairie Maspero in the Latin Quarter with Alfredo Guevara when we heard a great commotion in the street. We found ourselves witnessing the first big confrontation between French students and the police. What would become the famous rebellion of May 1968 began then, at the end of April, in the streets of the Latin Quarter.

From Paris I went to Cannes, where the younger directors were staging a militant protest. Jean Luc Godard, hanging from the curtain on the stage of the Palais de Festival, disrupted the screening and closed down the festival. All those in attendance had to return to Paris by bus or automobile because by this time both plane and rail service had been disrupted. The whole country was at a standstill. It was a euphoric moment.

A few days later, still charged up by the events in France, I went to Italy for the Mostra Internazionale del Nuovo Cinema at Pesaro. The mood there was equally militant, equally explosive. When they screened *The Hour of the Furnaces*, director Fernando Solanas was carried out into the streets on the shoulders of the crowd in a spontaneous demonstration of support. As the festival repeatedly spilled out into the street, there were many confrontations with the police. I remember tearing out telephones and throwing them at the police through the windows of the second story of the festival office. I remember fleeing en masse down the narrow cobbled streets of Pesaro with the police in hot pursuit. Two filmmakers, Carlos Alvarez, a Colombian, and Maurice Capovila from Brazil, were arrested and later released. It was a turbulent and exciting time, with a number of militant Latin American filmmakers in attendance, including Edgardo Pallero and Tomás Gutiérrez Alea and Julio García Espinosa from Cuba. Everywhere, film seemed to be at the forefront of those forces calling for a new social order.

Work on the *Marcha* Festival intensified. The 1967 program had been such a success that there was an immediate demand for distribution outside the capital. We found ourselves transporting the films in person by bus and restaging the festival at various cities and towns in the interior. By 1968 we realized that we had created a national film exhibition circuit for political cinema. That's when we decided it was time to begin production. Mario Handler's documentary short *I Like Students* was produced expressly for the 1968 *Marcha* Festival. Handler had already shot the footage, but he would not have been able to complete the film without the financial assistance he received from *Marcha*. The 1968 *Marcha* Festival was an even greater success than the preceding one. There, as at the First Exhibition of Latin American Documentary Film in Mérida, Venezuela, a few months later, crowds poured forth from the theaters into the streets in spontaneous protest demonstrations inspired by the screening of *I Like Students*. I was in charge of the film's international distribution. It generated considerable interest abroad because this was a period of widespread student unrest and activism. It was one of the first Latin American films to be shown on European television.

The enthusiastic reception of *I like Students* in Uruguay proved to us that, through the dissemination of political films, we had succeeded in creating an audience for that kind of cinema. We then began to think in terms of using that *pequeño gran público* we had generated as a base for short film production. We formed a group with Mario Handler, Marcos Banchero, Eduardo Terra, José Wainer, Daniel Larrosa, Mario Jacob, Walter Tournier, and other independent filmmakers who were just starting out. We used our association with *Marcha* as a kind of promotional base for our efforts to create a national film movement and, thanks to the efforts of Hugo Alfaro in particular, the magazine gave us generous coverage. The Departmento de Cine del Semanario Marcha soon became the Cine Club de Marcha. We continued to collaborate on preparation for the festivals and also initiated numerous supplementary activities.

On 8 November 1969, we inaugurated our own headquarters under the name Cinemateca del Tercer Mundo [Third World Cinemathèque], with a program in homage to Dutch documentarist Joris Ivens, who was present as our guest of honor. By that time our activities greatly exceeded those of a conventional archive or film society. In our own screenings, we always made a point to engage the audience in active debate. We had an archive of perhaps one hundred prints from Latin America and Cuba as well as Europe, the U.S., Africa, and Vietnam. Though the Third World Cinemathèque never officially affiliated itself with any political party, most of us supported the Frente Amplio [Broad Front] and assisted their *comités de base* [grass-roots organizations] in the provinces and in Montevideo, supplying them with films for political education and fund-raising activities. Mario Handler offered a course in filmmaking under the Cinemateca's auspices, enabling a group of aspiring young filmmakers to move from Super-8 to 16mm production. We started publishing a magazine called *Cine del tercer mundo*. We organized a national and international fund-raising campaign to enable us to purchase a moviola, since up to that time Uruguayan films either had to be manually edited or sent to Buenos Aires. With the proceeds from the campaign we bought a camera, a tape recorder, and a second-hand Italian moviola. Our activities thus ranged over the entire gamut—from archival and promotional to distribution and production. In addition, our offices were the local gathering spot for people interested in film and politics and the connections between the two.

One of the films we distributed was *Blood of the Condor*, by the Bolivian director Jorge Sanjinés. The film was a denunciation of forced sterilization in the indigenous communities of the Andes and sparked a national controversy, eventually forcing the U.S. Peace Corps out of Bolivia.

In October of 1970, I traveled to the United States with a print of *Blood of the Condor*, which I had arranged to have screened as part of the San Francisco International Film Festival. After the showing, which caused quite a sensation, and the subsequent discussion, I was approached by three young Argentines, residents of the Bay Area. They knew nothing about the movies, they told me, but they were committed to political change in Latin America and fervently believed that films like *Blood of the Condor*, if made available to U.S. audiences, could make a difference in American attitudes and policy toward Latin America. They were Gino Lofredo and Rodi and Carlos Broullon, and that conversation was the beginning of Tricontinental Film Center, later renamed Unifilm. The organization inspired by that first U.S. screening of *Blood of the Condor* would become the major North American distributor of Third World and political cinema until it shut down in 1983.

Pallero and I had met Sanjinés in Mérida in 1968 and again in Italy the following year when three Latin American features—*Blood of the Condor*, *Macunaíma*, and *The First Charge of the Machete*—were acclaimed at the Venice Festival. The RAI [Italian Radio and Television] was interested in producing a series of films made for television by directors of the emerging New Latin American Cinema movement—"Latin America as Seen by Its Filmmakers"—and they had approached Sanjinés. Pallero and I worked as producers on *The Courage of the People*, the pilot project and, as it turned out, the only film made for this series.

In our work together, we had always maintained our separate specialties clearly defined. In the Renacimiento Films experiment, Pallero would defer to me as the experienced distributor. In our production collaborations, I would bow to him as the expert in the field. Our collaboration on *The Courage of the People* was marked by this same division of labor. Pallero took charge of the production end in Bolivia; I negotiated the intercontinental problems, shuttling back and forth between La Paz, Rome, and Buenos Aires and Montevideo. The project was quite a challenge, since the shooting took place in the remote Siglo XX mines, high in the Andes. Footage was shipped to La Paz by bus or truck, then put on a plane to Buenos Aires, where our friend and colleague Mauricio Berú put it on another plane to Rome. In Rome it was developed and then sent back along the reverse route. Pallero was responsible for this minor miracle of executive production. The shooting was finished in less than two months—record time for such a project. Because Pallero covered his end so effectively, I was able to continue to do the other half dozen things I was involved in at the time— overseeing the distribution companies in Montevideo and Buenos Aires, flying to Europe to attend festivals and buy and sell films, helping manage the Third World Cinemathèque. Once finished, *The Courage of the People*—a documentary reconstruction of a massacre of miners and their families by government troops in 1967, in my opinion Sanjinés's best film—caused great consternation within the ranks of RAI, which cut certain sections and delayed the film's international release and distribution for years.

As the political situation in Uruguay became tenser, the Third World Cinemathèque increasingly became a target of official repression. Officially, there was no censorship in Uruguay, but the military began to intervene to ban a specific film in a specific region. Sometimes they would close down the screening; other times they would seize the print. Then our offices were sacked. By April 1972 our activities had been brought to a virtual standstill. In May, Eduardo Terra and I were arrested, imprisoned, and tortured. I was released after sixty days in response to an international campaign on my behalf. I remained in Montevideo for two months, but when the security forces came looking for me once again in September, I went into exile in Buenos Aires. Eduardo Terra was not released until several years later.

Many prints belonging to the Third World Cinemathèque were seized and destroyed, but others were recovered and smuggled out of the country in due time. We also managed to recover some of the confiscated equipment. But much was lost. More *compañeros* were arrested as the repression intensified and many others decided to leave. This exodus grew after the military coup of June 1973, a kind of underreported prelude to the Chilean coup the following September, which provoked much greater repercussions in the international press.

Despite the shutting down of the Cinemateca del Tercer Mundo, the severity of the repression, the loss of equipment, and the growing number of exiles, production continued for several months. While I was in prison, I had an idea for a film. One of the other political prisoners had written an illustrated short story for his young daughter explaining his situation metaphorically by using animals in the jungle. The result was very poignant and effective. I thought it should be filmed as an animated cartoon.

Upon my release I talked the idea over with Walter Tournier and other *compañeros*. Working from Buenos Aires, I financed and produced *En la selva hay mucho por hacer* [*In the Jungle There's a Lot to Do*, 1973]. The film took thirteen months to make. It was a very ambitious effort by filmmakers who had no prior experience with animation or 35mm. Made semiclandestinely, it was finished in early 1973 and even had one or two screenings at one of the Uruguayan film societies before the coup d'état. It has since been viewed around the world, and a book has been published in several countries.

There was no "Uruguayan cinema in exile" to compare with the impressive output of the filmmakers from Chile who were scattered throughout Europe and the Americas when General Pinochet overthrew

Allende. Exiled Uruguayan filmmakers now play an active role in countries like Venezuela, Peru, Mexico, and even Australia, making films that reflect the realities, interests, and problems of their adoptive countries. I don't want to overestimate our accomplishments in Uruguay, but I don't want to underestimate them, either. Our work demonstrated the validity of using distribution as a springboard to production. But our production was limited to documentary shorts, since a country of barely three million people does not have the resources to establish a feature-film industry. We successfully brought films into Uruguay that otherwise would not have been available there, and with those films we built an audience for our own documentary film production. We trained filmmakers and obtained equipment that had never existed in the country before. If we had not fallen prey to such severe repression, we would have continued our work on multiple fronts, and who knows what we could have accomplished. We had the foundation well laid.

I went to Venezuela in 1974 to attend a Reunion of Latin American Filmmakers at which the Comité de Cineastas de América Latina [Latin American Filmmakers' Committee] was founded. While there, I was offered a job with Dicimoveca [Distribuidora Cinematográfica Venezolana Compañía Anónima]. This was a 35mm distribution company founded by Edmundo Aray and Carlos Rebolledo the preceding year. They began by organizing a Cuban Film Week, which had considerable impact in Venezuela. At the time I joined them, they were beginning to acquire other Latin American titles. I brought several along with me—including Raymundo Gleyzer's *Los traidores* [*The Traitors*, 1973] and Miguel Littín's *The Jackal of Nahueltoro*. We obtained Patricio Guzmán's *El primer año* [*The First Year*, 1971] from another source, as well as several Brazilian films. With these we organized a Latin American Film Week.

I thought that my role should be to stimulate distribution in other parts of the country. Until that point, Dicimoveca's radius had been principally Caracas, Maracaibo, and occasionally Mérida. Its approach was to organize screenings in rented commercial theaters on a short-term basis. I saw the opportunity to expand its distribution network to student groups, workers' organizations, and *casas de cultura*. I began talking with Sergio Trabuco, an exiled Chilean friend who came to Venezuela in late 1975, about possibilities for 16mm distribution. We founded Palcine, a sort of 16mm sister company to Dicimoveca, from whose collection we struck a number of 16mm prints. We added many new films from other sources so that within a year's time we had accumulated approximately 130 titles. Some of these had been salvaged from the Third World Cinemathèque; other prints were obtained directly from the filmmakers. We were able to add sectors that Dicimoveca could not handle—the university circuits, for example—as well as offer new films to Dicimoveca clientele. We obtained a 16mm projector so that we could offer projection services to groups that did not have access to such equipment.

Palcine offered the most complete list of Latin American films available anywhere. No European company, not even Tricontinental/Unifilm in the United States, had as many Latin American titles as we did. We really established alternative cinema as a cultural presence in Venezuela, through the number and importance of the films we carried, and through the number of screenings we generated, not just in Caracas but throughout the country. In statistical terms, our record was quite impressive. Yet even though we had greatly expanded the distribution radius, we eventually faced the same dead-end as Dicimoveca and other similar film distribution companies—even Unifilm in the United States, despite its comparatively vast and affluent market. On top of overhead costs like the producers' percentage, office rent, staff salaries, film shipping and inspection costs, catalogue printing, and all the rest, we had to add a minimal percentage toward expanding our holdings and replacing existing prints as they wore out. We also had to keep our prices as low as possible, given the kind of distribution we were involved in. Since the films we were distributing do not have an unlimited market, we reached the inevitable point where our clients had exhausted our offerings. (The happy exception to this scenario in Latin America is Mexico's Zafra, an alternative distributor that has carved a space for itself outside the national distribution monopoly *and* managed to hold its own despite repeated currency devaluations.) Palcine folded in late 1979. Almost all our prints remained in Venezuela to be used by organizations like FEVEC [Venezuela Federation of Cultural Centers], the University of the Andes, and various solidarity committees.

By that time, however, I was no longer directly involved. In the late 1970s it became clear that the New Latin American cinema, if it were to be properly disseminated, needed a permanent European base. Alfredo Guevara, head of the Cuban Film Institute at the time, proposed that I take charge of their sales and distribution in Western Europe. The proposal made sense in professional and political terms. It was also appealing on a purely personal level, since life in Caracas was becoming quite a strain. In May of 1977, I moved to Europe.

My task was to develop a European market for Latin American cinema and thus generate funds to finance continued film production in Latin America. I chose Spain as my base of operations. After Franco's death, the country had begun the transition to democratic government. With the demise of the censorship policies that had kept our films from Spanish audiences, the time was ripe to import Latin American films on a large scale. Not long after my arrival, I organized a week-long Cuban film festival to mark the opening of the Alphaville cinema complex in Madrid. The festival then traveled to Barcelona and Valencia. My role at this point was not distributor but sales agent. As a result of the festival, three feature films were picked up for Spanish distribution.

I set up a company called Cinal [Cinematografía de América Latina] in Madrid, and from that headquarters I traveled throughout Western Europe as a sales agent for Cuban films. West Germany proved to be the best market; national television bought the largest package of Cuban films ever sold to a single buyer. I also sold films from Cuba and other Latin American countries in France, England, and Switzerland. A large percentage of these sales were for television.

By 1980, the Cubans had set up a sales organization capable of handling the other European countries, enabling me to concentrate my energies on Spain. I expanded the distribution side of Cinal, acquiring quality films from other European countries as well as a number of Hollywood re-releases like *The African Queen* and *Duel in the Sun*. With the inauguration of Felipe González's government, the Spanish national television network, TVE, came into the hands of genuinely cultured and committed people who have transformed national programming priorities. Where Hollywood products once dominated by an overwhelming margin and Latin American material was nonexistent, now the percentage of U.S. imports has diminished markedly while European and Third World cinemas have a significant presence on Spanish television screens. Films like *Lucía, The Jackal of Nahueltoro, Alsino and the Condor* have been shown on the leading channel during prime time, introduced by their directors, to audiences of at least five million viewers. Clearly, this is a cultural as well as an economic transaction.

Perhaps the cultural payoff is more important than the economic one, because the truth is that a plan that looked like a breeze on paper took many years to implement and perhaps was never fully realized. Latin American films sold relatively well, but they did not bring particularly high prices. Yet to operate at all, I had to maintain a basic infrastructure—office, telephones, staff, a travel budget—and these expenditures meant that the amount available for reinvestment in Latin American film production was proportionally diminished. Cinal's collection eventually numbered about eighty films. The audience for political cinema decreased in Spain as the democratic process advanced, converting the distribution of Nicaraguan newsreels, for example, or some of the Cuban and Chilean material, into an uphill struggle.

In the meantime, conditions in Latin America have been drastically transformed. Democratic government has returned to Argentina, Brazil, and also Uruguay. On January 30, 1985, I was allowed to return to my country after nearly twelve and a half years of exile. It is impossible to describe what I felt.

Two months later I returned once more, with Argentine filmmaker Jorge Denti, to shoot *Trece años y un día* [*Thirteen Years and a Day*], a documentary about the release of the country's political prisoners that is structured around an interview with writer and Tupamaro leader Mauricio Rosencraft, one of the hundreds freed. Since that time, I have been shuttling back and forth at a crazy pace between Madrid and the River Plate, and I plan to take up residence in Montevideo shortly.

Throughout my exile, I have maintained close ties with Uruguay in a variety of ways—by sending Spanish films to the Uruguayan Cinemateca, by securing film scholarships to Spain for Uruguayan students, by sending funds to support production. The Cinemateca recently completed the only feature-length film to be produced in Uruguay in the past five years. I negotiated its sale to TVE [Spanish Television] without covering my normal commission. I have recently secured TVE funding for two Latin American film projects—a feature-length documentary on liberation theology throughout Latin America to be directed by the Brazilian Geraldo Sarno, and a six-part history of Latin America based on the writings of Uruguayan essayist Eduardo Galeano, with segments to be directed by Tomás Gutiérrez Alea from Cuba, Jorge Sanjinés from Bolivia, Fernando Solanas from Argentina, Brazilian Geraldo Sarno, Mexican Paul Leduc, and Chilean Patricio Guzmán. I expect to dedicate the next three or four years to this latter project, a long-cherished dream of mine on the verge of becoming a reality.

I recently came across some interesting lines written by Hegel more than 150 years ago: "America is the land of the future. . . . All those who are weary of the historical museum that is old Europe long for this new land." Some say that the worldwide transformation of the mass media threatens the very survival of Third World cinema, yet in some senses the perspective for Latin American image-makers has never been more encouraging. The "third industrial revolution" being ushered in by the electronic media will produce different repercussions in different regions. When I left Uruguay thirteen years ago, there were one hundred movie theaters in Montevideo, a city of 150,000. Today only twenty-five remain. This tendency will continue. In the not-too-distant future, film theaters, like opera houses and concert halls, may open on a seasonal basis only. The introduction of home video equipment does not make film viewers disappear; it simply encourages them to change armchairs. What they once viewed in a theatrical space they can now see in their living rooms. The principal fact to keep in mind is that more films are being viewed, more images consumed, than ever before. In Latin America, there is an important future for alternative film and video distribution, as activity in Central America, Chile, Argentina, and Brazil clearly illustrates. In Brazil, for example, the churches currently control thirteen thousand alternative media outlets. The future belongs to the young people working in video, a medium that is cheap, versatile, and almost infinitely recyclable. The challenge before all of us is to adapt our mode of expression and our mode of production to these new technologies.

The recent enlargement of the Latin American Filmmakers' Committee to include representatives from all Latin American countries as well as the "clandestine nation" of Hispanics in the United States, the continued growth of MECLA, the Latin American Film Market, the recent founding of the New Latin American Cinema Foundation and of the Federation of Alternative Latin American Film Distributors, the organization of new festivals and the expansion of the annual Havana Festival of New Latin American Cinema to include video as well as retrospectives of American independent and African cinema—all these developments indicate our determination to meet the challenges that lie before us.

Chapter 18

Enrique Colina
(Cuba)

The Film Critic on Prime Time

Plate 22. Enrique Colina. Photo courtesy Dirección Extensión Cinematográfica

Cuban film critic Enrique Colina, whose articles have appeared frequently in the pages of *Cine Cubano*, is the host of a popular television show called "Twenty-four Times a Second," now in its second decade.

Jorge Silva's interview with Enrique Colina originally appeared in *Ojo al cine*, no. 2 (1976). This version is excerpted from Julianne Burton's translation, which was first published in *Jump/Cut: A Review of Contemporary Cinema*, no. 22 (May 1980).

Q: Could you describe your work as a film critic?

A: I do a prime-time program about film called "Twenty-four Times a Second," which appears on national television every Saturday night. This show, which we've been doing for several years now, attempts to establish a dialectical relationship with the films currently being shown around the country.

Q: What is the theoretical or conceptual basis of film criticism in Cuba and particularly of your work with the program "Twenty-four Times a Second"?

A: To discuss the theoretical assumptions behind this work, it would be useful initially to refer to the law that founded the Cuban Institute of Cinematic Art and Industry [ICAIC] and that was the first cultural legislation of the Revolution. One of its fundamental clauses cites the need to create a national cinema capable of bringing together the best of our cultural and revolutionary traditions. The law also stresses the need to decolonize our country's movie screens, thus signaling the need for a kind of informational and cultural orientation that would contribute, along with national film production, to the intellectual and cinematic development of our people. Cuban film criticism in general and our program in particular derive from this premise.

Before the revolutionary government came to power in 1959, more than 70 percent of the foreign films exhibited in our country came from the United States. Currently we exhibit between 120 and 130 North American films annually, but in totally different proportion. Today 50 percent of our programming comes from the socialist sector and another 50 percent from the capitalist sector. Obvious reasons of quantity, quality, and the need for information (because we do not exist in isolation from the rest of the world) compel us to program films from the capitalist sector; but in doing so, we must question the values implicit in many of these films. Filmic taste, which we are compelled to satisfy, exists in proportion to and in accordance with a country's level of cultural development. Our general level of cultural development has risen significantly in the past seventeen years, but this is a slow and complex process.

At one point, we were importing some films that bore no resemblance to the kind of movies we sought to make ourselves. For lack of a better term, we can call these "entertainment" films. The very conditions of our national cultural development mean that many sectors still equate "recreation" with these "entertainment" films. By applying a set of standards (which is not always absolute), we can ensure that the films we import are free from fascist or pornographic tendencies. Since these films are cultural expressions particular to the society that produced them, however, the expression of that society's values is implicit in their content. What kind of response do we provide to this kind of cinema, since we choose to continue making it available in Cuba? We confront it head-on, but without making the kind of "value judgment" that unintelligent film criticism makes.

Such criticism is primarily interested in addressing the critics' personal opinions while concealing the process by which those conclusions are arrived at. Such criticism deprives the reader of the "creative" participation that is in itself the greatest educational possibility and intellectual stimulus that film criticism can offer to national and personal cultural development, especially on a continent like ours.

This is why we never make value judgments on our television program. Instead, we deal with the factors that account for a film's success with the public. We begin to question these, showing the viewers how the visual material is structured, and questioning everything that is implicit and difficult to define. Many entertainment films only marginally possess or are *apparently* exempt from any type of ideological or political meaning. In fact, they all have an ideological dimension that we must point out and criticize, since we are part of a society that is trying to transform all inherited values. So we especially emphasize how ideological messages are conveyed directly or indirectly through film. We try to perform a kind of aesthetic and ideological "de-montage,"[1] taking apart what the filmmaker has assembled to reveal the film's inner workings.

We are living through a process that requires our people to seek out original, creative solutions. Once it has achieved liberation, independence from imperialism, and genuine sovereignty, a country like Cuba—which was underdeveloped before the Revolution and has limited resources—has to build socialism under very difficult conditions. To find the solutions that correspond to our limited material possibilities, we must cultivate our analytic and reflective capacities.

So we feel that our work in the field of film has what we might call a meta-goal: to enable people to take a more critical, more reflective and analytical attitude. We strive to encourage people to take on the kind of serious intellectual effort that is the precondition of that state of readiness that any transformation of reality requires. Our program thus goes beyond the realm of film culture through its use of film as a means of stimulating critical thought.

In film, messages are always conveyed through expressive forms. A filmmaker's choice of forms is conditioned by the ideological perspective from which he or she views the reality that he or she wants to reflect in aesthetic terms. So we put great emphasis on filmic language. Some programs, for example, are totally dedicated to camera style, to the way things are conveyed visually, to the expressive means used to create a certain atmosphere to indirectly transmit a particular message. We try to raise awareness about cinematic language to help people see how these messages are put together and how what is apparently lacking in meaning does, in fact, convey meaning—and an ideological one at that.

We also try to increase people's understanding of everything having to do with the distribution network, the commercialization of film as merchandise, and the political and ideological—as well as artistic—implications that this market imposes on the film product. We show how certain aesthetic effects derive from mercantile factors.

Q: You referred earlier to an ideological and aesthetic de-montage process, which exposes underlying mechanisms of consumer cinema. How do you achieve this?

A: In the case of a "thriller"—let's take *Bullit*[2] for example—we might take the hero as our point of departure. Who is he? What characterizes the hero of this kind of film? In most cases, such men are bandits. Let's try to define the particular expressive devices that prevent us from making a moral judgment about the hero when we see the film and instead lead us to identify with him in a positive way. We might try to do a de-montage of the personal life of the character, for example, of his relationship to women or of his personal values, analyzing his social behavior and how this person relates to particular institutions like the state. We would show how the film never questions the fact that it is situating the spectator in a Manichaean world of good and evil.

The program would illustrate such a process and also trace the forerunners of the particular genre in question—Hollywood *film noir*, for example. We use sequences from other films to demonstrate the ideological base of this particular conception of a character or hero. We might also refer to literary antecedents in our attempt to explain why this particular kind of hero is presented as entertainment in a capitalist society and to articulate what meaning this form of entertainment might have. And so we look at how a very banal story has an ideological backdrop that is clearly symptomatic of an entire social structure, one based on the exploitation of one human being by another. Starting from an isolated and apparently inoffensive phenomenon, you see, one can arrive at the de-montage of an entire social, political, and cultural context. This context accounts for the fact that these products are generated both as a kind of merchandise—and this is what's important—as the expression of an entire social system.

We feel that it is dangerous to set up value judgments. To say to people that a film is "good" or "bad" is like slamming a door in their faces if, in fact, our judgment goes contrary to their own taste. And taste is an essential factor of personality. So we try to encourage the spectator to take a critical stance. We try not to impose our own conclusions, though they are implicit in the de-montage technique; we prefer that they grow naturally out of the debate. We insist on the fact that we are not the sole purveyors of the truth. Whoever likes the film should continue to see it but should keep all these factors in mind. Spectators may continue to like a film even after this kind of analysis, but they are now conscious of the film's alienating mechanisms and they are armed to defend themselves.

Our goal is to develop the analytical tools that will permit spectators to defend themselves against cultural penetration. We are specialists; we've had the privilege of studying; but the great masses of our continent have not had access to the means of analysis that we have at our disposal. This is why they are practically defenseless against outside cultural penetration. We feel that an important function for the progressive intellectual is to contribute to the development of our own people. This critical awareness will serve the spectator and the film critic not only in viewing film and television but also in their lived experience, allowing them to recognize inconsistencies given them in the image of their situation, of their country, of their continent. Because this image is also the result of a certain class-determined perspective that dominates the mass media. We want knowledge to be a defensive as well as an offensive weapon.

Notes

1. *Desmontaje* might be translated as "deconstruction," but it seemed preferable to avoid associations with the critical methodology of that same name.

2. A fast-paced crime drama directed by Peter Yates and starring Steve McQueen (1968).

Chapter 19

Julio García Espinosa
(Cuba)

Theory and Practice of Film and Popular Culture in Cuba

Plate 23. Julio García Espinosa (with hat) greets one of his Vietnamese hosts during the filming of *Third World, Third World War*. Photo courtesy ICAIC.

In 1981 Julio García Espinosa relinquished his post as vice-minister of culture in charge of music and spectacles to succeed Alfredo Guevara as the head of the Cuban Film Institute (ICAIC). He was a founding member of ICAIC, and had been a vice-president of that organization from its establishment in 1959. He began working in radio and theater at an early age before going abroad to study filmmaking at Rome's Centro Sperimentale in 1952. A short Neorealist feature, *El mégano* (*The Charcoal Worker*, 1954) was produced collaboratively under his direction upon his return. During the guerrilla war, García Espinosa headed the insurgent film unit Cine Rebelde. More important than his four documentaries and five feature-length films has been his collaboration and consultation on many of ICAIC's most outstanding

244   Julio García Espinosa

Q: After nearly twenty years with the Cuban Film Institute [ICAIC], you were recently named to a vice-ministerial post in the Ministry of Culture, in charge of music, variety shows, nightclub acts and circuses. Surely that office is without counterpart anywhere else in the world. Could you give some background on the genesis of such an unusual post?

A: In the Ministry of Culture, which was founded in late 1976 but didn't really begin to function until 1977, five areas of cultural activity were initially defined and put under the supervision of a separate vice-minister: filmmaking, book publishing, artistic education and amateur activities, plastic arts and design, and, finally, a fifth sector comprising music, theater, dance, variety shows, and nightclub acts (which we designate by the term *"espectáculos"*), and circuses. I have always had a special interest in music and began working in theater at a very young age, so I was asked to take charge of the organization and administration of these and related activities.

Under Armando Hart, who had served for many years as minister of education before being named minister of culture, we began by trying to define some basic concepts related to artistic activity. It seemed to us that the entire field of culture had first to be defined as part of either the productive or the service sector. Education, for example, is one of the most widely recognized services, always offered free of charge in our country and never expected to generate revenue. Public health is another free service. Both of these areas are high on the national list of priorities, just as are the most important productive sectors: the sugar and tobacco industries, for example. But somehow artistic and cultural activities seemed to inhabit a gray zone between these two poles, without the prestige or the urgency of the other service and productive areas.

After separating out the service areas—artistic education, amateur movements, museums—which were to be provided free of charge, we

projects, including Humberto Solás's *Lucía* and Patricio Guzmán's *The Battle of Chile*. Outside Cuba, García Espinosa is best known for his provocative theoretical essay, "For an Imperfect Cinema." A collection of his theoretical pieces appeared in Havana in 1979 (Editorial Letras Cubanas) under the title *Una imagen recorre el mundo (An Image Encircles the Globe)*.

Julianne Burton interviewed Julio García Espinosa in Cuba in 1977 and again at the Third Havana Festival in December 1981. An abbreviated version appeared in *Studies in Latin American Popular Culture* 1 (1982), under the title "Folk Music, Circuses, Variety Shows and Other Endangered Species: A Conversation with Julio García Espinosa." The version included in this volume appeared in *Quarterly Review of Film Studies* 7, no. 4 (Fall 1982). A Spanish version appeared as "El reto de la masividad y la cultura popular" in *Areito* 8, no. 4 (Fall 1982). This interview is dedicated to the memory of Lourdes Casal, a courageous and committed Cuban-American scholar.

redefined the five areas of artistic production, separating music from what we call the *"artes escénicas"* [stage arts]. In contrast to the artistic services, these productive areas share an industrial component that it would be misleading and false to ignore, though the recognition of their capacity to generate revenue by no means implies the subordination of artistic activity to commercial ends.

According to this new definition, whereas all the other vice-ministers had a single area of artistic production in their charge, I had two—music and the "stage arts." Given the difficulty of adequately attending to such a large sphere, it was agreed that theater and dance would become the province of a new vice-ministry, and I would retain the rest. My official title is *viceministro de música y espectáculos*. *"Espectáculos"* covers everything from block parties and regional fairs to variety shows and nightclub acts. And of course I can't neglect to mention circuses, once the only form of organized cultural expression accessible to rural Cubans, and still an important one.

Q: It is probably hard for people who have not visited Cuba to comprehend just how important a role nightclub entertainment plays in Cuba's cultural life. Cabarets can be found in the most unlikely places, and the amount of amateur activity is staggering. This is the one form of cultural expression that most tourists see without fail, yet until very recently, it was also the cultural sector least changed by the revolutionary process.

A: The Cuban people's devotion to the cabaret tradition has a long and largely hidden history—hidden because it was never considered a worthy area of research. It has to do with the importance and dynamism of music and dance in Cuba's cultural life, with the urban emphasis of our culture, with our perennial openness to foreign influences (not least among them Meyer Lansky and other American gangster types who included sumptuous casinos and cabarets when they designed some of Havana's most luxurious hotels). In addition to the leading cabarets in hotels like the Nacional or the Capri, and Tropicana, the most famous nightclub of them all, there are at least fifty others in Havana alone. Many of our best singers and musicians, people like Benny Moré and Bola de Nieve, not only got their start but built most of their following performing in such clubs.

The sheer number of nightclubs throughout the country confers a mass status on this form of cultural expression. This fuels our commitment to search out and preserve the most culturally valid aspects of this tradition—not by "elevating" it to the level of ballet or opera or other "high cultural" forms, but by cultivating its own specificity and authenticity. Just how to go about discovering the artistic and cultural merits of a nightclub show—that's the problem we confront.

We believe that the challenge of mass culture is greater now than in any other period in history, that art forms that are genuinely popular and modern are necessarily and inevitably a mass phenomenon, and that in most of the world, unfortunately, it is the business executive rather than the artist who is addressing this challenge.

How does a society produce mass art that is still art? This question is relevant in most parts of the world today, but in the Cuban case in particular, the masses have gained an access to social life that prompts them to demand mass rather than elitist art forms. In their very origin, *espectáculos* have a mass base. They are thus obligated to confront this "challenge of massivity" and, in so doing, can both reaffirm the cultural legitimacy of that form of expression and indicate a possible pathway toward the reconciliation of artistic activity and the conditions of modern life.

Q: How, concretely, do you propose to go about this?

A: Just as bourgeois art has always had its vanguard, so must popular art. Like all vanguard movements, this one will be limited to minorities at first, but from the beginning those who break new ground must search for ways to cease being a vanguard and integrate themselves into a mass movement.

Take the New Latin American Cinema movement, for example. We cannot claim that this is the kind of filmmaking with which the masses in Latin America feel most identified today—not for deficiencies in content, style, or quality, but because of the practical obstacle of lack of access to commercial movie theaters.

Recently I asked a leading Italian film critic how many worthwhile films are produced in the entire world in a year's time. No more than forty or fifty, he answered. How then can we combat the thousands of alienating, dehumanizing, or simply mediocre films made each year for commercial gain? We have the responsibility of generating artistic products that have an impact on the population to counter the enormous quantity of alienating products that bombard that population from elsewhere. This is an impossible task unless we can develop new concepts and norms of artistic productivity that enable us to overcome the limitations imposed by underdevelopment.

In making documentaries, for example, we have to distinguish between those destined for conventional movie theaters and those designed for another kind of viewing space, because the viewing space inevitably conditions the kind of films viewed there. Informational and analytical documentaries should be presented within the workday environment, as a prolongation of it. Only when we offer films that posit a rupture with the workday environment, enriching it through entertainment and pleasure, which will give the workers renewed strength to contend with what awaits them outside the cinema, should we place our film products in conventional theaters, in direct competition with more commercial fare.

And in this competition, we have to resist the temptation to wage our fight with the same arms used by our competitors. In 1969, when I wrote "For an Imperfect Cinema," the Cuban film industry had recently produced a number of films that drew international recognition for their technical and artistic excellence—Tomás Gutiérrez Alea's *Memories of Underdevelop-*

ment, Humberto Solás's *Lucía*, the documentaries of Santiago Alvarez. Such widespread acclaim for the mastery that Cuban filmmakers had begun to demonstrate in their craft seemed to me to pose some urgent questions about what we intended to do with that craft and that art form.

For me, one of the key problems is the question of *la técnica*, which means both technology and technique. Today the technical aspect of filmmaking holds an enormous fascination. Most spectators are conditioned to be more responsive to a work's technical dimension than to its artistic qualities. And this is just as true of a piano concerto as it is of a feature film. But the technical aspect of a work of art should always be a means to an end rather than an end in itself. We are not opposed to using the most modern technologies, as long as we have the money to acquire them, but we have to be able to distinguish those that are most useful to and consistent with our own course of development. What I proposed in "For an Imperfect Cinema" was not poorly made films that reveled in their own lack of polish, but a kind of filmmaking whose modernity, relevance, and worth were a function of those elements that constitute the essence of artistic expression. The essay was motivated by what I saw as an urgent need to point out the dangers of technique for technique's sake.

Q: To what degree was that essay the direct outgrowth of the experience of filming *Las aventuras de Juan Quin Quin* [*The Adventures of Juan Quin Quin*, 1967]?

A: The experience of that film is directly responsible for several areas of deliberation in the essay. Mass versus popular culture, and process versus analysis are two of the most important.

In *The Adventures of Juan Quin Quin*, I wanted to work with genuinely popular characters. At the time the film was made, the leading folk hero in our culture was the guerrilla fighter. A traditional approach would have inserted this figure into a more lofty genre—the epic, in all probability. But I wanted to pair it with a "minor" genre, one that has been customarily devalued: the adventure story. This strategy seemed almost heretical at the time, because the act of consigning a semisacred figure to a picaresque adventure yarn would be seen as irreverent. From my point of view, however, adventure stories and other popular genres were the vehicles that offered the highest potential for genuine communication with a mass audience.

A second, related operation involved conceiving the film not only as a critical reflection of a given reality, but also as a critical reflection on cinema itself. Choosing the adventure story, for example, meant not only calling into question the reality I intended to depict through that genre, but also questioning the genre itself. Obviously, certain elements must be retained. The process of critique cannot be so sweeping that it obliterates the genre altogether, because the artist would be cutting out from under himself the common ground that ensures communication with the popular audience. Through the experience of *Juan Quin Quin*, it became clear to me for the first time that it is in fact impossible to question a given reality without questioning the particular genre you select or inherit to depict that reality. Normally, the artist's critique of the genre is done independently, and only the results of the process are shared with the viewer. The challenge I faced was to discover how this critical process itself, rather than simply the results of that process, could be integrated into the film.

In my former capacity as head of artistic production at ICAIC, and as consultant [*asesor*] to a number of Cuban filmmakers, I have participated in carrying out similar operations with a number of films. *Girón* [*Bay of Pigs*, Manuel Herrera, 1972], for example, was clearly inscribed within the war films genre, but by using Brechtian and other distancing techniques, we not only re-created historical situations and events, but also called the conventions of Hollywood-style heroism into question as well. Oscar Valdés's *El extraño caso de Rachel K* [*The Strange Case of Rachel K*, 1973] sets out to present a murder mystery/detective story while offering a critique of that genre. In this case, unfortunately, the director stopped in midstream; his film is fully convincing neither as a detective story nor as a critique of that genre. Enrique Pineda Barnet's *Mella* [1975] is another example of a largely unsuccessful effort to implant a similar approach. This period biography of a national hero uses a number of self-reflexive devices to call attention to the difficulties and contradictions of such an undertaking. Though some of these strategies are quite brilliant, their compound effect saturates the film and dilutes its impact.

Two of the most critically acclaimed examples of this approach are Sergio Giral's *El otro Francisco* [*The Other Francisco*, 1974] and Sara Gómez's *One Way or Another* [1974/1977]. I feel that Giral's film is engaged in a less honest operation than the others I have mentioned because it pretends to adapt a nineteenth-century abolitionist novel from a twentieth-century perspective. I would have preferred to see the critical analysis performed with greater spectator collaboration, with more juxtapositions between the novel's version of slave conditions and what we know today about the conditions of the period.

Since all these critical operations require new approaches to film directing, however, we cannot expect flawless results every time. Films built on the consecrated conventions of traditional dramaturgy are more likely to attain technical "perfection" than those necessarily "imperfect" attempts to challenge established conventions and search out new approaches.

Sara Gómez's *One Way or Another* is perhaps the best example of the trade-off between sterile technical perfection and the enrichment and innovation of an experimental work that is much less fully realized on a technical level. In this totally unconventional "love story," Sara opted for

Plate 24. An example of "imperfect cinema": Sergio Giral's *El otro Francisco*.
Photo courtesy ICAIC.

the second alternative with admirable, even inspiring, results. Unfortunately, her premature death from acute asthma prevented her from further developing her impressive talents.

Q: One of the things that often surprises foreigners who view Cuban films for the first time is their stylistic eclecticism, the way they freely draw on the most disparate cultural traditions, blending them into a synthesis that is uniquely Cuban. Within the Cuban cultural context, music seems to be the archetype of this process.

A: Cubans are an eminently musical people. Ours is also a very open culture for a variety of reasons—not simply because we're an island, but because of our particular geographical position as gateway to the Caribbean basin, which has been colonized and populated by people from so many different cultures, and because of the particular ethnic blending that has taken place in Cuba. Our forms of cultural expression have always been open to exchange and interaction with foreign cultural forms, without relinquishing their own particular flavor.

Ours is, as I've said, a musical culture; but whereas the Italians, for example, are a singing people, we Cubans are a dancing people. This does not mean that we don't produce excellent singers, but simply that, for us in general, dancing comes more naturally than singing.

I think that Cuba and Brazil are the only two countries in the world today where collective dance retains such a degree of cultural vitality. In Brazil it's the samba; in Cuba, the conga. Both are dances that involve great numbers of people dancing—singly, not in pairs—to the same rhythm.

The conga has two parts: the *paseo* [promenade] or *desplazamiento* [displacement], and the *evolución coreográfica*, where people display more individualized styles or movements while dancing in a fixed space. No Cuban can resist the conga rhythm; it moves us more than any other. People are capable of covering miles and miles in the *paseo* phase without tiring. In the years before the Revolution, our politicians would often use this rhythm to gather a crowd for their rallies. They'd send a sound truck through the popular neighborhoods and people would follow it like the Pied Piper of Hamlin. They had no idea where they were being led, but they just had to drop everything and follow that rhythm.

Q: Your film *Cuba baila* [*Cuba Dances*, 1960], made just after the Revolution and depicting, in microcosmic and broadly comic terms, class and generational conflict in prerevolutionary Havana, has a marvelous scene like the one you have just described. It seems that your fascination with the role of music in Cuban culture is a constant in your work; you've just chosen different ways to address the issue. In your present post, you are in a unique position to influence that musical tradition. How do you define that task, and what are some of the approaches you are using?

A: We are trying to break down the barriers separating "high brow" and popular music. For example, we staged a concert in a theater normally reserved for *espectáculos*. We put the national symphony orchestra on stage, seating them at random among the members of a jazz band and a group of folk musicians.

One of the themes of the concert was the *danzón*, a complex of popular music that harks back to the European classical tradition and that has given rise to a rich variety of other Cuban musical forms: the *danzonete*, the mambo, the chachacha. We had the folk orchestra play a *danzón*, followed by the jazz band playing a mambo. Finally, the symphonic orchestra played a mambo for symphony orchestra and jazz band. In this union of apparently separate forms, the musical integrity of these distinct traditions became obvious. Members of the audience who might prefer classical to popular music or vice versa found themselves reacting simply to the music itself, without conventional compartmentalizations.

We organized another concert with a very popular Afro-Cuban group, Los Irakere, and our most famous composer for classical guitar and contemporary music, Leo Brouwer. The program featured very popular contemporary music combined with compositions like the classical "Concierto de Aranjuez." Pieces that would ordinarily never appear on the same program assumed a remarkably organic unity.

Now Brouwer is helping us to organize a show called "Concert in B Major," featuring composers whose names begin with "B": Bach, Beethoven, the Beatles, Benny Moré, Brouwer himself—another strategy for subverting compartmentalization. The Irakere group is about to do a concert in which each of its members will be paired with a counterpart from a traditional folk group. We hope that this will prove to be another means of breaking new ground musically.

Q: Cuba is sometimes referred to as a *país de rumberos* [nation of rumba dancers]. What is the derivation of this expression?

A: Many people think that *rumba* is an African word, but in fact it comes from the Spanish expression "*mujeres de rumbo*" [women of the road]. In colonial times, the Spanish dismissed our popular celebrations as *fiestas rumbosas*, and that expression gave rise to the term "*rumba*" to designate a dance of the lower classes.

I've always asked myself why we still view this as such a derogatory term when it seems to me that it should be a source of pride, because we *are* in fact a *pueblo rumbero*, and the rumba is one of our most important rhythms. People think it refers to a single dance, but actually it designates a whole complex of dances and musical forms. The most important of these is the *guaguancó*, in which a male and a female dancer replicate the act of lovemaking in a manner more explicit than stylized. The *columbia* is danced by the man alone. Other variants are the *yambú* and the *tango-congo*. The latter, which sprang up around the ports, is tied not only to the origins of North American jazz, but also seems to have been the inspiration of the Argentine tango, transported there by the heavy ship traffic between the Caribbean ports and those of the River Plate.

Another reason that we Cubans may not be proud of the designation "*rumbero*" has to do with how the rumba was used and abused by nightclub entertainers who pandered to the foreign tourist trade. I don't mean to suggest that the rumba does not have a place on stage. In fact, for me there are two kinds of *rumba escénica*: one in the original context of the dock communities where the dance developed, where the same group of people is both performer and spectator; the other in a more theatrical setting, where there is a strict separation between performers and spectators and where the dancers have been formally trained. Each of these can be equally authentic; both are equally valid cultural forms. But what happened in the cabarets in the thirties, forties, and fifties was something else again: the authenticity of the form was lost to glittering bangles, cascading plumes, exposed flesh, and excessive sophistication. This is a "tradition" that we are still combatting.

Q: How much is known about the history of the cabaret tradition in Cuba? How and when did it become so widespread?

A: We're only now beginning to research this area. The gaps in our knowledge are enormous. Briefly, I think that the popularity of the cabaret tradition in Cuba has its roots in the *teatro vernáculo* [vernacular theater], a kind of "integrated" theater similar to the North American variety show in that it included music, dance, song, as well as acting and dialogue. Havana's El Alhambra was the most famous of these theaters. It functioned continuously, with the same company, from the turn of the century until well into the 1930s—probably a world record for a theater company.

I got my start as an actor in this kind of theater. From today's perspective, we might call them populist because any social criticism they offered tended to be superficial or opportunistic, but they had an enormous following, largely because of their use of music. Alejo Carpentier, who has done a great deal of research on Cuban music, acknowledges the important contribution made by the *teatro vernáculo* in the evolution of Cuban music and dance forms. The other component of their success was their use of the vernacular, of particularly Cuban forms of speech. This theatrical tradition constituted a reaction against and an alternative to the Spanish *sainete* [one-act farce] at a time when the Cubans had been fighting nearly thirty years to win their independence from Spain. It had a humorous, satirical, sometimes farcical tone conveyed through forms of speech that were not classical Castilian, but Creole. In the long and complicated process of defining Cuban national identity and culture, *mestizaje* [the blending of ethnic strains], which has always been the key, has revealed itself most clearly in two phenomena: music and speech. The *teatro vernáculo* encompassed both.

To trace the antecedents of this tradition, one has to go back to Europe during the transition from feudalism to capitalism. The rise of the bourgeoisie was contingent on the expansion of the city. Though the bourgeoisie appointed itself custodian of the forms of "high art" previously sustained by the nobility, it did not fully share the culture of its predecessors. In economic and even political terms, the bourgeois sector was ready to take power, but culturally it was less qualified. Besides, its very evolution and expansion as a class required more expansive art forms, capable of reaching a more massive public.

Initially, artists and performers from the popular classes had no designated space in the new urban centers. Singers, dancers, jugglers, sword swallowers simply performed in the streets. In the coming together in a single space of such diverse performers, we have the variety show in embryo. Inevitably, at a given moment a group of impresarios sprang up who began to offer performance space to these street artists, and gradually such institutions as the music hall and cabaret developed. If, on the one hand, these merchants provided an impetus to the development of these popular art forms by offering them designated space and a steady public, on the other, they also frustrated this development because their attention to a single criterion—profit—led them to pander to the coarsest tastes and most banal concerns. The corruption of these popular forms also served to deepen the apparent schism between popular expression and Great Art. The popular art forms that eventually gave rise to what we in Cuba call "espectáculos" were thus born under a contradictory sign: their worthy origins have been subject to constant manipulation by commercial interests.

I felt this very personally in my own career as an artist. I took a stand against imperialism long before I even had much political awareness because I saw firsthand how the old teatro vernáculo tradition, which by all rights should have evolved into a genuine national theater, was cut short by the drive to imitate U.S.-style radio and television. Since this was also where the money was, the best talents were syphoned off, and our popular theater tradition atrophied at precisely the time when it might have assumed an important role in addressing some of the more pressing and problematic aspects of contemporary Cuban reality.

Q: Can you describe your efforts in trying to improve cabaret shows and similar forms of entertainment?

A: First of all, since music and dance are the principal components of these shows, the impact of the decompartmentalization strategies I was describing in the musical sector will eventually be felt here, as well. We have tried to interest theatrical directors in directing espectáculos as a means of incorporating talented people with artistic training and a fresh perspective. To do this, we have to confer greater prestige on this particular cultural field. Conversely, success in bringing in more trained artists will elevate a genre that has until now been pretty disparaged by people trained in the arts.

Q: Let's discuss what you have been able to accomplish at Tropicana. Your film Son o no son (1980),[1] is set there and—again, in your typically humorous and highly accessible way—appears to be a critique of cabaret culture. Was that project in some sense a "practice run" for your job as vice-minister?

A: Son o no son is in fact much more of a meditation on the musical comedy form. Its purpose is to raise questions, not provide answers. Naturally, it completely breaks with the structure of the conventional musical. It begins well enough, but there comes a moment when it stops short and begins to ask itself why traditional Cuban musical revues are so poor, and why a country so rich in music has such difficulty producing musicals. In searching for the answer, the film borrows from a number of media and becomes itself something very different from what it apparently set out to be.

In the Cuban context, the *espectáculo musical* seemed the most appropriate space in which to experiment with the musical genre, which had intrigued me for years. Besides I'm not simply fascinated by musical comedies for their own sake; I see them as one more means of inquiring into the nature, function, and potential of mass culture. The film also refers to other mass media—movies, radio, television, comics. It is built around a series of rehearsals for a traditional musical review at Tropicana, which never seems to jell, in part because of the limitations imposed by underdevelopment, as seen, for example, even in the pronounced physical variations among the members of the chorus line. So the question becomes how to produce a staged or filmed musical with other components, less imitative of imported cultural models and more appropriate to our own condition as an underdeveloped Afro-Hispano-Caribbean island.

At ICAIC I have always argued that just as Hollywood directors must make the obligatory western, Cuban filmmakers should be required to make a musical. After all, it's pretty frustrating in a country with a musical tradition as rich as ours that we produce so few musical films. We have to be prepared to take some risks, to experiment.

Q: How have the nightclub shows changed since you assumed your post?
A: Tropicana and the other *centros nocturnos* are officially part of the National Tourist Institute [INTUR], but we have been able to establish an excellent working relationship with them. Together we analyze the plans for all the cabaret shows, with the participation of those responsible for the choreography and the artistic direction. This is an effective process, though not always an easy one.

One of the effects of the massification of contemporary musical culture is that the record industry provides access to new and foreign musical forms at such an accelerated pace that the hegemony of a new style is very short-lived, even as taste grows increasingly homogenized. Our audiences risk becoming saturated with a set of imported sounds that begin to constitute the canon of musical modernity. We risk the negation of even the most contemporary developments in Cuban music. There was a time when cabaret-goers were skeptical about the feasibility of putting together a successful show based on exclusively Cuban music. We have shown that if that music is imaginatively used, in a manner consistent with the specific requirements of the cabaret genre, even young audiences respond enthusiastically. One of the shows prepared last year was dedicated to Benny Moré; another commemorated one hundred years of the *danzón*. Both were so successful they've had to be revived.

Q: Where does your work with circuses fit in?

A: I've always been fascinated by the circus. My career as a performer began under a tent, in that same kind of naïve and primitive circus world that I tried to evoke in *The Adventures of Juan Quin Quin*. Cuban circuses were rather unusual. In addition to the standard acts, performers played out The Lady of the Camellias and the Life of Christ. Afterwards everyone ended up doing the rumba.

The circus is another manifestation of that popular urban culture that we were discussing earlier. Part of that tradition was channeled into the cabarets and corrupted there; the most modest strain, a whole spectrum of variety show performers who had nowhere else to go, remained in the circus.

We have seven permanent tents in the country, each with its own troupe. Except for its local season, each troupe spends most of its time on tour. We are putting special emphasis on circus activity right now, because we believe that it is an important proving ground for variety show artists. Remember that many great film comedians, people like Charlie Chaplin and Buster Keaton, with their marvelous physical control, derive in part from the circus tradition.

I've neglected to mention one other very important source of talent: the local and regional festivals. Each municipality and province has its own traditional celebrations. No two are the same. Carnival festivities in Santiago de Cuba, for example, are very different from the *parrandas* [revelry] *de remedio*, which take place at the same time in the interior. The city of Guantánamo, where the U.S. naval base is located, has a Carnival tradition called La Banda de los Perros [The Dogs' Band]. Only the most decrepit musical instruments are used. Each musician marches in the procession playing whatever tune comes to mind. The result, obviously, is unbelievably cacophonous, but people flock to the event.

We feel that these original folk customs must be continually encouraged because otherwise the people who invent and perpetuate them will simply begin to imitate what they see on television and suddenly that rich cultural variety will be absorbed into a single monolithic phenomenon. These diverse popular traditions are the taproot of a national culture with a genuine popular base and a source of enrichment for the more developed artistic sectors.

Q: Over the past decade you have written a series of theoretical essays on mass and popular culture in the developed and underdeveloped worlds, focusing primarily on film and television. Most of your films also reveal a theoretical bent, though often disguised by a comic spirit that accounts for their widespread popularity in Cuba. Since 1979, when your collected essays appeared under the title *Una imagen recorre el mundo*, have you been able to pursue your written reflections on these and related theoretical questions, particularly as they relate to your new position? This would seem to be an important means of both evaluating your practical experience in this unique post and making that experience more accessible to people outside of Cuba who are interested in strategies for promoting and protecting popular cultural traditions.

A: I would very much like to pursue some questions that continue to preoccupy me, but I've had to dedicate all my energies to my new job, which is extremely demanding. I'd like to undertake a more systematic study of the history of the *espectáculo musical*, for example, both in Cuba and elsewhere, and its relation to and impact on mass culture. I would like to continue evaluating the impact of the mass media technologies on pretechnological forms of cultural expression. Folk festivals, circuses, and musical shows risk being destroyed by what we call the *medios técnicos* [technological media], but there must also be ways for television and film to enrich these *living* forms. I refuse to believe that the only thing people want is to be shut up in their houses all day watching TV. People have an organic need to go out, to participate, to communicate with one another not through prepackaged images but through live activities. In the very near future, films will be exhibited in the home on screens large enough to make conventional theaters obsolete. I think that this will encourage cultural activities performed in the flesh, because people will seek out a more direct and human relationship to supplement if not replace that offered by the *medios técnicos*.

Here in Cuba we recognize that we must not let the culture of the capital city eclipse other national cultural manifestations, but it is also true—and this is another area that I would like to explore someday in greater depth—that, despite our being an agricultural country, our culture has an urban base. Our principal export crop, sugar, was traditionally produced under a plantation system that centralized its workers in communities that were more urban than rural in nature. In comparison to the richness, diversity, and dynamism of forms of cultural expression developed on the sugar plantations, on the wharves, and in the urban neighborhoods, peasant or *guajiro* culture has had a much more limited evolution. Perhaps these very urban roots of our culture have helped to ensure its continued vitality and viability in a modernizing society, in contrast to rural-based forms of cultural expression, which are endangered throughout the world.

These are some of the areas that concern me. I feel an urgent need to address such questions because, after all, what hangs in the balance is the survival of a rich national culture that has always had a strong popular base and a high degree of mass participation.

Note

1. The title puns on the famous Shakespearean phrase "to be or not to be" (*ser o no ser* in Spanish) and a Cuban musical form called the *son* (derived from *danzón*). *Son* is also the third person plural of the Spanish verb *ser*, "to be."

Chapter 20

Alfonso Gumucio Dagrón
(Bolivia and Latin America at Large)

A Product of Circumstances:
Reflections of a Media Activist

After training as a filmmaker initially in Madrid and later in Paris, Alfonso
Gumucio Dagrón has worked transferring his skills to peasant and workers'
organizations in Mexico, Nicaragua, and—intermittently—in his native Bolivia,
where adverse political circumstances have forced him to flee the country more than
once. In addition to several documentary films, few of which have been designed to
circulate outside the radius of their production site, Gumucio has published several
books of poetry, a history of Bolivian filmmaking (*Historia del cine boliviano*, La
Paz, 1982, and Mexico, 1983), a survey of film censorship in Latin America (*Cine,
censura y exilio en América Latina*, La Paz, 1979, and Mexico, 1984), and a
manual for workers' cinema (*El cine de los trabajadores*, Managua, 1981). He
returned to Bolivia in 1985 to direct CIMCA, the Centro de Integración de Medios
de Comunicación Alternativa (Alternative Mass Communications Coordinating
Center).

Excerpts of Julianne Burton's interview of Alfonso Gumucio Dagrón (conducted
in Mexico City in October 1983) appeared in Marc Glassman and W. W. Barker,
eds. *The Journal of Forbidden Films* (Toronto: Toronto Arts Group for Human
Rights), October 1984.

When people ask me what I do, I find it difficult to know how to answer any more. I can't come up with a convenient label. I am a poet who practices journalism out of necessity. I have done historical film research and scholarship because I discovered a vacuum that needed filling. I am a filmmaker whose films are unknown in conventional circuits—even "alternative" ones. I train others to make films and use various communications media, but I would never call myself a teacher. I practice a patchwork of vocations. In my eclecticism, I am the typical product of the circumstances and pressures that currently exist in Latin America.

Just by looking at me, you can tell that I come from my country's middle class. It is obvious that I am not of indigenous race. My primary education took place in private rather than public schools. Because my father sometimes held government and diplomatic posts, I've had the privilege of traveling a good deal, living in Spain and Uruguay. My situation corresponds to that of many Latin Americans of a similar social level who from an early age have enjoyed access to different environments, in contrast to those whose education and development are limited a priori because their socioeconomic position confines them to a very narrow terrain. From my early childhood, I was fortunate to have a vision of a wider world.

Studies

My father was determined that I should have a professional career. He dismissed my interest in poetry, literature, and cinema as mere "hobbies." I began studying medicine, but after the first year, I decided I had had enough, opting instead for literature. I had been writing poetry and short stories (very bad ones, to be sure) since I was a kid. As a high school student, I had edited some literary magazines. I began writing newspaper articles and was soon put in charge of the cultural page of one of the La Paz dailies. The newspaper I worked for supported President Torres, a progressive. When in 1971 a military coup replaced him with General Banzer, many of my colleagues faced persecution.

A few months earlier, I had gone to Spain to study television and film at the Faculty of Information Sciences in Madrid. Unfortunately, though perhaps predictably, the teachers were reactionary and the curriculum completely outdated. It was a total disaster. I shut myself up in my room to write. My three published books of poetry date from that period. The political situation in Bolivia made it impossible for me to go home, so I left Madrid for Paris in September 1972.

Things were quite difficult at the beginning, as they are for most newcomers, but I was finally admitted both to IDHEC [Institute of Advanced Film Studies] and the national university at Vincennes. If I had studied only at IDHEC, I don't believe I would have developed as versatile a set of professional tools or as intricate a vision. Though IDHEC is excellent from a technical standpoint, the program offers little theoretical content. Film is studied as an isolated phenomenon; it is not inserted into any sort of integrated vision of the arts, much less into any broad social vision.

Vincennes opened other avenues of inquiry for me. The campus was built in three months as a refuge (or a dumping ground) for all the dissenters from May 1968. It was a kind of island. People continued to live with the impetus of 1968, when in fact the rest of the country was in another place altogether. But it was a very valuable experience for me in my own ideological development because of the dynamic and constant circulation of opposing ideas about the world. (In another sense, Paris itself is an extension of this kind of experience.) When I enrolled at Vincennes, the faculty included members of the editorial boards of *Cahiers du Cinéma* and *Cinéthique*, two avant-garde film magazines, which were highly politicized during that period, in the aftermath of the events of May 1968. I developed close ties with the *Cahiers* group, taking classes from Jean Narboni and Serge Le Peron, and later even writing a few articles for them. In 1973 and 1974 the magazine began to change direction, partially in response to the influence of a number of exiled Latin American filmmakers who were then frequent visitors if not residents of Paris: Miguel Littín, Raúl Ruiz, and Helvio Soto from Chile; Jorge Sanjinés from Bolivia; later Glauber Rocha and Ruy Guerra from Brazil; and Fernando Solanas from Argentina. *Cahiers* published a number of interviews with them, and the ideas expressed by the Latin Americans had an impact on the outlook of the magazine's editorial group, which abandoned the rather orthodox "Cultural Front" stance in favor of a broader effort.

During this period, I put poetry aside and dedicated myself to the study of filmmaking and film criticism. I had already done some film criticism in Bolivia, but in a very improvised fashion, based exclusively on subjective impressions, since I had no knowledge of what film criticism was all about. I spent five years at Vincennes and three at IDHEC, trying not only to combine these two programs of study, but also to take advantage of other available resources like the courses at Nanterre and Le Musée de l'Homme given by documentarist Jean Rouch and his associates. Like a sponge, I began to absorb everything that might contribute to my goal of making films in Latin America.

While in France, I became very involved with solidarity campaigns for Bolivia, mounted photographic exhibits, and published books and bulletins about the Bolivian situation to inform people about what was going on in my country. But we were very short on material. We needed a slide show or a film that would combine actual images with a carefully structured account of Bolivia's history and the five years of the Banzer dictatorship. I decided to make such a film about Bolivia as my final project for IDHEC. The school only provided footage for a ten-minute short, but my documentary turned out to be seventy minutes long, so I also had to find other sources of funding.

I decided to do the narration first, laying out all the fundamental issues that needed to be addressed to understand the situation in Bolivia. I left the job of locating the images to illustrate each particular section for later. *Señores Generales, Señores Coroneles* is a kind of film-essay that attempts to provide all the necessary elements of analysis. One of my models was the great Argentine documentary *The Hour of the Furnaces* [1968]. The film is dense with information, but this is because I made it for a Latin American audience. The number of Latin Americans living in Paris at the time justified my decision to do the first version in Spanish; the French version came later. When the time came to find images to illustrate what I had laid out in essay form, however, I was forced to confront the total dearth of graphic and cinematographic records in and about my country.

The task of finding visual material to illustrate all the points I wanted to make in *Señores Generales, Señores Coroneles* was gargantuan. I wrote to dozens of people requesting photographic documentation. I combed the archives for footage. I couldn't find anything. I had to resort to making blowups of tiny newspaper photographs. Whatever I could find, I used. I would venture to say that the *photographic* history of Bolivia is also, almost inadvertently, presented in the film. In the section on the 1952 revolution, for example, I included almost all the extant photographs. In the section on the Chaco War, I used virtually all the surviving graphic documentation. The same with Che Guevara's 1967 guerrilla campaign in Bolivia. There are moments when the image seems very static—boring, if you like—because I refused to compromise what I wanted to say for the sake of aesthetic variation.

As it turned out, I had to make an unexpected trip to Bolivia that year [1975] because my father was very ill and I had also received a summons from the minister of the interior, asking me to report to the "Statistics Division," which everyone knew was a euphemism for the department in charge of interrogation and torture. My father did not want me to risk the trip, but I went and, fortunately, nothing happened. While I was there, I borrowed a camera from filmmaker Antonio Equino and filmed various sequences for *Señores Generales, Señores Coroneles*.

My first contact with the Super-8 format took place in France around that time. I was shooting an interview with former CIA agent Phillip Agee. We set up an appointment and I hauled over all the equipment from IDHEC— lights, camera, tape recorder, film stock, several assistants, etc. We spent the whole afternoon filming. Agee took advantage of the occasion to provide us with the names of the CIA agents then working in Bolivia. Since we were all also involved in solidarity work, and had good connections with Agence

France Presse and other news services, we were able to place this item on the wires immediately. It appeared the next day in newspapers all over the world and produced an enormous upheaval in Bolivia, prompting the U.S. embassy to make a number of personnel changes.

In the midst of the shooting of the interview, Alain Labrousse, a French documentarist who has lived and worked in South America for many years, arrived. He had told me that he was making a film about Uruguay and wanted to take advantage of my session with Agee to shoot some footage for his own film. "Two minutes is all I need," he had said, so I agreed. "Don't move anything," he said to the technicians. "I'll just shoot with everything as it is." So he knelt down with his little Super-8 camera in front of Agee and said, "Look, all I've got inside here is two and a half minutes of film, so you're going to have to synthesize things." I was amazed to see that Agee managed to cram almost all the information he'd conveyed to me during hours of shooting into the two and a half minutes which Alain allowed him. It was clear that the little camera elicited an entirely different attitude on the part of the subject, who felt more relaxed and more in control of the material. I saw that the filmmaker's attitude was also different, because he did not have to concentrate on a mass of preparatory technical detail. I realized then that I was witnessing something new, something I had not learned about in my years of apprenticeship at IDHEC.

Relatively early in my studies, I had begun to differentiate between those areas that would be most relevant to me as a filmmaker working in Latin America. It seemed pointless, for example, to study chemical processes when in Bolivia we don't even have a film lab. Lighting and cinematography, on the other hand, seemed extremely important to me, because I believe that Latin Americans must make films of high visual quality, so I put a lot of effort into the courses I had with cinematographer Nestor Almendros at IDHEC. I decided that I didn't need to spend five or six years in Europe to learn what I needed to know to work in Latin America. I realized that with a more synthetic one- or two-year course I would have been able to learn all that was necessary to implement the kind of projects I was able to develop later. I wanted less emphasis placed on technical detail and more on the larger conceptual questions: Why make films, how, and for whom? I also felt an acute need for an analysis of what had already been done in Latin American filmmaking.

Pioneering Histories

As I was posing these questions to myself, I came in contact with Guy Hennebelle, a leading French film critic known for his work on Third World filmmaking, particularly in Africa and the Middle East. In 1974 we decided to collaborate on a book that would trace the history and development of film in Latin America country by country. We knew that a lot of documentation already existed for some countries—Brazil and Mexico, for example—whereas for others very little was known. In the case of my own country, Jorge Sanjinés was the only filmmaker of international reputation, but I had the vague idea that there had been some prior activity in the field. I began to investigate the history of film in Bolivia and ended up spending almost six years on the project. The chapter I published in *Les Cinémas de l'Amérique Latine* [Paris, 1981], the book that Hennebelle and I co-edited, is an earlier, abbreviated version of what is in fact a much more detailed and ambitious volume, *La historia del cine boliviano*, published in 1983 by the Filmoteca of Mexico's National University. Ninety-nine percent of the information in the essay and in the book had never appeared in print. I culled it from widely dispersed sources, but primarily out of the memories and mementoes of the people who played a part in that history.

If I am considered a film historian, it is only by accident, because circumstances dictated. Investigating the history of filmmaking in my country was for me a necessary step in my preparation for becoming a filmmaker in Bolivia. Since no one before me had taken that step, it fell to me to do so. I have not been trained as a historian or as a researcher, either. I barely know how to make note cards. My research methods are unconventional, to say the least; I had to invent my methods as I went along.

I wanted to know how long people had been making films in Bolivia, and what the origins were, so I began searching through all the newspapers from the beginning of the century. Since we have no indices to these materials, I had to go through each newspaper page by page. I had a job at the time from eight in the morning to six at night. Since I had no access to research funding and had to support myself and my family, I had to do all my library work "after hours." As we say in Spanish, I singed my eyelashes reading late into the night. I would scan page after page, paper after paper, and every once in a while I would come upon a few lines: "Biograph today presents such-and-such a film in such-and-such a place." Photocopying technology is not widely available in a country like Bolivia. To have copied each of these notices by hand for the eighty-year period I intended to cover was unthinkable. But what else could I do? I decided to take a picture of every relevant item. I shot the pictures myself, developed the film myself, and made the prints myself. I have a monstrous archive of photographs of newspaper notices.

The project was tedious and grueling at times, but it was also very exciting because it had not been done before. There were no books and only a handful of articles dedicated to the topic. That meant that almost everything I found out was a discovery—a very different experience from reworking existing materials. Trying to track down the human survivors of this unknown history brought out the detective in me. For example, I found one of the early pioneers of Bolivian filmmaking, Don José María Velasco Maidana, alive and well and living in Houston, Texas.

Velasco Maidana is a fascinating man. Some might call him a dilettante, but like many Latin Americans who are determined to accomplish something in their countries, he was simply a man who did many things. A recognized painter in his own right, he was also the teacher of our leading contemporary painters; he was a violinist and orchestra conductor who, in the 1940s, toured Latin America as guest conductor of the leading national orchestras; he also founded the National Conservatory of Music.

In 1925 he made a film called *La profecía del lago* [*The Prophecy of the Lake*]. It had the dual distinction of being Bolivia's first feature film, and its first censored film. It ran for only one day before it was banned. Apparently banning was not enough; the authorities felt compelled to destroy the film. A judge ordered its incineration. In 1930 he made another film, *Warawara* [Aymara for "Stars"], the first Bolivian superproduction, set during the times of the Spanish conquest of the Incas. This large-cast costume drama, which even involved reconstructing several Inca monuments, also suffered an unfortunate fate. The Chaco War against Paraguay broke out, mobilizing the entire country and focusing all energies on the war. People were too busy to pay attention to Velasco Maidana's movie. This one has also been lost; only a few stills have survived.

This extraordinary man succeeded in bringing together all the most active, creative people—painters, poets, and so on—to act in his films. He stirred up a slumbering cultural milieu. But Bolivia is a small country, too small for a person of such broad horizons. After his musical tour of Latin America, he went to the United States. Few people remember him in Bolivia. I learned that our most famous sculptor, María Núñez del Prado, had been the apprentice and even perhaps the lover of Velasco Maidana. She was living at the time in Peru, but I caught her during a visit to Bolivia and asked her how long Velasco Maidana had been dead. "He's not dead," she answered. "He's living in the United States. I think I still have an address he gave me several years ago." Two years later, when I took my father to Houston for medical tests, I decided to track down that address, though I told myself it would probably be a wild goose chase. I explained in English to the man who answered the door that I was looking for someone who used to live there named Velasco Maidana. "Soy yo" [That's me] he answered in Spanish. It was quite a surprise.

He is just one of fifty people I managed to track down. I came across a reference to one Bazoberry, who had made a film in 1936 on the Chaco War, *La guerra del Chaco*. Since the name is an unusual one, I had little difficulty locating his son through the telephone directory. When he expressed his disappointment and outrage at how poorly his father was remembered, I encouraged him to share whatever information he had with me. In addition to other materials, the family conserved a print of the film, which the Bolivian Cinemateca is about to purchase. I also recovered a copy of the other major film from the thirties, *Hacia la gloria* [*Bound for Glory*], a feature made by three eighteen-year-olds just before the Chaco War broke out.

It has to be noted that from the beginning to the present, the history of Bolivian cinema is a story of pioneers. Everyone who has made films in Bolivia has done it the hard way, meter by meter, without support from anyone else, hitting up friends and family for funding. This is just as true of Jorge Sanjinés in the sixties and seventies as it was of Velasco Maidana in the twenties and thirties. Jorge Ruiz, the most important figure from the 1950s, is no exception. He began making 8mm films with Augusto Roca in the forties. A North American named Kenneth B. Wasson, who was interested in film, bought them a 16mm camera, which is what they used to make their first documentaries, including the first Bolivian color documentary. Jorge Ruiz is a professional only because he persisted, but it took him ten years before he could manage to make his living as a filmmaker. Aside from *La vertiente* [*The Watershed*, 1958] and *Vuelve Sebastiana* [*Come Back, Sebastiana*, 1953], Ruiz's films have been commissioned works. He doesn't have the explosive creativity of someone like Sanjinés, but he is an excellent technician with a high level of social awareness, because he has lived in the Bolivian countryside and knows its people well. But what is remarkable is the lack of continuity between these figures. Each one had to start from scratch.

Filming with Sanjinés

For the last two years I was in France (1973-1975), I acted as local representative for Sanjinés, overseeing distribution and exhibition of his films. In this connection I traveled to Belgium, Italy, Holland, and other European countries. My job involved contacting distributors and also making presentations at certain screenings. These tended to be large—five hundred or six hundred people—and extremely interesting, particularly those for rural audiences.

I had met Jorge Sanjinés while doing newspaper work in Bolivia in 1969 and 1970. Jorge has always been a very private person. If the reasons are obvious now, they were not back then. The other members of the group, in contrast, were much more accessible, so when I needed some information related to film, I would go to their office, La Productora Ukamau, to talk with Oscar Soria, Ricardo Rada, or Antonio Eguino. The Ukamau Group, formed after making the film *Ukamau* [*That's the Way It Is*, 1966], split in 1969 after the footage for their feature *Los caminos de la muerte* [*The Roads of Death*] was destroyed in a German laboratory. Jorge withdrew his share of the Sociedad Ukamau Limited and formed Grupo Ukamau, which did not have the same legal status. Eguino, Soria, and Rada kept Ukamau Ltd. In 1971 Radiotelevisione Italiana offered Jorge coproduction funding to make *El coraje del pueblo* [*The Courage of the People*], an interpretive documentary about a massacre of Bolivian tin miners, which he was anxious to make. He hired Soria to write the screenplay and Eguino as cinematographer. So they all started working together again despite the split, but no longer as part of the same group. Naturally, given the situation, there was a lot of resentment on both sides.

I began to work with Jorge because he was the one who had asked me to be his representative, and also because at the time, I found his films much more interesting than Eguino's. When Jorge decided to make *Fuera de aquí* [*Get Out of Here*, 1977] in Ecuador in 1975, I took on more of a producer's role, obtaining a camera and tape recorder and shipping them to Jorge in Ecuador. I was about to leave to join him, since I was to be assistant director on the film, when news came that Antonio Eguino had been imprisoned in Bolivia for possessing a print of *The Courage of the People*. I stayed in Paris to organize a campaign demanding his release, which in fact occurred two weeks later.

Filming *Get Out of Here* was an extremely important experience for me, as it was for Jorge, who had been used to working with a very tight script using indirect sound and postdubbing. *Get Out of Here* has not enjoyed much critical success, but I defend it to the limit for what it has to offer as an example of popular cinema. It breaks all the norms to which we are accustomed. Those of us who live urban lives are habituated to a certain celerity of pace; we grow impatient with slower rhythms. Western film and television implant and reinforce these expectations. But there is a vast rural population in Latin America that has not yet been deformed by Western film language. I believe that Jorge is trying to make films for this population, which in countries like Bolivia is clearly the majority. I respect his refusal to let middle-class expectations condition his language. He is looking for something different from the "international style," for modes of expression that correspond to the modes of perception of the Latin American peasant. In *Get Out of Here*, Sanjinés puts the film medium at the service of historical actors who have had no other means of expressing their history. This explains why the *campesinos'* collaboration is so impassioned and spontaneous.

I noticed a number of things that characterize Sanjinés's approach (in addition to sharing the living conditions of the people among whom we were working). His reliance on the long take avoids having to interrupt the historical actors when they are involved in redramatizing their own experience. In films that are more dependent on a fixed script, on the other hand, the action must be continually interrupted to change the angle and location of the camera. Jorge Vignati did the camera work, which was almost exclusively hand-held. Sanjinés would move behind him while he was shooting, whispering constant instructions about where he should turn next and how he should shoot. In this way, the camera adapted itself to the actions of the *campesinos*, rather than the reverse. To direct historical actors as one would direct professional or conventional actors is to denaturalize them, to block all that their memory might spontaneously offer. Sanjinés uses very different methods, thus making a contribution that has not yet been sufficiently acknowledged. In this kind of work, the long take is not an aesthetic a priori, like it might be in Miklos Jancso; it is mandated by circumstances.

Close-ups are almost totally absent from *Get Out of Here*; most of the shots are group shots. In his book *Teoría y práctica de un cine junto al pueblo* [*Theory and Practice of a Popular Cinema*, Mexico, 1979], Sanjinés explains that he wants to avoid underlining the importance of one character over the others because in Andean cultures the leaders grow out of and depend on the masses in a way that is constantly acknowledged. But in the act of filming, none of this seems quite so theoretical. Close-ups would be intrusive, fragmenting the integrity of the action that Sanjinés is constructing. It became quite clear to me how his theoretical positions grew out of his practical experiences—which is clearly the way things should be.

All this was very valuable to me in my subsequent work with Super-8 because I realized that in filming *Get Out of Here* Jorge was handicapped to a certain degree by concrete factors like the weight and general unwieldiness of the 16mm camera and the Nagra recorder. Super-8 has the obvious advantage of eliminating such complications. Sanjinés is caught between his commitment to an indigenous audience and his awareness that his films also have a national and international public. Until Super-8 enjoys mass distribution, filmmakers will have to make this choice between maximum flexibility in the filming and maximum exposure of what they film. In cases where the filmmaker is ready to define and limit his audience, Super-8 is eminently viable, but as long as filmmakers seek multiple audiences, they will have to continue using the larger formats.

We finished shooting the rural footage in late 1975. Because of a series of difficulties, the footage that was to be shot in Quito was not completed until the following year, 1976, which meant that the finished film was not released until 1977. I had made a commitment to a French publisher, Le Seuil, to do a volume on Bolivia and so I had to return to Paris as soon as the first phase of shooting was finished, but not before making a two-month "stopover" in Bolivia.

Back to Bolivia

The book I was contracted to write, called simply *Bolivie*, was part of Le

Seuil's Petite Planete series—a collection of volumes on the geography, culture, and society of various countries. Their policy was *not* to hire nationals on the theory that they were unable to present a sufficiently detached portrait of their own country. I am the only exception in the series. I insisted that they allow me to prepare some sample chapters, and they liked them well enough to offer me the contract. I spent most of 1976 and 1977 writing the text in Paris.

In early 1978 I returned to Bolivia to shoot the photographs for the book. While I was there, I also acquired some local filmmaking experience. Antonio Equino hired me to work on some publicity spots. These assignments had the added advantage of providing me with air transportation to several of the more remote areas at a time when I was trying to assemble a photographic record of all sections of the country.

I also had a chance to collaborate with Alain Labrousse, a French writer and filmmaker who has spent a good deal of time living, writing, and making films in Uruguay, Argentina, Peru, and Bolivia. We both arrived in Bolivia at a crucial moment: the hunger strike of January 1978, which was to precipitate the fall of the despised Banzer regime, in power since 1971.

Since press censorship was in full force, you couldn't read about the hunger strike in the papers; you had to find out through a much more informal information network. When I was told that Father Luis Espinal, our leading film critic, was participating in the strike, I went to see him at the offices of *La Presencia* newspaper. There I also found Domitila de Chungara, Javier Albó, and other people I knew from the mining region. They had been fasting for about ten days already and would go for another twenty without eating. I took some still photographs. The hunger strike had just ended when Alain Labrousse arrived and decided to do a film about it. We shot in the mining region and did interviews with the women leaders who had been fasting in La Paz. That film, called *La huelga de hambre* [*The Hunger Strike*] is the only visual document anywhere of that important event. Shot in Super-8, it has circulated widely in Bolivia through various political and social organizations. We also made another film called *Las elecciones sindicales en Viloco* [*Union Elections in Viloco*] to document the first free election in seven years.

These were my first practical experiences with Super-8. I couldn't help but be impressed by that format's enormous potential for rescuing and preserving the revolutionary resolve and potential of our people. I saw that people who had had no prior experience with being filmed were virtually unaware of the camera. They spoke and acted without any sign of intimidation, as if they were simply speaking in front of a microphone.

I completed the book in France in October 1978 and immediately left for Bolivia. This time I thought I was returning home for good. I had a position already set up at CIPCA [Centro de Investigación y Promoción del

Campesinado, Center for Peasant Research and Advancement], an institute founded in 1970 with the support of a number of priests and progressive agencies in Bolivia and elsewhere, with four branches throughout the country. CIPCA is quite political, though not in obvious ways. It has played an important role in the recent process of unification of the Bolivian peasantry, which has been accomplished despite vast regional differences. We provided support for peasant leaders like Genaro Flores, who was written up in the international press after an attack he suffered in the most recent coup left him paralyzed. CIPCA offered me an ideal opportunity to do something in film and communications that was directly tied to concrete and ongoing peasant organizing. Before I arrived, the institute's only audiovisual activities had consisted of leaflets and radio programs in the Aymara language. Within a few months, I had been able to put together a film lab, various photographic exhibits, a setup for making slide shows, and a Super-8 film workshop.

Selling Super-8

When I returned to Bolivia to work with CIPCA, I immediately started promoting Super-8. The major reason for the low level of filmmaking activity in the country was the shortage of funds to finance production. Bolivian filmmakers were forced to work in advertising to survive. I said to myself, we can't simply let Bolivian cinema atrophy for economic reasons; we can make our films in Super-8. So I tossed off a little mimeographed document called the *Manifesto de Cine Super-8*, which I distributed to all the national mass organizations. It was particularly well received in the Central Obrera Boliviana [COB, Bolivian Workers' Union], which asked me to be its media consultant [*asesor*].

It is very interesting how fast the Super-8 idea began to catch on. I don't take the credit for this phenomenon because I think that Alain Labrousse made a big contribution and that others also did their part. But the fact is that within a few months' time, Super-8 cameras began popping up everywhere. In the past, no matter how important the demonstration, you seldom saw a camera, and suddenly at every significant event you would see three or four cameras recording it. It is hard for people from developed societies to understand the importance of this because they are used to the constant and automatic visual recording of public events. In such countries, the store of historical images is immense; television has made it almost inconceivably complete. Countries like Bolivia, on the other hand, have lived through crucial periods for which there is almost no visual record. Of an event as important and relatively recent as the Revolution of 1952, only a few still photographs have been preserved.

After my first month at CIPCA, I accompanied my father to Houston for medical treatment and bought the film equipment for the Super-8 workshop. The first film I made for CIPCA was called *Tupac Katari, 15 de noviembre* [*Tupac Katari, November 15*], based on the celebration of the annual festival commemorating this Inca leader's rebellion against the Spaniards, festivities that had been banned during the years of the Banzer regime. I simply recorded the cultural as well as the political aspects of the festivities—the dancing and poetry readings in Aymara as well as the speechmaking. I got some very valuable footage of Genaro Flores and other younger peasant leaders.

We began showing this and other Super-8 films like *The Hunger Strike* to the *campesinos* who came by the CIPCA office. We were located in a very working-class section of La Paz, where *campesinos* new to the city would come and take lodging in the *tambos*, produce stalls that offer rooms for rent above. They would come by to make a presentation on one of the radio shows we produced, or for some other reason. When we had a film running, I would invite them in to watch it.

Experiences in the Field

Just to give an idea of how such films can be an outgrowth of popular demand, one day a group of *campesinos* came by the office all bruised and beaten. They wanted to use the radio show to make public what had happened in their community, Villa Anta. I happened to be screening *The Hunger Strike* and invited them to see it after they had taped their presentation. They came out of the screening fired with enthusiasm. "We want you to do the same thing in our community," they said. "I'd be happy to," I answered. "When?" "Tomorrow," they said firmly, and the next day we were off.

It seemed that a military detachment took a dispute over land rights as a pretext for invading the community, stealing property, and beating people up. The army could intervene again at any time. Many people were still fearful and reluctant to talk. On the whole, the women were more courageous about revealing exactly what had happened.

This was my first direct involvement with the *campesinos* as a filmmaker and my first real experience as director of this kind of film. I had to improvise a method as I went along. I knew we had only one day to complete the shooting. I began, out of personal curiosity, by trying to find out exactly what happened. As various people volunteered their versions, I began taping and filming them. Then I asked them to *show* me what happened. They took over and arranged everything, deciding who would play the roles of the soldiers and "costuming" them in caps. Their reconstruction of events was not an epic one, as in *The Courage of the People*; it was very natural, almost casual. You can even hear occasional background laughter on the soundtrack. Yet there are some wonderful scenes. The incident began when women from the community who were building a schoolhouse noticed that a small group of soldiers was beating up one of the local officials. They ran to his aid and started attacking the soldiers, who fled after the women successfully disarmed them. The sergeant, who was out cold, remained behind. The *campesinos* brought him water as he was coming to and began questioning him, genuinely puzzled, "Hey, you're a *campesino* just like us. Why do you treat us this way? Why do you attack us?"

I had no one to assist me except the driver of the car, who held the microphone and also served as my interpreter. I was very aware of my own linguistic limitations because even though I had taken some courses in Aymara, my rudimentary knowledge left me pretty helpless. The *campesinos* do speak Spanish; I was the one who insisted that we make the movie in their original language because the film was designed for use in the other rural communities of the *altiplano*, where many of the women do not speak much Spanish, which will always be regarded as the language of the colonizer.

Before the final cut was made, we showed the film in a number of other communities. Several *campesinos* were moved to make drawings of what had happened. I incorporated many of these at the end of the final version because their graphic symbolism is very interesting. I was satisfied that, because of the methods I used, the film was not mine but theirs. I had not imposed any structures or procedures on them; I saw my role as merely providing skills and technology and offering suggestions, though of course I had to play a more predominant role in the editing. That's how the film *El ejército en Villa Anta* [*The Army in Villa Anta*] was made.

Work in CIPCA was interesting because, in addition to filmmaking, I was also in charge of making slide shows. These could be about anything— planting potatoes, animal medicine, whatever—compelling me to educate myself about many everyday aspects of *campesino* life. We filmmakers tend to be a cocky bunch, assuming that we can take on any subject. The truth is that the results are often pretty superficial. Because of the level of expertise of my *campesino* audience, I had to impose high standards of information and accuracy on my own work.

The third film project took me to Charagua, a semitropical zone in the Chaco region inhabited by the Guarani Indians. They are a minority in Bolivia, but in neighboring Paraguay they form the majority of the population. For them that national border doesn't exist.

CIPCA's work in that area was extremely interesting. For many years, these Indians had been migrant workers [*trabajadores golondrinas*], spending three months harvesting sugarcane, then returning to their community for three months. This did not leave them sufficient time to cultivate their own lands properly. CIPCA was helping to organize them into work communities [*comunidades de trabajo*], which would be responsible for collectively cultivating designated plots of land. Though the project was only two years old, there were already a dozen participating communities. The two tractors they had purchased from their earnings were a concrete demonstration of the improving standard of living. They were beginning to talk about unionization.

I need to note here that Bolivia is a highly unionized country, and that the vast majority of our unions are democratic and progressive—even revolutionary. This is true for the *campesino* population and even more so for the workers. In Bolivia, the unions are not concerned exclusively with economics; their authority can range anywhere from mediating domestic conflicts to formulating positions on national and international policy. But the Guarani community had lived in isolation from this history.

Of the thirty settlements along the Izozog River, only a dozen were part of the CIPCA collectivization project. My task was to make a film that would help incorporate the remaining communities. I began by interviewing the oldest members of the communities to get a sense of their history. I discovered that the region had a long tradition of struggle. I talked to the traditional local authority, called the Capitán Grande, an eighty-year-old man who had walked all the way to La Paz in 1940 to secure the group's title to their lands. Another still recalled the period when the Guarani had been enslaved and described it in detail. I feared that unless these historical memories were recorded, they would soon be lost. I also interviewed the younger generation to get the necessary background about the contemporary situation, including how the work communities had been organized. The film then tried to posit a model for community organization in the region.

We had twelve prints made, which have been circulating in the region since 1979, uninterrupted even by the military coup of 1980. Reports from the region indicate that *Comunidades de trabajo* is still screened weekly. In the Villa Anta film, the reconstructions were more fragmentary, more elementary. Here we played with the fictional possibilities a little more freely. In the scene where a "headhunter" comes to contract workers for the cane harvest, for example, the acting was much more elaborate than it had been in the earlier film. The visual language of this film was also somewhat more sophisticated, with more long takes.

Most films released in Bolivia draw only about forty thousand to fifty thousand people. (The exception is Antonio Equino's *Chuquiago*, an all-time national hit with its four hundred thousand viewers—eighty percent of the population of La Paz.) My calculations, based on weekly showings of twelve prints to audiences of about fifty people, indicate that *Comunidades de trabajo* draws over thirty thousand spectators a year. The film only cost one thousand dollars; the equipment used to make it and others cost only twice that. Commercial films have to sink or swim in the first week or two of their release; the kind of alternative community filmmaking I was involved in faces no such imperative. You are not driven to recover your investment to pay off your debts because Super-8 filmmaking is remarkably inexpensive. What becomes important is how effective your film will be over the long haul. I was surprised to learn from people in Charagua that they have been able to get as many as a hundred screenings from a single print, since that is twice the conventional estimate for the life of Super-8 prints.

Most filmmakers are obsessed with reaching a large audience. I propose using different means to achieve the same end. Instead of making a film that costs a million dollars and reaches a million people, I would rather make a hundred films that cost ten thousand dollars apiece and that also reach a million spectators if each one has ten thousand viewers. The investment is the same, but the qualitative results are quite different. Any film that aims for an audience of a million people must be highly generalized in both topic and language. This is viable only if your audience shares a certain minimal economic level and class formation. If you want to direct your film to a peasant audience, you immediately have to acknowledge the differences between the cultural/perceptual apparatus of a French peasant and a Bolivian one, or even between a Bolivian peasant and another from Ecuador. You immediately have to contend with particularity. I believe that if you want to address issues in depth, you need to make concrete films for specific groups. The economy of the new technologies—Super-8 and video—encourages this.

The next film I made for CIPCA featured Domitila Barrios de Chungara, leader of the Comité de Amas de Casa [Housewives' Committee] of the Siglo XX mines, who became a nationally known figure in the hunger strike of 1978 and later, with the publication of her autobiography as told to Brazilian journalist Moema Viezzer [*Let Me Speak! Testimony of Domitila, A Woman of the Bolivian Mines*, New York: Monthly Review, 1978], an international one as well. *Domitila, la mujer y la organización* [*Domitila, the Woman and the Organization*], as the Super-8 version was called, simply records Domitila's speech on women delivered to an audience of *campesinas*. The original Super-8 version was only shown a few times before the coup. I managed to smuggle out the original, and I'm currently making a 16mm version, which will be called simply *Domitila*, for circulation outside of Bolivia.

Though *Domitila* was the last film I was able to complete in Bolivia, I had been simultaneously working on other projects outside of CIPCA. I have often felt like I'm in a race against time, driven to record many aspects of Bolivian life before it is too late. I began filming the muralist Walter Solón Romero, one of our most famous painters, who has had a fascinating career, working at one time with the Mexican muralist Siqueiros, and later traveling to China to learn Oriental techniques. My *compañera*, Eva Urquidi, and I had also been filming the Festival del Gran Poder [Great Power Folk

Festival], which involves dancing and parading in elaborate costumes representing figures from the time of the Spanish conquest. The second section of *Chuquiago* includes some shots of this festival, whose sociological implications are quite intriguing.

I was also doing some filming with Father Luis Espinal, founder and director of the progressive weekly newspaper called *Aquí*. I happened to be in Nicaragua on the day the national literacy campaign was launched. In the midst of the celebration, I learned that Espinal had been kidnapped, tortured, and murdered. I'll never forget the bittersweet mixture of emotions I felt that day. Back in Bolivia I made a pilgrimage to the place where his body had been found and I began to film a series of interviews for a film that I planned as a kind of homage. Different people covered different aspects of his life: Father Javier Albó talked about Luis as a priest; colleagues from the newsweekly *Aquí* talked about him as a journalist; Oscar Soria spoke of his activities as a film critic; Domitila Barrios talked about him as a personal and family friend. All this footage was lost in the coup, along with what we had filmed around the Festival del Gran Poder. I only managed to salvage a few of the rolls of Solón Romero.

During this time I was also working as a media consultant for COB, the Bolivian Workers' Union. In 1979 COB organized five *ampliados*—week-long conventions dedicated to discussing a specific theme, in this case the cultural question. I went to four of these conventions—the construction workers', the small businessmen's, the miners', and the teachers'. At each, I presented my Super-8 Manifesto and discussed the potential of this medium for their use. In Bolivia the workers' unions have control of a number of radio stations, which they use to disseminate their own news and views, but they have no access to audiovisual media.

In fact, it was the sample of miners' radio stations as they exist in Bolivia that convinced me that transfers of technology are possible. For the past two decades, Bolivian tin miners, who can barely read and write, have managed to finance, obtain, and set up their own radio transmitters, training themselves and their young people to plan programs, deliver broadcasts, etc. There are now more than twenty-five radio stations run by miners for miners. These broadcasts not only have a profound impact on the lives of the mining communities, where everyone feels free to utilize them according to their needs, but also, in times of crisis, on the lives of the rest of the country. During the most recent coup, since the miners' stations were the only ones that had not been taken over by the army, they were the sole source of reliable information about what was actually happening. Their broadcasts were also picked up in Peru and other neighboring countries. Once all the national radio and television stations and newspaper offices had been occupied by the military, who used them to declare that everything was under control, the miners' radio stations formed a broadcast chain that guaranteed that as soon as the army arrived to take a particular station over, another elsewhere would resume the broadcast. This kind of concrete demonstration of the effectiveness of alternative means of communication stands in direct contradiction to the "informed pessimism" prevalent in certain academic circles regarding the limited efficacy of such alternatives. These thinkers insist that the only effective transformation is a structural one, which can only take place after political power has changed hands. My line of reasoning is the opposite: we have to initiate these transformations from below to create the kind of spaces that will eventually guarantee the general structural transformation.

Four of the five *ampliados* approved proposals to create Super-8 film workshops. We were able to get some equipment from France. At the end of 1979, during the Natush coup d'état and the fifteen-day tenure of that regime, all that equipment was stolen in an attack on the COB offices. Subsequently, during the coup of 1980, the building itself was completely destroyed.

In addition to the kind of organizing and media activities I have described, I also published two books of poetry during these two years in Bolivia: *Antología del asco*, and *Razones técnicas*. Some of my short stories were anthologized in *Seis nuevos narradores bolivianos*. Finally, a fourth book, *Cine, censura y exilio en América Latina*, appeared in Bolivia shortly before events would force my own exile.

Looking back on it now, I find it hard to comprehend how I managed to do so many things at once. I was spending almost half my time in the field, but I still found time when I was in La Paz to supervise the books in press, do journalism, put together a radio show, produce some documentaries for television—all sorts of things at once. I was driven by a real sense of urgency, a fear (justified by subsequent events) that the historical dynamic would take a turn for the worse.

The succession of military coups cut off all these activities in midstream. It wasn't my film-related projects that put me in danger, since these were developed and utilized in the countryside, where information gathering and repressive control are less systematized, thus allowing a relatively higher degree of freedom. But CIPCA was forced to close, and most of its members were persecuted. I had also been working as one of the five journalists on the board of the weekly newspaper *Aquí*, whose director had been murdered several months before. We were all in grave danger. This is the reason behind my seeking asylum in the Mexican embassy in La Paz, my subsequent clandestine flight out of the country, and my eventual exile here in Mexico.

Exile

I have a certain sense that I have sacrificed a career as a filmmaker. I don't know whether or not it would have been a significant career, but I know that I would have liked to concentrate my skills and talents on expressing what I most care about, what is most personal—my own milieu, my people, my history. This is the first reflex of all creative people: to reflect what is existentially closest to them. I have sought this path in my poetry. Maybe this is my advantage compared to other filmmakers, since poetry does provide me with an outlet for my most personal concerns. Since I am also a journalist, I can use that kind of writing to develop and explore my political ideas and convictions. Filmmaking therefore becomes a zone in which I have a lesser degree of personal investment, which may be why I am able to offer my skills as a channel for other people, specifically peasants and workers, to express their most personal concerns in a medium to which they would not otherwise have access.

What matters most to me in film is its capacity to salvage popular memory and to rewrite history in visual images from the perspective of the marginalized classes in struggle, in contrast to written history, which has always been filtered through the lens of privilege. The history books in my country do not tell the story of the Bolivian *people*, but of a series of individuals who enjoyed temporary residence in the Governmental Palace. There is now *one* acceptable book, which traces the history of the Bolivian working class, but the *campesinos*, who have always constituted 70 percent or 80 percent of the country's population, are completely ignored. A people who lack a vision of their own history are incapable of progressing. This conviction explains why I am as committed as I am in this transition stage. Fortunately, many Bolivians are now seeing the importance of this visual reconstruction of history. This will eventually provide the basis for another kind of historical writing—oppositional and imagistic.

My role in the salvaging of popular memory is a transitory one. Such a task cannot be entrusted to a filmmaker of middle-class origins, nor even to several of them. It is essential that the *campesinos* themselves acquire the necessary means to enable them to record their own history as they see it. It looks like this is what is happening. I learned recently that Genaro Flores, the most important peasant leader, has just purchased a number of Super-8 cameras and has asked Alain Labrousse to offer a training course. The goal of such activity is not for the peasantry to reinvent cinema as we know it; they will develop another *kind* of expression based on more contemplative perceptual rhythms.

In Nicaragua

In a sense my work with the Central Obrera Sandinista [Sandinista Workers' Union] in Nicaragua gave me the opportunity to implement the kind of program that the military coups prevented me from putting into practice with its Bolivian counterpart, the COB. In June of 1980, prior to the Bolivian coup, I spent two weeks in Nicaragua as consultant for the United Nations, planning a workers' cinema training program. When I later returned to Nicaragua from my exile in Mexico, I came into a situation that had already been set up according to the plans we had developed earlier.

In fact, in some sense this particular situation threatened to be *too* favorable. In contrast to the circumstances I had to deal with in Bolivia, here I would be working in a country that was consolidating its new government after a massive revolutionary takeover; here I would also enjoy the full financial backing of the United Nations, the Nicaraguan Ministry of Planning, and so on. I decided that it was essential to impose some limits, lest the experiment we were about to carry out lose all connection to the realm of practical possibility as it exists today in most Latin American countries. From a purely personal standpoint, nothing would have pleased me more than the opportunity to spend three years working in Nicaragua under the sponsorship of the United Nations. But I insisted that the training course had to have a very limited time frame, since I wanted to prove that you only need a few months to successfully train workers in filmmaking techniques. I spent only six months in Nicaragua: one month was dedicated to preparation, another to teaching still photography, then three months on film apprenticeship; the final month was dedicated to tying up loose ends.

The second limitation I imposed had to do with equipment. The Super-8 Film Workshop [Taller de Cine Super-8] I set up was one of the cheapest projects of its kind that the U.N. has funded anywhere. Everything, including the equipment, the film stock, the cost of renovating our office, even my salary, amounted to only thirty thousand dollars. I insisted that we have but a single camera, a single moviola for editing, that there be only so many rolls of film, and so on.

I imposed these limits to accustom people to working under real as opposed to ideal conditions. I knew what had happened with other kinds of U.N. projects in the past. Two or three people are sent in to train a small group of nationals. After a year or more of work, they depart, leaving the equipment behind, but since in actuality *they* have retained control of everything, the people they have "trained" are incapable of doing anything on their own, so the equipment just sits in some closet gathering dust.

My goals were, first, to provide maximum apprenticeship in the shortest feasible time frame; second, to get maximum mileage out of a minimal amount of equipment; and third, to guarantee such an effective "transfer of technology" that after my departure, people would be completely capable of continuing on their own, without having to seek any additional assistance. I wanted to ensure that this first transfer of technology contained the necessary seeds for its own propagation in other groups, so I also trained my people to be able to teach others the skills I was teaching them.

There are several models for this kind of work. Jean Rouch's project in Mozambique is one of the most widely known. I happened to be in Mozambique when he first arrived to do some shooting in Super-8. Later, others from his group came and stayed about four months, teaching peasants and students from the University of Paputo. I saw that experiment firsthand and would criticize his method as growing out of a kind of "noble savage" theory. His assumption is that any transfer of technological knowledge "deforms" the native's own vision. You must simply give them the camera, show them which button to push, and tell them to shoot whatever they want. I am opposed to this approach. Since I am convinced that knowledge can never be a bad thing, my own approach is quite the opposite.

I began by trying to explain the nature and history of the medium. We screened classic and commercial films every evening, followed by sessions of film criticism. I encouraged the students to see all the movies they could. I wanted them to develop a profound sense of all that lay *behind* the screen, of how a particular image had been produced. Naturally, their first response involved a total immersion, which did not allow for critical distance. I used a very simple technique to disrupt that absorption: every time there was a cut, they all had to snap their fingers. That way I could be sure that they were alert to the way the images were assembled. A little later on, I began to ask them to name the various kinds of camera movements. I wanted them to be very aware of the components of film language so that the choices they would make as filmmakers would be informed and deliberate.

Initially, my students formed a very representative group: people from the Sandinista Workers' Union, the Association of Agricultural Workers, the Sandinista Youth organization, the Ministries of Planning and the Interior, and various women's organizations. We began with ten, but a number of people were transferred elsewhere or had to drop out for other reasons, so only five completed the course.

I was training a group of urban working people, with a long history of exposure to film and television, so it would have been absurd for me to expect them to erase that formation. I asked them to write brief critiques of the films we had seen after we had discussed them. At first these were mere plot summaries, and not always accurate at that, but it was remarkable how their critical awareness grew in just a few weeks. They began to see each film as an expression of a particular social, political, and historical context rather than as an isolated phenomenon.

We didn't use a single meter of film in the initial stages of training. I taught composition through still photography. Only one student had used a still camera before; none of the others had ever taken a single picture. We began by studying the Nikon itself—how it was put together, what optics are all about. Then we shot a roll of film together and developed it in our laboratory. The following week I asked them each to bring in three themes for a photoreportage. I had stipulated from the beginning that everything the Workshop produced had to be utilizable in the national Campaign for Economic Literacy, because the Workshop itself was part of that campaign. Nothing that we did was simply an exercise; everything had to face the test of its own usefulness in a larger context. I allotted each student a single roll of film and a single day to shoot it. They had to prepare their trajectory carefully beforehand, since they needed to cover every aspect of the particular theme they had selected, and to do it sequentially. I then told them to select the best fifteen shots, and handed out only eighteen sheets of printing paper apiece, which meant that they could only make three mistakes. The results were so impressive that we organized the official inauguration of our Super-8 Workshop around the exposition of those photo-reportages.

From there, it was just two short steps to filmmaking: we had to add movement and sound. I asked each student to prepare a script for a 5-minute documentary that could be shot in a single day. I allotted each of them 7 1/2 minutes of film. The members of the crew rotated jobs every day as each person in turn became the director-cinematographer, who would also later be the editor. One film dealt with a factory abandoned by its owners and then put back on line by the workers, another with housing, a third with the new urban markets, and so on. The official end of the course was marked with another public ceremony and the screening of the five documentaries.

While the documentary footage was being developed in Panama (there were no film labs in Nicaragua at the time), we began work on a collective feature film, to be called *Cooperativa Sandino*, which was conceived as a means of putting into practice all that they had learned. They would have to produce a much more structured screenplay, cast and direct actors, and do the kind of preparations necessary for making a fictional or semi-documentary film. I served as director, with the students filling the various technical positions. The film uses an imaginary cooperative to show what is happening in Nicaragua. We began by making a list of the most important issues facing the country: foreign debt, border attacks, internal subversion, reforestation, energy, food imports, and so on. Then we had to decide how to represent each of these issues in our film. The shooting lasted for two weeks. At each new location, we had to explain what the project was all about and enlist people's participation. The result is certainly not perfect: there are technical deficiencies, since the footage had to be processed outside the country and we weren't able to view it until two months later. We were working with a one-to-one shooting ratio; there was no chance of reshooting later what did not come out properly the first time. But the finished film also had a lot of humor and creative intelligence.

I have not gone back to see the progress that the group has made since I left, but I would like to. I understand that people are now working in video as well as Super-8. I began work on a film of my own in Managua, which I would like to finish. One of my students, Américo, himself a kind of crazy inventor who creates incredibly ingenious machines and dreams about three-dimensional cinema, brought his twelve-year-old son Carlos to the Workshop one day toward the end of the course. Carlos is a cartoonist who figured out on his own how to animate his drawings. He must have showed me fifty separate stories that day, composed of thousands of his own drawings and watercolors. He had even developed a primitive transparency technique. I made Carlos a proposition. "I know the techniques for filming animation," I told him. "You have made the drawings. Why don't we make a movie together?" I wanted to make a film about him, and through him, about childhood in Nicaragua. I am still looking for a way to finance this film. I only managed to shoot a portion of it and would very much like to finish it.

I don't know how people can assume that the working-class people are not creative enough to make their own movies when life gives us examples like Carlos and his father, people of enormous imagination and resourcefulness. If we "professionals" have eighty years of film history behind us, how can we begrudge workers five or ten or even fifteen years to develop their own tradition before jumping to the conclusion that they are incapable of doing so without our direction?

I also made a ten-minute short about the Workshop to use for fund-raising purposes. I had four copies made in New York and another four of *Cooperativa Sandino*. I sent three of each back to Nicaragua, but retained the remaining pair to show to whoever might be interested in providing financial support for the project.

Writing *El cine de los trabajadores* [*Workers' Cinema: Theoretical and Practical Support Manual for the Creation of Super-8 Film Workshops*, Managua, 1981] while I was working in Nicaragua was like diving headfirst into unknown waters. In its simple way, it was a call to transform the entire filmmaking process—not just production, but also distribution, reception, feedback, everything, through the transfer of technology. I don't believe that this transformation will be either quick or easy. These changes will take years to achieve. But I have made a commitment to this approach. Maybe that prevents me from having as much objectivity as I should, but I think all great transformations hinge on subjective factors like commitment and conviction. In the book I wrote in Nicaragua, and in my other writings and speeches, I am always insisting that we professionally trained filmmakers, no matter how progressive we might be, cannot constitute ourselves as the sole repositories of the power and potential of the film medium. We have to recognize that we are a small and privileged minority, but that the majority also have both the need and the ability to use the film medium as their own means of expression.

Viable Solutions

I'm not sure whether the new electronic media are going to make film obsolete, but my own view is broadening beyond film to include other communications technologies. Here in Mexico, I was recently hired as a consultant for the U.N.'s Food and Agriculture Organization [FAO] in a program for medium-sized regional peasant organizations. I realized that one cannot arbitrarily impose a particular communications medium on a particular sector. You have to study each situation with care before deciding what media solution is most viable.

I was assigned to work with a coffee and pepper producers' cooperative in Quetzalan, north of Puebla. I could have simply made a film about them, given it to them, and gone away satisfied that I had done my job. But that would have been a very limited response.

It was obvious from the start that there was a real lack of communication between the forty-four separate cooperatives that made up the main organization, since they were all located at some distance from one another, without effective means of transportation or the necessary resources to provide them. Some *campesinos* had to walk five or six hours to attend meetings. Few members even knew what the central cooperative was doing—where they were selling the pepper and for how much. The lack of information discouraged full participation. The organization was becoming less and less democratic as the decision-making power became increasingly limited to a smaller number of centrally located people.

I began to evaluate the means of communication these communities had at their disposal and how they utilized them. There were no theaters or movie projectors, so film was out of the question. Television was rare. The radio programs that reached the zone originated in Puebla and had virtually nothing to do with local concerns. The central cooperative put out a little mimeographed newspaper, an arid and unimaginative document. To make matters worse, it was published in Spanish although half the people in the region still speak Nahuatl and few are skilled at reading Spanish. None of the women either speak or read Spanish.

I had noticed that all the houses had radio-cassette machines. Apparently they are marketed only as a dual unit. Since no one in this region had cassettes, the tape recorder potential went unused. I decided to change that. We asked each of the forty-four member cooperatives to name a correspondent. We arranged a meeting of the correspondents in which the lack of information exchange between groups was demonstrated and discussed. I proposed that they begin to record a weekly news update [*noticiero*] on cassettes. We rigged up a recording system using local machines, familiarized everyone with the use of the microphone, and began asking what were the most important news items concerning the cooperative.

They made a list of ten items, which I asked them to rank in descending order of importance. Then we began to discuss various means of presenting each item: through interviews, from a written text, in dramatized form, etc. They decided that the interview format was the most viable for most of their needs. One of them would make up a list of questions and then track down the cooperative member with the most knowledge about that particular topic and conduct the interview.

The first *noticiero* was a half-hour long. We recorded it onto the other cassettes. On each cassette we wrote the name of one of the cooperatives, using a different color code for each. Inside the case we listed instructions, stipulating that the cassette could either be broadcast by loudspeaker in each community, played at the weekly or monthly assembly, or simply circulated from house to house, and that people were encouraged to make their own copies of the tape. The instructions also stipulated that on side B, which was blank, they could record news from their community and comments on the *noticiero* recorded on side A. The second *noticiero* was made up of a selection of the best feedback items, and so the system perpetuated itself, using the same forty-four cassettes. We saved only one original as a record, recycling all the others. The only financial outlay was the purchase of the first forty-five cassettes. They system is fully capable of perpetuating itself indefinitely without any additional expenditures except for the one cassette each week that is saved for a record.

Conclusion

I can no longer think of myself only as a filmmaker. Circumstances have compelled me to be much more eclectic. I am, as I said at the beginning of this interview, a kind of privileged victim of the reigning conditions in my country and on my continent. I cannot be indifferent to the persistent popular demand for means of bearing witness, of reconstructing the past and transmitting the present. This is just one example of what I mean when I maintain that each situation requires its own particular communications medium. A community "newspaper" or cassette is another form of conserving the popular memory and writing history from an alternative viewpoint.

I recognize that in this regard countries like Bolivia offer certain concrete advantages. The generalizations I make from that experience may not be relevant to other kinds of countries with other kinds of conditions. The very disparateness of my country, its lack of integration, provides more options for creating alternative communicational spaces. In countries like Argentina or Brazil, the situation is much more complex and problematic. Interestingly enough, my four months' experience working for FAO in Mexico has shown me that, despite all the differences, the situation in the Mexican countryside is not markedly superior to Bolivia's. The Mexican peasantry is just as economically disadvantaged as the Bolivian peasantry, and even more disadvantaged in political terms because it has been subjected to a degree of media conditioning and indoctrination that the Bolivian *campesinado* has up to now managed to escape. I have strolled late at night through a village in the most remote corner of Nayarit, where all was enveloped in silence and darkness except for one malevolent blue eye, which pulsated from one of the huts and the sound of "Charlie's Angels" spouting Spanish into the primordial stillness. To work in alternative media with people whose aspirations and values have been so distorted by the mass media presupposes a prior process of "de-mediatization." It is a process that will not be easy.

When the films made within the kind of alternative tradition I have been describing are shown to the group or groups for and with and by whom they were made, they need no introduction. But when I show one of them by way of example in another context, I always preface the screening by saying, "This film is not important. What *is* important is that this film represents a new tendency, a new line of action within the framework of *cine popular* [people's or popular cinema]." Each film is merely one example of a larger process.

Clearly, the approach I am proposing takes documentary filmmaking as its principal concern, although I am convinced that there will come a stage, once they have had a certain level of experience making films, when workers and peasants will begin to throw themselves into more imaginative modes of expression. It is only natural; it is only human. This imaginative capacity for fiction making exists in all of us. But I'm not about to predict what that kind of fictional filmmaking will look like, for we've barely entered into the first testimonial, documentary stage.

For Further Reading

Until recently, English-language writing on Latin American films and filmmakers was largely confined to magazines and professional journals. These occasional pieces remain an important informational source. (For a full listing and capsule summary of these articles organized chronologically by country and director, see my *The New Latin American Cinema: An Annotated Bibliography* [New York: Smyrna Press, 2d edition, 1983; forthcoming 3d edition.].) In the 1980s, a number of indispensable book-length works have come into print, beginning with Guy Hennebelle and Alfonso Gumucio Dagrón's country-by-country compendium history, *Les cinémas de l'Amérique Latine* (Paris: Lherminier, 1981). The first important work to appear in English was Randal Johnson and Robert Stam's *Brazilian Cinema* (East Brunswick, N.J.: Associated University Presses, 1982), a collection of historical, theoretical, and critical essays by Brazilian and North American authors. In 1983, the British Film Institute and Channel Four Television published an attractive oversize pamphlet, *Twenty-Five Years of the New Latin American Cinema*. Edited by Michael Chanan, this publication made the principal theoretical essays by the leading Latin American filmmakers widely available in English for the first time. Jorge A. Schnitman's institutional study, *Film Industries in Latin America: Dependency and Development*, which examines historical and contemporary patterns in film production in Argentina, Mexico, Chile, and Bolivia, appeared in 1984 (Norwood, N.J.: Ablex). That same year, Randal Johnson published *Cinema Novo x Five* (Austin: University of Texas Press), the first sustained auteurist study of Latin American directors to appear in English. Michael Chanan's *The Cuban Image: Cinema and Cultural Politics in Cuba* (London: BFI Publishing, and Bloomington: Indiana University Press), which appeared the following year, carried the national cinema history to a new level of comprehensiveness and intellectual sophistication.

During the same timespan, a number of important volumes have appeared in Spanish and Portuguese, with Mexico and Brazil the sites of much of this activity. In the English-speaking world, journals like *Jump/Cut: A Review of Contemporary Media* (Chicago and Berkeley), *Film Comment* (New York), and *Framework* (London) have devoted special issues to aspects of Latin American film. Foreign-language as well as English-language books, special journal issues, monographs, and dissertations are all listed and described in *The New Latin American Cinema*, mentioned at the beginning of this section.

Appendix
Films and Writings by Latin American Directors

Note: Appendix is restricted to people and works mentioned in the text.

Argentina
Aristaraín, Adolfo
  Tiempo de revancha
Birri, Fernando
  Che, Buenos Aires (composite; in-
  cludes *Buenos días, Buenos Aires*)
  Los inundados
  Org
  La pampa gringa
  Tire dié
  "For a Cosmic Cinema, Raving and
  Lumpen"
  "For a Nationalist, Realist, and
  Popular Cinema"
  *La Escuela Documental de Santa
  Fe*
Bonacina, Diego
Cedrón, Jorge
del Carril, Hugo
Denti, Jorge
  Trece años y un día
Favio, Leonardo
  Crónica de un niño solo
  El romance de Aniceto y la Francisca
Getino, Octavio
  La hora de los hornos
Gleyzer, Raymundo
  Los traidores
Goldenberg, Jorge
Solanas, Fernando
  La hora de los hornos
Vallejo, Gerardo
  La hora de los hornos

Bolivia
Bazoberry García, Luis
  La guerra del Chaco
Eguino, Antonio
  Amargo mar
  Chuquiago
  Pueblo chico
Gumucio Dagrón, Alfonso
  Cooperativa sandino
  Domitila
  Domitila, la mujer y la organización
  Comunidades de trabajo
  El ejército en Villa Anta
  Las elecciones sindicales en Vilolco
  Señores generales, señores coroneles
  Tupac Katari, 15 de noviembre
  "Super-8 Manifesto"
  *Cine, censura y exilio en América
  Latina*
  El cine de los trabajadores
  Historia del cine boliviano
Roca, Augusto
Ruiz, Jorge
  La vertiente
  Vuelve Sebastiana
Sanjinés, Jorge
  ¡Aysa!
  Las banderas del pueblo
  ¡Basta ya!
  Los caminos de la muerte (unfinished)
  El coraje del pueblo
  El enemigo principal
  ¡Fuera de aquí!

Sanjinés, Jorge (*continued*)
  Revolución
  Ukamau
  Yawar Mallku
  Teoría y práctica de un cine junto al pueblo
Velasco Maidana, José María
  La profecia del lago
  Warawara

Brazil
Bruno Bareto
  Dona Flor e seus dois maridos
Capovilla, Maurice
  Subterrâneos do futebol
Carneiro, Mário
Carolina, Ana
de Andrade, Joaquim Pedro
  Macunaíma
  Os inconfidentes
  O padre e a moça
Diegues, Carlos
  Bye bye Brasil
  Chuvas de verão
  Ganga Zumba
  A grande cidade
  Joana francesa
  Os herdeiros
  Quando o carnaval chegar
  Xica da Silva
dos Santos, Nelson
  O amuleto de Ogum
  Como era gostoso o meu francês
  Estrada da vida
  Fome de amor
  Memórias do cárcere
  Quem é Beta?
  Rio cuarenta graus
  Rio zona norte
  A tenda dos milagres
  Vidas secas
  "The Manifesto for a Popular Cinema"
Giménez, Manuel Horácio
  Nossa escola do samba
Guerra, Ruy
  Os fuzis
Hirszman, Leon

  Maioria absoluta
Jabor, Arnaldo
Mauro, Humberto
Muniz, Sérgio
Neves, David
Rocha, Glauber
  Antônio das mortes
  Barravento
  Cabeças cortadas
  Claro!
  Deus e o diabo na terra do sol
  A idade da terra
  Der leone have sept cabeças
  Terra em transe
  "The Aesthetics of Hunger"/"The Aesthetics of Violence"
Saraceni, Paulo César
  Capitú
Sarno, Gerardo
  Viramundo
Sganzerla, Rogério
  A mulher de todos
Soares, Paulo Gil
  Memória do cangaço
Solberg-Ladd, Helena
  The Brazilian Connection
  Chile: By Reason or by Force
  The Double Day
  The Emerging Woman
  A entrevista
  From the Ashes... Nicaragua Today
  Home of the Brave
  Meio dia
  Simplemente Jenny
Yamasaki, Tizuka

Chile
Francia, Aldo
  Valparaíso, mi amor
Guzmán, Patricio
  La batalla de Chile
  Manuel Rodríguez (unfinished)
  El primer año
  La respuesta de octubre
Kaulen, Patricio
Littín, Miguel
  Actas de Marusia

Alsino y el condor
El chacal de Nahueltoro
Recurso del método
La tierra prometida
La viuda de Montiel
Ruiz, Raúl
   Colloque des chiens
   La colonia penal
   Des grands evénéments et des gens
   ordinaires: les elections
   Diálogo de exiliados
   La expropriación (unfinished)
   L'Hypotèse du tableau volé
   Le jeu de l'oie
   Militarism and torture (unreleased)
   Petit manuel d'histoire de France
   ¿Qué hacer?
   Realismo socialista
   The Territory
   Tres tristes tigres
   La vocacion suspendue
Soto, Helvio

Colombia
Rodríguez, Marta
   Campesinos
   Chircales
   Planas: testimonio de un etnocidio
   Nuestra voz de tierra, memoria y
   futuro
Silva, Jorge
   (same as Rodríguez)

Cuba
Alvarez, Santiago
   Hanoi, martes 13
   Noticiero latinoamericano
   Now
Díaz, Jesús
García Espinosa, Julio
   Las aventuras de Juan Quin Quin
   Cuba baila
   El mégano
   Tercer mundo, tercera guerra mun-
   dial
   Son o no son
   "For an Imperfect Cinema"

Una imagen recorre el mundo
Giral, Sergio
   El otro Francisco
Gómez, Manuel Octavio
   La primera carga al machete
   Ustedes tienen la palabra
Gómez, Sara
   De cierta manera
Gutiérrez Alea, Tomás
   Las doce sillas
   La muerte de un burócrata
   Memorias del subdesarrollo
   La última cena
   Una pelea cubana contra los demonios
   Dialéctica del espectador
Herrera, Manuel
   Girón
Pineda Barnet, Miguel
   Mella
Solás, Humberto
   Cantata de Chile
   Cecilia
   Lucía
   Manuela
   Minerva traduce el mar
   Simparele
   Un día de noviembre
Valdés, Oscar
   El extraño caso de Rachel K
Vega, Pastor
   Viva la república

Mexico
Cazals, Felipe
   Canoa
de Fuentes, Fernando
Fernández, Emilio
Fernández Violante, Marcela
   Azul
   Cananea
   De todos modos Juan te llamas
   En el país de los pies ligeros
   Frida
   Misterio
Leduc, Paul
Navarro, Berta
Toscano, Carmen

Toscano, Carmen (*continued*)
Memorias de un mexicano
Ronda revolucionaria

Nicaragua
Caldera, Franklin
Ibarra, Carlos Vicente
Lacayo, Ramiro

Peru
Chambi, Manuel
Carnaval de Kanas

Uruguay
Handler, Mario
Carlos: cine-retrato de un caminante
Elecciones
En Praga
Me gustan los estudiantes

Liber Arce, liberarse
Uruguay 1969: el problema de la carne
Maggi, Carlos
La raya amarilla
Mantarás Rogé, Alberto
Punta del Este, ciudad sin horas
Miller, Alberto
Cantegriles
Musitelli, Feruccio
Piriápolis
Tournier, Walter
En la selva hay mucho por hacer
Ulive, Ugo
Como el Uruguay no hay
Crónica cubana
Elecciones
Un vintén pa'l Judas

Index of Films

A la cola (Get in Line), 5
Actas de Marusia (Letters from Marusia), 199
The African Queen, 234
Alsino y el cóndor (Alsino and the Condor), 234
Amargo mar (Bitter Sea), 48 n.2, 161
O amuleto de Ogum (The Amulet of Ogum), 133, 134, 135-136
Angeles del arrabal (Slum Angels), 196
Antonieta, 204
Antônio das Mortes (O dragão da maldade contra o santo guerreiro), 106-107, 109-113, 177, 225
Las aventuras de Juan Quin Quin (The Adventures of Juan Quin Quin), 247-248, 255
L'avventura, 144
¡Aysa! (Landslide!), 35
Azul (Blue), 197
Azyllo muito louco (The Alienist), 133

Las banderas del amanecer (The Banners of the Dawn), 36
Barravento (Turning Wind), 105
Barren Lives, 53, 133, 177, 225
¡Basta ya! (That's Enough!), 36
La batalla de Chile (The Battle of Chile), 49, 50-58, 59, 62-66, 76, 244
The Battle of the Ten Million, 68 n
Bicycle Thief (Ladri di bicicleti), 4
Black God, White Devil, 106, 224, 225, 227

Black Orpheus, 137
Blood of the Condor, 22, 36, 40-41, 43-47, 48 n.7, 146, 161, 162-163, 229-230
Un boliche (A Tavern), 5
The Brazilian Connection, 97-99, 100
The Brickmakers, 25, 26-29, 31, 32, 78
Bullit, 240, 242n
Bye Bye Brasil, 171, 177-178

Cabeças cortadas (Severed Heads), 144 n.4
Calcutta, 53, 155
Los caminos de la muerte (The Roads of Death), 41, 166, 266
Campanas rojas (Red Bells), 204, 205
Campesinos (Peasants), 25
Cananea, 198, 199-200
Canoa, 199
Cantata de Chile, 143, 149, 152-153, 157, 211
Cantegriles, 18
Capitú, 85, 88
Carlos: Cine-retrato de un caminante (Carlos: Cine-Portrait of a Vagabond), 19-20
Carnaval de Kanas, 18
Cecilia, 143
El Chacal de Nahueltoro (The Jackal of Nahueltoro), 78, 146, 186, 211, 214, 215, 217, 232, 234
Che, Buenos Aires, 7
Chile: By Reason or by Force, 97, 99-100

Chircales (The Brickmakers), 25, 26-
    29, 31, 32, 78
Chuquiago, 48 n.1, 161, 164, 166-
    167, 273, 275
Chuvas de verão (Summer Showers),
    175, 176, 178
Colloque des chiens (Dogs' Dialogue),
    192, 193
La colonia penal (The Penal Colony),
    187
Como el Uruguay no hay (There's No
    Place Like Uruguay), 18
Como era gostoso o meu francês (How
    Tasty Was My Little Frenchman),
    133, 134, 139
Comunidades de trabajo (Work Com-
    munities), 272-273
El conventillo, 5
Cooperativa sandino, 280
El coraje del pueblo (The Courage of
    the People, 36, 41-42, 48 n.5, 78,
    161, 163, 167, 168, 230-231, 267,
    271
Crónica cubana, 19
Crónica de un niño solo (Chronicle of a
    Boy Alone), 224
Los cuarenta cuartos (The Forty
    Rooms), 8
Cuba baila (Cuba Dances), 250

Death of a Bureaucrat, 120, 121, 225
De cierta manera (One Way or An-
    other), 78, 120-121, 127, 248-249
Des grands événements et des gens
    ordinaires: Les élections (Of Great
    Events and Ordinary People: The
    Elections), 182, 184, 191, 192, 193
De todos modos Juan te llamas (What-
    ever You Do, It's No Good), 198-
    199, 200
Deus e o diabo na terra do sol (Black
    God, White Devil), 106, 224, 225,
    227
Diálogo de exiliados (Dialogue of
    Exiles), 188, 192, 193
Un día de noviembre (A Day in
    November), 153, 154

Las doce sillas (The Twelve Chairs),
    19
Domitila, 274
Domitila, la mujer y la organización
    (Domitila, the Woman and the Or-
    ganization), 274
Dona Flor e seus dois maridos (Dona
    Flor and Her Two Husbands), 137
The Double Day, 81, 88-92, 95, 98
Duel in the Sun, 234
Dune, 204

La educación no se interrumpió (Edu-
    cation Was Not Interrupted), 78
El ejército en Villa Anta (The Army in
    Villa Anta), 272
Elecciones (Elections), 20, 227
Las elecciones sindicales en Viloco
    (Union Elections in Viloco), 269
The Emerging Woman, 81, 85, 87-88,
    98
En el país de los pies ligeros (In the
    Land of the Light Feet), 203
El enemigo principal (The Principal
    Enemy), 36
En la selva hay mucho por hacer (In
    the Jungle There's a Lot to Do), 231
En Praga (In Prague), 14
A entrevista (The Interview), 81, 82-84
Estrada da vida (The Road of Life),
    133
La expropriación (The Expropriation),
    187
El extraño caso de Rachel K (The
    Strange Case of Rachel K), 248

La fievre monte a El Pao, 174
The First Charge of the Machete, 58,
    121, 151, 225, 230
The First Year, 49, 54, 58, 59, 232
Fists in the Pocket (I pugni in tasca),
    224
Fome de amor (Hunger for Love), 133
Frida Kahlo, 198
From the Ashes . . . Nicaragua Today,
    81, 93-97
¡Fuera de aquí! (Get Out of Here!), 36,

267-268
Os fuzis (The Guns), 177

Ganga Zumba, 172, 174, 176, 177, 178
Gayosso da descuentos (Gayosso Gives Discounts), 197
Giordano Bruno, 140
Girón (Bay of Pigs), 121, 248
A grande cidade (The Big City), 176, 178
La guerra del Chaco, 265

Hacia la gloria (Bound for Glory), 266
Hanoi, martes 13 (Hanoi, Tuesday April 13th), 74
Harakiri, 224
Harlan County, U.S.A., 76
Os herdeiros (The Heirs), 106, 108, 172, 174, 175, 176, 179
Hiroshima, mon amour, 145
The Home of the Brave, 100, 102
Un homme et une femme (A Man and a Woman), 227
La hora de los hornos (The Hour of the Furnaces), 23, 53, 228, 262
How Tasty Was My Little Frenchman, 133, 134, 139
La huelga de hambre (The Hunger Strike), 269, 271
L'Hypotèse du tableau volé (The Hypothesis of the Stolen Painting), 189, 192, 193

A idade da terra (The Age of the Earth), 105
I Like Students, 22, 23, 53, 228-229
Os inconfidentes (The Conspirators), 134
La inundación de Santa Fe (The Flooding of Santa Fe), 7
Los inundados (Flooded Out), 1, 223

The Jackal of Nahueltoro, 78, 146, 186, 211, 214, 215, 217, 232, 234
Jaws, 125
The Jazz Singer, 2

La jetée, 68 n
Le jeu de l'oie (Snakes and Ladders), 193
Joana Francesa (Joanna the Frenchwoman), 176, 177

The Lady Vanishes, 224
Land in Anguish, 106, 107, 108, 172, 225
The Last Supper, 119, 121, 122-123, 158, 211, 216, 218
Der leone have sept cabeças (The Lion Has Seven Heads), 114 n.3
Letter from Siberia, 68 n
Liber Arce, liberarse, 23
Lucía, xiv, 143, 148-151, 153, 225, 234, 244, 247

Macunaíma, 106, 108, 172, 225, 230
Maioria absoluta (Absolute Majority), 226
The Man from Maisinicú (El hombre de Maisinicú), 145
Manuela, 143, 147-148, 150
Manuel Rodríguez, 58
La Marseillaise, 74
El mégano (The Charcoal Worker), 115, 123, 243
Me gustan los estudiantes (I Like Students), 22, 23, 53, 228-229
Meio dia (Noon), 85
Mella, 121, 149, 150, 158, 248
Memória do cangaço (Memory of the Cangaço), 9
Memorias de un mexicano (Memories of a Mexican), 196
Memórias do cárcere (Prison Memoirs), 133
Memories of Underdevelopment (Memorias del subdesarrollo), xiv, 115, 116-119, 121, 129-130, 145, 246
Mercado de abasto (Public Market), 5
Militarism and Torture, 187
Minerva traduce el mar (Minerva Translates the Sea), 144
Misterio (Mystery), 201-203
Monimbó es Nicaragua, 76

La muerte de un burócrata (Death of a Bureaucrat), 120, 121, 225
La mujer de nadie (Nobody's Woman), 196
A mulher de todos (Everybody's Woman), 85

La negra Angustias (Angustias the Black Woman), 196
Nossa escola do samba (Our Samba School), 9
Noticiero Latinoamericano (Latin American Weekly Newsreel), 75
Now, 226
Nuestra voz de tierra, memoria, y futuro (Our Voice of Earth, Memory, and Future), 26
Nuncia, 5

One Way or Another, 78, 120-121, 127, 248-249
Org, 1, 5, 10-11
Ossessione, 146
El otro Cristóbal (The Other Christopher), 225
El otro Francisco (The Other Francisco), 121, 248

O padre e a moça (The Priest and the Girl), 85
El palanquero (The Pile Driver), 7
La pampa gringa, 1, 7
Patria libre o morir (Free Homeland or Death), 70, 71
Una pelea cubana contra los demonios (A Cuban Struggle against the Demons), 122, 130
Petit manuel d'histoire de France (Handbook of French History), 190
Piriápolis, 223, 224
Planas: Testimonio de un etnocidio (Planas: Testimony about an Ethnocide), 25
La primera carga al machete (The First Charge of the Machete), 58, 121, 151, 225, 230
El primer año (The First Year), 49, 54, 58, 59, 232
La profecía del lago (The Prophecy of the Lake), 265
Pueblo chico (Small Town), 48 n.2, 161, 163-166
El puente de papel (The Paper Bridge), 7
Punta del Este, ciudad sin horas (Punta del Este, City without Hours), 223

Quando o carnaval chegar (When Carnival Comes), 174, 178
¿Qué hacer? 183
Quem é Beta? (Who Is Beta?), 134
Que Viva México, 203

La raya amarilla (The Yellow Line), 223
Realismo socialista (Socialist Realism), 187, 188
El recurso del método (Reasons of State/Viva el presidente), 211, 216-217, 218
Red Desert (Il deserto rosso), 146
La respuesta de octubre (October's Answer), 49, 59
Revolución, 35, 48 n.3
Rio cuarenta graus (Rio Forty Degrees), 18, 133
Rio zona norte (Rio Northern Zone), 17
El romance de Aniceto y la Francisca (The Ballad of Aniceto and Francisca), 20, 224, 227
Rome, Open City (Roma, città aperta), 4
Ronda revolucionaria (Revolutionary Round), 196

Señores generales, señores coroneles, 262
Simparele, 143, 153
Simplemente Jenny, 81, 92, 95
Son o no son, 253-254, 257 n
Subterráneos do futebol (Soccer Underground), 9

Sunday in Peking, 68 n

Tenda dos milagres (*Tent of Miracles*), 133, 134, 137, 138-141

Tercer mundo, tercera guerra mundial (*Third World, Third World War*), 52, 53, 65

Terra em transe (*Land in Anguish*), 106, 107, 108, 172, 225

La terra trema, 4, 146

The Territory, 193

Il tetto, 4

Tiempo de revancha (*Time of Revenge*), 206

La tierra prometida (*The Promised Land*), 211

Tire dié (*Throw Me a Dime*), 1, 5, 6-7, 18, 222

Tootsie, 204

Los traidores (*The Traitors*), 232

Trece años y un día (*Thirteen Years and a Day*), 234-235

Tres tristes tigres (*Three Sad Tigers*), 185, 186, 187, 211, 214

La trotacalles (*The Streetwalker*), 196

Tupac Katari, 15 de noviembre (*Tupac Katari, November 15th*), 271

Ukamau (*That's the Way It Is*), 36, 39, 40, 44, 162, 163, 266

La última cena (*The Last Supper*), 119, 121, 122-123, 158, 211, 216, 218

Under the Volcano, 204

Uruguay 1969, el problema de la carne (*Uruguay 1969: The Meat Problem*), 23

Ustedes tienen la palabra (*Now It's Up to You*), 120

Vaghe stelle dell'orsa, 146

Valparaíso mi amor (*Valparaíso My Love*), 186

La vertiente (*The Watershed*), 37, 266

Vidas Secas (*Barren Lives*), 53, 133, 177, 225

Un vintén pa'l Judas (*Two Bits for Judas*), 18

Viramundo, 9, 20

Viridiana, 117

La viuda de Montiel (*Montiel's Widow*), 211

¡Viva la República! (*Long Live the Republic!*), 53

La vocation suspendue (*The Interrupted Vocation*), 182, 186, 187, 189, 192

Vuelve Sebastiana (*Come Back, Sebastiana*), 18, 37, 266

Warawara, 37, 265

With Babies and Banners, 88

Xica da Silva, 140, 171, 175, 178, 179

Yawar Mallku (*Blood of the Condor*), 22, 36, 40-41, 43-47, 48 n.7, 146, 161, 162-163, 229-230

Zéro de conduite, 85

General Index

Achugar, Walter, 14, 20, 21, 22, 221-236
Actors: nonprofessional/social, xii, 17, 41, 148, 149, 152, 267-268; professional, 6-7, 85, 201-202, 211-218; working with improvisation, 146-148, 187
Adaptation, from literary works, 117-118, 137-138, 142, 186, 189, 201, 202, 216-217, 248
Almendros, Néstor, 263
Alsina Thevenet, Homero, 222
Alvarez, Santiago, 31, 74, 75, 226, 247
Alvear, Marta, 143
Alves, Cosme, 20
Andrade, Rudá, 8
Añon, Plácido, 14
Antonioni, Michelangelo, 145, 146
Argentina Sono Film Studios, 3
Aristaraín, Adolfo, 206
Auteurism, xiii, xvi, 136, 182, 204
Avant-garde, 110, 154, 185, 186, 261

Banchero, Marcos, 229
Bareto, Bruno, 137
Barrios de Chungara, Domitila, 90-91, 269, 274, 275
Bazin, André, 16
Bazoberry García, Luis, 265
Beato, Affonso, 89, 98, 99
Bernardet, Jean Claude, 83
Bertolucci, Bernardo, 175
Bethânia, Maria, 178
Birri, Fernando, xiii, 1-11, 17, 18,

222, 223
Bolivia: military coup of 1971, 48 n.2, 163, 260; revolution of 1952, 262, 270
Bonacina, Diego, 8
Bondarchuk, Sergei, 204
Borges, Miguel, 173
Botet, Jaime Francisco, 222
Brazil: coup d'état of April 1, 1964, 9, 82, 83, 134; Institutional Act No. Five, 1968, 134, 172
Brechtian ("distancing") techniques, 42-43, 109, 122, 138, 165-166, 200, 215, 248
Buarque, Chico, 178
Buñuel, Luis, 116, 174
Burrill, Christine, 89, 92

Cahiers du Cinéma, 16, 173, 261
Caicedo, Andrés, 26
Caldera, Franklin, 73
Camus, Marcel, 137
Candomblé, 137
Cangaçeiro, 106, 111, 112-113
Capovilla, Maurice, 8, 9, 12 n.3
Carneiro, Mário, 83
Carolina, Ana, 84
Casal, Lourdes, 244
Castilla, Patricio, 61
Castilla, Sergio, 61
Castro, Miguel, 16, 223
Cazals, Felipe, 199
Cedrón, Jorge, 8
Censorship, xvi, 7-8, 20, 39, 101, 111,

Censorship (*continued*)
112, 138, 198, 204, 233, 259, 265, 269

Central Obrera Boliviana, Bolivian Workers' Union (COB), 270, 275, 276

Central Obrera Sandinista (Sandinista Workers' Union), 277

Centro de Integración de Medios de Comunicación Alternativa, Alternative Mass Communications Coordinating Center (CIMCA), 259

Centro de Investigación y Promoción del Campesinado, Center for Peasant Research and Advancement (CIPCA), 269-276

Centro Sperimentale di Cinematografia, 3, 5, 115, 243

Centro Universitario de Estudios Cinematográficos, University Center for Film Education (CUEC), 195, 196-197

Chambi, Manuel, 17, 18

Chanchada, xii

Chaplin, Charlie, 73, 224, 255

Chaskel, Pedro, 53, 61, 64

Chile: coup d'état of September 1973, 50, 52, 62-65; Films, 58, 59, 60-61

Christie, Ian, 181

Cine, censura y exilio en América Latina, 259, 276

Cine cubano (Cuban film magazine), 52, 143, 219 n

El cine de los trabajadores (*Workers' Cinema: Theoretical and Practical Support Manual for the Creation of Super-8 Film Workshops*), 259, 281

Cinema, mobile, 7, 59, 76-77; popular, xiv, 10, 135, 136, 281, 284

Cinema Novo, xiv, 82, 83, 84, 105, 114 n.1, 125, 133, 134, 135, 141, 146, 171, 172, 179, 206, 225, 226

Cinéma verité, xiii

Cinemateca. See Film societies

Cine rebelde (Cuba), 243

Cine urgente, 13

Coad, Malcolm, 181

Colina, Enrique, 237-241

Colombia, history of *la violencia*, 26, 3 n.1

Color, 18, 37, 74, 75, 108, 110-111, 122, 266

Comedia ranchera, xii

Comité de Cineastas de América Latina (Latin American Filmmakers' Committee), 232, 236

Commissão de Auxílio à Indústria Cinematográfica, Commission to Aid the Film Industry (CAIC), Brazil, 84

"Communicability," 40, 43, 125

Compadrazgo, 28, 34 n.3

CONACINE (Mexican state-owned film production company), 201, 202

Corrieri, Sergio, 144

Cuba, takeover by Castro forces, January 1959, 74

Culture: mass, xiv, 244-255; popular, 108, 111, 133, 135, 138, 142, 143, 152, 153, 175, 177, 185, 243, 245-256, 267

Dassori, Walter, 16

de Andrade, Joaquim Pedro, 83, 85, 106, 108, 114 n.1, 134, 172, 179, 225

"Deconstructive": cinema, 119-120, 121-122, 247-249; criticism (*desmontaje*), 239-241, 242 n.1

de Fuentes, Fernando, 17

del Carril, Hugo, 17

Demaré, Lucas, 17

Denti, Jorge, 234

Departamento de Inteligencia Nacional, National Department of Intelligence (DINA), 64

De Sica, Vittorio, 4, 15, 156

Desnoes, Edmundo, 117

Dialéctica del espectador, 115

Díaz, Jesús, 76

Dicimoveca (Distribuidora Cinematográfica Venezolana Compañía Anónima, Venezuelan Film Distribution Company, 232

Diegues, Carlos, xiv, 82, 85, 106, 108,

114n, 140, 171-179
Distancing techniques. *See* Brechtian
    techniques
Distribution, 15, 165, 166, 205, 206,
    223-224, 228, 232-233; in Cuba,
    125-126; independent, 28, 29, 30-
    31, 92-93; international, 111, 268;
    Super-8, 268
Documentary: methodology, 5-6, 19,
    20, 21-22, 26-27, 53-55; reconstruc-
    tion, 27, 41-42, 267-268, 271-272,
    277
dos Santos, Nelson Pereira, xiv, 17, 53,
    114 n.1, 133-141, 171, 172, 179, 225

Eguino, Antonio, 48 n.2, 161-169, 262,
    266-267, 269
Eisenstein, Sergey, 203
Elton, Federico, 49, 56, 64
Embrafilme, xiv, 134, 135
Equipo Tercer Año (Third-Year Group),
    Chile, 49, 56-57, 63-65
Escuela de Cine y Televisión (School of
    Film and Television), Cuba, 1
Escuela Documental de Santa Fe (Doc-
    umentary Film School of Santa Fe),
    5, 9, 11, 18, 222, 223; formation of,
    4-8; history of, 4-8
La Escuela Documental de Santa Fe,
    12 n.2
Espina, Luis, 26
Espinal, Luis (Father), 269, 275
Exhibition, 15, 136, 205, 225, 227,
    228, 273-274; in Cuba, 238; quota
    system, 114 n.2; via television, 234
Exile, 10, 36, 167, 188, 191-192, 193,
    218, 231, 260, 276
Experimental Film Group, Chile, 61

Faria, Betty, 177
Farias, Roberto, 135
Farkas, Tomaz, 8, 9, 225
Favio, Leonardo, 20, 224
Federación Venezolana de Centros de
    Cultura, Venezuelan Federation of
    Cultural Centers (FEVEC), 233
Feminism, 92, 150-151

Fernández, Emilio, 203
Fernández, Joseíto, 160
Fernández Violante, Marcela, 195-207
Ferrara, Juan, 201
Figueroa, Gabriel, 203
Film festivals: Europe: Biarritz, 203;
    Cannes, 224, 228; Krakow, Poland,
    84; Leipzig, 23, 35; London, 182,
    198; Moscow, 198; Oberhausen,
    198; Pesaro, Italy, 228; Populi,
    Italy, 84; Sestri Levante, Italy (Colum-
    bianum), 224; Venice, 230; Latin
    America: Festival de Cine Indepen-
    diente del Cono Sur (Festival of
    Independent Film from the Southern
    Cone), 20; Havana Festival of the
    New Latin American Cinema, 2, 11,
    13-14, 69, 75, 76, 206, 236, 244;
    Mar del Plata (Argentina), 223;
    Marcha (Uruguay), 19, 20, 21, 225,
    226-227, 228; Mérida (Venezuela),
    22, 25, 228; Punta del Este (Uruguay),
    15; SODRE (Sociedad Radio-Eléc-
    trica, Radio-Electric Broadcasting
    Society of Uruguay), 6, 12 n.1, 17,
    20, 37, 222; Viña del Mar (Chile),
    20, 53, 214, 226; North America:
    Chicago, 203; FilmEx (Los Angeles),
    203; Museum of Modern Art "New
    Directors, New Films," 198; New
    York, 203; San Francisco, 230
Film societies, 3, 15, 16, 74, 84; Cine-
    Club del Uruguay, 16; Cine-Club
    Núcleo (Argentina), 222; Cine-Club
    Universitario (Uruguay), 16, 222;
    Cinemateca del Tercer Mundo (Third
    World Cinematheque), Uruguay, 23,
    24 n, 225, 229, 232; Cinemateca do
    Museu do Arte Moderno, São Paulo,
    8; Cinemateca do Museu do Arte
    Moderno, Rio de Janeiro, 20, 82,
    85, 173; Cinemateca Uruguaya, 16,
    235; Cineteca Nacional de México,
    205
Flaherty, Robert, 17
Folbré, Nancy, 36
Ford, John, 179

Francia, Aldo, 186
Frente Sandinista de Liberación Nacional, Sandinista National Liberation Front (FSLN), Nicaragua, 69, 70; Equipo de Prensa y Propaganda (War Correspondents' Corps of), 69, 71, 73; Office of Information to the Exterior of, 71

García Espinosa, Julio, xiv, 52, 53, 65, 71, 78, 115, 123, 131 n.4, 228, 243-256
García Joya, Mario, 122
García Márquez, Gabriel, 9, 191
García Riera, Emilio, 9, 205
Gatti, Armand, 225
Genre, 240; contemporary issues, 120; epic, 109; *film noir*, 240; historical, 120-121, 158, 190, 191, 277; multiple, 202; musical, 253-254; "road movie," 177; subversion of, 121, 247-249
Getino, Octavio, xiii, 53
Giménez, Manuel Horacio, 8, 9
Giral, Sergio, 248
Gleyzer, Raymundo, 8, 232
Godard, Jean-Luc, 107, 124-125, 174, 179, 228
Goldenberg, Jorge, 8
Gómez, Manuel Octavio, 58, 120, 225
Gómez, Sara, 78, 120, 131 n.1, 248-249
Grey, Lorraine, 88
Grierson, John, 16, 17
Grupo Experimental de Cine Universitario, University Experimental Film Group (GECU), Panama, 73
Grupo Tercer Año (Chile), xiii, 51-55, 59
Grupo Ukamau, Bolivia. *See* Ukamau Group
Guerra, Ruy, 114 n.1, 261
Guevara, Alfredo, 64, 222, 226, 228, 233, 243
Gumucio Dagrón, Alfonso, 259-284
Gupta, Udayan, 162
Gutiérrez Alea, Tomás, 18, 115-130, 211, 225, 228, 235, 246

Guzmán, Patricio, xiii, 49-66, 76, 232, 235, 244

Haber, Roberta, 87
Handler, Mario, xiii, 13-23, 53, 226, 227, 228, 229
Hanstra, Bert, 17
Harnecker, Marta, 55, 59, 64
Hawks, Howard, 179
Herrera, Manuel, 248
Herzog, Vladimir, 8, 12 n.3
Hirszman, Leon, 53, 114 n.1, 173, 226
Historia del cine boliviano, 259, 264-266
Hollywood, xii, xiii, xiv, xvii, 3, 4, 16, 111, 123, 126, 128, 151, 163, 204, 234, 248. *See also* Mode of production, industrial
Huston, John, 204

Ibarra, Carlos Vicente, 69-70, 72-79
Identification, 43, 93-95, 117, 119, 212, 240
IDHEC, 3, 260-263
Una imagen recorre al mundo, 244, 255
"Imperfect cinema,", xiv, 29, 52, 71
Instituto Cinematográfico Boliviano, Bolivian Film Institute (ICB), 39, 48 n.4, 162
Instituto Cinematográfico de la Universidad de la República, Film Institute of the University of the Republic of Uruguay (ICUR), 14, 20
Instituto Cubano de Arte e Industria Cinematográficas, Cuban Institute of Cinematic Art and Industry (ICAIC), 10, 18, 64-65, 76, 114, 121, 127-130, 142, 143, 154, 158-159, 224, 226, 233, 238, 243, 244, 248, 254
Instituto Nacional de Cine, National Film Institute (INCINE), Nicaragua, 69, 71, 73, 75, 77, 93
International Women's Film Project, 89, 102
Istmo Films (Costa Rica), 70
Ivens, Joris, 17, 229

Jabor, Arnaldo, 82, 173, 179
Jacob, Mario, 226, 229
Jaiwaco, 45-46
Johnson, Randal, 133
Junco, Víctor, 201
Júnior, Fábio, 177

Kaulen, Patricio, 17
Keaton, Buster, 255
Kopple, Barbara, 76

Labrousse, Alain, 263, 269, 277
Lacayo, Ramiro, 73, 93
Landau, Saul, 183
Landeta, Matilde, 196
Larrosa, Daniel, 229
Leacock, Richard, 17
Leão, Nara, 178
Léaud, Jean-Pierre, 176
Leduc, Paul, 235
Legrá, Adela, 148
Lelouch, Claude, 227
Lillienthal, Peter, 76
Littín, Miguel, 60-61, 78, 89, 146, 167,
    186, 189, 199, 211, 214, 232, 261
López Portillo, Margarita, 201, 205

Maggi, Carlos, 223
Maholik, Melanie, 81, 87, 89
Malle, Louis, 53, 156, 173
Manifestoes: "The Aesthetics of Hun-
    ger"/"The Aesthetics of Violence"
    (Glauber Rocha), 105, 146, 159
    n.2; "For a Cosmic Cinema, Raving
    and Lumpen" (Fernando Birri), 10;
    "For an Imperfect Cinema" (Julio
    García Espinosa), 52, 65, 78, 244,
    246-247; "The Manifesto for a
    Popular Cinema" (Nelson Pereira
    dos Santos), 135; "For a Nationalist,
    Realist, and Popular Cinema" (Fer-
    nando Birri), 10; "The Super-8
    Manifesto" (Alfonso Gumucio Da-
    grón), 270, 275
Mantarás Rogé, Alberto, 16, 223
Marker, Chris, 17, 53, 55, 58, 59, 64,

68 n
Marxism, 110, 139, 156, 184-185,
    189, 212
Maselli, Francesco, 4
Mauro, Humberto, 17
Menz, Bernardo, 56, 57
Mercado de Cine Latinoamericano,
    Latin American Film Market (ME-
    CLA), 236
Meyer, David, 97, 99, 101
Miller, Alberto, 18
Miranda, Carmen, 176
Mode of production: artisanal, xiii, xvi,
    187; collaborative (with mass partici-
    pation), 28, 41-42, 46, 78-79, 267-
    268; coproduction, 9, 76, 134, 225;
    independent, 97, 205; industrial, xii,
    xvi, 77, 107, 166, 182, 187, 205-
    206; state participation, xv, 129-
    130, 204, 205; for television, 95, 97-
    99, 235
Montaldo, Giuliano, 141
Moreau, Jeanne, 177
Movimiento de Izquierda Revoluciona-
    ria, Movement of the Revolutionary
    Left (MIR), Chile, 60, 185, 187
Movimiento Nacional Revolucionario,
    National Revolutionary Movement
    (MNR), Bolivia, 164, 169 n
Mraz, John, 195
Muller, Jorge, 56, 57, 59, 63
Muniz, Sérgio, 8
Music, xii, 21, 108, 111, 143, 179, 185,
    212, 244, 245, 249-252, 254
Musitelli, Feruccio, 223

Nabor, Príncipe, 177
National Film Board of Canada, 77
National identity/national reality, xiii,
    5-6, 11, 19, 47, 206, 214, 252
Navarro, Berta, 76
Neorealism, Italian, xii, 3, 16, 123,
    156, 179, 185, 186
Neorealist model, 17, 127, 167, 223, 243
Neves, David, 82
New Latin American Cinema Founda-
    tion, 236

New Latin American Cinema movement, xi, xv, xvii, 2, 11, 14, 15, 206, 223, 233, 246
Newsreel (*noticiero*), 75, 80 n, 282-283
New Wave, French (Nouvelle Vague), 124, 144, 173, 179, 185
Nicaragua, Sandinista takeover of, July 1979, 69

"One Hundred Years of Struggle" ("Cien años de lucha"), Cuba, 150

Palcine (Venezuela), 232-233
Pallero, Edgardo, 9, 222, 228, 230
Participatory observation, 6, 19, 29, 32, 41, 78, 79, 121
Pennebaker, Donn, 17
Photodocumentary/photoreportage, 4, 5, 6, 27, 279-280
Pineda Barnet, Enrique, 149-150, 248
Pino, José, 56
Pitanga, Antonio, 178
"Popular memory," xiii, 36, 42, 273, 277, 283
Popular Unity coalition/government (Chile), 49, 57, 187, 188
Producine (Nicaragua), 73, 74, 77

Race: blacks, 136, 138, 140, 158, 174-175; indigenous peoples, 38-47, 100, 139, 164, 165, 167, 177, 194 n, 200, 203, 267, 272-274
Rada, Ricardo, xiii, 45, 48 n.2, 162, 266-267
Radio, 12, 28, 40, 61, 73, 252, 254, 271, 275
Radio Sandino, 73
Radio-Televisione Italiana, Italian Radio and Television (RAI), 163, 230-231, 267
Radio Venceremos Film and Video Collective, xv
Reception (how a film relates to audience and vice versa), 28-29, 42-43, 107-109, 119, 126-127, 128, 151-152, 162, 166, 237-241, 284

Reconstruction. *See* Documentary: reconstruction
Religion, Afro-Brazilian, 136-137, 138
Renoir, Jean, 74
Repression, 135, 231, 276; response to, 10, 95-97, 101, 164, 168, 172, 174. *See also* Exile
Resnais, Alain, 145, 173
Revuelta, Raquel, 148
Rivera, Pedro, 73
Roca, Augusto, 266
Rocha, Glauber, xiv, 84, 89, 105-114, 125, 134, 146, 167, 172, 173, 179, 224, 225, 227, 261
Rodríguez, Marta, xiii, 11, 26-33, 78
Rodríguez Vázquez, Emilio, 69-78
Rouch, Jean, 17, 261, 279
Ruiz, Jorge, 17, 37, 266
Ruiz, Raúl, 59, 181-194, 211, 214, 261

Salles Gomes, Paulo Emílio, 8
Sanjinés, Jorge, xiii, 35-47, 48 n.2, 78, 162, 164, 229, 230-231, 235, 261, 264, 266-268
Saraceni, Paulo César, 83, 85, 88, 114 n.1
Sarno, Gerardo, 9, 20, 235
Saura, Carlos, 204
Sequeyro, Adela, 196
Sganzerla, Rogério, 83, 85
Sheridan, Beatriz, 201
Silva, Jorge, xiii, 11, 26-33, 78, 237
Soares, Jofre, 178
Soares, Paulo Gil, 9
Solanas, Fernando, xiii, 53, 167, 228, 261
Solás, Humberto, xiv, 143-160, 211, 225, 244, 247, 261
Solberg-Ladd, Helena, 81-102
Soria, Oscar, 35, 37, 48 n.2, 162, 163, 266-267, 275
Soto, Helvio, 261
State, role of, in film production. *See* Mode of production, state participation
Stevens, George, 16
Sucksdorff, Arne, 17

Super-8, xiv, xv, 229, 262-263, 268-282; Film Workshop (Taller de Cine Super-8), 278-281

Technology, transfer of, 275, 278-281, 282-283
Televisa, 202, 205
Television, 16, 22, 52, 61-62, 63, 78, 95, 100, 137, 138, 163, 173, 177, 181, 182, 190, 196, 201-202, 205, 206, 214, 234, 254, 255, 256, 260, 267, 270, 276, 279, 284; CMQ-TV (Cuba), 17; TVE (Televisión Española), 234, 235; "Twenty-Four Times a Second" (Cuban TV show), 237-241
Teoría y práctica de un cine junto al pueblo, 268
Terra, Educardo, 229, 231
Third cinema, xiii
Torres, Miguel, 106
Toscano, Carmen, 196
Tournier, Walter, 229, 231
Trelles, Danilo, 14, 17
Tropicalism, 108, 133, 172

Ukamau Group (Bolivia), 36, 48 n.2, 78, 146, 162, 266
Ulive, Ugo, xiii, 16, 18-19, 20-21, 222, 227
Umbanda, 137, 139
Unidad Popular, Chile, 49, 57, 187, 188
Uruguay, history of, 15-21, 22, 23; coup d'état of June 1973, 23, 231

Valdés, Oscar, 248
Vallejo, Gerardo, 8
Van der Horst, Herman, 17
Vega, Pastor, 53
Velasco Maidana, José María, 265, 266
Vertov, Dziga, 52
Video, xiv, xv, xviii, 78-79, 235, 236, 274, 280
Vignati, Jorge, 267
Vigo, Jean, 85
Villagra, Nelson, 149, 211-218
Visconti, Luchino, 146

Wainer, José, 21, 226, 229
Wilker, José, 177, 178
Wyler, William, 16

Yakir, Dan, 171
Yamasaki, Tizuka, 84
Yanahuaya, Marcelino, 44-45
Yates, Peter, 242
Yatiri, 45-46, 48 n.7
Yelin, Saúl, 64, 224, 226

Zafra (Mexico), 76, 233
Zambelli, Zaira, 177
Zavattini, Cesare, 4